CELTIC
ART

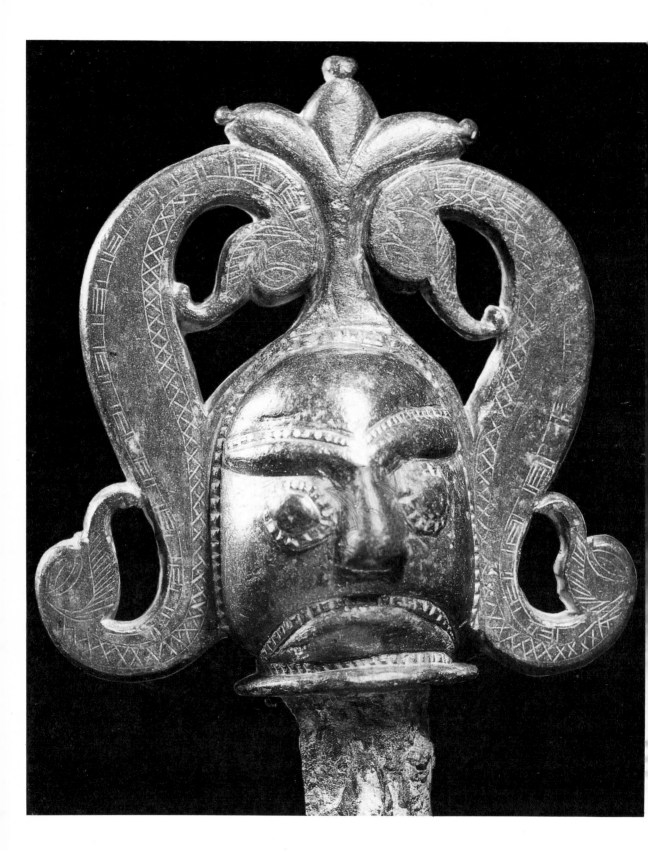

Ruth and Vincent Megaw

CELTIC ART

From its beginnings to the Book of Kells

With 452 illustrations, 24 in colour

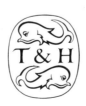

Thames and Hudson

In affectionate memory of Glyn Daniel
and Walter Neurath, who first introduced
us to the world of publishing

Title page: *Oberndorf/Ebene-Unterradelberg, St Pölten,
Austria. Iron linch-pin with bronze head. L. 18 cm. This
anthology of fifth-to-fourth-century Early Celtic art elements
is one of several recent spectacular finds from Lower Austria,
an area formerly thought to be too far east for such material.
The face is similar to those on several early brooches, such as
that from Slovenské Pravno (colour plate VIII), and is
surmounted by a typical bud or palmette motif; it is flanked
by two S's ending in the heads of birds of prey. The engraved
decoration is like that on the Stupava plaque (ill. 72) or the
Hallstatt grave 994 scabbard (ill. 92). La Tène A, late 5th/
early 4th c. BC.*

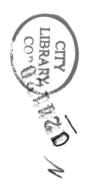
Printed and bound in Spain by Artes Graficas Toledo S.A.
D.L.TO: 2017–1988

Contents

Preface

Long, long ago, beyond the misty space
Of twice a thousand years,
In Erin old there dwelt a mighty race,
Taller than Roman spears . . .

THOMAS D'ARCY MCGEE (1825–68) *The Celts*

THE COMMON PERCEPTION OF Celts and Celtic art is of the art and culture of early historic Ireland. But Ireland is not the whole of Celtdom and in the past was very much on its western fringe. This book is only incidentally concerned with the reconstituted imagery, the popular symbolism of insular nineteenth-century romanticism and the recent growth of a Celtic nationalism. Never shared by the Celts of antiquity, it fogs any serious attempt to observe the true nature of the Celtic twilight. Our central theme is the prehistory of the Celts of the continent and basically, this book is as much archaeology as it is art history. Much of this material continues to defy analysis, confound the synthesizer and even daunt archaeologists and prehistorians, who, in the words of a recent President of the Royal Irish Academy, claim to determine a man's culture, race and language from the shape of his sword. The objects of Celtic prehistory exhibit, as Françoise Henry, the great interpreter of insular Celtic art, once wrote, 'multiple symbolic meaning'.

We have chosen in this book to concentrate on pre-Roman Celtic art, extending the temporal scope in the Epilogue up to the period of western Viking expansion. In the later historic period, survival of pre-Roman motifs is in fact only one of several threads in Early Christian art. We have also throughout occasionally included non-Celtic material – choosing as a rule of thumb only such examples as have been found within or on the borders of the Celtic world itself. There are of course gaps in coverage, territorially as well as temporally. We have for instance largely omitted Iberia and the nature of what is particularly Celtic in that region – a topic on which there is still much debate. On the other hand we hope on this occasion to have done more justice to central and eastern Europe.

The heart of this book lies in its illustrations; here we have tried to strike a balance between the necessary hardy perennials and material less well known or new photographs of old pieces. Although the photograph can be as much a personal interpretation as a line drawing, we have preferred the latter only when absolutely necessary to elucidate details not easily seen through the eye of the camera. A general survey such as this is no place for detailed footnoting. We have, we hope, added nonetheless sufficient bibliographical signposts to the objects illustrated in our Bibliography to allow the curious – or sceptical – to take matters further; more detailed indications of some of the views expressed here can be found in J.V.S. Megaw's *Art of the European Iron Age* (1970).

A NOTE ON CHRONOLOGY

It is necessary to warn readers that dates in years BC/AD where cited are often no more than guesses inspired by hope. Even where the objects discussed are found in association with other material which may be ascribed fixed dates by analogy or because it represents dated objects imported from the 'civilized' world of Greece and Rome, fine chronology is largely unobtainable. A simplified table of Iron Age relative chronology is appended, but this is of little help, for example, for much of prehistoric Celtic art which is found in isolated contexts. Absolute chronology established by independent means – dendrochronology or radiocarbon (C14) dating – is also of limited assistance. Even with the coming of the Romans this remains true, particularly in insular contexts where, even more frequently than on the continent, objects are isolated finds. The chart (p. 258) – which still follows the successive division of the Celtic Iron Age into 'Hallstatt' and 'La Tène' phases first proposed at the end of the last century – will, however, act as some kind of chronological sheet-anchor.

Leicester – Marburg/Lahn – Hyde Park, South Australia 1987

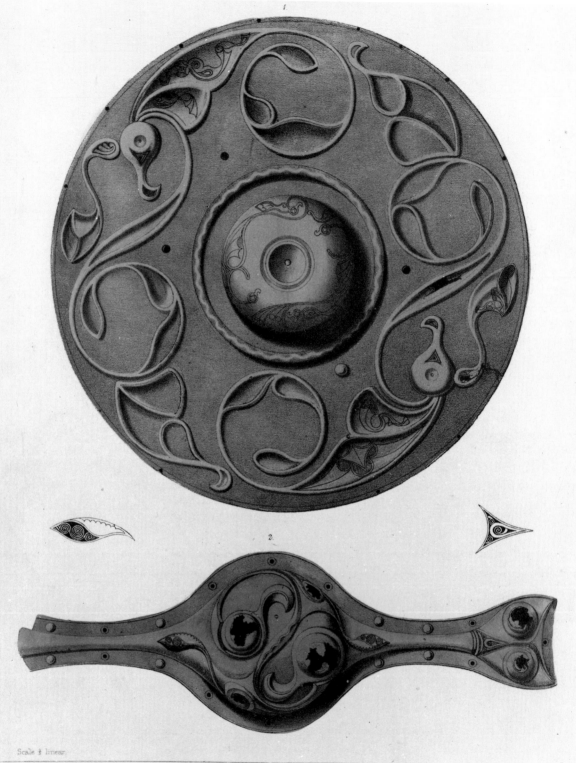

1

2

Scale ½ linear

O. Jewitt, Sc. et lith.

Vincent Brooks imp.

Introduction

IN SEARCH OF THE CELTS

NO SIMPLE DEFINITION of the word 'Celt' is possible. In modern times it has been used in a romantic nationalist sense of the Irish, Scottish, Welsh and Bretons, some of whom still speak forms of Celtic languages. In ancient times, however, the term *Keltoi* was given by Greek writers to the 'barbarian' peoples of temperate Iron Age Europe, but was never applied to the British Isles. There is no evidence that these people thought of themselves as a unified group called 'Celts', rather than as members of regional tribal units – in later prehistoric times, for example, as Helvetii in Switzerland, Scordisci around Belgrade, Boii in Italy and Bohemia or Arverni in France among many others. At their most far-flung, Celts settled across Europe into Asia Minor, terrorized infant Rome and attacked sacred Delphi.

The common traits obviously seen by Greek and Roman commentators are hard to pin down. 'Race' is a concept no longer very acceptable to scholars; the genetic and cultural mingling of Celtic peoples with those among whom they settled makes it an imprecise notion at best. The Celtic 'Belgae' of late pre-Roman France are sometimes, for example, thought to be an amalgam of Celtic and Germanic peoples. Nor is language any very certain indicator until the Roman and post-Roman periods. In some areas Celtic languages may go back to a millennium before Christ, but there is little close geographical correspondence with regions recorded as 'Celtic' by classical sources or with those which archaeologically have produced Celtic objects or art.

Linguistic evidence is often an uncertain matter concerned largely with theoretical arguments as to how far back in prehistory one may trace, for example, topographical names which are clearly of Celtic origin – rivers in the Iberian peninsula, place names in Switzerland and Hungary, the prehistoric roots of the considerable amount of written and epigraphic sources which becomes available from the early stages of Roman dominance over central and western Europe. There have been claims that around the thirteenth century BC, during the Bronze Age, a form of Celtic was being spoken just north of the Alps. Eastern France, northern Switzerland and south Germany – all areas important in the development of the early, or Hallstatt, Iron Age – appear to be part of this zone on the basis at least of similarities in material culture to that of the Alpine area. But current thinking tends largely to reject this as evidence for such groups being 'proto-Celtic'.

1 *(Opposite) Two bronze shield mounts from the River Thames at Wandsworth (see also ills. 319 and 336). Lithograph by Orlando Jewitt published in* J.M. Kemble, A.W. Franks and R.G. Latham, Horae Ferales, or Studies in the Archaeology of the Northern Nations *(London 1863).*

9

Certainly the name 'Celt' was employed by the classical writers from the sixth century BC onwards to describe a people following a particular way of life and was not used to describe the language spoken by such people. It was not until the sixteenth and seventeenth centuries AD that scholars, including the Welsh antiquarian Edward Lhwyd, one of the first professional museum men, made the linguistic link between the descriptions and names applied to the ancient Celts and the surviving Celtic languages of western Europe. Though the term 'Celt' was in fact never applied by the ancient writers to the population of the British Isles and Ireland, it is nonetheless in Ireland that one can trace linguistically the oldest surviving form of spoken Celtic. Traditionally, this was considered – again with little evidence – to have developed perhaps as early as the first millennium BC from a putative parent 'common Celtic' which in turn had its origin somewhere in the west Alpine region.

Most modern scholars regard prehistoric Celtic society as an amalgam of traits. The economy was largely based on cereal-dependent agriculture with associated animal-herding. Horses and wheeled transport were important in both war and peace. Yet social structure varied, at certain times and in certain places, from hierarchical to egalitarian to oligarchic. Trade with the Mediterranean areas is apparent both early and late in Celtic development, but was of no significance from the mid-fourth century till the late second century BC.

Celtic society and culture are generally seen as emerging around 500–450 BC, particularly in the Middle Rhine and northeast France, in the so-called Early La Tène period. Some observers also see the earlier, violently destroyed, sixth-century BC Hallstatt D culture of southeast Germany, near the Danube headwaters, and eastern France, especially Burgundy, as the first that is recognizably Celtic. Hecataeus of Miletus, a sixth-century BC writer whose works survive only in much later Byzantine versions, seems to indicate that the population in the hinterland of the Greek colony of Massalia (Marseilles) was Celtic, as too was that of ancient Noricum (Austria). Herodotus, in books II and IV of his fifth-century BC history, says that Celts lived in the region of the Danube, as well as 'beyond the pillars of Hercules', a reference which has been interpreted as showing settlement in southwest Iberia.

Later Celtic expansion southwards into Italy and eastwards to the Balkans and Asia Minor is historically and archaeologically attested; archaeology also indicates Celtic spread into western France and the British Isles. In these new areas their culture mingled with and drew upon the traditions of older inhabitants among whom Celts settled. Later, as Dacians reclaimed eastern European territory or Roman expansion dominated Celtic lands, further new influences were brought to bear on economy, society and material culture. Celtic society and art were never static, but display constant adaptation, development and evolution throughout the thousand-year period before Celtic conversion to Christianity.

This book concentrates on the art of the pre-Roman Celts of Europe and the British Isles, though it briefly extends the story to Hiberno-Saxon art of

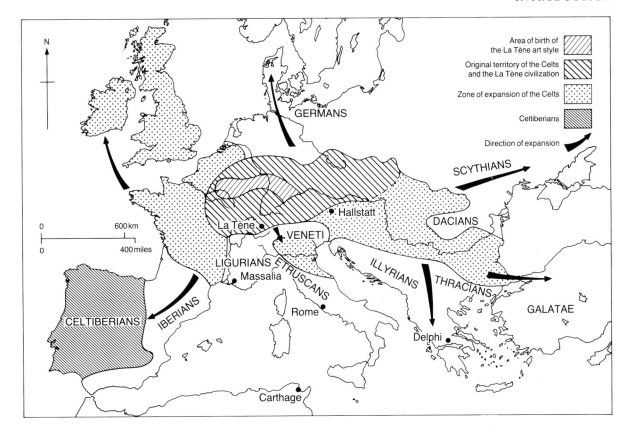

the post-Roman period. The prehistoric Celtic strand is in fact only one of three which are interwoven to create the art commonly thought of in modern times as 'Celtic'; the other two are the animal interlace of the Germanic invaders of Britain in the fifth century AD and the influence of Mediterranean Christianity.

Three main types of sources are available on the early Celts. Some written accounts have come down to us from classical observers. Of these, some are second- or third-hand, many are fragmentary and all see the 'barbarian' Celts through the distorting lens of their own preconceptions. Julius Caesar, for example, though a first-hand observer, tends to understand the Celts of Gaul and Britain in terms of his own society, relating their political, social and religious institutions to those of Rome; his *De Bello Gallico* was written to justify and glorify his conquest of Gaul for a Roman readership. Celtic written sources are mainly Irish and Welsh hero tales and codes of law, committed to writing in the Early Christian period around the seventh century AD. How accurate a picture they provide of Celts in other lands and over a thousand years earlier is extremely doubtful.

Finally, there is the record of the material past provided by archaeology. This too has its problems. We cannot tell how representative the objects discovered are, since much depends on chance or money as to whether a grave or settlement is excavated or not. Probably less than five per cent of

2 The territories occupied by Celts from the fifth century BC until the Roman conquests.

the material remains of the pre-Roman Celts are currently known to us. Again, despite increasingly sophisticated attempts in recent years, the social, intellectual and political structures of the Celts are remarkably hard to infer either from graves containing weapons or ornaments, except in the very crudest terms, or from the settlement sites, which are mostly known from the first century BC. Yet the finds associated with Celtic art provide the clearest evidence we have for such matters as date or stylistic influences. This book will thus have to be in part, however incompletely, an archaeological survey as well as an investigation of Celtic art. Without such chronological and social frameworks as archaeology provides, Celtic art must remain largely meaningless, except in terms of our own aesthetic responses – which reveal little about about the Celts. Attempts to enlist disciplines such as anthropology, systems theory or human geography have generally been seriously flawed both theoretically and in terms of the data available. Though their aim of putting people as well as objects back into the prehistoric past is admirable, it has not yet succeeded.

This book therefore will largely confine itself to verifiable information, rather than with unprovable speculation about the Celtic past: with realities rather than romanticism. Occasionally material is included which is demonstrably non-Celtic, though generally from within or on the borders of the Celtic world. This is in part to show the influences exerted on Celtic art.

THE EARLY STUDY OF
CELTIC ART AND ARCHAEOLOGY

In central Europe, Celtic studies were very much the product of the age of Romanticism and its associated nationalism. In archaeology, as in many other areas, it was an age of discovery of the past and of its reinterpretation to buttress modern identity. From the late eighteenth century a desire grew to associate a growing number of sites and artefacts with recognized modern peoples or cultures – Germans, Slavs or Celts. Interest in the Celts, whether as ancient Britons or ancient Gauls, had begun in the Renaissance, largely as the result of a reading of classical sources. In the nineteenth century this interest, coinciding with the growth of philological studies, developed into a positive disease of Celtomania, with regional strains of the virus. The English obsession with the Druids, for instance, has continued to this day – manifested above all in their supposed, but completely erroneous, link with megalithic monuments such as Stonehenge.

Like the Jews, the Celts formed in the past, as today, a loosely-knit cultural grouping rather than a single ethnic unit. They were linked more by religious and political beliefs than by economic or technological systems. It is perhaps surprising nonetheless, in looking at the history of Celtic art and archaeology, to note just how late the truly indigenous and distinctive nature of the material was recognized. Johann Georg Ramsauer, surveyor for the Hallstatt salt-mines, began the first systematic excavations at the cemetery in Hallstatt in Austria in 1846, claiming the graves he found as 'Celtic', an interpretation which is still a matter for dispute. When, however, the first of the indubitably Celtic Rhineland La Tène Iron Age chieftains' burials were discovered in the years around 1850, they were largely ascribed to the Roman period, and even while imported objects were identified – quite correctly – as coming from Italy, so too was the native Celtic material. An alternative view current at the time, that such finds were to be attributed to local Teutonic tribes, is understandable in the context of mid-nineteenth-century movements in German nationalism.

It was in fact left to an Englishman, Augustus Wollaston Franks, on the staff of the British Museum and Keeper of the Department of British and Medieval Antiquities and Ethnography from 1866 to 1896, to publish in John Kemble's posthumous *Horae Ferales* in 1863 a collection of insular Iron Age masterpieces which he defined as 'Late Celtic' and with continental Celtic antecedents.

As early as 1859 after the canalization and artificial lowering of the Jura Lake system, investigations had begun at the site of La Tène itself on the banks of Lake Neuchâtel in Switzerland, but the fine decorated sword scabbards and related material found there were not at that time regarded as Celtic and serious work on the site did not begin until 1874. In the same period, from 1858 to 1881, the first attempts at chronological and typological ordering of what was later to be termed 'La Tène' material (that characteristic of the second half of the pre-Roman Iron Age) was established by Ludwig Lindenschmidt. He was, however, still imprisoned by the shackles of a conviction that no barbarians were capable of producing masterpieces of craftsmanship, and so ascribed to the Etruscans the material now recognized as La Tène Celtic metalwork.

Early consideration of the routes by which trade with Italy and particularly with the Etruscans could have taken place did, however, initiate much discussion of the factors by which cultural contact and exchange affected the growth of local groups. For many years it was thought that it was only through the Greek trading centre of Massalia – established by East Greek colonists around 500 BC – that such contacts were made, but in 1874 Hermann Genthe in his *Über den Etruskischen Tauschhandel nach dem Norden* emphasized the importance of the ancient transalpine passes in this context. The first historically documented mass movement of Celts was, of course, southwards over the Alps in the early fourth century BC and it was the Frenchman, Gabriel de Mortillet, who in 1871 recognized the archaeological evidence for those incursions. He saw the close parallels between metalwork found in graves in the area of the Etruscan city of Marzabotto near Bologna and that which was being discovered in the Marne region of northeastern France.

By 1872 the Swede Hans Hildebrand had divided the pre-Roman Iron Age into two parts. The first, named after the Hallstatt complex of prehistoric salt-mining activities and its associated cemeteries in western Austria, was based largely on the enormous amount of material unsystematically recovered before Ramsauer began his investigations. The second of Hildebrand's phases was named after the site of La Tène. His system was further elaborated by Otto Tischler in 1881. Tischler divided the Hallstatt phase into two and in 1885 he allocated three phases – Early, Middle and Late – to the La Tène material in a paper based particularly on the changing forms he observed in swords and brooches. Significantly, Tischler saw no cultural break between Hallstatt and La Tène, which is another point still being debated today. He also drew attention to the similarity between the decoration of later Celtic sword scabbards – such as those already known from La Tène itself – and contemporary Celtic coins.

At last the true nature of early Celtic art and its differences from classical examples were being acknowledged. In 1870, Ernst aus'm Werth had recognized 'Gaulish copies' of Etruscan motifs amongst the fine metalwork of a barrow grave opened the year before at Waldalgesheim, Kr. Mainz-Bingen. In 1889 Adolf Furtwängler, the classical archaeologist and excavator of Olympia, gave the first thorough analysis of prehistoric Celtic art, describing finds from Schwarzenbach, Kr. St Wendel, excavated forty years earlier. He still did not attribute them to native Celtic workmanship but rather, on analogy with East Greeks working for Scythians in the Black Sea region, wrote of the native objects from Schwarzenbach as products for Celtic use produced in Massalia, through which centre the imported finds in the Celtic area came. Nonetheless, he clearly demonstrated the ways in which this metalwork borrowed and transformed Greek motifs.

It was another pioneering Englishman who, in a series of six lectures given in Edinburgh in 1895, made a remarkable summary of what he termed *The Origins of Celtic Art*. Sir Arthur Evans, the excavator of Knossos, observed in his Rhind lectures not only Etruscan and archaic and classical Greek influences in the development of early Celtic art but also those from the non-Celtic eastern Hallstatt areas of the head of the Adriatic and, in addition, elements transmitted through Scythian art. Arthur Evans and his father, Sir John, had worked on material from a cremation cemetery excavated in 1890 at Aylesford in Kent which they recognized as 'late Celtic'. Sir John Evans had also participated in the earlier uncontrolled examination of the Hallstatt cemeteries and in 1849 had made a pioneering study of native Celtic coinage in Britain which anticipated in its typology the evolutionary principles of Charles Darwin. Evans' knowledge of Hallstatt made him the first scholar really to recognize the importance of the east Alpine region for the development of Celtic culture. In contrast, Paul Reinecke, a pupil of Furtwängler's, in his *Zur Kenntnis der La-Tène-Denkmäler der Zone nordwärts der Alpen* of 1902 showed his allegiance to the classical bias of the time. While his divisions of the La Tène phase into four lettered subphases has remained fundamentally unchanged to the present day – though being based strictly on material from central and southern Germany – Reinecke still looked to archaic Greek influences of the sixth century BC, transmitted through Massalia and mingling with native Hallstatt traditions, to produce a new style somewhere in the area of the Greek colonies of the west Mediterranean.

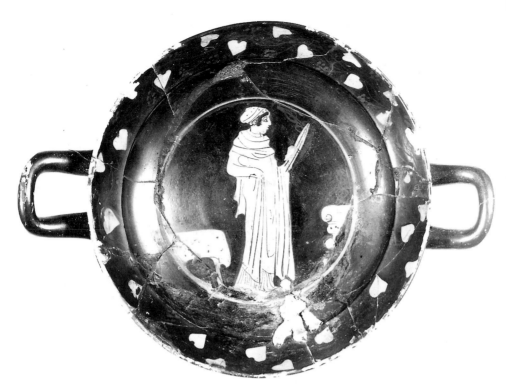

It was Paul Jacobsthal, another classical scholar, who in his *Early Celtic Art*, which he published as a refugee from Nazi Germany in 1944, set the ground rules for all recent discussions of La Tène art. Jacobsthal had started his research in Germany by once more looking at the question of Italic and Greek imports into the Celtic world. As he wrote:

One day in the cold and hungry winter of 1921 when I was studying Greek vases in Stuttgart, I was attracted by the painted Attic cup from the Klein Aspergle chieftain-grave, not because of its beauty or its importance for the history of Greek vase-painting . . . what struck me was the fact that a Greek cup had been found in this Hyperborean country, and the gold plaques of a strange style mounted on it; there were similar gold ornaments and Italic bronzes, all from the same tomb (*Early Celtic Art*, vi).

Jacobsthal noted not only an indigenous but also a Graeco-Etruscan strand in the growth of Celtic art – an art which he stated had no genesis, by which provocative remark he meant that in the La Tène phase of the Iron Age, it had no discernible and gradual evolution. But, like Evans, Jacobsthal also saw a nomadic and oriental or 'orientalizing' element. All of these he detected in varying degrees in four main 'styles', although he used the term 'style' in a rather all-embracing manner. Thus his 'Early Style' was that largely associated with the Early La Tène chieftains' graves of the fifth and earlier fourth centuries, making much use of classical plant motifs. What he

3 Attic cup with Celtic gold openwork net from Kleinaspergle, Kr. Ludwigsburg, Germany. W. (including handles) 22 cm. Cup c. 450 BC. Gold LT A, later 5th c. BC.

saw as a succeeding 'Waldalgesheim Style' – named after the grave site near Bonn – developed a much more individual use of classical non-representational form. Then, in the early third century, Jacobsthal envisaged an overlapping development with two separate groups. One he termed the 'Plastic Style', with a somewhat Germanic use of the adjective to indicate a much more three-dimensional use of form, often incorporating stylized human or animal forms. The second substyle he called the 'Hungarian Sword Style', restricted both regionally and in its use of largely engraved variations on basically classical – or rather Hellenistic – plant forms for decorating weapons, particularly iron sword scabbards.

The time and circumstances in which Jacobsthal was writing have given his work a western bias and various attempts to refine his terminology have been made, notably by Paul-Marie Duval in his superbly illustrated *Les Celtes*, published in 1977. Duval wrote of an evolution from an early 'strict style' through a 'free style' to a 'free graphic style' – more or less equivalent to Jacobsthal's Waldalgesheim and Sword 'styles' – through to a 'free plastic style'. But, for the reasons already suggested, it is still impossible to arrive at a totally satisfactory periodization of Celtic art styles and those who expect to find such in the present study will search in vain.

WAYS OF SEEING

In dealing with Celtic art, it is necessary to abandon post-Renaissance definitions, which are as meaningless in understanding the Celts as they are for most other prehistoric or ethnographic material. Distinctions developed in our own society between 'high art', popular art, and craft are alien to most other peoples at most other times. In particular, the view that 'real' art, as distinct from craft, must exist primarily in the realm of ideas, and have no demonstrable practical use, is a very modern concept. Much Celtic art is found on everyday objects – pottery, weapons and horse-harness. Of surviving wooden carvings, many have the eminently practical purpose of asking a deity for help or healing. Stone carving is rare, and apparently also usually connected with religion, certainly with a system of ideas and beliefs, but one of which we have little real understanding.

The idea of an avant-garde group, regularly and consciously challenging the techniques or subject-matter of 'established' art, is really a nineteenth-century invention not applicable to most traditional societies, where continuity is valued and preserved. Appropriate though it is to a society in a state of major and rapid social and technological change, it has little to offer the study of Celtic art, where the assumption that art is only 'art' when it consciously challenges accepted norms is an anachronism. The romantic view of the artist as an isolated genius, drawing inspiration from an inner vision, not from society, and increasingly inclined to ignore or patronize patrons and audience is also inapplicable. Few save the most conservative of art historians would now deny that there are inescapable connections between artist and society even in modern times. Most modern artists seek

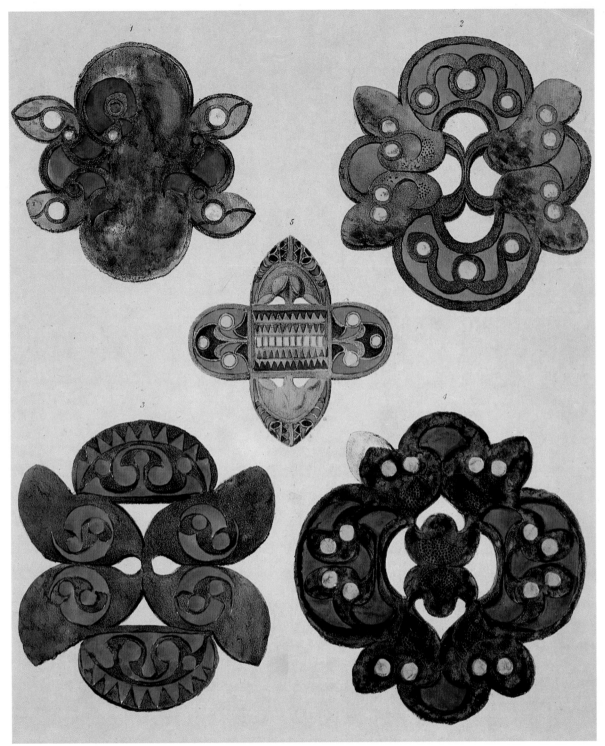

I *Enamelled trappings from the 'Polden Hills' hoard (see ills. 365, 366). Lithograph by Orlando Jewitt published in J.M. Kemble, A.W. Franks and R.G. Latham,* Horae Ferales, or Studies in the Archaeology of the Northern Nations *(London 1863).*

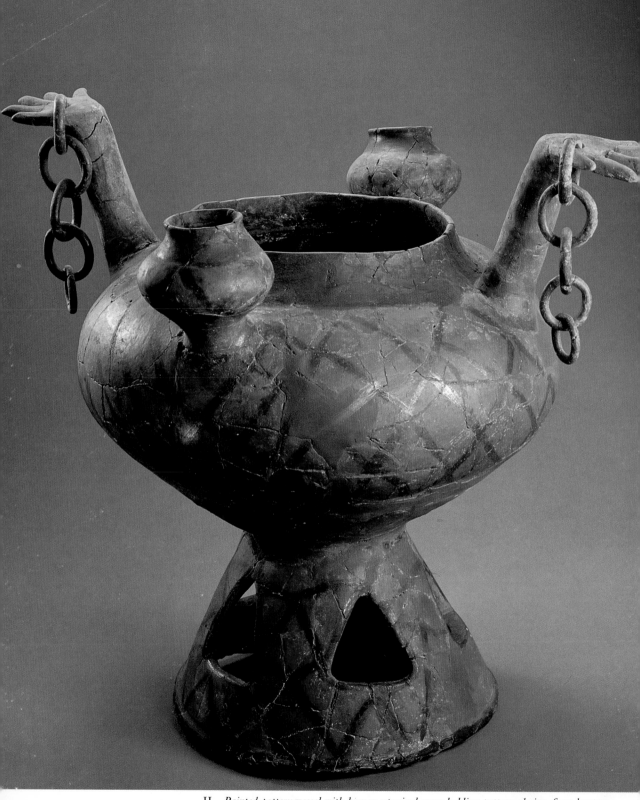

II   *Painted pottery vessel with human upraised arms holding pottery chains, from barrow VI, Dunajská Lužná, okr. Bratislava-vidiek, Czechoslovakia. H. 48 cm. Ha C2/D1, c.600 BC.*

markets, and become involved in the mechanisms of art dealerships, galleries and patrons. Most are influenced too by the technology available to them – in the colours they use, or the increasing impact of electronics or new technology. Most seek audiences with whom to communicate; even those who define art as process rather than finished object often record that very process on video.

It is difficult even today to make generally accepted aesthetic judgments about objects from different cultures. For example, what the Western buyer of modern Aboriginal painting or Eskimo carving considers to be of high quality is often quite different from the value judgments applied by the producers of the objects. Value judgments applied to what we define as prehistoric art are liable to carry even greater distortions. It may well be possible to assess technical skill or technical incompetence, but it is also possible that the Celts were sometimes more concerned with the symbolism of a motif on a scabbard or brooch than with the degree of skill with which it was carried out, the message being more important than the medium. Here we have another problem, for we cannot tell the precise meaning to a Celt of even some of the commonest motifs, such as the three-armed triskel or whirligig or, amongst more obvious animal representations, the boar. Some may have been like a three-leaved clover, a charm; others may be heraldic symbols like the American bald eagle or the Tudor rose; yet others may have a significance as profound as a crucifix has for a Christian. While not knowing the belief systems of Celtic society, we can still recognize repeated symbols, but we cannot fully understand them, or respond to them in the same way as did the Celts. Aesthetic response usually presupposes a shared value system or way of creating an image, so that a two-dimensional flat canvas is interpreted as a three-dimensional portrait or narrative; the narrative again usually assumes that both artist and viewer know the same 'story'.

A minimal working definition of Celtic art is that it encompasses elements of decoration beyond those necessary for functional utility, though these elements represent a form of symbolic visual communication which is only partially accessible to us. Much Celtic art is in the form of highly skilled metalwork, and the capacity to command the time and training – even perhaps the perceived magical powers – of such metalsmiths belonged in general to the elite members of Celtic society. This implies a degree of economic specialization, on a predominantly agricultural base, with the generation of sufficient economic surplus to sustain such specialization. Most Celtic decorated metalwork is on weapons of war, fine drinking vessels and personal ornaments, again representing the major preoccupations of a warrior elite which traded for wine with the Mediterranean. Stone and wood carving appears to have been more directly concerned with Celtic religion and ritual. Its rarity is perhaps because wood survives less easily than metal, but the general impression is that carving was a less specialized craft than metalworking.

In examining Celtic art it is possible to distinguish between the techniques used and the subject-matter. Thus birds' heads or bulls can be produced in metal by repoussé (beating up sheet metal from the reverse side), by casting, by use of wrought iron, by incising lines on sheet metal or by die-stamping. Subject-matter or motifs such as human heads or animal figures, whirligigs or plant tendrils can be clearly picked out.

'Style', like aesthetic judgment, is another elusive concept. At times in this book it is employed in the cruder sense as used by Jacobsthal of 'belonging (perhaps) to a specific period'. More properly it consists in the precise combination of technical and iconographic elements to produce a particular form or effect. For identification of close groupings linked in time or space – possibly even from the same workshop or hand – it is often the apparently minor details, such as edgings, punch marks and the like, which are of most value. These almost unconscious, conventionalized artistic fingerprints are frequently the best, though by no means foolproof, clues we possess to help us answer the obvious questions, 'what is its date?', 'what are its stylistic affinities?', and 'by whom was it made?'

Unfortunately, for the pre-Roman Iron Age these questions must sometimes remain unanswered in view of the partial nature of the material available to us and our lack of knowledge of the methods by which Iron Age art was both produced and distributed. Thus, while there is some meagre archaeological evidence for workshop practices, we cannot always be certain whether, for example, skilled craftsmen moved from centre to centre receiving commissions as they went, whether particular individuals would call upon the services of particular specialized gold-, bronze- or ironsmiths, or whether it was the objects rather than the craftsmen that travelled. Again, within each workshop it seems likely either that masters employed pupils for minor tasks on major pieces or that such apprentices were themselves responsible for individual pieces which modern scholars might easily confuse as older – or later – works of one particular 'school'. Ethnographic analogy also strongly supports the view that the organization of, for example, fine pottery manufacture would have been very different from that of gold-, bronze- or ironworking. Finally, one must beware of equating the presence of Celtic material necessarily with the presence of Celts. The adoption of Celtic weapons or jewellery in areas such as the Alpine region, eastern or northern Europe does not mean that one is dealing with Celts themselves. As Otto-Herman Frey has put it, blue jeans, sneakers and a baseball cap do not make the wearer an American.

THE NATURE OF CELTIC ART

Among the most noticeable features of Celtic art is its determined non-narrative quality, despite the demonstrable availability of models in the form of imported narrative art from Greece and her colonies, from Etruria and in the art of the *situlae* from the area at the head of the Adriatic. Oral traditions of story-telling and song are attested from classical and later Irish and Welsh sources among the Celts, so narrative in words was not unfamiliar. Furthermore, Celts were certainly able to adapt and transform, as, for example, in the case of plant motifs – some in turn derived by the

Greeks from the Middle East – such as palmettes, lotus-buds or blossoms, or acanthus tendrils. Thus foreign artistic models were assimilated only if they fitted in with Celtic visual symbolism and syntax.

Representations do exist, particularly of certain animals: horses, boars, cattle, sheep, dogs, birds are all common throughout the Celtic world in all periods. Such animals obviously played a part in everyday economic life, though in some cases – the boar for instance – a more profound symbolism was apparently involved. More mythical beasts such as sphinxes, griffons, lions, dolphins, even perhaps crocodiles, were adapted from classical prototypes. Very few full-length human figures are known, and virtually no unequivocally female representations. Yet the human head is omnipresent, frequently mask-like and 'severed' in appearance, often reduced to cartoon-like abstraction, or elusively buried, 'Cheshire-cat' like, in foliage. It has to be presumed that the head had major symbolic importance, and that there may even have been some kind of taboo on the representation of human form or on narrative sequences – as in Jewish or Moslem art.

Vivid colour was obviously appreciated, at first in the use of imported coral and then of red glass or enamel. By the first century BC, true enamelling in several colours was widely employed in the British Isles. This was not a trait apparent in the classical world.

Despite such borrowings of motifs from the classical world, it is essential to recognize that Celtic art owed as much, if not more, to its own internal development and its European background. Greeks, Etruscans and Romans also all borrowed heavily from the arts of other peoples. Such behaviour does not in any way imply the inferiority or 'degeneracy' of Celtic art, just as Picasso's use of African models does not diminish his standing as a twentieth-century artist. The early domination of Celtic art studies by classical scholars, and by those of diffusionist views, has tended to emphasize the role of classical art, sometimes at the expense of comprehending Celtic processes of transformation, and to see it purely as an offshoot of artistic and technological processes passed from a 'higher' to a 'lower' civilization. The eclecticism of Celtic art is not, however, mere copying, but the sign of a society open to such change as it chose to accept and adapt on its own terms. Though stylistic features were borrowed, the messages transmitted seem to have been affected by internal factors only.

Thus though Celtic art is essentially aniconic, it should also be regarded as basically religious. Despite the difficulties of reconstructing the beliefs of prehistoric societies, everything we know of the Celts from contemporary and later sources indicates 'a culture imbued with a deep reverence for the arts, for intellect and for learning, and for the gods and the ritual attendant upon them', as Anne Ross has expressed it, emphasizing the ever-present and, even when seemingly benign, dangerous nature of Celtic deities. The unbroken line between this world and the afterworld, the past and present, is not of course restricted to Iron Age Europe and it certainly explains the often menacing element which can be perceived even today in Celtic art.

Much more difficult is the specific identification in pre-Roman Celtic art of apparent representations of gods and goddesses and their attributes.

Nonetheless, there appear to be certain observable constants which allow one, however tentatively, to make such attributions. Julius Caesar, whose tidy Roman mind reduced the changing and changeable nature of Celtic religion to an over-rigid equation with the classical pantheon, refers to the Celtic 'Dis Pater', the divine ancestor whom Celtic scholars today would equate with the Irish Dagda, the giver of life, the warrior with his cauldron of plenty, the universal tribal deity. The natural veneration of a basically pastoral people for the animal world is expressed by the frequent appearance in Celtic iconography of bulls, deer and birds and also of human figures with animal attributes, notably horns or antlers. Goddesses and, particularly in the period of contact with the Roman world, triple personifications seem to have been associated predominantly with water, the land, generation and procreation.

It is now generally agreed that, like all folk traditions subsequently formalized, the Old Irish and Welsh hero tales, first written down in the Early Christian period, represent a virtually indecipherable palimpsest of myth, reality and interpretation. Nonetheless, as with other forms of ethnographic and historic analogy, one may use traditional accounts to suggest models of past behaviour. The Celtic scholar Proinsias MacCana quotes an Old Norse text of the middle of the thirteenth century AD entitled *Konungs Skuggsjá* or 'King's Mirror'. It contains a number of legends or 'wonders', almost certainly based on oral traditions collected in the eastern part of Ireland, and reflecting tales which were first written down in Latin versions in the eighth or ninth century AD. One such 'wonder' is set in the monastery of Clonmacnois where one day as the congregation was at Mass an anchor and rope were seen to come dropping from the air. The fluke of the anchor caught on the church door and, on looking up, the people saw a ship with men in it floating in the air. A man leapt overboard and dived down towards the anchor, moving his hands and feet as if he were swimming. As he tried to loosen the anchor some of the people on the ground wanted to restrain him, but the bishop, who happened to be present, prevented them, saying that if they did so the man would die just as if kept beneath water. And so the man was released and regained his ship where the crew cut the rope and sailed away. This legend, as with so many manifestations of Celtic mythology, as MacCana has pointed out, adds a sense of ambiguity, an extra dimension where time and space no longer form the natural boundaries of rational relationships: so too with the Celtic world of the dead, an Otherworld of infinite variation with no firm boundary between it and the world of the living.

This fluidity of concept is that which in other 'wonders' enabled young girls to change into swans, or brave heroes into a salmon, an eagle or a hawk. The same shape-changing ambiguity, of motif rather than myth, is present in pre-Roman Celtic art where seemingly abstract decoration becomes imbued with human and animal forms reduced to the merest visual formulae. Such ambiguity is only in the mind of the outsider looking in. The point of the story of the ship of Clonmacnois is that the real world is as you see it. For the people in the ship the Otherworld was the monastery, for those below, the ship in the air was the Otherworld. Against such a background, with gods who were men and men gods, both able to change with ease into birds of the air and fish in the streams, it is scarcely surprising that, in the last generation of Celtic independence on the continent of Europe, Julius Caesar should try to contain the many-faced local deities of Gaul within the readily assimilated orders of the Roman pantheon. Celtic religion, like Celtic art and the Celts themselves, was stubbornly resistant to assimilation, adapting only so far as was necessary for survival.

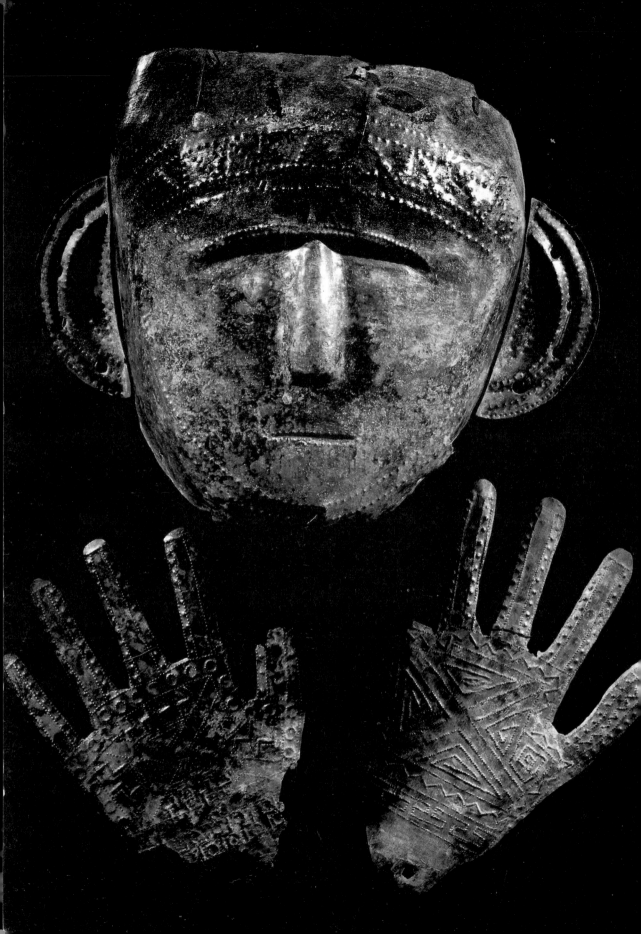

I
The Antecedents of Celtic Iron Age Art

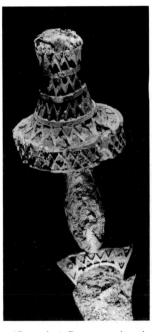

WATERBIRDS SWIM UP the legs of a bronze cauldron stand. A stylized horseman surmounts a small cast bronze axe. Over two hundred pieces of Baltic amber are inset in a geometric design into the African ivory on the pommel of a long iron sword.

These three objects all come from cremation graves at Hallstatt in Austria, the salt-mining metropolis whose name is applied to the period when ironworking first reached Europe, around the eighth century B C. These immediate precursors of truly Celtic art illustrate the iconography and preoccupations of an aristocratic horse-riding society whose art owed as much to war as to peaceful tranquillity, and whose trading connections were widespread.

Changes in climate and in social and political structure, as well as in the economy and technology, mark this Hallstatt period in Europe north of the Alps. It extends to the end of the sixth century B C, yet late Celtic art, little changed from its prehistoric prototypes, is still frequently found on weapons as late as the sixth century A D in Ireland. Birds' heads and horses appear on metalwork in Britain and Ireland long after the Romans came to – or left – the British Isles.

Some aspects of the art of the Hallstatt C period, of the earliest Iron Age in the eighth and seventh centuries B C, are geographically widespread. Swans with cygnets appear on a bronze flesh-hook of a locally made type from as far west as a peat-bog at Dunaverney, Co. Antrim, in Ireland. Crested waterbirds similar to those found in the Hallstatt cemetery itself appear on a bronze pendant from a fortified settlement at Smolenice in Slovakia. Swords such as that from Hallstatt come from as far north as southern Sweden and as far west as Oss in the Netherlands.

Development of iron technology obviously modified the economic life of Europe, since the new metal was more widely available than the combination of copper and tin necessary for bronze. Since iron is harder and keeps a better edge, it was increasingly used for tools and weapons. Bronze, however, continued to be used for decorated objects: it is more easily cast or worked with hammers and corrodes less readily. The blacksmith took a central place in Iron Age society, but the iron sword frequently had its ornate scabbard of bronze.

Wheeled vehicles, known sporadically from earlier periods, became more common, attesting to the importance of horses and of local and long-distance trade. Other new cultural elements in this period include

4 *(Opposite) Bronze mask and hands from the Kröll-Schmied-Kogel, Kleinklein, Steiermark, Austria. W. (of mask) 23 cm. Ha C, 7th c. BC.*

5 *(Above) Iron sword pommel with ivory and amber inlay from Hallstatt, Salzkammergut, Austria, grave 573. W. (of pommel) c. 9.5 cm. Ha C, 7th c. BC.*

inhumation burials with funerary wagons in wooden chambers. Warriors were buried with horse-gear and with weapons: the long iron sword in the west and the socketed axe from central Austria eastwards.

The horses themselves were a new type, larger than those previously found in Europe. They were increasingly used as cavalry mounts and not merely for traction. Such horses and burials were formerly seen as evidence for wholesale westward migration by the largely pastoral populations of the south Russian steppes. It is now more widely thought that there were only small groups of settlers or invaders from the east and that change was due as much to the influx of new ideas as of new populations.

The growth of a series of nuclear communities, each under the control of a local centre of power, can be traced from the first emergence of the new burial customs in eastern central Europe – in the territory bordering that of the westernmost of the horse-rearing nomads related to the Scythians mentioned in Herodotus' *Histories*. Thence the new communities spread, in the seventh century BC, into western Czechoslovakia and Bavaria, and, in the succeeding century, deeper into southwest Germany.

This so-called Hallstatt culture is not a uniform or undifferentiated phenomenon. There is a division in particular between the western and eastern zones, visible in the art as well as in other aspects.

The type-site of Hallstatt itself sits virtually on the boundary between these two zones. It is close to copper ores in the Tyrol and to iron ores to the east. Salt was mined more or less continuously from the late Bronze Age until Roman times. The early Iron Age cemetery associated with the eastern salt-mining complex was abandoned, perhaps because of natural disasters, in the fifth century BC. The graves were unsystematically excavated in the nineteenth century and much of the material given away without record. It seems, however, that this was not merely a seasonal workplace, since the 2,000 individuals, from some 1,300 known graves, included women and children, though few infants.

Much of the fine metalwork from Hallstatt comes from cremation graves, over half of it from a small number of warriors' burials. Thus the waterbirds mentioned at the beginning of the chapter come from cremation grave 507, whose occupant possessed yet another amber- and ivory-inlaid long sword, another horse-decorated axe and four bronze pails, two of which have tally marks, or simplified writing, on their rims.

The axe with a horseman comes from a poorer grave, cremation grave 641, which otherwise contained only a straight-shanked pin. The rider appears to be wearing a short tunic and trousers as well as the neckring so characteristic of later Celts; he may once have carried a weapon. Horses and riders of clay are also known, for example from Gemeinlebarn in Lower Austria, or from Speikern in Bavaria. These may have been token burials for those not rich enough to take with them to the grave a horse and all its accoutrements.

Cattle figurines in bronze from Hallstatt grave 671 (long-horned *bos longifrons*), or pottery cattle from Austrian barrow cemeteries such as Kleinklein or Gemeinlebarn, may also have been substitutes for the

6 (Below) *Bronze container and stand from Hallstatt, Salzkammergut, Austria, grave 507. H. 36 cm. Ha C, 7th/6th c. BC.*

7 (Right) *Bronze axe with horse and rider from Hallstatt, Salzkammergut, Austria, grave 641. L. 10.9 cm. Ha C, c. 600 BC.*

8 (Below right) *Pottery figurine of horse and rider from Speikern, Ldkr. Lauf an der Pegnitz, Germany. L. (of horse) 8.7 cm. Ha D, 6th c. BC.*

9 (Bottom) *Bronze 'flesh-hook' with swans and ravens from Dunaverney Bog, Ballymoney, Co. Antrim, Northern Ireland. L. 60.7 cm. ?8th c. BC.*

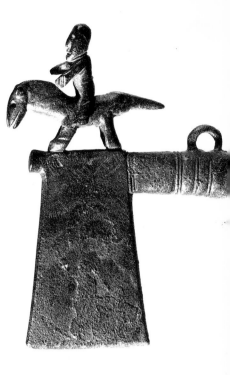

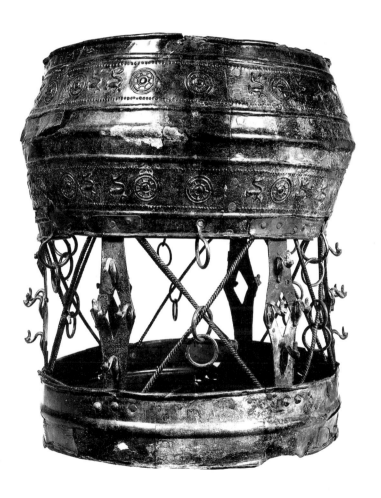

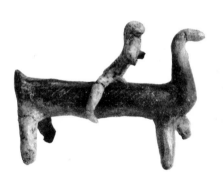

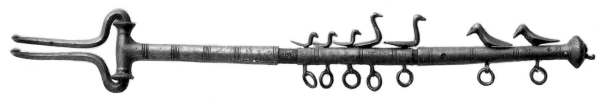

27

animals themselves. Cattle representations are to be expected in a herding society, and, like horses, have a long life in Celtic art. In the Hallstatt period they also form handles of bronze or pottery vessels. Of these the finest is perhaps the cow with her calf, also from Hallstatt grave 671; the amber beads in this grave suggest it was a woman's burial.

One spectacular, and much discussed, cast bronze bull comes from Býčí skála cave in Moravia. Brand marks of iron are inlaid on his forehead and shoulders. Both the limestone cave itself and the artistic influences on the bull have caused controversy. Býčí skála contained the skeletons of some forty individuals and at least four wheeled vehicles decorated with characteristic Hallstatt-period geometric designs. This used to be interpreted as macabre evidence of the ritual slaughter of women and animals to accompany the dead warrior to the grave, in the manner of Scythian burials. More recently, if more prosaically, it has been interpreted as either a dynastic cemetery in use for over a century or – improbably again – a metalworking site in which the bodies were trapped by a roof fall.

The bull himself, though stylized, is an accurately observed specimen of *bos primigenius*, the local type of cattle at that time. Despite claims that he is either an actual import from Asia Minor or, at the very least, influenced by eastern nomadic art, the steppe nomads made no freestanding animal figurines. His squared-off snout and limbs are firmly within the tradition of Hallstatt three-dimensional art, and foreshadow later, accomplished, Celtic stylizations of animals.

10 (*Below*) *Detail of handle of bronze bowl showing cow and calf from Hallstatt, Salzkammergut, Austria, grave 671. L. (of cow) 14.4 cm. Ha D, 6th c. BC.*

11 (*Below right*) *Painted pot with bovine heads from Dunajská Lužná (formerly Nové Košariská), okr. Bratislava-vidiek, Czechoslovakia, barrow VI. H. 29 cm. Ha C2/D1, c. 600 BC.*

12 (*Bottom right*) *Bronze bull figurine with iron inlay from Býčí skála, okr. Blansko, Czechoslovakia. H. 10.1 cm. ?6th/5th c. BC.*

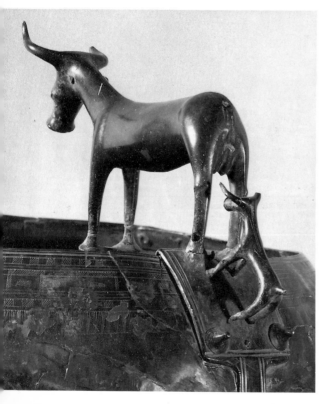

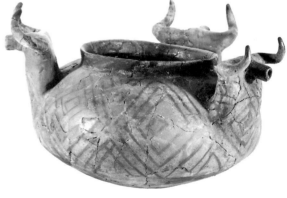

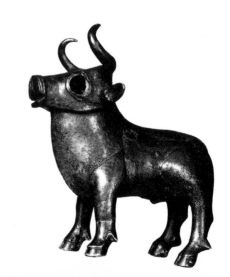

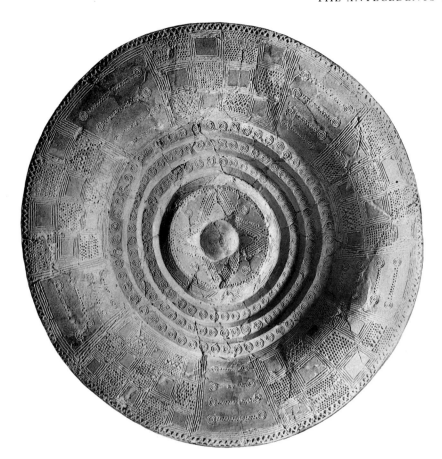

13 *Stepped Alb-Salem pottery plate, stamped, incised and painted with black and red from Gomadingen-'Sternberg', Kr. Reutlingen, Germany, barrow I. D. 55 cm. Ha C1, early 7th c. BC.*

Geometric designs are found throughout the eastern and western cultural zones, on both pottery and metal. The Hallstatt axe carries pendent triangles formed by zig-zag or tremolo lines, executed by rocking a chisel-ended engraving tool from side to side, a long-lived technique in the Celtic Iron Age. The bowl with the cow and calf from Hallstatt also shows incised pendent triangles as well as rectangles and meanders.

Sometimes the geometric designs are carried out in 'chip-carved' technique, derived from woodcarving. V-sectioned grooves are cut or impressed into pottery or metal, as on the hand-made Alb-Salem stepped dishes from the Swabian region. These pots also show the use of a stamp with concentric circles, another enduring technique on pottery. Graphite and red oxides provide the painted colour.

Chip-carving can be seen too on the Hallstatt sword from cremation grave 573, in the fashioning of the settings for the amber inlay. These long Mindelheim swords with their characteristic 'cocked-hat' pommel are found only in the western Hallstatt zone, mostly in Austria, southwest Czechoslovakia or south Germany. Another such sword, with gold and bone or ivory inlay, was found in barrow 9 at Gomadingen in Germany. It is so like the Hallstatt example that it may have been made by the same hand.

Such techniques, designs and iconography can be seen throughout both eastern and western zones. There are, however, some significant differences between the art of these two areas.

THE EASTERN HALLSTATT PROVINCE

The classic archaeological division has been that the eastern zone used the socketed axe, while the western zone used the long sword. The eastern settlements and cemeteries in Hungary, eastern Austria and Slovenia are also very much larger than those in the western area. As to the art, while the shape of high-status pottery is similar in both eastern and western zones, the western zone shows almost exclusively geometric designs, while some eastern pots occasionally carry narrative scenes. Metalwork in the east more frequently depicts full-length human figures and also uses narrative art, which is quite foreign to the western zone and indeed to Celtic art of later periods.

Properly speaking, the art of this easterly province cannot be regarded as 'Celtic' in the sense used in this book until the incursions of Western Celts during the fourth century or later. There are, however, some good reasons for including it here. One is that it gives us some rare depictions of certain aspects of material culture shared by both zones in the Hallstatt period. Secondly, it provides a basis on which the art of the western invaders later built. Finally, it is important in that it shows types of artistic models available to, but rejected by, Celtic artists, and the means by which certain features passed into Celtic art.

The most remarkable series of narrative scenes of early Hallstatt date is that on a group of handmade urns in burnished black paste from the present-day border between Hungary and Austria. Sopron is the more southerly of two major Hallstatt centres linked by minor settlements and their attendant cemeteries, and was first excavated between 1890 and 1892. It lies at the intersection of the Danube with the so-called amber route from the Baltic to the Adriatic, and appears to have been occupied from the late Bronze Age (Hallstatt B) until the first century BC. Some two hundred Hallstatt-period barrow burials line the approach to Sopron-Burgstall, an upland settlement surrounded by major fortifications. Such 'hillforts' are another characteristic of the eastern Hallstatt zone. The burials belong to the Kalenderberg culture, a subgroup of the eastern Hallstatt culture which extends into neighbouring Slovakia, northeast Bavaria, southern Silesia and Bohemia.

The basic pottery form is the wide-bodied, small-footed urn with inward-sloping neck. It is decorated with a combination of circular stamps and incised lines, but some pots also depict weaving, the droving of cattle, music-making with pipe or lyre, horse-riding and the use of a four-wheeled wagon. The human figures are exceedingly stylized and men can be distinguished from women only by the fact that their bell-shaped clothing is less exaggerated.

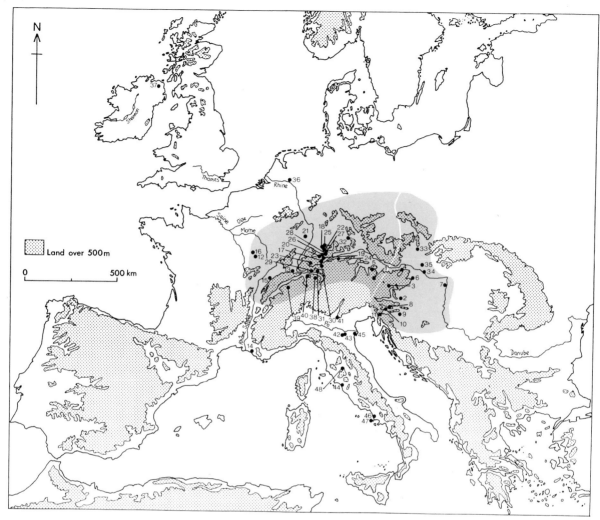

14 *Map of principal sites
mentioned in Chapter 1. (Tint
indicates region in which classic
Hallstatt material culture is
found, divided into Western and
Eastern areas.)*

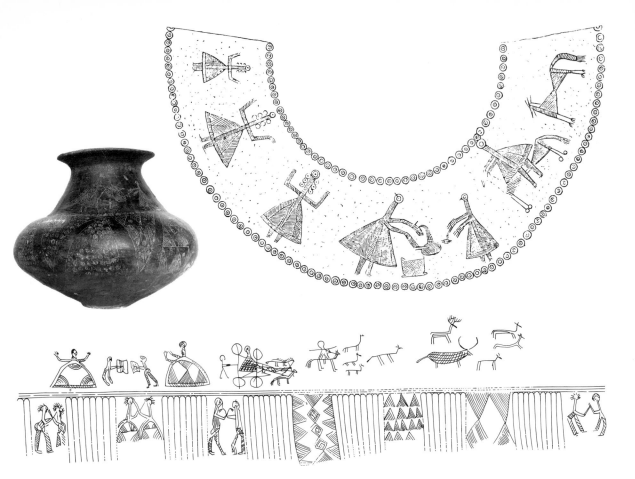

15,16 *(Top left and top right)*
Pot from Sopron-Várishegy,
Györ-Sopron, Hungary, barrow
3, and drawing of the scenes
incised on its shoulder. H. 41.5
cm. Ha C, late 7th c. BC.

17 *(Above) Drawing of 'life-*
scenes' on an incised pot from
Sopron-Burgstall, Hungary,
barrow 28 (127). Max D.
63.2 cm. Ha C2, late 7th c. BC.

Ritual rather than domestic activities can be seen as for example on an urn from barrow 3 of the neighbouring barrow group of Sopron-Várishegy. Here a sacrificial offering seems to be being made. Many of the Sopron Hallstatt C pots show women with hands upraised; these may be mourners, or even dancers and singers since they may have accompanying lyre-players. Pairs of men confront each other with swords, or simply with empty hands as in a duel or boxing match.

In Slovakia, similarly shaped pots are not incised but painted with graphite and red and yellow oxides, as are those from Dunajská Lužná (formerly Nové Košariská) near Bratislava. Here, six Hallstatt C barrows yielded cremation burials within chambers built from wooden logs. Barrow I produced five painted pots including three narrative Kalenderberg urns. Barrow VI contained some seventy pots, of which thirty were painted; it also produced a unique piece which has been termed an 'offering bowl'. This consists of an urn on a pedestal, to the rim of which are attached two miniature urns and two upraised arms – like those of the 'praying' women of Sopron – from whose fingers hang chains with links of fired clay.

This raised-arm stance can be seen on pottery in Austria and, at its furthest west, in northeast Bavaria. Here the figures, following local traditions, are decorated with rectilinear impressions using a toothed stamp, and their bodies are indicated by two triangles joined at the apex.

These westerly examples do not however narrate activities, though one from Fischbach, Kr. Burglengenfeld, shows figures, probably male, below the rim, and highly schematic horses with riders near the bottom.

There has been considerable discussion about the origins of this representational and narrative pottery. The great eighth-century Dipylon Greek vases show similar narrative scenes, with hour-glass figures and burial processions with four-wheeled biers, while many of the non-figural geometric designs can be found on East Greek pottery from the first half of the seventh century, much closer to the date of these particular Hallstatt pots. But a more easterly, rather than southeasterly, influence is also possible: the 'Bosut' and 'Basarabi' pottery from eighth- and seventh-century barrow burials in northeast Jugoslavia and Romania also displays boxers and dancers with hour-glass profiles and upraised arms. Southern influence from the area of northern Italy and the head of the Adriatic is also a possibility, particularly for the depiction of the playing of lyres and the double pipes.

In considering external influences, however, one must not forget the indigenous culture of this eastern Hallstatt area. The double pipe has, in fact, a long history in eastern Europe and the Balkans and can be seen in the early Hallstatt period in a little bronze musician from Százhalombatta, south of Budapest. Similarly there is a good local pedigree in the Hallstatt area for the four-wheeled, as well as for the rarer two-wheeled, vehicles. The influence of neighbouring cultures may indeed be traceable, but it was at work on a demonstrably local substratum.

One of the most intriguing of all Hallstatt-period works of art again shows a woman with raised arms. This is the bronze cult model from a male cremation burial with axe, spear and three horse-bits under a barrow at

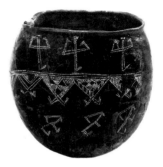

18 (Above) Round-bottomed pot, decorated with human and animal figures from Fischbach, Kr. Burglengenfeld, Germany, grave 1. H. 24.5 cm Ha C, 7th c. BC.

19 (Below) Bronze cult wagon from Strettweg, Steiermark, Austria. H. (of goddess) 22.6 cm. Ha C, 7th c. BC.

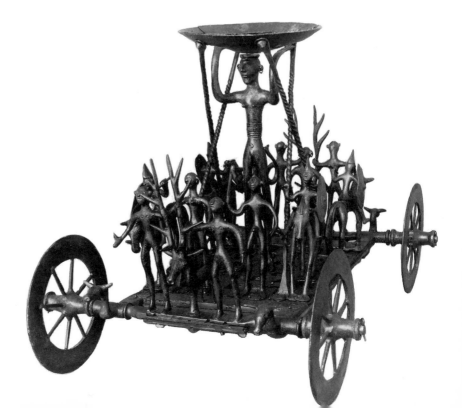

Strettweg near Graz in Austria. The pottery, described in 1934 but now lost, is considered to be of late sixth-century date, while the other material could well belong to the seventh; in any case the possibility of the model being an heirloom must be kept in mind. The most striking figure on the model is the central woman, naked but for a belt and earrings; she supports a small dish in the manner of the large offering dishes. The other figures, separately cast and riveted on to the base plate, form a symmetrical pattern front and back. Two figures, again probably female, support a stag behind which are a male and female pair, the women with earrings, the ithyphallic men with axes. Flanking these on the outer sides are pairs of mounted warriors with spears, shields and pointed helmets. The base rests on twin axles with ox-head protomes; the wheels, with eight spokes and large hubs, copy the pattern of wheeled vehicles of the period. Despite claims that the central 'goddess' would be stylistically 'unthinkable apart from Greek geometric bronzes' and the citation of a seventh-century figure of Zeus from Olympia, and despite also the 'geometric' look, especially of the horses, this piece is locally made, though it again demonstrates the possible absorption of external influences.

METALWORK OF THE EASTERN ZONE, AND THE ART OF THE SITULA

As in the western Hallstatt zone, sheet bronze metalwork was often decorated. It is, however, frequently worked in punched dots, as in the face and hands from the large barrow cemetery of Kleinklein in the valley of the Sulm in eastern Austria.

This forms part of the cluster of seven hundred smaller barrows excavated out of a probable several thousand, together with fifteen larger ones, grouped round the 500-m-high Burgstallkogel. One of the four large barrows at Kleinklein is the 'Kröll-Schmied-Kogel', a warrior burial under a stone cairn in a chamber which was probably lined with wood. The dead man had with him the typically eastern Hallstatt weaponry of spears and socketed axe. Other eastern military fashions represented were the breastplate and the helmet with double ridges and provision for a crest.

The face and hands were probably attached to a coffin, and while the face may well recall the much earlier gold 'mask of Agamemnon' from Mycenae, it has parallels closer in both time and space in the slightly later gold sheet masks found in the cemetery at Trebeniŝte near Lake Ohrid in Jugoslavia.

Thirty or so bronze vessels found in these Kleinklein barrows also show dot-punched, repoussé and stamped decoration in their narrative scenes. These include, as on the eastern pottery, boxer figures, horse-riders, and lyre- and pipe-players. One bucket or chest lid shows friezes of waterbirds – possibly swans – and of axe-carrying, helmeted, nude warriors, displaying their sex like the horses on the lowest register.

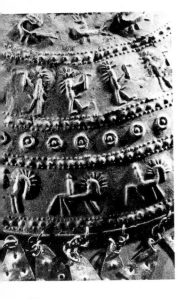

20 Detail of bronze ?chest lid from a barrow grave at Kleinklein, Steiermark, Austria. D. 35.7 cm. Ha C, 7th c. BC.

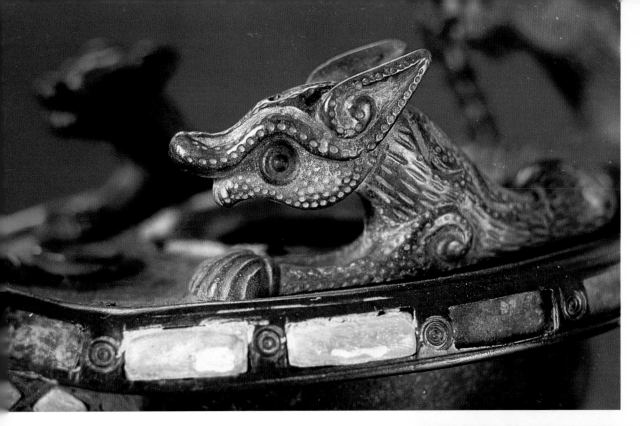

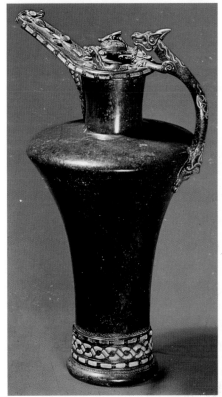

III, IV *Second of a pair of bronze flagons with coral and enamel decoration from Basse-Yutz, Moselle, France. The detail (above) shows a handle attachment in the shape of a dog or wolf. H. of flagon 38.7 cm. LT A, late 5th or early 4th c. BC.*

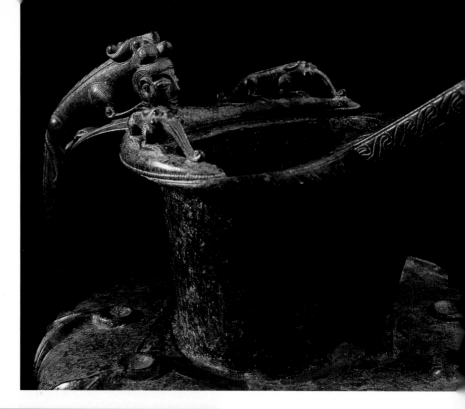

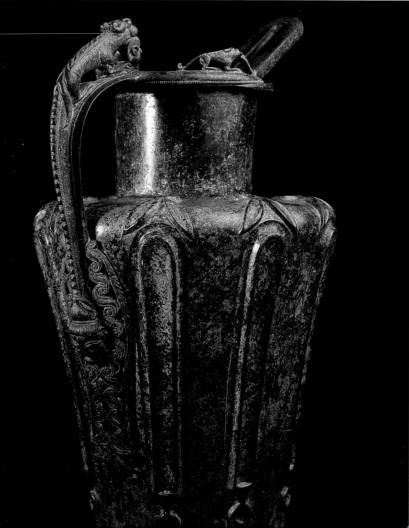

V, VI   *Bronze flagon from grave 112, Dürrnberg bei Hallein, Ld. Salzburg, Austria. The detail (above) shows a cast beast forming a handle attachment. H. of flagon 45.8 cm. LT A, late 5th c. BC.*

Though these vessels are locally made, as is shown by the punch-dots and the absence of portrayals of women, they also recall the art of the *situla*, or bronze bucket for wine-mixing, stemming from northern Italy.

The beginning of the tradition of representational scenes on bronze vessels, and sometimes on belt-plaques, goes back to the later seventh century and the orientalizing phase of Etruscan art. From Etruria this spread north to Este at the head of the Adriatic and thence into eastern Hallstatt areas where it continued relatively unchanged until about 400 BC. Some later situlae are archaizing, depicting artefacts and probably customs a century old at the time of their manufacture. They are, however, of great importance to the later development of La Tène Celtic art in the western Hallstatt province, since they became one of the major means of transmission from the eastern into the western Celtic zone of so-called oriental or orientalizing elements such as sphinxes, griffons and lions, together with certain forms of hatching, and backward-looking pairs of animals. These are all elements which were absorbed into the 'Early Style' of La Tène Celtic art dealt with in the following chapter.

Elements of archaic Greek mythology and of Greek decoration are visible in situla art; for example 'Corinthian' lions, grazing deer and rosettes appear as fill-in on the arcades of plant-based forms which often separate representational scenes. It was through Etruria, however, that this Greek legacy was transmitted, perhaps via the Euboean colonies of Pithekoussai and Cumae, established in the eighth century, rather than directly from such Corinthian foundations as Apollonia, established at the head of the Adriatic at the end of the sixth century BC.

The earliest situla known is that from the Villa Benvenuti at Este, from around 650 BC. Of almost the same early date, and also from Este, though found at Hallstatt, are the lids of situlae from cremation graves 696 and 697. That from grave 697 clearly shows the proto-Corinthian rosettes as well as a frieze of dogs with raised tails. On the example from grave 696, the orientalizing sphinx and lion with hatched wings and mane alternate with stags. The latter, characteristically, have plants hanging from their mouths while in the lion's mouth is a half-eaten animal. Among the other contents of the rich grave 696 is a locally-made belt-plaque showing a waterbird with adaptations of the proto-Corinthian rosettes. The *fibulae*, or safety-pin brooches, and the antennae-hilted dagger from this burial give a sixth-century date for the grave; the situla itself dates from around 600 BC.

Though the use of narrative and many of the motifs of situla art are derived from Etruria, the situlae or buckets themselves go back to Bronze Age bucket shapes. The situlae proper are generally decorated with repoussé work with subsequent engraving, though some are engraved only. Situla art depicts life as seen from a masculine viewpoint, in which women are servants or sex-objects; most of the scenes which include humans are of the feasts in which the situlae themselves figure, of the hunt or of war.

In the sixth and fifth centuries, situlae were also produced in the northern Slovene area of Jugoslavia, south of the eastern end of the Alps, where there appear to have been at least two separate workshops, one at

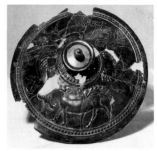

21 *Bronze situla lid showing winged lions from Hallstatt, Salzkammergut, Austria, grave 696. D. 23.7 cm. Early 6th c. BC.*

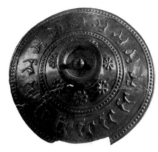

22 *Bronze situla lid showing dogs and 'Corinthian' rosettes from Hallstatt, Salzkammergut, Austria, grave 697. D. 22.9 cm. 6th c. BC.*

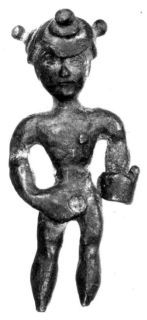

Vače and the other at Magdalenska gora. On a belt-plaque from Magdalenska gora, barrow IIB, are two ithyphallic boxers with miniature dumb-bells, confronting each other across a helmet on a stand, watched by a horseman. The belt-plaque from Vače shows the confrontation of two axe-wielding horsemen, one with long flowing hair, each backed by a shield-carrying foot soldier; at the right a civilian in a wide-brimmed hat seems remarkably unconcerned. Both date from about the fifth century BC.

From Vače again, from a barrow excavated in less than model fashion in 1927, comes a cast bronze warrior figurine. It was probably found in a grave where the only identifiable weapon was a spear. The figurine may have been mounted on a staff by means of a cylindrical bronze ferrule which also survives. The figure is naked save for his helmet; he may once have held a spear in his left hand, with the right hand grasping his (separately attached) penis, now missing. The helmet itself is of an eastern Hallstatt type found in eighth- and seventh-century graves at Smarjeta in Slovenia. It is also portrayed in much later representations, notably on the splendid late situla from grave 68 of the Certosa Cemetery at Bologna, dated to about 500 BC. The Vače figurine, on the grounds that its body outline is similar to that of some Greek *kouroi* – nude male statues – has been claimed as a Greek artefact, portraying archaic Greek armour, and to be as early as the seventh century BC. It is more probably a local Slovene product of the sixth century, showing Greek influence but not of Greek origin.

23 Bronze figurine from Vače, Slovenia, Jugoslavia. H. 24 cm. c. 500 BC.

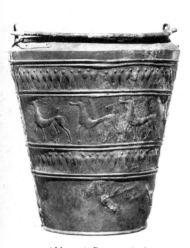

24 (Above) Bronze situla no. 1 from Novo mesto-Kandija, Slovenia, Jugoslavia, grave IV/3. H. 21 cm. c. 400 BC.

25 (Right) Bronze situla from Certosa di Bologna, Italy, grave 68. H. (of panels) c. 7 cm. Early 5th c. BC.

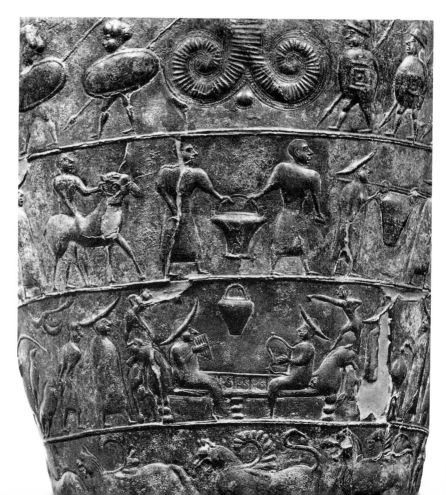

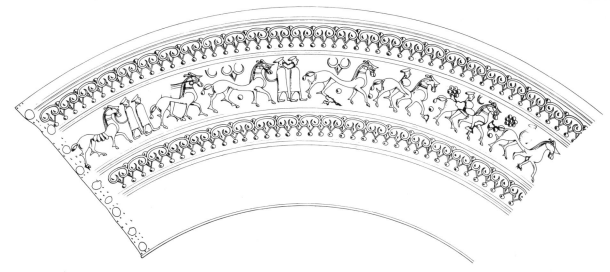

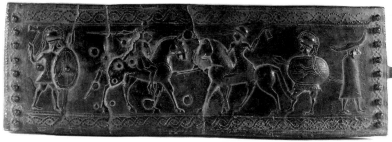

The last of the major Slovene sites to adopt its own local situla art was
Novo mesto, where recent excavation has thrown a great deal of light on the
later prehistory of the eastern Hallstatt zone, as well as on the effects of
Celtic La Tène settlement from the west in the third century BC. The
Kandija group of four large barrows at Novo mesto produced several
situlae. One, barrow IV grave 3, was the central one of twenty-six burials
arranged in a ring. With the chieftain in his timber-lined chamber were
horse bones and harness, including horse-bits of the so-called 'Scythian'
Szentes-Vekerzug type, a ridged local east Alpine Negau-type helmet –
deliberately damaged before burial about 400 BC – an axe and spears.

The two situlae from barrow IV grave 3 are probably local and display
friezes of animals and flowers; a similar pair came from a woman's grave in
barrow II. Local pottery from the Kandija barrows includes crude white-
encrusted urns whose stylized designs and lop-sided manufacture make
them poor descendants of earlier pottery.

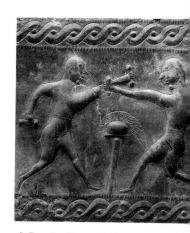

28 Detail of bronze belt-plaque
from Magdalenska gora,
Slovenia, Jugoslavia, barrow
IIB. W. 10.4 cm. 5th c. BC.

THE WESTERN ZONE IN
THE LATE HALLSTATT PERIOD

In the Hallstatt D period, which follows Hallstatt C, there was no major
change in the art or culture of the eastern Hallstatt area, but there were
dramatic developments in the west. These include the emergence in eastern

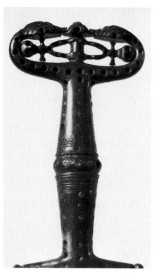

29 *Bronze hilt of an antennae-dagger from Hallstatt, Salzkammergut, Austria, grave 116. W. c. 5.4 cm. Ha D, 6th c. BC.*

OPPOSITE

30 *(Above) Detail of bronze belt-plate from Kaltbrunn, Kr. Konstanz, Germany. W. 17.5 cm. Ha D1, early 6th c. BC.*

31 *(Below) Detail of punch-decorated sheet bronze from couch-back, showing combat with swords and horse-drawn wheeled vehicles, from Eberdingen-Hochdorf, Kr. Ludwigsburg, Germany. W. 13.8 cm. Ha D1, mid-6th c. BC.*

France, southern Germany and Switzerland of new, so-called 'princely', settlements, associated with extremely rich burials. These graves display gold ornaments, particularly neckrings, which are interpreted by some archaeologists as emblems of supreme earthly – and possibly spiritual – rank. The settlements appear to have traded widely with other parts of Europe, especially the Mediterranean, importing bronze vessels for wine from Greeks and Etruscans, as well as a great deal of Greek black-figure pottery, possibly from Massalia (modern Marseilles), founded at the mouth of the Rhône in the sixth century BC. Certainly Mont Lassois in Burgundy contains the largest quantity of such wares; its situation would make it the most easily reached from Massalia. The Heuneburg, the great settlement on the headwaters of the Danube, displays a mud-brick wall of bastion construction suggesting the use of Greek craftsmen or Greek influence; it is possible that similar construction methods were also used at the Britzgyberg in Alsace.

In this period, the short dagger replaced the long sword in male graves in the western Hallstatt region; these daggers were quite probably not fighting weapons but symbols of rank. A few long swords are still found, but other weapons or defensive armour vanish almost entirely from graves in the western area in this phase. Another feature which distinguishes the Hallstatt D period is the widespread adoption of the fibula, or safety-pin brooch, as a means of fastening clothing, as opposed to earlier, simpler, pins. The evolution of these brooches has been used to subdivide the Hallstatt D period into three subphases based on a relative chronology.

The absolute chronology of Hallstatt D is less securely established. The most common view is that it corresponds more or less to the sixth century BC, with each subphase occupying roughly a generation. The most recent study of Hallstatt D in the princely area, by Konrad Spindler, on the basis of a dendrochronological date for the largest of all Hallstatt burial mounds (though by no means the richest), the Magdalenenberg bei Villingen in the Black Forest, sets the start of Hallstatt D1 at 550 BC and the end of Hallstatt D3 at 350 BC. The Magdalenenberg date, however, has already been twice revised, while for the 350 BC date even Spindler produces virtually no justification. Though some overlap between Hallstatt D3 and La Tène A periods is possible – and much discussed – there is clear evidence of La Tène culture by the middle of the fifth century BC. Here, it will generally be taken that Hallstatt D roughly corresponds to the sixth and early fifth centuries BC.

One example of the short swords or daggers from the Hallstatt cemetery is illustrated here. It is of iron with a bronze sheath and has a typical 'antennae'-shaped openwork hilt, while the brooch found with it was a 'serpentine' fibula. The hilt and scabbard are inset with bead-shaped bone pieces, and on the hilt two backward-curved birds' heads enclose two tiny human figures. In Aichach in Bavaria a dagger was found which is so similar – with horses replacing humans – that it probably came from the same workshop.

Some characteristic features of the princely area – as well as some aspects reminiscent of the art of the eastern zone – can be seen in a recently excavated grave in Baden-Württemberg, a satellite of the as-yet-unexplored Hohenasperg. The barrow of Eberdingen-Hochdorf was originally around 60 m in diameter. Its ramp, leading down from an entrance in the stone walls, has parallels in the tomb architecture of the eastern Hallstatt zone. All but three of the other graves in the mound had been destroyed by ploughing, but the wooden central chamber had survived both agriculture and the tomb-robbing to which many of the rich Hallstatt graves were subjected in prehistoric times.

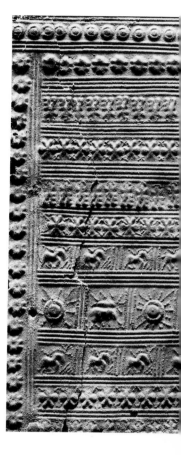

The forty-year-old 'prince' of Hochdorf was well supplied for the funeral feast. The walls of the chamber were lined with hangings and the floor covered with textiles; nine drinking-horns hung at the southern end. On the four-wheeled wagon were three bronze bowls and nine bronze plates, as well as an axe, a knife, harness for two horses and a bronze-decorated yoke. The 6-foot-tall (*c*. 1.83 m) chieftain was covered with gold from head to foot. His neckring, belt, armring and brooches were of gold; his antennae-hilted dagger and even his shoes were covered in gold leaf. All the gold was produced with the same punch, and debris of gold- and bronzeworking was also found within the burial mound, so presumably it was locally made specifically for the burial. The neckring carries rows of tiny horses with riders – a motif similar to the horses alternating with sun and duck symbols on the bronze belt-plaque from Kaltbrunn, Kr. Konstanz.

Such sheet bronze repoussé belt-plaques, it is worth noting here, were a feature of Hallstatt metalwork in the western area. No two are identical, suggesting that they were specially commissioned pieces, individual badges of rank perhaps. Many have been found with remnants of organic material from the belts still adhering. The Kaltbrunn example comes from a barrow containing eighteen skeleton burials and the remains of a funeral pyre; fine Alb-Hegau pottery was also found.

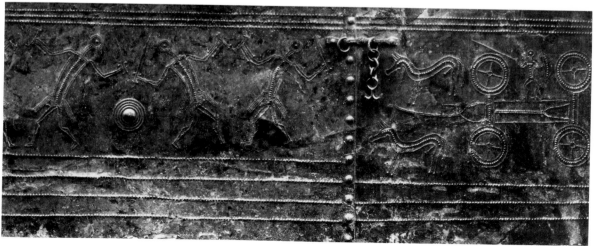

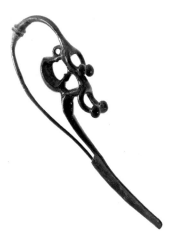

32 Bronze serpentine brooch from the Magdalenenberg bei Villingen, Schwarzwald-Baar-Kreis, Germany, grave 81. L. 15.5 cm. Ha D1, early 6th c. BC.

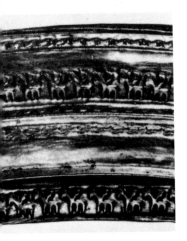

33 Detail of gold neckring from Eberdingen-Hochdorf, Kr. Ludwigsburg, Germany. D. 25.3 cm. Ha D1/D2, mid-6th c. BC.

The most unusual feature of the Hochdorf burial was the 3-m-long couch, with traces of upholstery, placed along the western wall of the chamber and embellished with punch-dot decorated sheet bronze reminiscent of the Kleinklein material. The body lay on this, rather than, as is usual, on the wagon, and the copper acetate salts have preserved some of the organic material well, including some striking coloured embroidery. The idea of drinking while reclining on a couch – as well as the flat conical birchbark hat worn by the prince – recalls the art of the situla, but the technique is more like that on the Kleinklein vessels from the eastern Hallstatt zone. At each end of the couch backrest is a schematic four-wheeled wagon drawn by two horses, with a driver carrying a sword and spear. In between are three pairs of long-haired figures, apparently armed with true swords and fighting or dancing – again recalling eastern Hallstatt narrative and situla art. The feet of the couch were formed of eight cast bronze female figures with upraised arms, like those of the Strettweg cult wagon, all with bone- and amber-inlaid decoration indicating neckring, armrings, anklets and belt, and with pierced ears. Six were mounted on wheels, so that this extraordinarily eastern-looking couch was virtually on castors.

The classical connection is represented by a bronze cauldron some 1 m in diameter and 0.8 m high, once containing mead, found in the northwestern corner of the grave chamber. The usual classical tripod had apparently been replaced by a wooden structure covered by badger skin. Two of the three couchant lions and the three massive bronze handles soldered on the rim appear to have been adapted from a much larger vessel, imported from the Greek colonies in southern Italy or from Greece itself. The third lion, nicknamed 'The Rat' by its excavators, seems to have been separately, but more expertly, cast by Celtic imitators. One of the original lions has an incised mane, apparently unfinished, which may also have been added by its northern owners. This foreshadows the process of selection, imitation and transformation by which Celtic craftsmen, faced with the stimulus of classical imports, transformed Hallstatt art into that of the La Tène period.

The two gold serpentine brooches date Eberdingen-Hochdorf to the transition period between Hallstatt D1 and D2; a related type is the fine bronze brooch with two stylized bull's heads from a woman's grave, one of 125 satellite burials under the Magdalenenberg.

Gold was probably imported to the western Hallstatt zone, possibly as bars or as massive roughed out pieces. Bohemia is one possible source, though the Iberian peninsula is another, for the gold bowl found under a stone slab together with some pottery – all that survives from a rich burial at Altstetten, near Zürich – may be a finished import from Iberia. Certainly Iberian imports have been found at the Magdalenenberg in Germany, and possibly too at La Butte and Vix in eastern France. The Altstetten bowl sets a frieze of alternating animals with sun and moon symbols against an all-over pattern of repoussé gold dots.

Later pottery in the western chieftainly zone continued to be handmade till the introduction of the potter's wheel from the Mediterranean at the

34 (Right) One of eight figurines supporting the bronze couch from Eberdingen–Hochdorf (ill. 31). H. 35 cm. Ha D1/D2, mid-6th c. BC.

35,36,37 Two of the three bronze lions from the rim of the cauldron from Eberdingen–Hochdorf. (Below) Imported lion no. 1. L. 33.8 cm. (Bottom) 'The rat' (lion no. 3) probably locally made. L. 34.4 cm (Bottom right) Incised mane of no. 1 lion. Ha D1/D2, mid-6th c. BC.

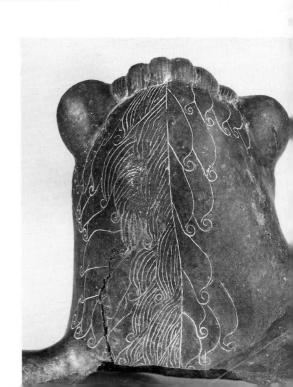

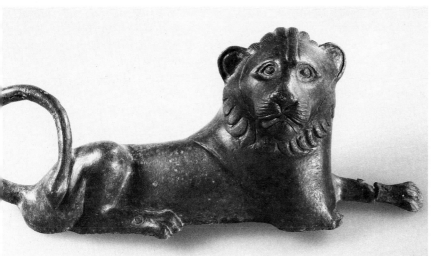

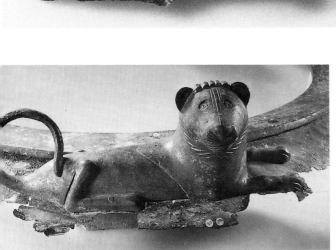

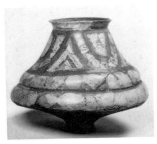

38 *Pot painted in red and white from 'Burrenhof', Marking-Erkenbrechtsweiler, Kr. Nürlingen, Germany, barrow 2, grave 1. H. 22 cm. Ha D, early 6th c. BC.*

39 *(Below) 'Alb-Hegau' style pottery, incised and painted in red and black from Nenzingen, Kr. Konstanz, Germany, grave I. H. (of largest pot) 29.4 cm. Ha D, 6th c. BC.*

very end of the Hallstatt period. It shows greater use of colour and more complex designs than that of the earlier phase. From the Heuneburg itself comes a range of small-footed, wide-bellied urns, similar in profile to those from Sopron, and made in the period of the Greek-derived mud-brick wall. These are more finely executed than the more easterly pots, very possibly made with the aid of a turntable, and they are painted in red and white.

In Switzerland, on the peninsula running northwest of Konstanz, a number of barrow cemeteries were constructed during the first part of Hallstatt D. These contain examples of fine polychrome and white-encrusted pottery, the so-called Alb-Hegau style, here illustrated from Nenzingen, Kt. Konstanz. Their decoration has been compared to the lozenge-based designs on contemporary metalwork and also with embroidered textiles, which occasionally survive. Such a textile fragment was found in the chieftain's tomb, grave 6, of the 14-m-high Hohmichele, to the southeast of the Heuneburg, perhaps the last resting place of the Heuneburg's ruling dynasty. It incorporated silk thread, which had perhaps come from the Far East, via Persia and the northern Balkans. The Hohmichele is roughly contemporary with Eberdingen-Hochdorf, and similar in layout and burial rite. Hochdorf's textile remnants include embroidery in blue and yellow, incorporating Greek key and swastika designs similar to local pottery, as at the Hohmichele.

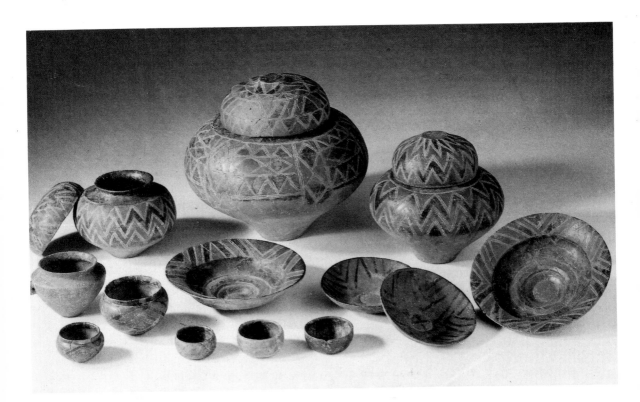

A different style of pottery is represented by the red and grey designs found at the 'Burrenhof', Kr. Nürlingen in southern Germany. This has been nicknamed 'Batik' style, though the technique has, of course, nothing to do with that for producing southeast Asian cloth patterns. It has such close parallels with pottery from the Heuneburg itself that it may perhaps have been produced in a workshop there. Visible within the design is a highly stylized human face, foreshadowing the elusive Cheshire-cat faces of La Tène art, though it is not easy to accept a theory that the very origins of this later style are to be found in such south German material.

One unique piece of stone sculpture from late in the Hallstatt period comes again from Germany, from the tumulus of Hirschlanden in the region of the Hohenasperg. A life-size figure of a naked warrior, carved from the local Stuben sandstone, was found by the stone kerb of a 'dynastic' barrow containing two central graves and sixteen satellites. The few associated finds suggest the barrow was created around 500 BC or later, the start of the 'century of crisis' in the old Hallstatt area. The figure has been broken off at the feet, but the neckring and dagger he wears are clear symbols of power in the late Hallstatt world.

At one time the figure must have stood on top of the barrow. The pointed helmet and aggressively ithyphallic posture recall once more Strettweg and the eastern Hallstatt area. The contrast with the earlier and simpler sandstone figures in the region is striking, and the hunched shoulders, exaggerated hips and well-muscled thighs and calves show southern influence. One may dismiss recent suggestions that the contemporary male statues of archaic Greece, the kouroi, offer a parallel, or that the Hirschlanden figure was carved by a sculptor from mainland Greece or adapted locally from a kouros. The resemblance to the sixth-century figure of a warrior from the central Italian cemetery of the Vestini at Capestrano and the curious position of the left hand with outstretched thumb, which can be seen on contemporary Etruscan funerary urns as well as on a funerary stele from Chiusi, point to a more probable Italian source of inspiration. The cultural and trading links with Italy are clear and the period is one when communities north of the Alps were becoming remarkably receptive to southern influences. Seasonal patterns of movement, including transhumance, probably contributed to such exchanges. The Hirschlanden figure may be the work of a local stonecarver conversant with transalpine styles or of an immigrant sculptor trying to adapt his skills to local customs and local materials.

Whichever may be the case, the transition from the sixth to the fifth century sees a time of political turmoil; the increase of what may be described as 'amulets' in graves of the period may reflect also a period of psychological turmoil. Significant in this context, in Ludwig Pauli's view, are pairs of miniature naked bronze men and women, the former always in a state of sexual arousal, since explicit sexuality is rarely shown in Celtic art.

The finest and certainly most spectacular of the imports into the Hallstatt world were associated with drink, and none were so spectacular as the great bronze *krater*, or wine-mixing jar, from Vix. It was over 1.5 m tall,

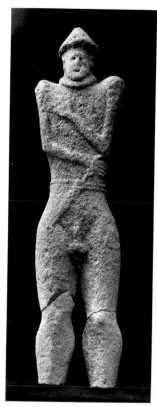

40 *Sandstone statue of nude warrior from Hirschlanden, Kr. Leonberg, Germany. Extant H. 1.5 m. Ha D3, late 6th/early 5th c. BC.*

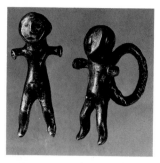

41 Bronze nude figurines on finger-rings from Stuttgart-Uhlbach, Germany. H. 2.7 cm. Ha D3, late 6th/early 5th c. BC.

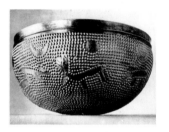

42 Gold bowl from Altstetten, Kt. Zürich, Switzerland. D. 25 cm. Ha D2, late 6th c. BC.

with a capacity of some 1,250 litres, and was found in a 'princess's' grave of about 500 BC, below the local late Hallstatt stronghold of Mont Lassois near Châtillon-sur-Seine. The princess, buried on a dismantled four-wheeled wagon, has been claimed as a Hallstatt 'transvestite', a prince with female attributes; the anatomical evidence is, however, for a 35-year-old woman. Notwithstanding this, claims have been made that this and some other late Hallstatt burials, such as Bad Cannstatt, do not so much reflect sexual practices as the need to establish male power in a matriarchal society.

One of the most striking objects in the Vix burial was found on the skull and was thus originally interpreted as a diadem. It is more likely to be a torc or neckring, made of hollow 24 carat gold and weighing some 480 g. The ends of the ring are fashioned as lion's paws resting on spheres. On the back of the paws a pair of winged ponies stand on filigree pads. Much has been made of the apparent similarities of the ponies to steppe horses, this supposedly supporting an origin in a Graeco-Scythian workshop in the Black Sea region. Since filigree is a common technique of ancient Italian jewellers, an Etruscan origin has also been suggested. The form and technique of the ring have parallels in Iberia, too. In view of other definite imports from this area, or from Italy, which have been found in late Hallstatt contexts, it seems better to reject an eastern origin for the little Pegasus horses in favour of one in the western Mediterranean, albeit unidentified as to precise location.

The krater, old when buried, was made either in the Greek settlement area around Tarentum in south Italy or possibly in Corinth, in mainland Greece itself, most probably some time in the second half of the sixth century. Two related, though smaller, mixing jars come from the Jugoslav cemetery of Trebenište, as does a 'Droop' cup, the nickname for a particular type of Attic black-figure drinking cup decorated by the so-called 'Wraith' painter around 520 BC, which was also found in the Vix burial – a popular export line occurring in some numbers in contemporary Massalia. The krater had been assembled with the aid of location marks incised in Greek characters. This may have been just part of the workshop practice, since it is known to occur on other bronzes, but it is also possible that the Vix krater was taken apart for transportation. It is not mere fancy to suggest that it was accompanied on its journey by, if not a Greek, then someone conversant with Greek. He may well have come to Vix not via the Adriatic and over the Alps – certainly the route followed more and more from the sixth century onwards with the increase in Etruscan imports – but rather through Massalia. The considerable trade up the Rhône and to Mont Lassois near the head-waters of the Saône, possibly in exchange for north European tin, was at a time when Greece and her colonies were losing control of the western seaways, and Vix heralds the end of an era not only for the western Hallstatt area but for Massalia.

Also in the tomb were a beaked bronze wine flagon and bronze dish, both Italian products of that Etruscan metal-producing centre, Vulci. The flagon is of a type in production for about a century from around 550 BC and particularly popular either as imports or as local copies in later Celtic rich

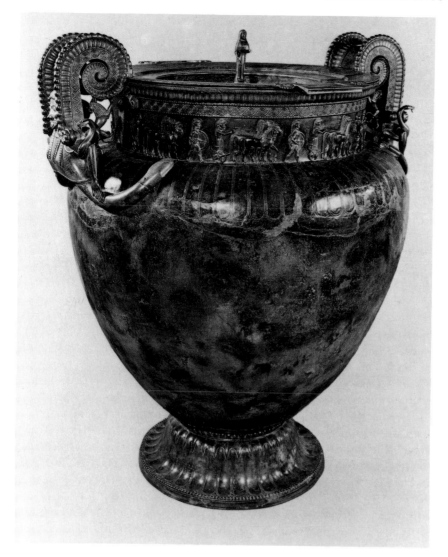

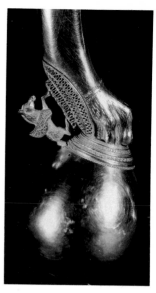

43 (Left) Bronze krater of Greek origin from Vix, Côte d'Or, France. H. 1.64m. c. 530 BC.

44 (Above) Terminal of a gold neckring with winged horse and animal paw from Vix, Côte d'Or, France. H. of terminal c. 2.5 cm. Ha D3, c. 500 BC.

graves. The bases of the cast handles of these flagons are often in the form of bearded Silenus or satyr heads and part of a clay mould for one such flagon handle was found on the Heuneburg. Although unfortunately without datable context, stylistically it must belong to the earlier part of the fifth century. Again, it strongly suggests either an emigrant craftsman or – even more significant in the context of observing how local artisans were adapting motifs by producing imitations of Etruscan bronzes – a relic of a native workshop.

Although contact with Greece and her colonies occasionally manifested itself at the beginning of the later or La Tène Iron Age, it is Italy, a country where motifs grew like weeds, which politically, economically and artistically became ever more dominant in the development of Celtic culture.

ANCIENT PATTERNS OF CULTURE

Before, however, we leave the late Hallstatt D culture of these first western Celts or proto-Celts, we must say something about the rise and fall of their sway in western Europe, the society they created and the art they produced.

The use of gold and the apparently greater social stratification of this period, with its less widespread interment of weapons or defensive armour, suggests perhaps a more stable and strife-free world than that of Hallstatt C. The art itself clearly reflects the widespread exchange connections of this late Hallstatt western world and its increasing contacts with the classical world of the expanding Greek trading colonies around the Mediterranean basin and with Etruria; this is clear from the pottery of southern Germany, the Hirschlanden statue and the connections shown by the Vix burial.

Following Franz Fischer, some writers have seen these imports as the start of a pattern of 'gift-exchange'; the donation of luxury items as a mutual recognition of status between those of high rank, the *keimelia* recorded by Homer. In modern times such a pattern is seen in the exchange of symbolic, largely useless, gifts by heads of state. It must, however, be emphasized that such gift-giving, even in Homer, is rarely reciprocal, and that it tends to symbolize an already existing political or commercial relationship. It may supplement existing patterns of interaction but rarely exists without them. Other archaeologists, then, reconstructing the nature of Iron Age society prefer to emphasize the significance of the Greek or Etruscan entrepreneur in the growth of long-range commerce. Greek colonists and Etruscan merchants actively sought markets for goods; it is more probable that they travelled in search of their markets than that northern Europeans travelled in search of southern goods. The placing of Hallstatt D settlements near water routes or Alpine passes is unlikely to be accidental. What the northerners exchanged for southern merchandise, which increasingly included wine as well as the vessels in which to serve it, is not clear. The western zone produced no salt; agricultural produce, minerals or slaves are possibilities but have left no real trace in the archaeological record.

Some writers have seen both the rise and the decline of the late princely Hallstatt culture as due to trade with the south. Fifteenth-century African patterns of controlling wealth and power by monopolizing trade with the outside world and redistributing that wealth to secondary settlements have been used as analogies to account for the rise of such great Hallstatt centres of power as the Heuneburg, Mont Lassois, the Britzgyberg in Alsace and the Camp-le-Château in the Jura and also for the increase in social differentiation.

Leaving aside the value of models so far removed in space and time from our proto-Celtic subjects, it seems unlikely that such development would itself be possible without an improved agricultural base and perhaps increased population in these areas. Trade with the outside world was obviously not the sole nor even the primary means of economic survival or political control, and its prominence in the archaeological record as we know it should not blind us to the fact that at most its role is likely to have been auxiliary rather than central to the economic and political life of the area.

The same applies too to the collapse of the Hallstatt D cultures, which we can certainly read in the archaeological record. Many of the old chieftainly centres, most notably the Heuneburg, were actually destroyed; many of the Hallstatt graves were robbed and the custom of barrow burial temporarily vanished. Population and power shifted to new areas – to western Switzerland, the Marne region in France, and the Hunsrück-Eifel area west of the Middle Rhine – in the succeeding La Tène period, which may have overlapped with the end of the Hallstatt D era. The richer graves in the Hunsrück-Eifel often contain two-wheeled vehicles rather than four-wheeled wagons, a hint perhaps of increased Etruscan influence. The settlements too are smaller and more scattered, extending eastwards into Bohemia and to the southern Netherlands.

The reasons for the downfall of the western Hallstatt D society are obscure, but are likely to be more complex than merely the loss of control of external trade. Internal revolution against hated tyrants, a fundamental change in political or religious systems leading to the rejection of old hierarchies, epidemic disease, the failure of local agriculture, are all possible explanations which the archaeological record fails to illustrate, since they leave no material remains. The grave-robbing and destruction of the Hallstatt D tombs and settlements do, however, suggest a violent rejection of the old way of life, rather than a peaceful emigration or transfer of power and population. The archaeological record produces no evidence for external invasion or pressures as an explanation.

The attraction of the iron ores of the Hunsrück-Eifel is equally unlikely to be the major cause of the shift, though they may account for the wealth of this Rhineland area. There are no similar mineral deposits in the Marne area, which shows simultaneous settlement, while in central Europe, where ores are available, there was no contemporary shift in political power. The exploitation of the iron in the Hunsrück-Eifel seems to have been a consequence rather than a cause of population movements.

It is perhaps not coincidental that the Early La Tène, or indisputably Celtic, period in western Europe, sees a growing dependence on trade with the Etruscans rather than with the Greek colonies. At this time Etruria found its southern expansion blocked by the Greek colonies in Italy, while the Greeks themselves increasingly found that Carthaginian dominance of the western Mediterranean forced them also to look north for commercial expansion, to areas at the head of the Adriatic and round the Black Sea. It was when Greeks and Etruscans found new markets in the fourth century that the early La Tène Celts themselves embarked on a period of expansion and conquest, perhaps to gain continued access to products from the south.

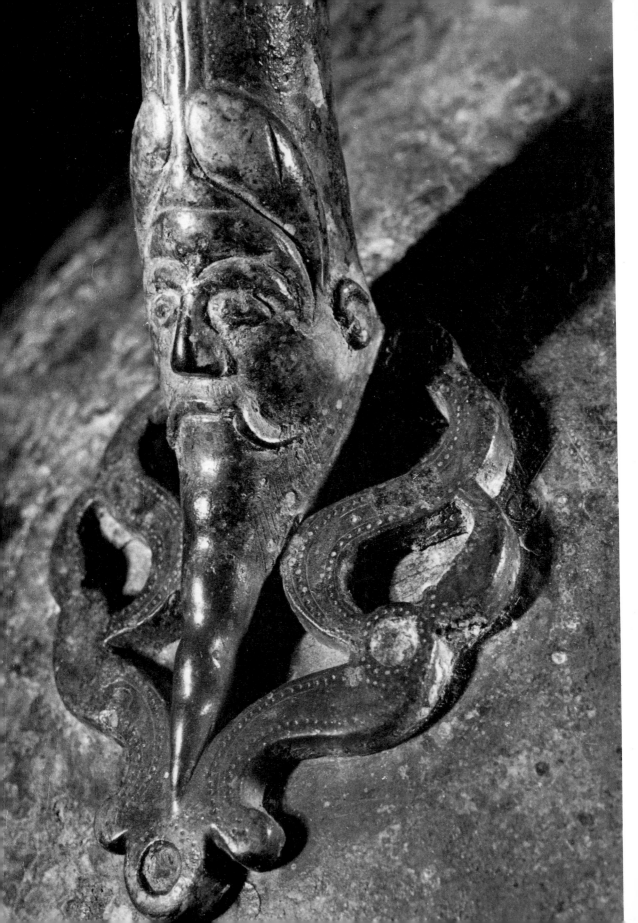

2
The Chieftainly Art of
the Early La Tène Celts

IN WESTERN EUROPE IN the fifth century the first quite definitely Celtic art is discernible. Its apparently sudden appearance and fantastic imagery caused its most distinguished student Paul Jacobsthal to describe it as 'an art without a genesis'.

Much of the richest and most characteristic material comes from the hundred or so rich barrow graves in the Middle Rhine and Hunsrück-Eifel. Such very wealthy graves are rare in the other areas, such as the Marne, southern Belgium or western Czechoslovakia, which also produce art of this Strict, or Early La Tène, style. The Rhineland areas seem to have been the most innovative artistically as well as the richest and most hierarchical materially.

Despite the difficulties of tracing a precise ancestry, it is possible to identify the main influences at work. These include the translation into Celtic terms of certain imported classical and orientalizing elements, which were grafted on to the root-stock of the late Hallstatt art of the west.

The Rhineland areas in particular maintained and extended their wide trading links with the Mediterranean. Attic pottery and Etruscan bronze wine vessels attest to the continuing Celtic passion for wine and for the wherewithal to serve it at feasts both in this world and in the afterlife. Mediterranean coral appears on Celtic flagons, brooches, scabbards and neckrings. Exports probably continued to be such basic necessities as ores, slaves and, from further east, salt. The agricultural base must have been efficiently exploited, since population seems to have increased markedly in the course of the fifth century, contributing an impetus to Celtic territorial expansion in the fourth century. In these areas where Greek and Italic imports are concentrated, Celtic craftsmen began to copy the designs, which were available in profusion and over a long period of time. This was a highly selective process, since elements such as narrative art were not adopted from classical prototypes, while more congenial aspects such as plant designs were transmuted into purely Celtic forms.

There is a marked distinction in this development between the westerly regions of the Rhine, Moselle and Marne and the more easterly and southerly areas of the former western Hallstatt region round the Rhine-Danube, which have been described as a separate 'eastern style Province' in this fifth- to fourth-century period. It extends through the old Hallstatt areas, from Austria through Switzerland to Bavaria and Baden-Württemberg, to overlap with the western area in Alsace. Though there

45 (Opposite) *Head on the handle base of a spouted bronze flagon from Waldalgesheim, Kr. Mainz–Bingen, Germany. H. (of head)* c. *4 cm. Late LT A/ early LT B1, mid-4th c. BC.*

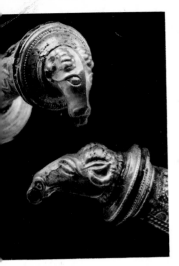

46 Rams' heads on the terminals of gold drinking-horns from Kleinaspergle, Kr. Ludwigsburg, Germany. L. (of lower head) 1.8 cm. LT A, mid-5th c. BC.

was obviously considerable interchange between these two Celtic areas, and some elements of western styles can be found also in the Rhine-Danube province, the distribution of grave goods between male and female is different and while pottery was deposited in graves in the east, this was rarely the case further west.

The single most productive site in this more easterly zone is the Dürrnberg-bei-Hallein, above the Salzach River, in Austria. Apparently developed or expanded in the seventh century to mine salt, perhaps in competition with Hallstatt itself, the site occupies a key geographical position; it is also just to the west of the old division between the Hallstatt-period eastern and western zones. There is no apparent break in occupation at the Dürrnberg at the end of the Hallstatt era. Between the fifth and third centuries BC it seems to have been a major trading and cultural exchange centre. Continuing excavation is still extending the extraordinary range and number of finds. There is also increasing evidence for local specialized craft production on the Dürrnberg. This, together with the continuity of occupation and of burial patterns, suggests that it represents an indigenous population over many generations, rather than incomers from outside. Despite strong links with southwest Germany in the late Hallstatt period, there was no destruction at the Dürrnberg and the inhabitants were apparently receptive to the changes which heralded the start of the La Tène era. It continued to maintain strong connections with southwest Germany and Bohemia in particular.

Some of the imported influences and their Celtic transformations can be shown in the contents of a rich barrow grave which was found, unusually, in an old Hallstatt centre of power. This is the Kleinaspergle, below the Hohenasperg defended settlement in Baden-Württemberg. The main grave chamber had been robbed, apparently in the Middle Ages, before the barrow was excavated in 1879. A side chamber, however, remained intact and contained cremated remains, possibly of a woman, though the pair of drinking-horns are a feature more usually associated with men. The funeral feast is represented by these horns, with their gold leaf covering, a plain bronze cauldron, an Italic cordoned bronze bucket, an Etruscan bronze *stamnos* (a tall two-handled vessel with cast decoration on its handle plates), two Attic pottery drinking-cups and a Celtic beaked bronze flagon which imitates Etruscan forms. The lack of local antecedents for the material and the secondary position of the burial in the mound suggests rather that this is a foreigner to the region, arriving by marriage or conquest, than that it is evidence for local development in this area.

One of the stemless drinking-cups shows a priestess before an altar and was painted by the so-called 'Amphitrite' painter in Attica, around 460–450 BC. The majority of the datable classical imports were made in the first half of the fifth century and, allowing some time for importation and use, suggest dates between 450 and 400 BC for such early rich graves as Kleinaspergle, Somme-Bionne, or Dürrnberg grave 44/2. In the absence of suitable timbers for dendrochronological dating or of a systematic radiocarbon dating programme, these imports offer at present the most

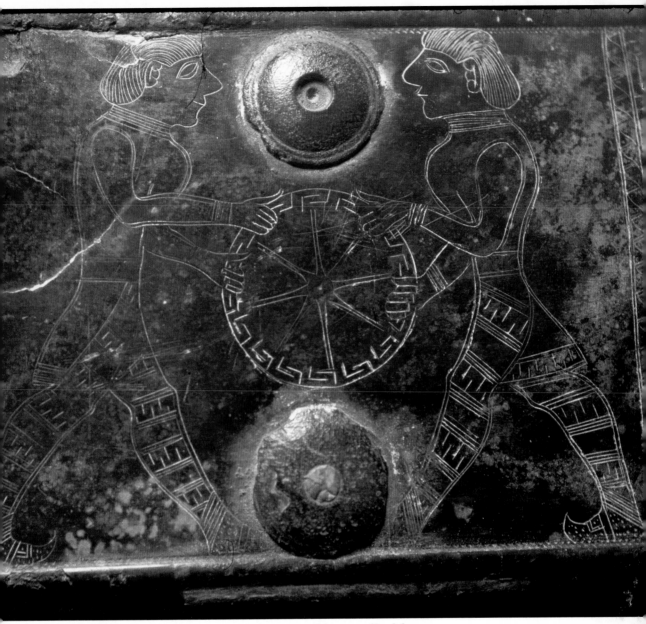

VII   *Confronted men holding a wheel, a detail from an iron and bronze scabbard from grave 994, Hallstatt, Austria. W. 5 cm. LT A, 400–350 BC.*

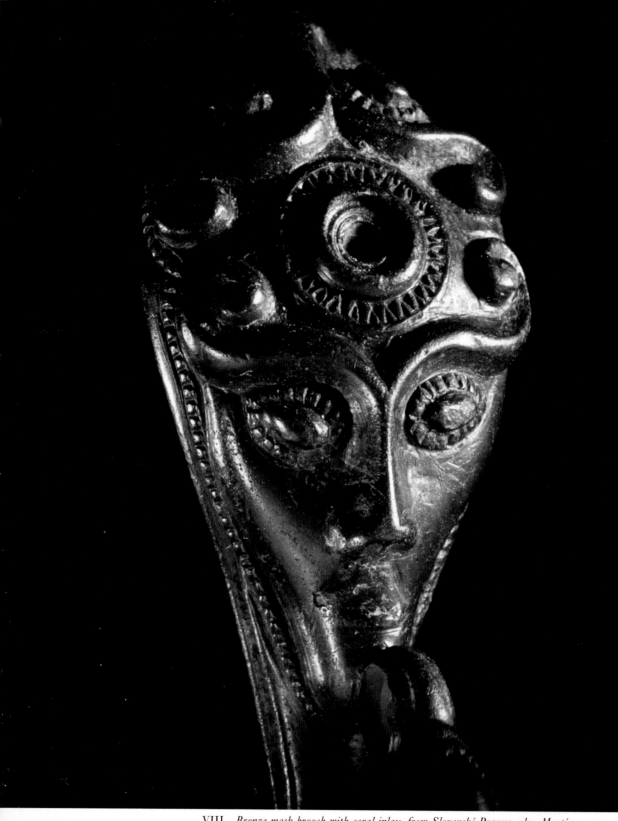

VIII *Bronze mask-brooch with coral inlay, from Slovenské Pravno, okr. Martín,*
Czechoslovakia. Total L. 6.2 cm. Late LT A, mid-4th c. BC.

secure chronological benchmarks for early Celtic Europe. Other works by the Amphitrite painter occur in northern Italy, which may show that Greek products came via Italy rather than by way of the Greek colony of Massalia at the mouth of the Rhône.

The value placed on the cups can be seen from the Celtic sheet goldwork which had been used to repair them, using palmette shapes based on classical plant motifs. Use and transformation of palmettes, lotus-buds or lotus-blossoms, themselves derived by the Greeks from Near Eastern prototypes such as the palm frond, are an important feature of the Celtic Early Style. Translated over time into a continuous form, they were to become the basis for the emergence of the later 'Vegetal' or Waldalgesheim style of Celtic art in the late fourth century BC.

Kleinaspergle also yielded a plaque, possibly part of costume or belt decoration. This is of openwork gold on an iron backing, with provision for coral inlay held in place by bronze rivets. It too displays classical plant motifs, this time lotus-buds at either end. The beaded edging is another characteristic of Early La Tène goldwork, particularly in the Middle Rhine region.

The use of drinking-horns, and the decoration of their terminals with sheep, are among a number of features which have been interpreted as oriental or orientalizing in the Celtic world. Here, the terminals may represent a ram and a ewe. Such 'eastern' features as the portrayal of sphinxes, griffons and backward-looking pairs of animals, as well as of the sheep from Kleinaspergle, and the route of their arrival in Celtic iconography, will be examined below.

Finally, the grave goods clearly show the Celtic adaptation of imported forms. The flagon is more concave in profile than its Italian prototypes. The separately cast handle branches over the rim as is the case on some Etruscan examples, displaying two prick-eared dog-like faces, instead of the more usual Etruscan lions. The face at the base of the handle, with its pointed ears, huge oval eyes and pursed mouth, is an adaptation of those on the handles of Etruscan stamnoi. One such import from the Rhineland barrow 2 grave at Weiskirchen offers an even closer parallel than the stamnos from Kleinaspergle itself. The forked beard and the spiral fill-ins above the ears of this satyr face are derived from late sixth-century Greek motifs transmitted to the Celts by way of Etruria, and used in the western area as one of two main prototypes for mask-like human faces in this period. Human heads appear in highly stylized form on a wide range of Celtic metalwork; they were apparently of central importance in Celtic iconography. Later written sources indicate that, to the Celts, the head was the seat of the soul as well as of the intellect.

The linear and floral geometric Hallstatt patterns persist into this new Celtic art, though they are scarcely evident on this Kleinaspergle material. They now generally, however, occupy the role of decorative fill-in rather than of central design elements.

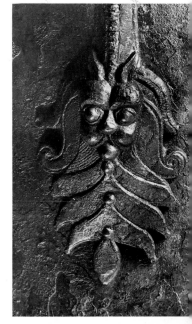

47 *Handle attachment of a bronze flagon from Kleinaspergle, Kr. Ludwigsburg, Germany. H.(of face) 7 cm. LT A, later 5th c. BC.*

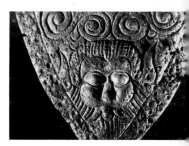

48 *Detail of handle attachment of a bronze Etruscan stamnos from Weiskirchen, Kr. Merzig-Wadern, Germany, barrow 2. H. (of face) 2.7 cm. 450–400 BC.*

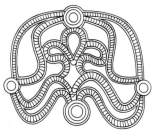

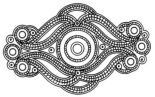

49 *Gold openwork band from a ?drinking-horn from Eigenbilzen, Limburg, Belgium. L. 22 cm. LT A, c. 400 BC.*

50 *Gold plaque on bronze and iron backing, from Chlum, okr. Rokyčany, Czechoslovakia. W. c. 5.3 cm. LT A, late 5th c. BC.*

PLANT MOTIFS: THE RHINE-MOSELLE AREA

Palmettes and lotus-buds frequently occur on other sheet goldwork from the rich graves of the Middle Rhine, such as the openwork gold covering for a wooden bowl from Schwarzenbach barrow I, one of a dozen burial mounds on the southern edge of the Hunsrück-Eifel. This male grave contained an Etruscan bronze amphora dating to the second quarter of the fifth century BC. Four gold plaques display tiny clean-shaven faces wearing comma-shaped headdresses like those on the Kleinaspergle flagon handle face. Another pair of gold discs at Schwarzenbach show the long-lasting Celtic pattern of triple whorls or triskels, linked into a continuous chain and enclosing curved-sided triangles in the manner of later La Tène B art. The beading which outlines each element is highly characteristic of Rhineland work generally, and in this particular case the considerable amount of gold sheet appears to be the output of a single skilled craftsman.

Standardization of chariot parts, together with such related gold- or bronzework as this, suggests that in the Rhineland there may have been fixed workshops or craft centres which were under princely patronage and thus had access to imported materials like coral and gold. If this is correct, the occurrence in Belgium, Switzerland and Czechoslovakia of very similar items demonstrates trade or gift-exchange rather than the existence of travelling craftsmen making goods to order.

Palmettes, lotus-buds and beaded edging certainly appear again on the openwork gold, perhaps a mount for a drinking-horn, found in 1871 at Eigenbilzen in Belgium – a northern extension of the Rhineland chieftainly grave area. Two similar tiny gold brooch-mounts were recovered from a barrow grave near the Uetliberg, a fortified settlement south of Zürich. This is one of the relatively few areas where life seems to have continued without much interruption from Hallstatt into Early La Tène times. To the east in Austria, the second salt-mining complex of the Dürrnberg produced similar discs from grave 44/2, and a sheet gold plaque on iron backing with a silvered engraved reverse from a warrior's grave at Chlum in Bohemia once

51 *(Right) Sheet gold disc showing chain of triskels or three-armed whirligigs from Schwarzenbach, Kr. St Wendel, Germany, grave I. D. 5 cm. LT A, later 5th c. BC.*

52 *(Opposite) Map of principal sites referred to in Chapter 2. (Regional divisions in burial customs of the Early La Tène period: 1 Marne – Mosel area; 2 Western Rhine – Danube area; 3 Eastern Rhine – Danube area; 4 Burgundy – Lorraine 'group'.)*

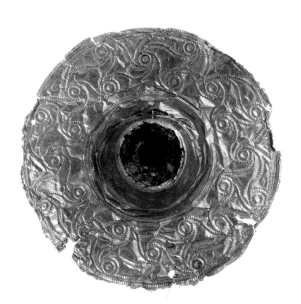

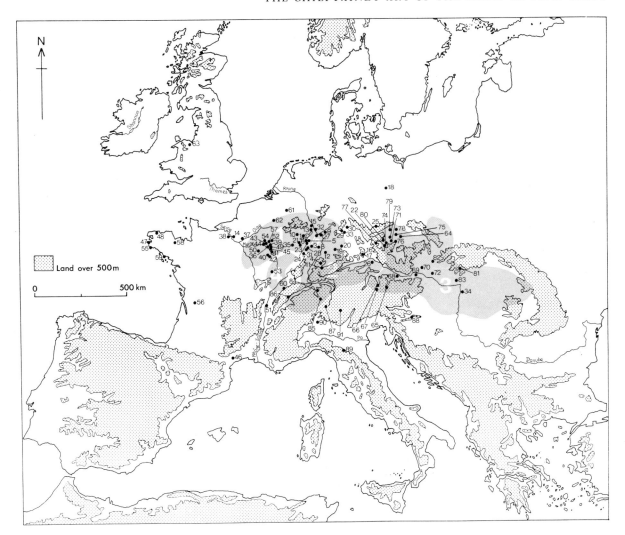

N

Land over 500m

0   500 km

Agris 56
Aignay-le-Duc 53
Ameis-Siesbach 6
Amfreville 38
Auvers-sur-Oise 37
Bad Dürkheim 8
Basse-Yutz 35
Berlin-Niederschönhausen 18
Berru 54
Besançon 60
Besseringen 21
Bexbach 31
Bormio 91
Braubach 32
Cerrig-y-Drudion 63
Chlum 71
Chynovský Háj 64
Courtisols 45
Criesbach 19
Cuperly 36
Dürrnberg-bei-Hallein 66
Ecury-sur-Coole 40

Eigenbilzen 61
Ensérune 46
Erstfeld 85
Ferschweiler 10
Freisen 28
Giubiasco 87
Glauberg 9
Golasecca 90
Hallstatt 65
Heidelberg 12
Hénon 58
Herzogenburg 68
Hölzelsau 67
Holzgerlingen 11
Hoppstädten 24
Hořovičky 73
Kärlich 15
Kélouer-en-Plouhinec 47
Kernavest 59
Kleinaspergle 4
Kleiner Gleichberg 33
Kleinmittersdorf 17
Komjatice 83

Kšice 77
L'Eglise 62
Leichlingen 14
Les Saulces Champenoises 52
Libkovice 79
Losheim 23
Mâcon 51
Mainz 27
Mairy 42
Manětin-Hrádek 80
Mannersdorf 69
Marson 41
Matzhausen 22
Nová Hut' 74
Oberwittighausen 20
Ostheim 29
Panenský Týnec 75
Parsberg 16
Pfalzfeld 13
Polešovice 82
Pössneck 30
Prunay 43
Puisieulx 44

Radovesice 78
Reinheim 7
Rodenbach 3
Roseldorf 70
St Jean-sur-Tourbe 57
St Jean Trolimon 55
St Pol-de-Léon 48
San Polo d'Enzo 89
Schwarzenbach 5
Sengkofen 26
Slovenské Pravno 81
Šmarjeta 88
Somme-Bionne 49
Somme-Tourbe 39
Stupava 72
Szentenre 34
Uetliberg 84
Val-de-Travers 86
Vert-la-Gravelle 50
Waldalgesheim 2
Weiskirchen 1
Zelkovice 76

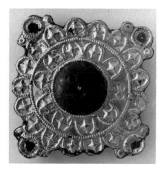

53,54 *Compass-designed plaques of gold sheet on bronze and iron backing with coral inlay. (Above) Hochscheid, Kr. Bernkastel-Wittlich, Germany, barrow 1. L. c. 4.8 cm. LT A, mid-5th c. BC. (Right) Weiskirchen, Kr. Merzig-Wadern, Germany, barrow 1. W. 8 cm. LT A, late 5th/early 4th c. BC.*

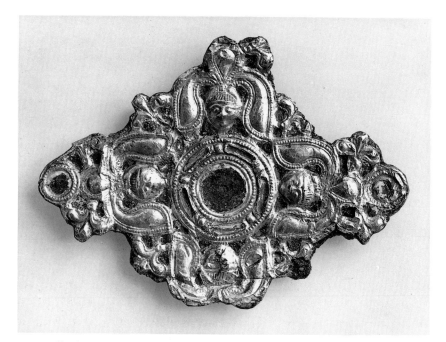

OPPOSITE

55 *(Left) Silvered engraved reverse of gold plaque (ill. 50) from Chlum, okr. Rokyčany, Czechoslovakia. W. c. 5.3 cm. LT A, late 5th c. BC.*

56 *(Centre) Bronze scabbard-plate with provision for coral inlay from Ameis-Siesbach, Kr. Birkenfeld, Germany. W. 4.7 cm. LT A, late 5th/early 4th c. BC.*

57 *(Far right) Engraved bronze scabbard showing ?bulls standing on their hindlegs from Hochscheid, Kr. Bernkastel-Wittlich, Germany, barrow 2. W. c. 4.9 cm. LT A, 450–400 BC.*

more displays the beaded edging and curved triangles visible on the Schwarzenbach triskel disc. This last plaque, which comes from a grave containing a beaked Etruscan flagon – an import rarely found so far east – once contained coral in circular settings and shows fat lobed shapes.

Such lobed shapes appear on the coral-set brooch from Weiskirchen barrow 1 in the Hunsrück-Eifel, which has given its name to this whole group of discs and brooches. The lobed shapes here are more curved and droop downwards, forming a headdress for the four little clean-shaven human faces. Coral combines with amber to decorate a brooch from the warrior grave of Hochscheid in the Rhineland; the arcaded pattern is executed in beading and recalls not only the Eigenbilzen gold but older, Hallstatt, patterns. This whole group of material appears to have originated in the Rhineland, possibly in a single workshop or else in several closely allied ones.

Classical plant motifs are also used on material such as the sword scabbard from a warrior burial at Ameis-Siesbach, once again in the Hunsrück-Eifel. Here a palmette is supported by lyres and lotus-buds and the whole is inset with coral. Another sword scabbard from the same region, from Hochscheid, shows chains of dissected half-palmettes and a lyre shape, together with two beasts with the shoulder curls that are a so-called orientalizing feature.

Such adoption of classical plant motifs is a speciality of the Middle Rhine and Marne regions, and is most noticeable in those areas which also display the greatest concentration of imported Mediterranean pottery and bronzes. In the more easterly Rhine-Danube province, such imports occur only rarely and the use of these floral elements is correspondingly unusual, though not entirely lacking.

Rhineland engraving again shows the plant motifs. A coral-inlaid scabbard from the same grave as the Weiskirchen brooch shows a discontinuous chain of feathery S-shaped tendrils, each enclosing a half-palmette, engraved with the same rocked-chisel technique which was encountered on Hallstatt-period material. A beaked flagon from this burial had apparently first been put together by Celts from at least two imported Italian bronze vessels and then engraved. This time, however, the engraving was much less accomplished and the design shows an older, more geometric, repertoire of motifs, including arcades, zig-zags and half-moons.

Other imported flagons were also engraved by their new Celtic owners, whose tastes seem to have run to more elaborate decoration than that which appealed to their Italian suppliers. Those from Reinheim, Eigenbilzen and Besançon were similarly engraved with varying degrees of skill.

One feature of much early Celtic art is visible on the silvered reverse side of the Chlum plaque. The engraved design here was laid out with the aid of compasses. The use of compasses may, like the potter's wheel and the plant motifs, have been borrowed from the Mediterranean region, but they were put to very Celtic uses. Possibly a quarter of all Early or Strict Style Celtic art is based on compass design, a feature once again at its most common and most elaborate in the chieftainly areas of the Marne and the Hunsrück-Eifel. Though the use of compasses disappeared from continental European material at the end of the La Tène A period, it re-emerged as a major feature in the Celtic art of the British Isles in the late first century BC.

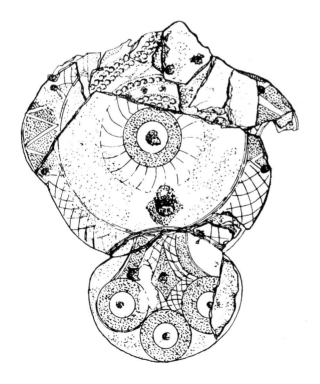

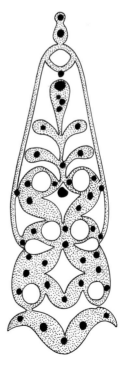

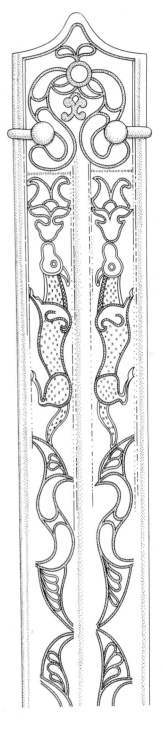

PLANT MOTIFS: EASTERN FRANCE

On the chalk lands of the Marne, Celtic art produces fewer pieces of rich goldwork than does the Rhineland. Horse-harness is found in greatest profusion in this area, though two-wheeled chariots or carts are found throughout the Celtic region, as far east as western Czechoslovakia. Local fine pottery, now more widely made on the wheel, is commoner in the region running from the Marne directly eastwards to Czechoslovakia than it is in southern Germany, Switzerland or other parts of eastern France.

Plant designs are strongly to the fore in this region as well. A bronze terminal for a chariot pole from the grave called La Bouvandeau at Somme-Tourbe displays a double three-leaved palmette. It also shows a simple pattern of arcs and circles similar to that of stamped pottery in the east of the Celtic region discussed below. An openwork palmette decorates what is possibly a helmet cheek-piece from a chariot grave at Cuperly where the outward-looking animals are orientalizing griffons.

Lyres adapted from palmettes are visible in the U-section openwork mounts, perhaps again for a chariot pole or yoke, from La Bouvandeau. These were inlaid with coral, and the design was emphasized by rows of dots set within two parallel lines.

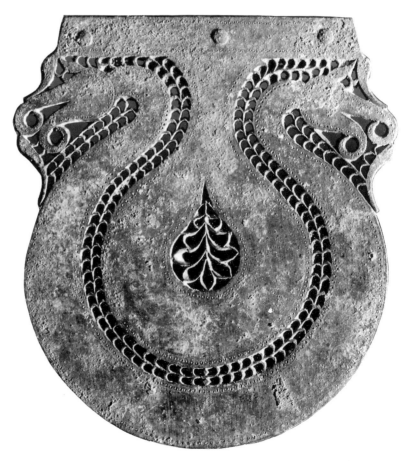

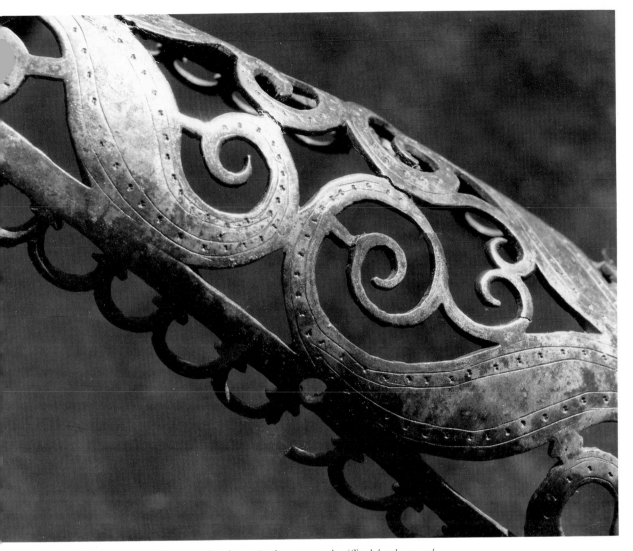

58 (Left) Bronze mount with openwork palmette in the centre and griffons' heads at each side from Cuperly, Marne, France. H. 9.1 cm. LT A, later 5th/early 4th c. BC.

59 (Above) Bronze openwork ?chariot-mount with coral inlay from La Bouvandeau, Somme-Tourbe, Marne, France. H. (of detail) 2 cm. LT A, late 5th c. BC.

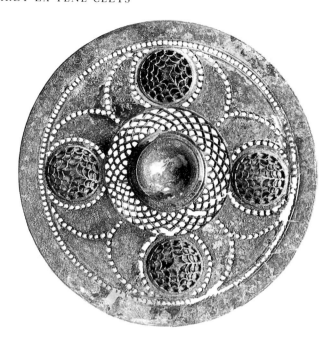

Compass design is visible on an enamel-decorated disc which may have been attached to a helmet from a chariot grave at Cuperly: the layout required only three different radii. It also appears on a disc from one of the most spectacular of the early chariot graves of the Marne region, L'Homme Mort at Somme-Bionne, discovered in 1877. The imports here included an Attic red-figure stemless cup of about 420 BC which puts the burial probably in the earlier fourth century BC. Amongst the harness fittings was a cast bronze openwork disc. Though the work is not mathematically precise, the design had been originally laid out with compasses, as a drawing shows, producing lotus-bud elements from the sickle-shaped segments. The dots within parallel lines as seen on the openwork mounts from La Bouvandeau are also visible here as outlining elements.

Compass design is clearly the basis for a harness mount from a chariot grave at L'Eglise in southern Belgium. Here the graves of the Early La Tène settlers share with the Marne the rite of inhumation and certain angular pottery forms. The mount is, however, either an import or the product of a travelling craftsman. Openwork Celtic harness mounts come also from further north, from Anloo in the Netherlands, which is well beyond the main Celtic area so that they are unlikely to be the products of travelling craftsmen.

Openwork harness pieces have been recovered from the Rhine at Mainz and from the Danube, the former example being once again a freehand copy of a compass-based design. Whether these were chance losses or the result of ritual deposition in water is not clear; many fine objects of the pre-

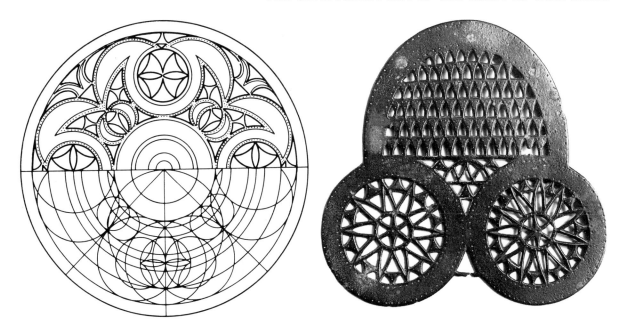

Roman Iron Age have been found in streams, lakes, rivers or wells, especially in the British Isles – a fact which makes them very hard to date. The Danube piece is so small that it has been suggested it may have been for a deer, not a horse; grave 34 of the Marnian cemetery of Villeneuve-Renneville has indeed yielded a stag, carefully buried with all the harness usually associated with the burial of horses.

Not all the material from the Marne region shows curvilinear designs. Two of the most impressive examples of the use of Hallstatt rectilinear patterns in the Early La Tène period come from this area. The sword scabbard from Vert-la-Gravelle shows a plaited zig-zag, once again executed in rocked-chisel tremolo and edged with the ubiquitous Marnian dots-and-ring motif. Another rectilinear design, again created from tremolo lines, appears on the pointed 'Berru' type bronze helmet, decorated with coral, from La Gorge Meillet, another of the Somme-Tourbe graves. The helmet originally lay between the feet of the warrior, who was buried with weapons and the wherewithal for the funeral feast, including joints of pork and beef; his companion, a charioteer, was buried above him.

There seems indeed to have been a school of specialist engravers active in eastern France in this period. Two less accomplished pieces were harness mounts from Ecury-sur-Coole. The helmet from Berru itself exhibits engraved designs, this time based upon classical motifs. Familiar palmettes can be recognized in the band of decoration round the brim, where dotted infilling is used to give the effect of light and shade. It is perhaps worth

61 *(Above left) The compass decoration of a bronze openwork disc from L'Homme Mort, Somme-Bionne, Marne, France. D. 6.9 cm. LT A, last quarter 5th c. BC.*

62 *(Above right) Bronze openwork plaque from the River Rhine at Mainz, Germany. H. 9.6 cm. ?LT A, 5th c. BC.*

mentioning that the pointed Berru type helmets have been regarded as of eastern origin and compared to those of fourth-century Persians. With the exception of one found in the rich Dürrnberg chariot grave 44/2, all come from the Marne region, with no intermediaries. It seems therefore more likely that, as with other orientalizing features discussed below, Italy is the most probable source for the transmission of this military fashion.

The triumph of early French La Tène engraving skill is, however, the Celtic decoration of an unprovenanced Etruscan flagon from France, now housed in the museum of Besançon. This, together with other pieces from the Marne region, may be used to illustrate the mid-fourth-century Celtic transformation of side-by-side classical plant elements into more continuous patterns, and will be further discussed later.

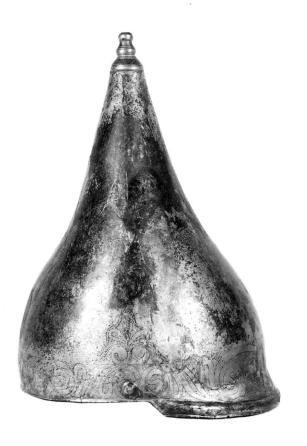

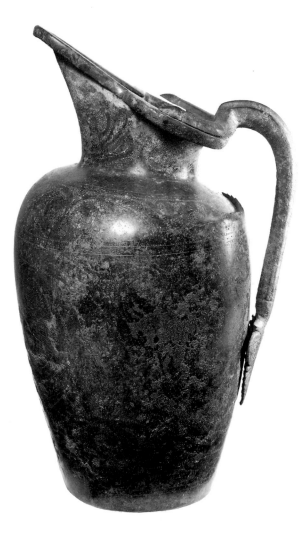

63 Bronze helmet with incised decoration from Berru, Marne, France. H. 29.5 cm. LT A, second half 5th c. BC.

64 (Right) Unprovenanced beaked Etruscan bronze flagon with Celtic incised decoration (ill. 143) now in Besançon. H. 25.5 cm. LT A, mid-4th c. BC.

ORIENTALIZING ELEMENTS
IN CELTIC ART: EAST OR WEST?

Considerable debate has raged over the route by which certain 'oriental' elements, briefly referred to above, infiltrated Celtic art: claims have been advanced that these features are owed to the animal-based art of the Royal Scythians centred to the northwest of the Black Sea and to the Achaemenid Persians under Darius and Xerxes, who were present in Greece, Thrace and southern Russia from the later sixth century BC until their defeat by the Greeks at Plataia in 479 BC.

It is undeniable, as we have seen, that in the late seventh century semi-nomadic Scythians (though not the later Royal Scythians of the Black Sea) and related groups moved westwards; in eastern Czechoslovakia and in Hungary their cremation graves are found side by side with the inhumation burials of the indigenous population. No Persian or Scythian material has ever been found, however, within the area of the genesis of La Tène art. The westernmost occurrence of such material is the Scythian gold hoard discovered a century ago at Vettersfelde, now Polish Witaszkowo, dating perhaps to the later sixth century BC or Darius' raids on the Danube. Even this nomadic art is heavily influenced by central European traditions and also contains material either made by East Greeks or influenced by their style. Enterprising Ionian Greeks indubitably made products for Scythian clients in the same way as other Greeks made goods for the western markets. The 'oriental' elements in this nomadic Scythian material, however, did not necessarily come directly from Royal Scythians or Achaemenid Persians, but may have taken a more indirect route via Greece and Italy. There is no evidence for Persian artefacts any further west than Thrace, present-day Bulgaria.

Despite determined attempts to bridge the gap between Celts at the head-waters of the Danube and Persians at its mouth, no concrete evidence of contact has been produced. Proponents of direct eastern influence have been reduced to hypotheses about eastern material in as-yet-undiscovered Celtic graves or settlements. On the other hand, there is indeed evidence that these 'oriental' elements can be found in the earlier orientalizing art of the Etruscans, in the art of the Atestine area of Italy and the art of the situla. Celtic contacts with such areas can be clearly demonstrated. Therefore, as Castriota has recently summed up the position, 'In the absence of any specific archaeological or historical evidence for contact between Persians or Scythians and Celts at the beginning of the La Tène period it is simply unnecessary if not erroneous to insist upon a direct Oriental source for such zoomorphic ornament in early La Tène art.'

The Kleinaspergle drinking-horns, with the cable-edged arcading typical of Rhineland sheet goldwork, are local pieces. Drinking-horns were found in the Hochdorf burial in Hallstatt times, are illustrated in Etruscan vase painting and can be found in the spheres of influence of western Greek

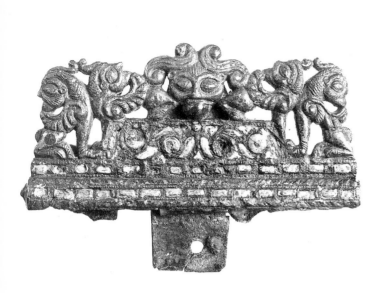

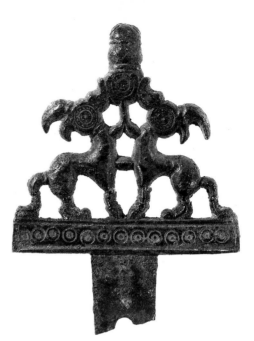

65 (Above left) Bronze belt-plaque with coral inlay from Weiskirchen, Kr. Merzig-Wadern, Germany, barrow 1. W. 7.5 cm. LT A, late 5th c. BC.

66 (Above right) Bronze belt-terminal from L'Homme Mort, Somme-Bionne, Marne, France. W. 6.3 cm. LT A, early 4th c. BC.

67 (Below) Bronze brooch with mask-terminals and twin griffons on catchplate from Kr. Parsberg, Germany. L. 8.8 cm. LT A, c. 400 BC.

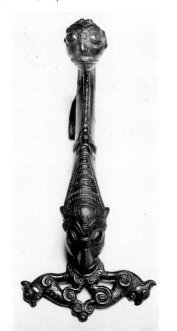

colonies in Iberia, as well as in East Greek goldwork. One East Greek piece does indeed appear to have reached the Middle Rhine from the region of the Black Sea. This is the very thin gold leaf ring from a drinking-horn found in barrow 2 at Weiskirchen. Sphinxes with curling horn-like locks form a fringe round it; their wings have a sickle shape characteristic both of Greek, and of early Etruscan orientalizing, art. This horn mount can be dated to around 500 BC. Similar West Greek ivory sphinxes with amber faces were found in the late Hallstatt Grafenbühl barrow below the Hohenasperg. Sickle-winged sphinxes and lions also appeared on a sixth-century situla lid found in the Hallstatt cemetery.

There are thus Italian, West Greek and East Greek models in the Celtic world for the Siamese twin sphinxes on an Early La Tène belt-plaque from Weiskirchen barrow 1. Here they support a human head on an ornate buckle, inlaid with rectangular pieces of coral rather than with the more usual round inserts. Such belt decorations in the Hunsrück-Eifel are apparently restricted to males, and certainly the disembodied head sports fine moustaches. Wide lateral eyes, narrow chin and the crowning twin S-curls show its Italic ancestry. The twin sphinxes or griffons have horns and sickle wings but extremely Celtic faces; the outward-facing pair wear shoes with upturned toes, an Italian fashion seen also on a number of miniature Celtic brooches, notably from the Dürrnberg.

Twin backward-looking griffons also decorate the catchplate of a complex bronze brooch from a skeleton grave from under a barrow in the region of Parsberg in the Rhine Palatinate. The indication of the beasts' pelts by dashes, and the spirals forming the shoulder joints are details often seen as being of Scythian origin. Yet if one wishes to look for more westerly forerunners, spiral joints can be seen on a situla lid from Villa Benvenuti

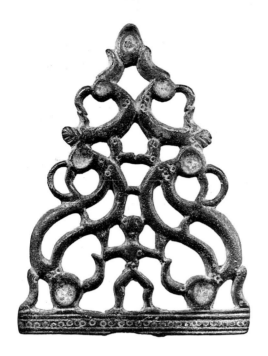

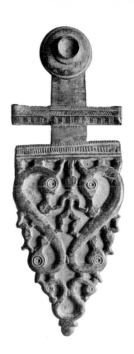

grave 124 at Este and dashing on the terminals of the Vix diadem, while winged griffons can be found in Etruria in about 600 BC.

Griffons appear, too, not only on the mount from Cuperly in the Marne mentioned briefly above, but also on an openwork belt-hook from the Somme-Bionne chariot grave. This belt-hook has an almost precise parallel in one found in grave 152 of the Fondo Rebato at Este. Simpler trefoil belt-hooks in the form of a cloverleaf or palmette-bud are found in several Marnian burials and occur also in northern Italy, as far east as Slovenia and at Ensérune in southwestern France. The belt-hooks are among the clearest archaeological evidence for Marnian Celtic infiltration of and perhaps settlement in northern Italy, before the historically documented major invasion of Italy.

Triangular belt-hooks with a tiny human figure struggling with intertwining birds of prey have been found in the canton of Ticino in southern Switzerland. Here, and down into the Ossola and Mescotina valleys, in the fifth and early fourth centuries, was the native, non-Celtic Golasecca culture, an important bridge between Italy and the northern Celts. This area produced evidence for the use of an early form of the Celtic language. A belt-hook similar to the Ticino examples was found in a cemetery at San Polo d'Enza, near Reggio Emilia in northern Italy, while from further north, from Hölzelsau in Austria, comes a hook where the tiny human is supported by a lyre ending in a horse's head while waterbirds swim on the margin. Again, a tiny brooch supposedly from Hallstatt adds a backward-turned griffon head to the body of what is most probably a dog. A Swiss bird-headed brooch from the site of Val-de-Travers has a pendant openwork plaque also with griffons; tiny human heads decorate the bow.

68 (Above left) Bronze belt-hook from San Polo d'Enza, Reggio Emilia, Italy. L. 8.1 cm. Late LT A, mid-4th c. BC.

69 (Above right) Bronze belt-hook from Hölzelsau, Kufstein, Austria. L. 16.2 cm. Late LT A, early 4th c. BC.

70 (Below) Bronze brooch in the shape of a dog or a griffon from Hallstatt, Salzkammergut, Austria. L. 2.7 cm. LT A, c. 400 BC.

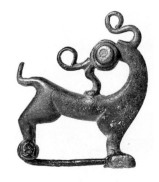

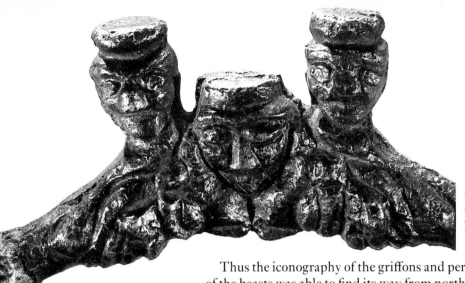

71 *Detail of fragmentary bronze neckring from Glauberg bei Stockheim, Kr. Büdingen, Germany. H. (of heads) 1.5 cm. LT A, late 5th/early 4th c. BC.*

Thus the iconography of the griffons and perhaps of the eastern mistress of the beasts was able to find its way from northern Italy both to the Marne and north through the Alpine passes to Austria. Italy again offers an alternative to the eastern route for the arrival of such motifs in Celtic art.

Griffons with sickle wings appear yet again in the most easterly of the orientalizing pieces, the plaque from Stupava in eastern Czechoslovakia, in the engraving visible when the face is turned upside down. This area is one into which Celtic settlers appear to have moved in the course of the fourth century, as they did into eastern Austria and northwestern Hungary. These first settlers from the west appear to have included some from the Rhineland, an interpretation to which the Stupava plaque lends support. The engraving on it is like that found, though rarely, in the Hunsrück-Eifel and Middle Rhine. It can be seen, for example, on a sieve from a warrior's grave at Hoppstädten or on the bronze sword scabbard from Hochscheid barrow 2 with its pairs of bulls just sniffing the lotus flowers. The Stupava griffons are like those on a chariot mount from Bad Dürkheim, shoulder

72 *Bronze belt-plaque with cast human head and engraved griffons from Stupava, okr. Teplice, Czechoslovakia. 6.6 × 3.3 cm. LT A, c. 400 BC.*

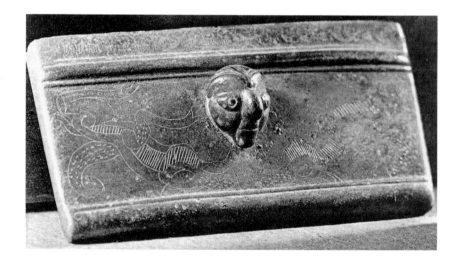

curls and all, and the face, too, is very similar to that above the catchplate on the Parsberg brooch.

One other piece of orientalizing art is the section of a bronze neckring found in the outerworks of a defended settlement, the Glauberg in Hesse. Unusually, the ring has been cast from a two-piece mould. When the three flat-capped heads are reversed, as they would have been for the wearer, the central head can be seen to rest between the open jaws of two lions whose outstretched bodies form the arc of the ring. This piece, in the depiction of the lions' manes and the disposition of their bodies round the ring is, of all Celtic works, the closest to Achaemenid Persian originals; it has been described as 'possibly the work of an artisan from the East, employed by the Celts'. The heads, however, display the technique of reducing the face to a series of protuberances which is, as we shall shortly see, widely found in early Celtic art.

THE HUMAN FACE
IN EARLY LA TÈNE ART

Human heads are ubiquitous in Early Style art: peering from the foliage of the Middle Rhine gold leaf, decorating finger-rings and neck- and armrings of gold and bronze, visible on the bases of flagon handles, on belt-plaques, sword scabbards, chariot fittings, and safety-pin brooches. Full-length representations are, however, rare, and it is the 'masks' which are characteristic; 'the beasts and masks', said Jacobsthal, 'give the Early Style the stamp.'

Faces are particularly typical of the Rhineland region, and the areas of Czechoslovakia into which western Celts were spreading by the fourth

73 (Below) Celtic mask-faces and their relationship to Italic bearded and clean-shaven prototypes. (A) Etruscan gold finger-ring found near Vulci. (B) Silver bucket handle-mount of the 7th c. BC from the Tomba Castellani, Praeneste. (C) Detail of an unprovenanced bronze stamnos handle in Munich. (D) Detail of a 4th/3rd c. BC Etruscan gold bracelet from 'Italy' in the British Museum. (E,F,G) Handle details of bronze flagons from: E Kleinaspergle, Kr. Ludwigsburg, 5th c. BC; F Basse-Yutz, Moselle, c. 400 BC; G Dürrnberg bei Hallein, grave 112, 5th c. BC. (H,I) Gold finger-rings from: H Rodenbach, Rheinpfalz, 5th c. BC; I ?Sardinia, 5th c. BC.

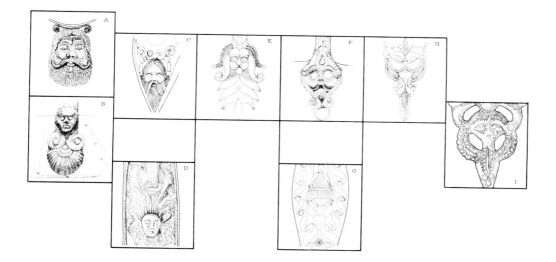

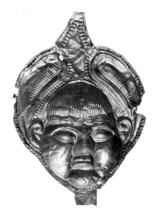

74 *(Above) Sheet gold face with leaf crown from Schwarzenbach, Kr. St Wendel, Germany, grave 1. H. 3 cm. LT A, later 5th c. BC.*

75 *(Right) Bronze harness disc with iron binding strip from Hořovičky, okr. Rakovník, Czechoslovakia. D. 12 cm. LT A, late 5th/early 4th c. BC.*

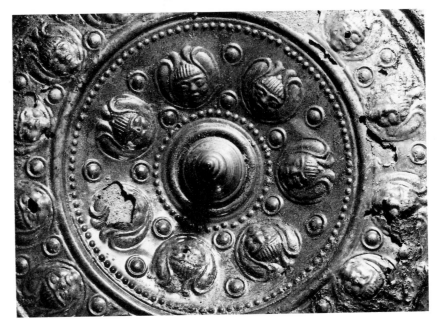

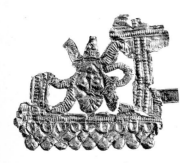

76 *Sheet gold openwork fragment showing reversible face from Bad Dürkheim, Kr. Neustadt, Germany. H. (of head) c. 1.7 cm. LT A, late 5th/early 4th c. BC.*

century. They are relatively uncommon in the Marne region, whose art is generally more abstract and less representational in this period.

Despite an enormous number of Celtic variations, the ultimate prototypes are two somewhat different Etruscan types of face. One is the bearded Silen already seen on the Weiskirchen stamnos handle; the other is clean-shaven (though Celtic versions may display moustaches) with straight hair in a fringe.

In one instance, from a woman's grave at Bad Dürkheim in the Hunsrück-Eifel, both faces appear in a reversible image which replaces the central element of a lotus blossom on a gold leaf fragment. The clean-shaven Celt with palmette headdress becomes a bearded old man. Whether this shape-changing is a mere visual joke or perhaps represents youth and old age or a female and male is impossible to say.

Of the Rhineland faces, the most common is the beardless variety. On those pieces which have already been illustrated in other contexts, it appears in uncharacteristically plump-faced form on the gold fragment from Schwarzenbach; the tiny chins of the Weiskirchen barrow 1 gold mount or the coral-inlaid belt-plaque are more characteristic. Faces very similar to those of the Weiskirchen gold, but with more oval eyes, appear on a pair of sheet bronze harness mounts from Hořovičky in Bohemia. Here the 'crown' of comma-leaves has become a frame in which the twenty-one faces are cradled like flower-buds. The other grave goods in this cremation, like the presence of horse and chariot fittings, indicate that this Bohemian Celt was, if not a settler from the west, then from a community with close links with that region.

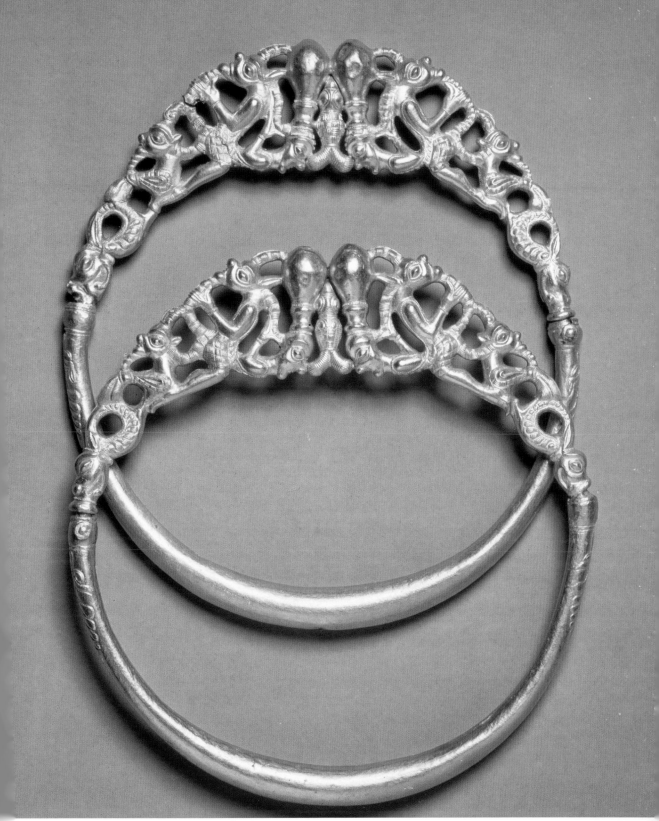

IX *Gold neckrings nos. 1 and 2 from Erstfeld, Kt. Uri, Switzerland. D. 13.6 and
14.8 cm. LT A, 5th to early 4th c. BC.*

X, XI *Bronze-covered iron helmet with gold and coral from Agris, Charente, France. The general view (*right*) lacks the recently discovered knob from the top. The detail (*below*) is of the openwork coral-inlaid cheek-piece. H. of helmet 21.4 cm. LT A/B1, mid to late 4th c. BC.*

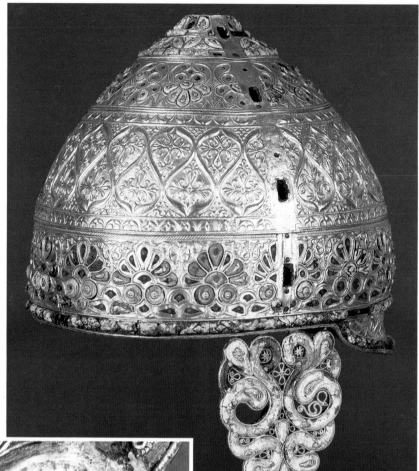

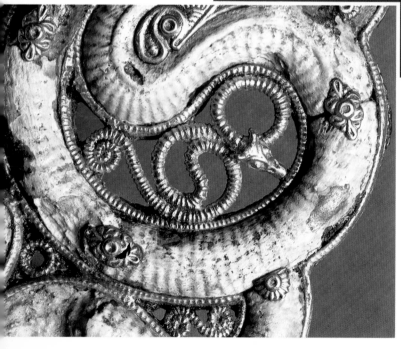

The tiny 'horns' which sprout from the centre of the Hořovičky head may be vestigial satyr ears. They appear again on a gold finger-ring from a warrior's grave at Rodenbach in the Rhineland Palatinate. Finger-rings are rare in the Celtic world and decorated ones even more so. Etruscan jewellery does, however, provide the example of 'Janus' rings with twin heads in the fifth and fourth centuries BC. Etruscan too are the wig-like crowns which on Italian bronzework betrays in turn the influence of Egyptian fashions. The moustached faces of the Rodenbach ring, with their flanking 'Hathor' wigs, are similar in type to the Weiskirchen and Hořovičky faces, though more exuberant. Similar Janus faces appear on a ring now in the Victoria and Albert Museum, which is recorded as coming from Sardinia, well outside Celtic territory: nothing, however, is known of the circumstances of its discovery.

The satyr ears are again visible on a tiny gold leaf mount from Ferschweiler, where the face is flanked, like those on the Rodenbach ring, by a Hathor wig, serving as a beard. They appear too in the three pairs of Janus faces on a gold armring from the woman's grave at Bad Dürkheim which contains the reversible face. These are otherwise rather more naturalistic faces than usual; the buffer junction between the heads recalls those visible also on the Kleinaspergle drinking-horns. The most animalistic ears attached to a definitely human face are those on a bronze sword pommel found in a small flat grave cemetery at Herzogenburg in Lower Austria: the ears are like those of a hare – or possibly of a horse – while the arms end in birds' heads which once contained inlay.

Other early pieces important for their renditions of human faces are found outside the Rhineland. An inhumation warrior's grave from Marson, near Châlons-sur-Marne (which contained an openwork trefoil belt-hook like those discussed above) produced a sword scabbard plate carrying three 'negroid' heads. The faces have been compared to those on the Glauberg torc, while the edging also strongly suggests a Rhineland origin. The face on a cast bronze belt-hook, an isolated find from the vicinity of a Bohemian chariot grave at Želkovice, is a descendant of that on the Rodenbach finger-ring: the tremolo engraving shows a Greek key pattern. Unlike the Stupava plaque, it is a much more likely candidate for identification as a local Celtic product. Four tiny cast bronze heads from the major Slovenian site of Smarjeta, however, must have been imports, since Celtic settlement did not reach this region until the first half of the third century BC.

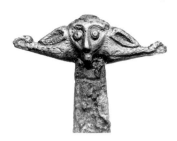

77 Bronze sword-hilt from Herzogenburg-'Kalkofen', Lower Austria, grave 11. H. (of face) 1.1 cm. LT A, late 5th/early 4th c. BC.

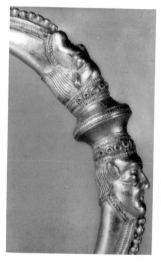

78 Detail of gold armring from Bad Dürkheim, Kr. Neustadt, Germany. L. (of pair of faces) 2.8 cm. LT A, late 5th/early 4th c. BC.

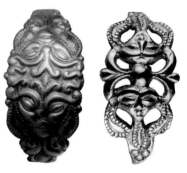

79 (Far left) Gold finger-ring with Janus heads from Rodenbach, Kr. Kaiserslautern, Germany. D. 2.1 cm. LT A, later 5th c. BC.

80 (Left) Gold finger-ring from ?Sardinia. D. 2 cm. LT A, later 5th c. BC.

73

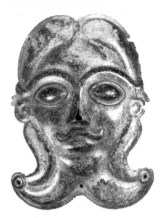

81 *Bronze mount from wooden flagon from Dürrnberg bei Hallein, Austria, grave 44/2. H. 8.3 cm. LT A, 400–350 BC.*

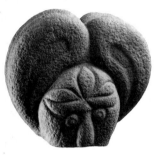

82 *Fragmentary stone head from Heidelberg, Baden, Germany. H. 31 cm. LT A, late 5th/early 4th c. BC.*

One feature of some Celtic heads from this early period is the reduction of the face to a simplified number of protuberances, a cartoon-like abstraction which is an ancestor of the later 'three-dimensional' style which Jacobsthal named as 'Plastic'. This is, naturally enough, more obvious on cast bronze or gold objects than in those created by repoussé work, particularly in gold leaf.

The lobed crowns or headdresses visible on some metalwork faces such as Hořovicky, Weiskirchen and Ferschweiler appear also on the mount from a wooden flagon found on the Dürrnberg, in the rich chariot grave 44/ 2. Similarities exist in the grave material to the rich chieftains' graves of the Marne. An Attic stemless black-glaze cup made around 450 BC dates it to a similar period as Somme-Bionne; the Dürrnberg grave indeed contains a Berru type helmet as did La Gorge Meillet.

Similarly stylized human features are also visible on the small number of examples of stone sculpture – mostly from southwestern Germany, the old Hallstatt area – which one can attribute with any degree of certainty to the Early La Tène period. None can be dated except on stylistic grounds. These include the Janus heads of the Holzgerlingen sandstone pillar statue – whose faces are otherwise strongly reminiscent of the Kleinklein mask. Much more obviously of La Tène date is the Heidelberg fragmentary sandstone head – perhaps again from a pillar statue. The leaf crown on this is of the type seen on the Hořovicky disc as is the face on one side, carrying a lotus-bud above the eyebrows. The reverse, though at first glance seemingly representing nothing more than a simple star pattern, may represent a second, highly stylized, face.

A broken four-sided pillar stone from Pfalzfeld may once have been surmounted by a head such as Heidelberg. Each side carries a lugubrious face once again with the leaf crown and the lotus-bud on the forehead; the fat S-curves are also definitely Celtic, while the forked beard of the Silen mask has become another bud. Though the idea of pillar stones may have been inspired by Etruscan carved stones from northern Italy, this piece is definitely in the Early La Tène decorative style, despite its cabled edging, and is carved from local sandstone.

Since these possibly phallic pillars are probably connected with ritual, the headdresses and lotus-buds must also have some specific significance when found on metalwork, though it is not possible to determine their meaning from the evidence available to us.

One Janus head from Leichlingen, carved of basaltic lava from the Eifel, probably once also topped a pillar stone and is one of the few Rhineland examples of stone sculpture. Its button eyes and bulbous nose are like those of the pop-eyed clean-shaven faces found on Rhenish metalwork. It has a hint of a torc or neckring, an ornament which in the Rhineland, in this Early La Tène period, is confined to women.

It is worth remembering that much sculpture must have been made of wood, which survives only in exceptional circumstances and from later contexts. The lower part of the Holzgerlingen figure, for instance, has a carefully cut rebate for fitting into a base, which suggests carpentry techniques.

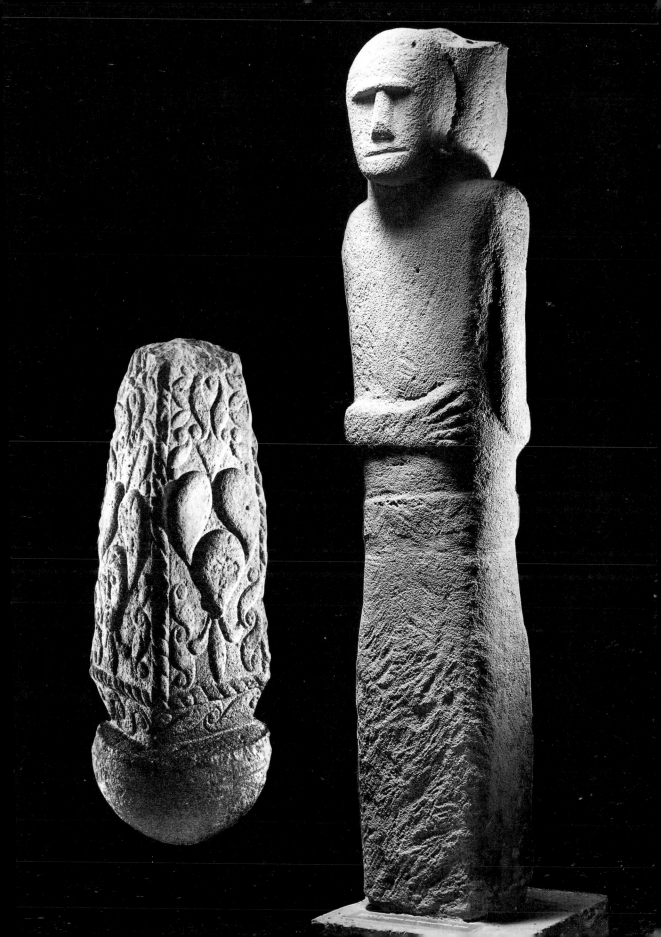

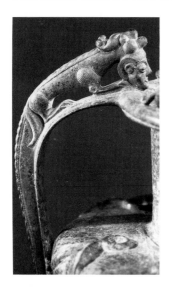

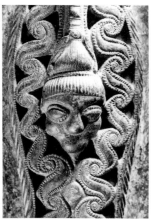

85,86 *Details of the flagon from the Dürrnberg bei Hallein, Austria, grave 112 (Pls. V, VI). (Top) Top of the handle. (Above) Face on the handle attachment. LT A, second half 5th c. BC.*

CELTIC ART AND CELTIC THIRST: THE DÜRRNBERG AND BASSE-YUTZ FLAGONS

Three great masterpieces of Celtic art combine most of the key features of early Celtic art we have already examined, and demand detailed study. These are the bronze flagon from the Dürrnberg and the pair of flagons found by a gang of railway navvies in 1927 at Basse-Yutz on the Moselle, on the edge of the Hunsrück-Eifel/Middle Rhine zone.

Because the discoverers of the Basse-Yutz flagons did their best to falsify the details of the find, we do not now know for certain whether this unique pair comes from a grave or a trader's hoard. They were, however, accompanied by two Etruscan bronze stamnoi, one dating from about 450 BC, the other from late in the fifth century. The Dürrnberg flagon comes from one of only three chariot graves so far found on the site, and was excavated in 1932. Apart from the chariot and flagon there were few grave goods; these include a disc-footed fibula, which suggests a date for the burial at the end of the La Tène A period, in the fourth century BC, though the fibula may come from a later burial than the flagon, which has been placed as early as 450 BC.

The concave profile of these flagons is very different from the more rounded shape of their Etruscan prototypes, though it can now be matched in the profile of the recently reconstructed Borsch and Kleinaspergle jugs, each claimed as the earliest flagon made by Celts following the general Etruscan form, and in two beaked pottery flagons, one from the Dürrnberg itself and one from Hallstatt – further examples of the comparatively few Early La Tène finds so far recorded from the area of Hallstatt.

All three flagons share a similar manufacturing technique. The bodies, including the sharply carinated shoulder and the neck, were beaten up from a single sheet of bronze. The base was left open while the ribbed design of Dürrnberg was hammered up from inside on wooden formers, and the foot collar of Basse-Yutz, with its inlaid coral in place, was slipped over the bottom. The cast base then had its edges turned up to cover the sides and was put in place. The beaked spouts of the Basse-Yutz flagons were set into U-shaped cut-outs in the body and attached with rivets. The mouthplates were then affixed and turned over the tops of the flagons, and the separately cast handles, with their branching rim animals, attached. Amazingly, the bases on all three jugs were apparently held on by nothing but faith, hope and resin, which in the Basse-Yutz examples lines the whole of both flagons and almost fills the pouring spouts.

Despite their similarities in basic construction, Dürrnberg and Basse-Yutz display quite different decorative elements, with no close points of comparison.

The twin-leaved floral elements on the shoulder of the Dürrnberg flagon are found also on local stamped pottery, and on bronze mounts for a wooden flagon from the same site. At the foot of each rib appears a lotus-bud. There is a sinuous S-design round the turned-over edge of the spout. The stack of interlocked fat S-commas supporting the basal handle face

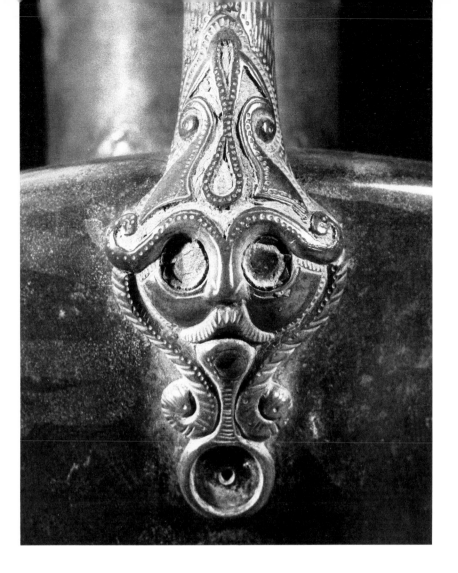

87,88 Details of the pair of bronze flagons with coral and enamel decoration from Basse-Yutz, Moselle, France (Pls III, IV). (Left) Face on handle base of Flagon 1. W. 3.6 cm. (Below left) Duck on spout of Flagon 1. LT A, late 5th/early 4th c. BC.

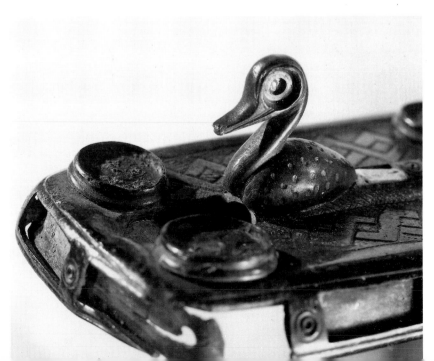

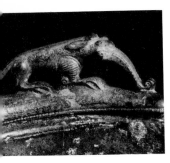

89 One of the two animals on the rim of the Dürrnberg bei Hallein, grave 112, flagon (Pls. V, VI and ills. 85, 87). LT A, second half 5th c. BC.

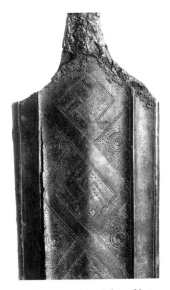

90 Bronze scabbard from Vert-la-Gravelle, Marne, France. W. (max.) 5.5 cm. LT A, later 5th c. BC.

91 (Right) Detail of the incised decoration on a bronze helmet from La Gorge Meillet, Somme-Tourbe, Marne, France. H. (of helmet) 38 cm. LT A, later 5th c. BC.

ends again in a lotus-bud and recalls those of the Pfalzfeld pillar stone, while their beaded edging is also reminiscent of Middle Rhine goldwork. The two faces, one at the base of the handle and the other on the rim, display the bulbous nose, ridged lenticular eyes, small chin, fringe and 'caste mark' we have seen above, particularly in the Rhineland; if the handle is reversed the four S-commas below the true face offer perhaps another elusive hint of a Celtic physiognomy.

Nightmarish imagery too lurks on the Dürrnberg piece. Over the 'severed' head on the rim crouches a monstrous beast with bushy tail reaching down the handle and long, almost bird-like, claws. Its face is made up of bulbous protuberances, like several of the beasts, part man and part monster, on the brooches discussed below, many of which have been found on the Dürrnberg itself. It is unnecessary to argue whether this beast is a wolf, or a lion like those on the Glauberg torc, and futile to try to disentangle its precise meaning.

The curious beasts on the flagon rim have incomplete shoulder spirals, as does the handle animal. They sport bulbous human faces with animalistic ears and immensely long, elephant's-trunk-like, curling, beards – a feature which some observers have interpreted as a stylized limb or tendril hanging from their mouths, another 'oriental' motif often found in situla art.

The keynote of the Basse-Yutz flagons is baroque extravagance, in contrast to the greater restraint of the Dürrnberg example. They display a veritable pattern book of early Celtic art elements, fused into a magnificent whole. From the earlier Hallstatt repertoire comes the plaited interlace recalling the Marnian Vert-la-Gravelle sword and the Marnian helmet from La Gorge Meillet, engraved in slapdash fashion on the mouth covers, and also the chequer-meanders visible on the bronze settings of the foot collars. Unconcerned by the crouching canines, a cheerful duck swims on the river of wine in the spout – yet another waterbird whose artistic ancestry stretches back to the Bronze Age.

Compass-based design can be seen on the enamel-decorated stoppers, where it forms a continuous pattern of four stylized lotus-buds. These stoppers originally had a bayonet fitting, but when this rusted, they were

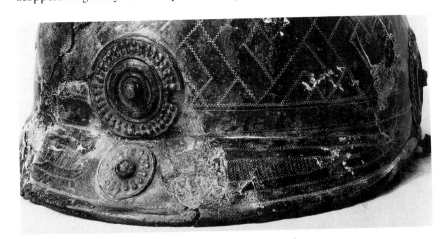

attached, in antiquity, by a chain to the jaws of the handle beast; they must therefore have been in use for a considerable time before their burial.

The cable design of the coral-inlaid bronze foot collars can be found on Etruscan stamnoi of the same Giardini Margherita type found with the flagons, though the Basse-Yutz stamnos itself lacks this feature. The faces at the base of the handles are very close to those on the Rodenbach finger-ring, the Rodenbach armring and the belt-plaque from Weiskirchen; the Weiskirchen piece, in addition, shares with Basse-Yutz the inlay of coral in rectangular pieces rather than in the more usual round studs. The Basse-Yutz handle faces, if reversed, show yet another pseudo-face, as on the Dürrnberg flagon. Further pseudo-faces lurk, both upright and reversed, in the coral-inlaid throat panels.

Palmettes appear too: in elongated form on the backs of the handle and rim animals, similar to those on a La Bouvandeau chariot mount. Indeed, these palmettes are also outlined by dots, as on the Marnian material. On the coral-encrusted throat panels the palmettes have moved yet further from their classical prototypes.

The Basse-Yutz handle and rim animals, with their dashed pelts and shoulder spirals, have been taken as proof of further orientalizing influence, though these features, as we have seen, have a respectable Italian pedigree. It is not clear whether they are dogs or wolves; moreover the handle beast appears to sport a vestigial mane. Whatever the truth, they are certainly from a less fearsome bestiary than those on the Dürrnberg flagon.

Polychromy was a feature that the Celts appear to have invented for themselves. The lavish use of imported red Mediterranean coral on the Basse-Yutz flagons is unparalleled. Coral is hard to distinguish with absolute certainty from other similar substances, and the Basse-Yutz insets have faded, as is so often the case, to white. Coral was used by the Celts from the sixth century until the mid-third century BC. In the La Tène A period it was used both in the Rhineland and in the Marne regions, though by the fourth century it was used more commonly in the Marne. The closest parallels for the use of coral in Basse-Yutz come from Weiskirchen barrow I in the Middle Rhine, from La Bouvandeau in the Marne and from the Dürrnberg.

Enamel – or, rather, opaque red glass, since it is not fused to the metal – was also used on these flagons, on the stoppers and the animals' manes. Despite suggestions that this technique was imported from the Black Sea area, it may have been a purely Celtic invention, used from the late fifth till the early third century BC, mostly in the Alpine area, with a few exceptional finds in the Middle Rhine and Marne. Very rarely – on some twenty-one known objects – are both coral and enamel used on the same artefact.

All in all, despite some tantalizing Marnian connections, these magnificent flagons have their strongest connections with the Middle Rhine area, from which Basse-Yutz itself is not far distant. The Dürrnberg flagon, however, despite its similarity in manufacturing technique, is extremely different in its decoration. Cogent arguments have been put forward to support the theory that it could well have been made on the

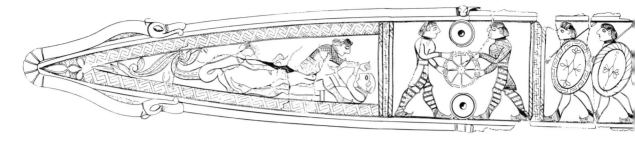

92 Engraved iron and bronze scabbard with remains of coral studs from Hallstatt, Salzkammergut, Austria, grave 994. L. 68 cm. LT A, 400–350 BC.

Dürrnberg itself, where certainly there is increasing evidence for local skilled craft production. The Dürrnberg flagon, though, also has Rhineland connections in some of its features, and one is tempted to think that the artist who created it might well have been trained in that area.

Two Celtic trinities are fused in the Basse-Yutz and Dürrnberg flagons – plant, animal and human, and Hallstatt (on Basse-Yutz at least), classical and 'oriental' motifs or influences – to form major masterpieces of unmistakably Celtic art.

RIDERS AND WARRIORS

Narrative art was never attractive to the Celts, nor was pictorial realism. Thus we have few portraits of them or of their way of life. However, a number of Etruscan grave markers, relief carvings, and metalwork from Este, do clearly illustrate Celts.

The sword scabbard engraved with narrative scenes which was found at Hallstatt in grave 994 – one of the handful of Early La Tène graves so far identified in the area first excavated in the nineteenth century – is undoubtedly Celtic. The warrior was laid on an oval stone platform with an iron helmet, knife and casting spears, and a bronze wire sieve. His sword was hanging high on the right side, since Celts seem to have slung their swords over their shoulder rather than from a waist belt: the dead man must presumably have been left-handed. The coral-decorated sword is of typical Early La Tène shape. Two griffons' heads with inlaid eyes decorate the chape while the T-shaped grip ends in inlaid birds' heads.

Bands of tremolo engraving across the sword are executed in a combination of rectilinear interlace and Greek key designs, similar to those on the Vert-la-Gravelle scabbard and the Basse-Yutz flagons. These divide the sword into four zones, the longest panel of which is flanked by two showing two pairs of confronted men, holding a wheel between them, as on the transalpine situla art. Between them is a row of four mounted men and three foot-soldiers. The figures' tunics, trousers and shoes with upturned toes are Celtic fashions which occur on other pieces. The weapons – oval shields, hemispherical helmets and the sword slung over the left shoulder of the third rider – are of types which can be matched from Celtic graves; so too can the discs visible on the horses' reins. The three foot-soldiers carry spears, as do the riders. Large oval shields cover their bodies. Despite the

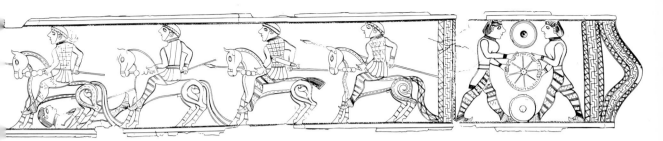

fact that the foot-soldiers' spears are not at the ready, we seem to be witnessing a battle or its aftermath, since one of the horsemen is despatching a fallen figure with his spear. It is thus clear that Celtic warfare was conducted on horseback at a period when the Greeks used their horses merely as a means of transport, dismounting to fight on foot once they arrived at the battlefield. The tip of the scabbard has been much damaged, but appears to show two unarmed figures struggling hand-to-hand. This may record either a real event, perhaps one in which the dead warrior took part, or possibly a mythological battle tale.

Haunch spirals are visible on the horses. The only real use of plant motifs is in the bushy 'tail' of a fragmentary third figure behind the struggling pair on the tip; on closer examination this is a tendril pattern like those from the western chieftains' graves.

It is hard to pinpoint the artistic influences under which the Hallstatt scabbard engraver may have worked. The piece obviously owes much to situla art in the idea of narrative, the way it is presented in friezes and the pairs of confronted men. Celtic stylistic influences are also apparent, however, for the human heads are not unlike the three-dimensional faces of the Dürrnberg flagon. Certain details of the engraving, such as the rectilinear patterns, are found on flagon mounts from the Dürrnberg, on the Basse-Yutz flagons and on a wire sieve from Hoppstädten in the Middle Rhine, while the tendril and even the profiles of the faces also recall the Middle Rhine region. Such a combination of influences suggests an itinerant craftsman, assembling an eclectic pattern book of style on his travels. This is not totally inconsistent with the existence of fixed workshops, either at such central sites as the Dürrnberg or under princely patronage, particularly in the rich Middle Rhine area. Craftsmen might have moved between such workshops, or visited those in other areas to work or train there. There seems no reason to suppose however, that the Hallstatt sword was made far from its findspot, though the Dürrnberg may be a more likely source than Hallstatt itself. The Dürrnberg rather than Hallstatt, in this Early La Tène period, was a major centre; goods and people from the Atestine area of the art of the situla, as well as from the western centres of Celtic power, must have found their way there, and mingled with each other – an obvious means by which elements from the eastern zone or the area of situla art were passed into Celtic art. The date for the manufacture of the scabbard is probably late fifth or early fourth century BC.

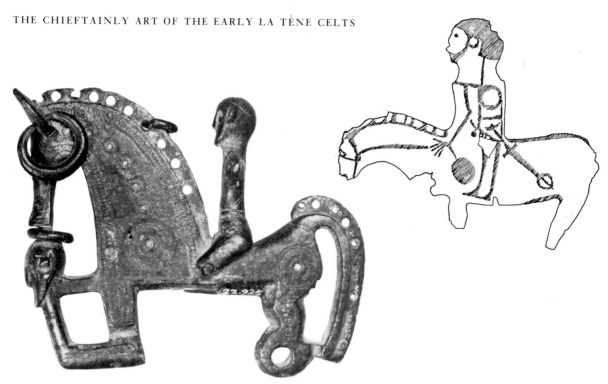

93 (*Above left*) *Bronze brooch from Iberia showing rider carrying severed head. H. 7.3 cm. ?5th/4th c. BC.*

94 (*Above right*) *Sheet bronze rider from Kärlich, Kr. Koblenz, Germany, chariot grave 3/1928. L. 4.8 cm. LT A, 5th c. BC.*

OPPOSITE

95 (*Above left*) *Bronze horse-head from Taunus, Germany. H. 10.2 cm. LT A, 5th/4th c. BC.*

96 (*Above right*) *Bronze brooch from Iberia. L. 5 cm. ?5th/4th c. BC.*

97 (*Centre*) *Bronze brooch from Sengkofen, Kr. Regensburg, Germany. L. 4.8 cm. LT A, 5th/4th c. BC.*

98 (*Below*) *Bronze horse figurine from Freisen, Kr. St Wendel, Germany. L. 12 cm. LT A, 5th/4th c. BC.*

One representation of a Celtic knight from the western chieftainly area comes from a chariot grave at Kärlich, Ldkr. Coblenz. It is probably a mount from a bronze frieze on a wooden flagon or other vessel. Details are only roughly outlined with punched dots, and are hard to distinguish. The figure has a typical short La Tène sword with oval chape, and may be wearing a hemispherical helmet. In his left hand he carries a round object which may be a 'pilgrim flask' of the type found at Rodenbach and the Dürrnberg; it could, on the other hand, be a severed human head. Such gruesome battle trophies were certainly described by later classical observers of the Celts such as Livy and Diodorus Siculus. Unlike the Hallstatt sword warriors, however, the Kärlich figure is naked, and his penis is erect, like that of the earlier Hirschlanden statue. Another naked mounted warrior appears on an unprovenanced bronze brooch from Iberia, on which the horse's muzzle surmounts a definite severed head. Though the rider and the geometric patterns recall Hallstatt-period axes, the brooch is of later form and the severed head has affinities with the more realistic of the Early La Tène mask-faces.

In the search for evidence of mounted Celts, it must be observed that horse bones are rarely found in Early La Tène graves, though horse-harness is. There are, however, a few small horse figurines, including that from a high-status craftsman's chariot grave at Freisen in the Hunsrück with horse-bits but no bones. Such finds, like a number of horse brooches – a speciality, apparently, of the region around Parsberg in northeastern Bavaria, though at least one example comes from as far afield as Iberia – may indicate token burials or talismans, representing what was clearly a highly prized and widely venerated asset.

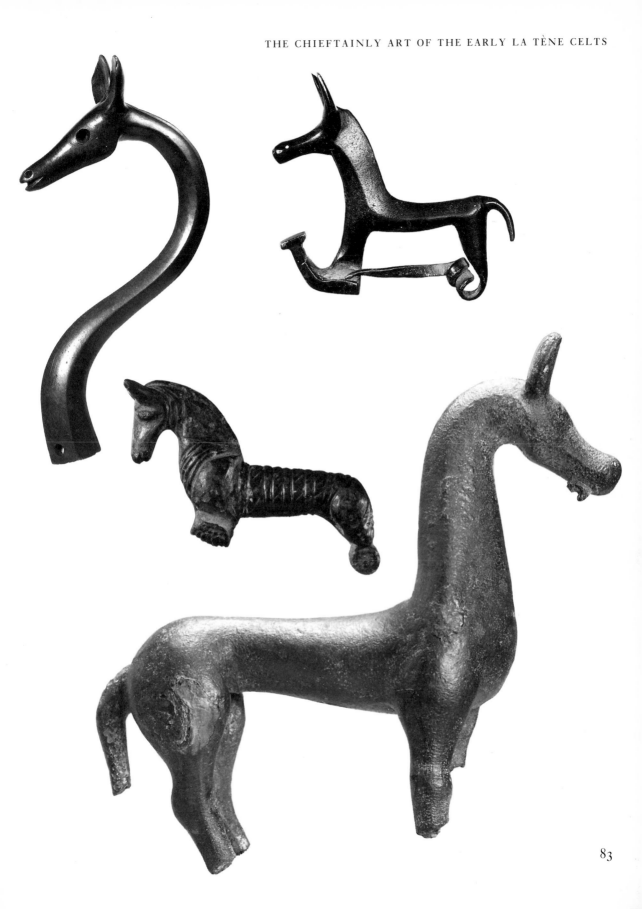

Apart from the warrior figures, there are few known full-length representations of humans, and none which can be definitely identified as women. One of the few instances is the recently found fibula from Dürrnberg grave 134. With his pointed shoes, trousers and jerkin he is not unlike the Hallstatt sword figures. Similar costume can be seen on a brooch found in 1967 at the small cemetery site of Maňetín-Hrádek in Bohemia. This has circular settings for coral and amber inlay, reminiscent of the Hochdorf 'castor' figures or the Strettweg cult figures; his bulbous face and fringed hair are, however, similar to other La Tène faces. The associated material suggests a date towards the end of the La Tène A period for this probably Bohemian-made product.

Despite occasional ithyphallic males exhibiting the proven link between aggression and erection, explicit sexuality is rarely seen in Celtic art. From the period of transition from Hallstatt to Early La Tène culture there are, however, a few pairs of tiny pendants attached to finger-rings. These are female and male, both nude, with the males depicted in a state of sexual arousal.

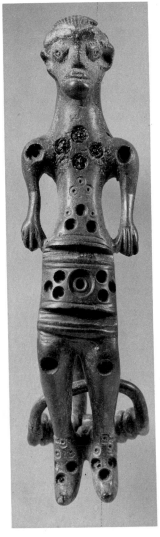

99 *Bronze brooch inlaid with amber from Maňetín-Hrádek, Plzeň-sever, Czechoslovakia, grave 74. L. 8.8 cm. LT A, 5th/4th c. BC.*

MYTHOLOGICAL MASTERPIECES IN MINIATURE

Human masks and beasts predominate in the decoration of the widespread fibulae or safety-pin brooches. These are found throughout the western and central Celtic world, both in settlements and cemetery sites, but in greater profusion in the Rhine-Danube zone, from Bavaria and Baden-Württemberg eastwards, than in the Marne and Middle Rhine.

Of more than 550 brooches with representational decoration now known, from Jugoslavia in the east to Spain in the west, by far the largest class – some 270 – depicts birds, and particularly waterbirds. Three-quarters of the brooches come from burials, but more than 100 have been found on settlement sites of various types. Evidence for different regional preferences is clear; for example, in the Middle Rhine decorated brooches are predominantly a male attribute, in northwestern Bavaria female, while of some 40 from the Dürrnberg a greater number come from male, and particularly warrior, graves than from female. As to actual types, strictly symmetrical or double-headed brooches are a feature of the Middle Rhine and Hunsrück-Eifel region while those with a mask or head at the foot or clasp end extend from the latter region to as far south as the Dürrnberg. Brooches which incorporate a human head above the spring and another human or animal above the foot are again found particularly on the Dürrnberg and in Baden-Württemberg.

The basic form of some brooches suggests contact with Italy, whence the idea of the safety-pin brooch had been introduced early in the first millennium BC. In the eastern Hallstatt zone, brooches with animal heads (especially horses) or in the form of dogs or wolves (sometimes chasing waterbirds) were produced in the sixth and fifth centuries BC: these are occasionally found at such sites as Hallstatt or the Dürrnberg.

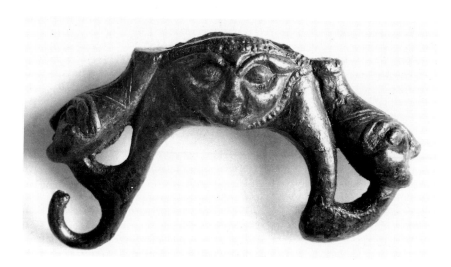

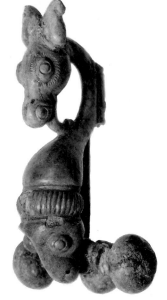

The earliest definitely Celtic versions of ornately decorated brooches are those from the chieftainly graves of the Hunsrück-Eifel and Middle Rhine. The Weiskirchen barrow I warrior, for example, had a coral-inset brooch with four tiny human faces or masks. Two are set Janus-like in the centre with one at each end. This type of inlaid brooch is characteristic of the Middle Rhine, as also are those with simple terminals in the form of a duck's head.

By contrast, in the Rhine-Danube area, decorated brooches occur in female graves and as many as twelve have been found in a single burial. The Dürrnberg itself has produced more brooches and more types of brooch than any other site. These safety-pins may indicate status and identity and were perhaps intended to ward off harm – a more complicated version of the lucky horseshoe or the shamrock. Several, with clean-shaven faces, may well depict women rather than men.

Local specialization of types is certainly apparent. To the east in Transdanubia a ringed animal-headed brooch was developed as a local response to the kind of fantastic beasts one can see on the Bavarian brooches. As indicated already, northeast Bavaria produced horse brooches as did the Dürrnberg. Connections between these two areas, Franconia and the Rhine Palatinate can be seen in the distribution in these areas of brooches on which the catchplate is decorated with two or three balls, like a miniature pawnbroker's sign. These appear on horse brooches and human mask brooches alike; on the Dürrnberg they even decorated one in the shape of a boar.

One site with brooches in this style has provided evidence that production of such items in the Rhine-Danube area was certainly not centralized, whatever may have been the case in the Middle Rhine. In the hilltop fortification of the Kleiner Knetzberg in Bavaria, several decorated brooches were found, together with one which is a rough, unfinished, casting. A human head can be made out at each extremity of this casting, and a bird's head at the end of an elongated 'neck' extending from the head

100 (Above left) Bronze quadruple mask-brooch with provision for ?coral inlay from Weiskirchen, Kr. Merzig-Wadern, Germany, barrow I. L. 4 cm. Later LT A, early 4th c. BC.

101 (Above) Silvered bronze brooch with ram's-head and horse-head terminals from Dürrnberg bei Hallein, Austria, grave 37/2. L. 4 cm. Late LT A, mid-4th c. BC.

102 One of a pair of non-identical animal-headed bronze brooches joined by a bronze chain from the River Danube at Szentendre, Komárom, Hungary. L. 5.6 cm. LT A, ?mid-4th c. BC.

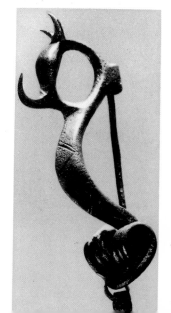

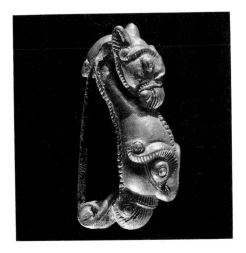

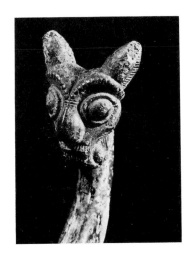

103 (Above left) Bronze brooch from Oberwittighausen, Kr. Tauberbischofsheim, Germany. L. 3.3 cm. Late LT A, late 5th/early 4th c. BC.

104 (Above right) Detail of bronze brooch with coral inlay from Chýnovský Háj, Libčice, Prague, Czechoslovakia. Total L. 7 cm. Late LT A, mid-4th c. BC.

105 (Right) Bronze brooch with double bird-of-prey heads and pendant from Val de Travers, Ct. Neuchâtel, Switzerland. L. 9.4 cm. LT A, c. 400 BC.

106 (Below) Bronze brooch from Nová Hut', Plzeň-sever, Czechoslovakia. L. 3.5 cm. LT A, c. 400 BC.

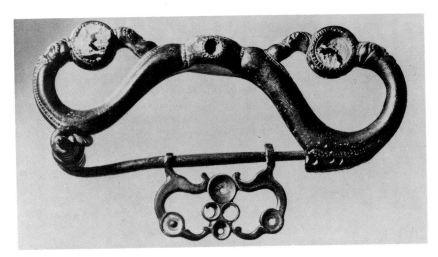

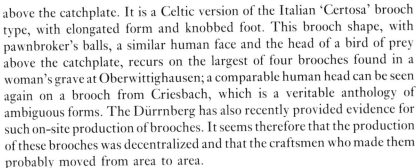

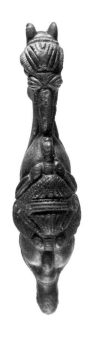

above the catchplate. It is a Celtic version of the Italian 'Certosa' brooch type, with elongated form and knobbed foot. This brooch shape, with pawnbroker's balls, a similar human face and the head of a bird of prey above the catchplate, recurs on the largest of four brooches found in a woman's grave at Oberwittighausen; a comparable human head can be seen again on a brooch from Criesbach, which is a veritable anthology of ambiguous forms. The Dürrnberg has also recently provided evidence for such on-site production of brooches. It seems therefore that the production of these brooches was decentralized and that the craftsmen who made them probably moved from area to area.

Other brooches seem sometimes to have been imported from outside the region where they were found, at other times to have been copied locally from unfamiliar styles, occasionally incorporating multiple imagery. An example from Nová Hut' in Bohemia, with Janus faces on the bow, is in the tradition of the Middle Rhine Rodenbach ring, but modelled by a craftsman apparently uncertain of his artistic sources. By contrast, a single

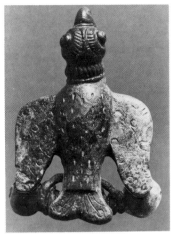

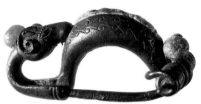

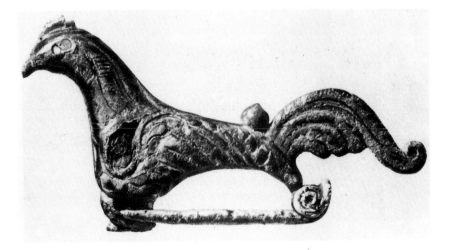

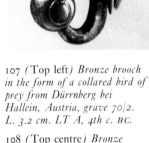

brooch from Chýnovský Háj near Prague carries a face so like that on one of the three smaller Oberwittighausen brooches that it is probably an import.

One brooch has clean-shaven heads and a reversible crouching animal-cum-double-bird growing out of the catchplate. It was actually found in a Roman settlement of the second century AD at Slovenské Pravno in western Slovakia. It could be an antique souvenir imported by a provincial Roman colonist, or the very long-term result of trading down the line from one Celtic community to another. Certainly its stylistic relatives lie to the west, for example with the fantastic imagery of the rim animals of the Dürrnberg flagon.

Some of the imagery of the brooches is relatively straightforward, such as the frequent use of birds' heads, and particularly those of ducks. Of the more than five hundred decorated brooches now known, more than half have birds' heads or, less commonly, entire birds. The hen, an introduction from India in Hallstatt times and identified on the Heuneburg, appears on a coral-inlaid brooch from the Rhineland princess's grave at Reinheim. Birds

107 *(Top left) Bronze brooch in the form of a collared bird of prey from Dürrnberg bei Hallein, Austria, grave 70/2. L. 3.2 cm. LT A, 4th c. BC.*

108 *(Top centre) Bronze brooch with coral inlay from Aignay le Duc, Côte d'Or, France. L. 3.7 cm. ?LT A, 5th c. BC.*

109 *(Above left) Bronze brooch with coral inlay from Reinheim, Kr. St Ingbert, Germany, barrow A. L. 6.4 cm. Late LT A, mid-4th c. BC.*

110 *(Above) Bronze brooch from Oberwittighausen, Kr. Tauberbischofsheim, Germany. L. 10.7 cm. LT A, late 5th/early 4th c. BC.*

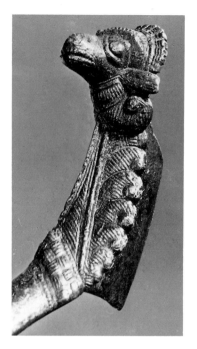

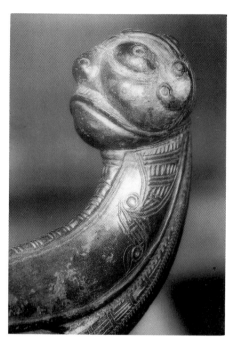

111 *(Right) Foot of a bronze brooch with a collared bird of prey on spring end from Panenský Týnec, okr. Louny, Czechoslovakia. L. (of ram's head) c. 1.3 cm. LT A, 5th c. BC.*

112 *(Far right) Detail of the bronze brooch from Kr. Parsberg, Germany, ill. 67. LT A, c. 400 BC.*

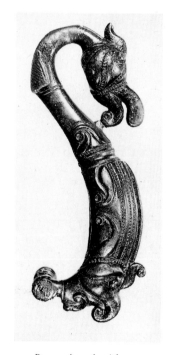

113 *Bronze brooch with griffon's-head terminals from Ostheim, Ldkr. Mellrichstadt, Germany. L. 8.8 cm. LT A, late 5th c. BC.*

of prey, wearing collars in a possible early hint of falconry, make their debut in Celtic iconography on a brooch from the Dürrnberg, and on the spring end of the sheep-headed brooch from Panenský Týnec – another piece often claimed to exhibit orientalizing forms like the Kleinaspergle horn terminals. As we have noted, boars appear on the Dürrnberg, as do horses, while griffons may be seen on the Ostheim brooch or on the catchplate of the magnificent human-headed Parsberg brooch. Yet it remains almost impossible to say with precision what these symbols, singly or in combination, meant to those who made and wore them. Their function is obviously more than the practical one of fastening clothes, and the nightmarish imagery which intrudes would seem to fit in with Ludwig Pauli's theory that Early La Tène art was imbued with magical properties, and evolved at a time of social and political instability. The individual nature of the brooches may thus indeed represent a visible attempt to retain identity at a time of general upheaval.

WOMEN AND WEALTH: RING ORNAMENT IN THE SAARLAND AND THE ALPS

The richness of the Middle Rhine area in material goods and artistic skill can be further seen in a series of superb gold neck- and armrings from the Middle Rhine graves and from a hoard in Switzerland. These combine the plant motifs of the Rhineland sheet goldwork with an extraordinary imagery of beasts and humans in a fashion which, again, has sometimes been seen as 'oriental'.

Of these, the earliest comes from the warrior's burial inserted into a Hallstatt-period barrow at Rodenbach, containing an Etruscan bronze basin and a beaked flagon. The grave can be dated by its two-handled Attic pottery *kantharos* made in the latter half of the fifth century. This is an example of the so-called 'Motte-St Valentin' type also found in Este at the head of the Adriatic. As well as the usual weapons, there was a bronze pilgrim flask shaped like a water bottle, another Italic piece, decorated with an animal frieze related to the situla style. The grave contained in addition the Janus-headed gold finger-ring we have already seen and a splendid gold armring. This armring has a central moustached face remarkably like that at the base of the Basse-Yutz flagon handles; two further tiny faces peer from the foliage, supported by dissected half-palmettes, about an eighth of the way round the circumference. The central face is flanked by two couchant rams or ibex with backward-turned heads. A quadrant away on each side are two, not quite identical, reversible heads; in one aspect they appear griffon-like, while reversed they are another pair of sheep or caprids. The balusters were separately cast and soldered on.

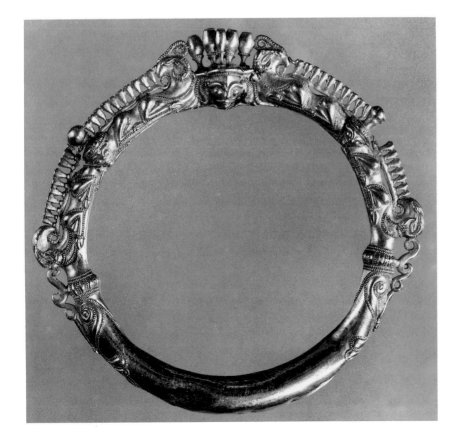

114 Gold armring from Rodenbach, Kr. Kaiserslautern, Germany. D. 6.7 cm, LT A, later 5th c. BC.

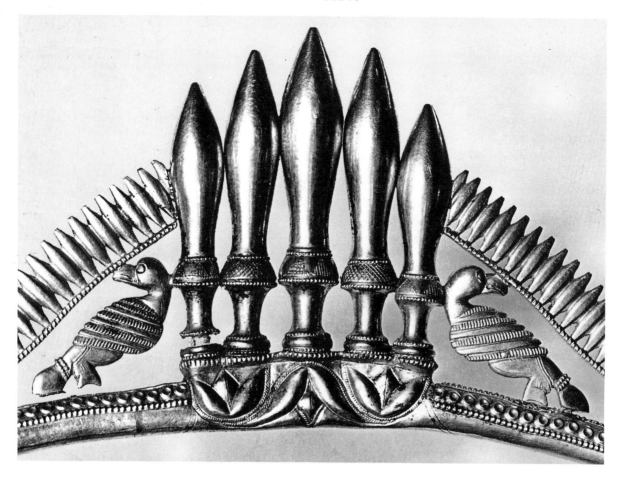

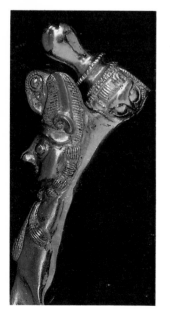

115 (Above) *Detail of gold neckring from Besseringen, Kr. Merzig-Wadern, Germany. W. (of central feature illustrated) 3.9 cm. LT A, 5th c. BC.*

116 (Left) *Detail of gold neckring from the 'princess's' grave at Reinheim, Kr. St Ingbert, Germany, barrow A. D. 14.2 cm. Late LT A, mid-4th c. BC.*

Balusters appear in sharper and more elongated form on a gold neck-ring found with chariot fittings at Besseringen in a woman's cremation grave. Lost during World War II, the ring is now known only from photographs. The five central balusters rest on three lotus-buds and are supported by a backward-looking pair of birds of prey, which are probably wedge-tailed eagles. Analysis of the gold used for this neckring and for the Rodenbach armring shows that it came from the same source as the jewellery from the Reinheim 'princess's' grave in the Saarland, close to other rich burials such as Weiskirchen and Schwarzenbach, as well as to Rodenbach and Besseringen.

The Reinheim princess comes from the very latest in date of the Rhine-Moselle chieftainly burials and was discovered in sandpit operations in 1956. Her body lay in a wood-lined chamber within the barrow. Trappings for the funeral feast included two bronze basins, the gold mounts for a pair of drinking-horns and a spouted gilt-bronze flagon. To the right of the body was a bronze mirror of Celtic workmanship, one of the rare examples from continental Europe. On her other side were the contents of what must have been a jewellery box, containing over two hundred items, among which were many beads, including some of polychrome glass as well as over a hundred of amber. The glass beads indicate a date late in the fourth century on analogies with western Swiss finds. There were also two gold-on-iron disc brooches, three finger-rings (two of gold wire, one of bronze), a brooch in the form of a hen and another with a human head. Two gold armrings and a gold neckring, obviously far from new when buried, completed her finery.

The twisted neckring was made not from solid gold, but from beaten sheet gold, as were the armrings. All three show certain similarities in decorative details, for example, the balusters and the beading, which relate them to the craftsmen or workshop responsible for the Rodenbach and Bad Dürkheim armrings and the Besseringen neckring.

Similar, though not identical, hands can be recognized at work on the Reinheim neckring and the larger armring. Underneath the terminal balusters of both are prick-eared beaked faces in which the ultimate prototypes, the orientalizing lions, have undergone a Celtic metamorphosis into owls, supplied with bib-like outward-curling leaves, as are the human heads on the torc. Here too is the palmette-bud of the Pfalzfeld pillar faces in another guise. On the armring, the owls have a single outstretched wing, possibly attached to the shoulders of the outward-gazing pair of humans, who have their arms raised over their chests. The clean-shaven human faces – particularly on the armring, with the hands folded over the 'stomach' formed by the plant motif – do look female. Mantling their wings

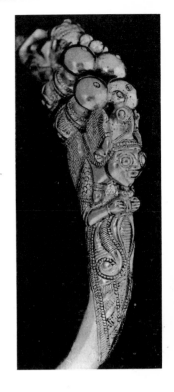

117 *Gold armring from the 'princess's' grave at Reinheim, Kr. St Ingbert, Germany, barrow A. D. 8.1 cm. Late LT A, mid-4th c. BC.*

118 *(Left) Detail of ill. 117, showing owls on armring terminals.*

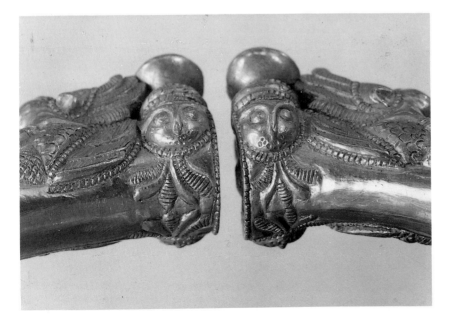

over both pairs of faces are, once again, the birds of prey which make their first appearance in the European art of this Early La Tène, or La Tène A, period.

Predatory birds, beasts, humans neatly shod with pointed shoes, monsters and plants are all inextricably entwined on three out of four neckrings found with three other gold rings at Erstfeld, Kt. Uri – outside the Celtic zone, but on the route between northern Italy and the Celtic world. Found under a boulder by a bulldozer operator in 1962, the neckrings come from just north of the St Gothard pass. Details of construction technique and gold analyses suggest strong similarities with the Reinheim and Bad Dürkheim rings: they are once more formed of beaten sheet gold in two half-shells, joined together over a core of clay or other non-metallic material. Here, again, are the terminal balusters, the armring-wearing hands, the bead-and-reel backbones, the cable edging, and the feather tails formed from half-palmettes. We appear to be looking at a school of craftsmen, fixed or mobile, separate from that which produced the sheet goldwork described earlier. The seven Erstfeld rings are themselves products of a single workshop, though the poorer quality of one neckring suggests an apprentice's hand.

119,120 Part of the hoard of gold neckrings found at Erstfeld, Kt. Uri, Switzerland. (Below) Neckring no. 4. D. 15.7 cm. (Below right) Detail of neckring no. 3 (the so-called 'apprentice' ring). D. 15.4 cm. LT A. ?5th/4th c. BC.

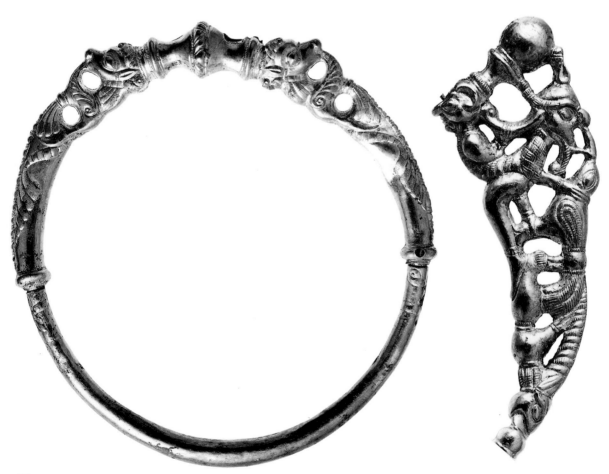

Siamese twins share the same well-turned leg, with pointed Italian shoe, on the better-made of the twin neckrings. They stand on a backward-facing beast with a horned head, but the body of a long-tailed bird – a feature made more explicit on the apprentice's ring. Below this again is a beast with sweeping circular horns, a sheep or goat perhaps. Where the otherwise plain ring section is joined by two catches to the decorated zone, are the eye and beak of a predatory bird – on the apprentice's ring translated into a big-nosed mask – from which sprout feathery tendrils.

The fourth Erstfeld neckring is 'waisted' above the face of a benign outward-looking animal, possibly a bovine rather than a caprid; such 'waisting' is also a feature of the Bad Dürkheim neckring. Below is a very long-tailed, almost headless, bird with grasping talons, apparently attempting to devour the outward-looking beast.

The purpose of this strange imagery is obscure. It has been suggested that it represents this world and the next, but, in the absence of any written records, such interpretations must remain speculative. Rings such as Erstfeld may have represented myths or stories, or played some exorcizing role, since obviously for Celts there were beings both to worship and to fear.

How such late fifth- or early fourth-century Celtic finery came to be in a southern Swiss valley is unclear. It may have been the stock-in-trade of some enterprising Rhenish craftsman on his way south to the new land of Celtic opportunity in Italy, for its connections with other Rhineland pieces are far too strong for it to have come from Italy, as has been suggested. It may have been buried, in fear of attack, by a trader who never had the opportunity to recover it. Explanations which suggest that it was buried to propitiate some mountain god or goddess do little to explain how the rings got there in the first place from so distant and foreign a region.

DECORATIVE POTTERY OF THE RHINE–DANUBE AREA AND ITS WESTERN COUSINS

Persistent geometric, rather than floral, patterns, and the continued influence of situla art are evident in what has been called the 'eastern style province' of Early La Tène art, especially in its pottery.

Increasing use of the wheel enabled fourth-century Celtic potters to develop new forms. One of these is a range of flasks, with squat, widely flared bases and tall narrow necks, to which the German name *Linsenflasche* has been given. These were particularly widespread in northeast Bavaria, northern Austria, southern Bohemia and western Hungary; there are several from graves on the Dürrnberg. One of the finest comes from the family burial of a man, a woman and a child in one of a group of fifty barrows at Matzhausen, Ldkr. Parsberg. Associated grave goods such as the brooches of 'Certosa' form indicate a date in the earlier part of the fourth century BC.

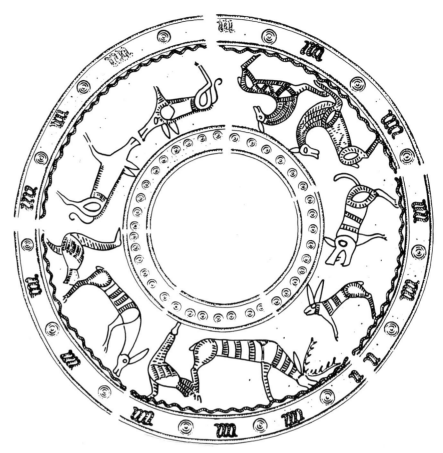

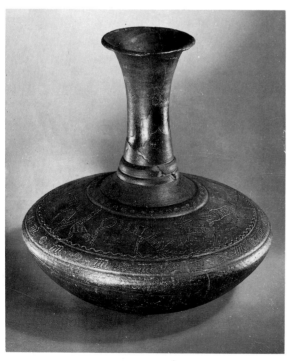

121,122 (Above and left)
Pottery flask with incised
decoration of pairs of animals
and birds from Matzhausen, Kr.
Neumarkt, Germany. H. 23.8
cm. LT A/B1, early 4th c. BC.

123 (Right) Swans painted in
red on a pottery 'Braubach' dish
from Radovesice, okr. Teplice,
Czechoslovakia. D. c. 28 cm.
LT A, c. 400 BC.

124 (Far right) Pottery
fragment, stamped with hares,
from Libkovice, okr.
Most, Czechoslovakia. L. (of
hares) c. 2 cm. LT B1, later
4th c. BC.

The Matzhausen flask had been placed by the woman's right shoulder. Incised decoration shows antithetically placed boars, a pair of hinds looking over their shoulders while a third grazes, a stag, and a pair of geese or bustards; these have been interpreted as a series of male-female confrontations. A hare pursued by a dog is also visible. This is a motif going back to Greek proto-Corinthian antecedents, whence it passed into situla art. Hares appear earlier on one situla-style belt-plaque from Vače in Slovenia; they appear too as a stamped frieze on a pottery sherd from an Early La Tène settlement site at Libkovice, near Duchcov, and on an openwork pendant from the Hochscheid chieftain's grave in the Middle Rhine. The stags, the backward-looking animals and the idea of narrative friezes also have their origins in situla art.

Figural decoration such as this is rare on pottery, but appears again on the inner surface of a wheel-turned 'Braubach' bowl, with a raised central dimple, which came from an extensive settlement at Radovesice in northwest Bohemia. The majority of such bowls are stamp-decorated, but here even the S-shapes are painted instead in red pigment. Red-painted pottery is common in this region in late Hallstatt times and by no means unknown in the Early La Tène period. The bowl was dated to about 400 BC by its excavator, who found it in a hut which may have served some religious purpose. The swans depicted are perhaps migratory wild swans, which may have played a major role in early Celtic myth and symbolism, as such birds most certainly do in later folklore.

Geometric designs as well as figural decoration are evident on the Matzhausen and Libkovice pottery: arched on the former and in waves or 'S's and concentric stamps on the latter. Stamped decoration was, as seen above, a feature of Hallstatt-period pottery in both eastern and western areas. In the Early La Tène period, however, it is much more common in burials in the Rhine-Danube area than it is in the Rhine-Moselle-Marne regions to the west; in these latter areas native pottery was seldom deposited in graves. Geometric stamped designs can again be seen on a locally made bowl from the Early La Tène Krautacker settlement at Sopron in Hungary,

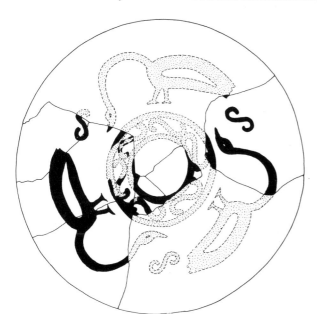

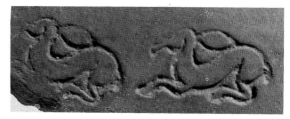

95

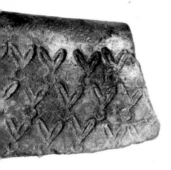

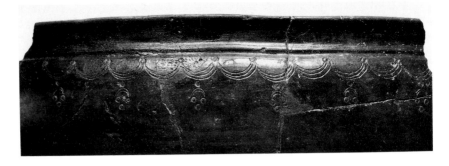

125 (Above) Stamp-decorated pottery fragment from Šakvice, okr. Breclau, Czechoslovakia. L. 15.5 cm. LT A/B1, mid- to later 4th c. BC.

126 (Above right) Stamp-decorated pot from Sopron-Krautacker, Györ-Sopron, Hungary. H. 31 cm. LT B1, mid-4th c. BC.

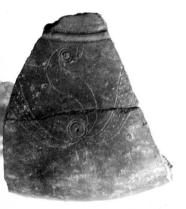

127 Stamped and incised pottery fragment from Polešovice, okr. Uherské-Hradiště, Czechoslovakia. L. c. 5 cm between stamps. LT A/B1, mid-4th c. BC.

or on the shoe-shaped pot from the grave of a young girl at Mannersdorf in Lower Austria.

Sometimes potters borrowed techniques and designs from the more prestigious metalsmiths. For example, a pottery fragment from the Moravian settlement site of Polešovice adds compass-drawn lines to stamped decoration to produce a curvilinear design which is in fact a flying bird. From the same site comes a rare find of one of the bone tools actually used to produce such stamped decoration, consisting of a floral or plant-derived motif of two comma-leaves.

Repeated use of a single stamp below the rim of a pot from a settlement at Šakvice, south of Brno in Moravia, produces a delicate network. This can be compared with the similar leafed motif on the shoulder of the Dürrnberg flagon. The double-petalled floral motif, basically a simplified lotus-bud, occurs on other pottery both from the Dürrnberg itself and from western Czechoslovakia. Such plant designs are sometimes claimed to be exclusively a feature of the western Celtic zone, but in this more eastern Celtic region, which lacks the Greek and Etruscan imports of the western part, such adaptations of classical motifs attest to continued contacts with the region south of the Alps. Fine pottery, though less prestigious than metalwork, seems also to have been traded and exchanged in the west, as recent laboratory analysis of the clay fabrics has shown. Braubach bowls, for example, of the end of Early La Tène, were brought from their centre of production in the region of Bonn to the Hunsrück-Eifel, as is evidenced by one buried with a woman in barrow XX of the Losheim, Kr. Merzig-Wadern, cemetery – evidence perhaps of marriage outside the area.

The non-floral 'eastern' motifs occur also on metalwork exhibiting complex compass designs. These can be seen on the pilgrim flask from Dürrnberg grave 44/2, a local version of that found in the Rodenbach burial. Two half-shells are joined together with a binding strip to form a disc shape which stands on four human feet, well shod in pointed shoes, each foot carrying a staring eye at the ankle. Like other tributes to Celtic thirst – the imported stamnoi from Weiskirchen grave 2 and from Kleinaspergle – this flask contained traces of resinated wine, laced this time with hemp. Purely geometric decoration appears on its neck, its stand and the central area of its body. Within the raised concentric ribs is a design laid

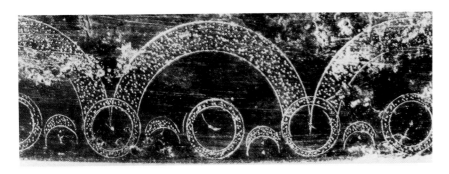

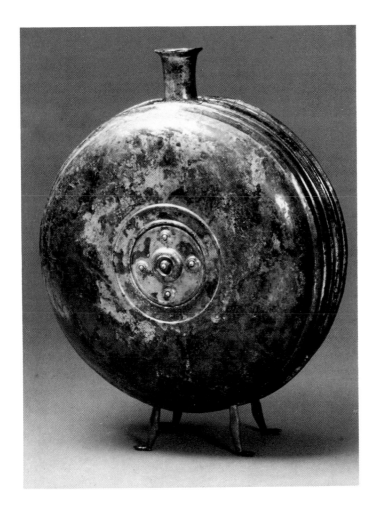

128,129 *Detail of engraving (above left) on bronze 'pilgrim flask' from the Dürrnberg bei Hallein, Austria, grave 44/2 (left). H. 51.8 cm. LT A, first half 4th c. BC.*

130 *(Below) Stamped pottery shoe, from Mannersdorf, Niederösterreich, Austria, grave 4. H. 10.5 cm. LT B1, mid-4th c. BC.*

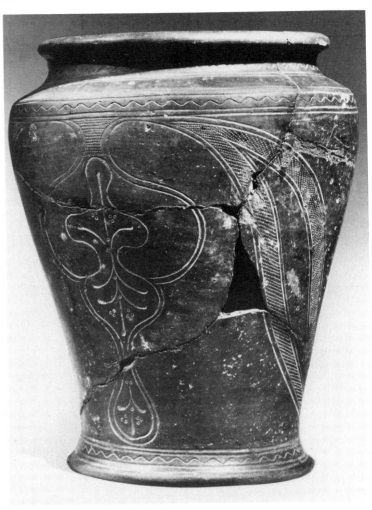

131 *Incised and stamp-decorated pot from St Pol-de-Léon, Finistère, France. H. 26 cm. ?Early LT B1, 4th c. BC.*

132 *Detail of stamped decoration on a pot from Castellou-Peron en St Jean-Trolimon, Finistère, France. Total H. 16 cm. Late Ha D/LT A, ?5th c. BC.*

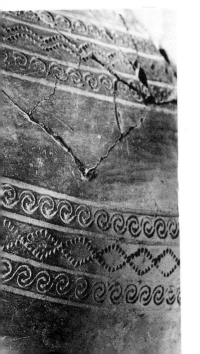

out with compasses and filled with stabbed dots; the motifs are the metalworker's version of the stamped arcades on the pottery. Such pieces may fill the apparent distribution gap caused by the absence of comparable stamped pottery in southwest Germany and western Switzerland perhaps influenced by different burial practices, since in these regions, pottery was less often placed in graves.

POTTERS OF THE FAR WEST

Very much further to the west, in Brittany, the wheel-turned pottery is possibly contemporary with that from the Rhine-Danube area, though it cannot be dated with certainty. It too shows a correspondence in shape and motifs between metalwork and pottery, the continuance of Hallstatt patterns and later borrowings from the central repertoire of plant-based

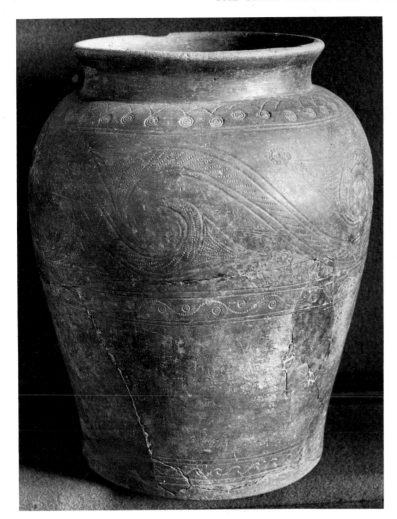

133 Incised and stamp-decorated pot from Kélouer, Finistère, France H. 31 cm. ?Early LT B1, 4th c. BC.

western La Tène art, features which were even more marked in the later Breton pottery. The stamped geometric decoration on a pot from Castellou-Peron, St Jean-Trolimon is, for example, very similar to the stamped design on the hilt of a bronze dagger sheath from Kernavest. Other pots from this region combine incised with stamped decoration in a manner reminiscent of eastern French metal engravers and so close is the resemblance that the term 'Metal Style' has been coined to describe them. Two such examples come from barrow graves in Finistère. That from Kélouer-en-Plouhinec was apparently used as a cremation container. It combines at least six circular and toothed stamps; the main sinuous wave pattern strongly recalls that on the Besançon jug discussed below, while the simpler, overlapping elements round the rim are straight out of the repertoire of the stamped wares of the east. The second comes from St Pol-de-Léon and has a double palmette motif like that on the throat of the Basse-Yutz flagons; it also displays undulating leaves with toothed stamp infilling.

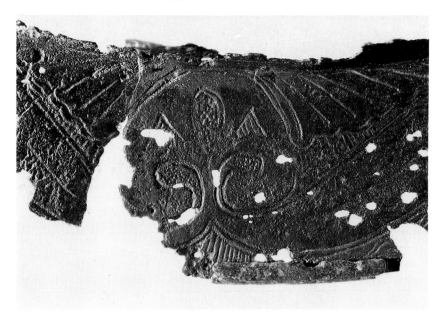

134 (Above) *Fragmentary rim of a bronze bowl or lid from Cerrig-y-Drudion, Clwyd, Wales. W. (of fragment) 3 cm. ?4th/3rd c. BC.*

This later pottery probably dates from the latter half of the fourth century. Metalwork found across the English Channel, at Cerrig-y-Drudion in the mountains of north Wales, has often been compared with the Breton pots. These Welsh fragments are in all likelihood from one or more lids: they show a split palmette motif linked by long fleshy leaves as on the French pots, though there are other details to indicate that they were made in Britain rather than being imported from France. It is in this late fourth-century period that the first scattered hints of Celtic art appear in the British Isles, as we shall see later on.

OPPOSITE

135 (Top right) *Detail of silver neckring from ?Mâcon, Saône-et-Loire, France. H. (of head) c. 1.7 cm. LT A/B1, mid-4th c. BC.*

136 (Left) *Intricately engraved bronze spouted flagon from Waldalgesheim, Kr. Mainz-Bingen, Germany. H. 35 cm. Late LT A/early LT B1, mid-4th c. BC.*

137,138 *Details of a gilt-bronze spouted flagon from Reinheim, Kr. St Ingbert, Germany, barrow A. (Centre) Human-headed horse on the lid. (Below right) Human head at the top of the handle. H (of flagon) 51.4 cm. H. (of horse) 5.7 cm. Late LT A, mid-4th c. BC.*

ENGRAVERS TO THE RHINELAND CHIEFTAINS

Two masterpieces of Celtic engraving come from two of the last of the 'royal burials' in the Rhine-Moselle area. They are both women's graves; one is a chariot burial at Waldalgesheim and the other is that of the Reinheim princess. Both produced Celtic spouted flagons with swollen bellies and splayed bases, whose profiles, rather than copying southern metal flagons, are much more similar to those of wheel-turned pedestalled pottery from the Marne. Pottery versions of spouted and handled jugs are also known from the Dürrnberg and the Ticino. Other such tubular-spouted flagons have been found at Eigenbilzen and at Le Catillon, St Jean-sur-Tourbe, in the Marne region.

Both flagons have cast quadrupeds standing on the lids; on the Reinheim example this is a human-headed horse, and on that from Waldalgesheim a somewhat sheepish-looking horse with orientalizing shoulder curls. Both also sport cast handles which display versions of the human face at the attachment end and, in the case of Reinheim, at the rim, where it sits above a ram's head. This moustached face, with its oval eyes, boasts a palmette headdress, not unlike that of the Bad Dürkheim reversible face. It is repeated at the base of the Reinheim handle, palmette and all, but extended to fit the taper so that the beard is grotesquely pulled out and offset against an S-decorated mounting plate shaped like a shield.

The beard on the Waldalgesheim handle face is also long and pointed: this face sports a leaf crown like those on other Celtic heads. It is one of the most naturalistic of Celtic faces and is full of character. The openwork attachment plate is similarly S-decorated, with provision for inlay; like the Basse-Yutz flagon handles and some Marnian work, it shows outlining with dots and, when reversed, birds' heads. At the top of the handle is yet another ram's head.

The closest comparisons to the old man of Waldalgesheim and perhaps to the lower Reinheim face are on a silver neckring, of Rhenish manufacture, found near Mâcon in eastern France and on a bronze brooch fragment from a disturbed grave at Kšice in central Bohemia.

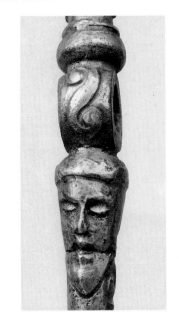

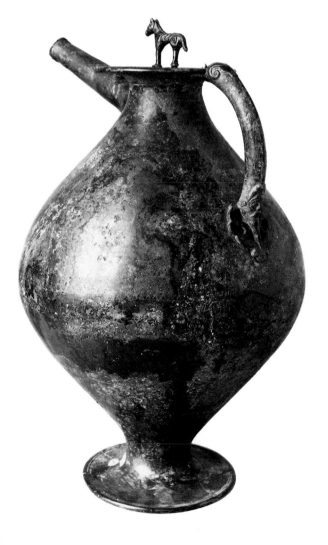

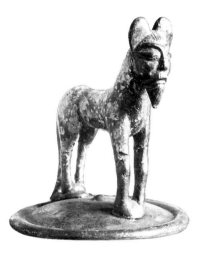

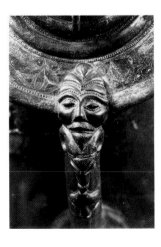

It is, however, the related engraving on both flagons which is their most important feature, carried out in each case in a different layout. On the Reinheim flagon it is limited to three zones, one under the rim, one around the fattest part of the belly and one on the foot. The elements used are the plant motifs found on Middle Rhine goldwork, executed with mathematical precision and without a single error. Palmettes, lotus-buds, comma-leaves or S's are found, together with geometric zig-zags, all so tiny as to suggest extreme near-sight in the artist.

The Waldalgesheim flagon has, as recent restoration work has revealed, even more extensive engraving almost entirely covering the body. This time the design is produced from dotted lines rather than the tremolo line characteristic of the rocked engraving tool. Lotus-buds, chains of whorls and comma features link the design to that on Reinheim and to the sieve from Hoppstädten barrow II in the Middle Rhine. Intersecting concentric circles recall designs on stamped pottery and also on the bronze biconical vessel from Eigenbilzen.

THE MOVE TO THE END OF THE 'STRICT STYLE' OF EARLY LA TÈNE ART

From early in the development of La Tène A art, certain characteristics which became fundamental features of the later 'Vegetal' or Waldalgesheim style can be clearly seen. Three final objects from France can be used to illustrate this development.

139 Disc of sheet gold placed over two bronze discs and inlaid with ?coral from Auvers-sur-Oise, Val d'Oise, France. D. 100 cm. LT A, early 4th c. BC.

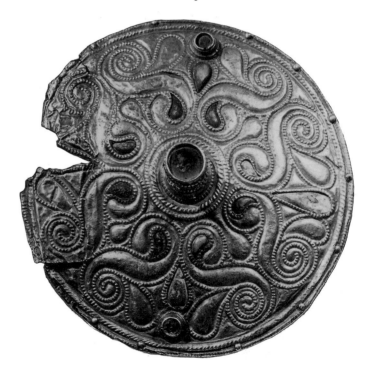

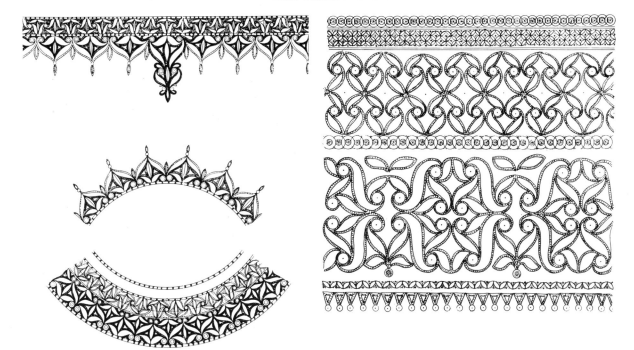

One is the magnificent gold-covered bronze disc from Auvers-sur-Oise. This bears some resemblance to the miniature gold discs from the Uetliberg, including the use of Rhineland cable or beading, created by a goldsmith's hammer working on an anvil. Half-palmettes have been reduced to fat S-shapes which form lyres: these are scarcely separated, and at some points actually share the beaded lines dividing them. Such swashbuckling S-shapes can be seen elsewhere, for example on a sherd from the Dürrnberg, on bronze leaf shield mounts from Le Mont Blanc at Etrechy and on a piece of bronze appliqué from grave 47 at Mairy. At the rim of the disc, the lyres are separated by lotus-buds formed of a central droplet flanked by a pair of comma-leaves. At first sight, the Auvers disc looks like an exercise in abstraction, but within each lyre is the hint of a face with eyes, nose and outward-curling forked beard. Such elusive Cheshire-cat faces, partially concealed in plant motifs, became a characteristic feature of the later La Tène B vegetal art.

The tendency towards continuous pattern was also evident on the base of the Schwarzenbach bowl, or on the Schwarzenbach triskel discs. Transformation of static into continuous design can actually be seen on the openwork edge of a large, coral-inlaid, bronze disc from a Marnian wagon grave at St Jean-sur-Tourbe. Lyres are formed from double S-shapes which run into one another; the lyres, moreover, shift shape into a sinuous wave or 'running dog' pattern.

Celtic engraving on the unprovenanced flagon now in the Besançon museum covers almost the entire surface, including the base. The first

140,141 Details of the engraving on spouted flagons. (Above left) Reinheim, Kr. St Ingbert, Germany, barrow A, ills. 137–8. (Above right) Waldalgesheim, Kr. Mainz-Bingen, Germany, ill. 136. Late LT A, mid-4th c. BC.

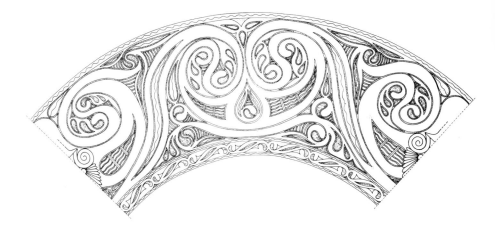

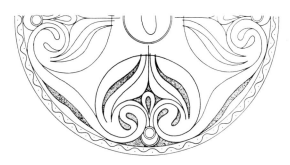

142 *(Left) Incised decoration on a bronze disc from Écury-sur-Coole, Marne, France. D. 14.3 cm. Late LT A, early 4th c. BC.*

143 *(Above) Celtic incised decoration on the Besançon Etruscan flagon, ill. 64. H. 25.5 cm. Late LT A, mid-4th c. BC.*

zone, below the neck, shows a palmette flanked by S-scrolls reminiscent of the Berru helmet, and demonstrating the flagon's debt to Etruscan metalwork. On the central zone, two fat comma-leaves revolve around a central point in a design of yin-yang commas enclosing and supported by half-palmettes. These also display a Cheshire-cat pseudo-face peering out of the foliage. Dismembered tendrils and enclosed curved-sided triangles take on lives of their own. The frieze looks continuous, though it is not entirely so, with the exuberance of the Auvers disc translated into a sense of restless movement. On the base is another example of movement around a central point by four dismembered, but totally interlinked, tendrils.

Minor decorative details link this flagon with Marnian pieces, including the use of random dot infilling and the enclosing of the design with parallel lines containing a row of dots, as on the St Jean-sur-Tourbe disc, the Vert-la-Gravelle sword or the openwork harness mount from La Bouvandeau.

The Besançon flagon, together with the helmet from Berru and similar objects from France, marks a turning point in the Celtic assimilation of classical designs. Selective adaptation and transformation of imported elements during the fifth and early fourth centuries is very apparent. Narrative elements available on Mediterranean imports for Celts to adapt obviously had no appeal and were ignored. Motifs such as the palmette or lotus-bud, which the Greeks themselves had inherited from the Near East, and the Etruscans from the Greeks, were mutated into a unique and quite unmistakably Celtic artistic vocabulary.

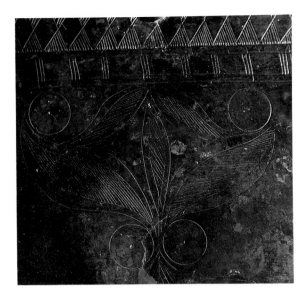

144 *(Left) Detail of the incised decoration on a bronze helmet from Prunay, Marne, France. LT A, second half 5th c. BC.*

145,146 *Bronze disc (bottom, detail below) with openwork at edge and centre from St Jean-sur-Tourbe, Marne, France. D. 24.5 cm. LT A, 450–370 BC.*

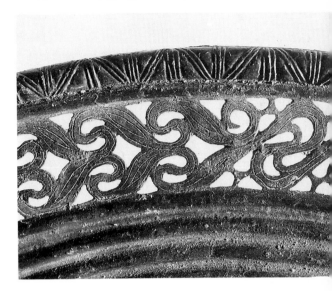

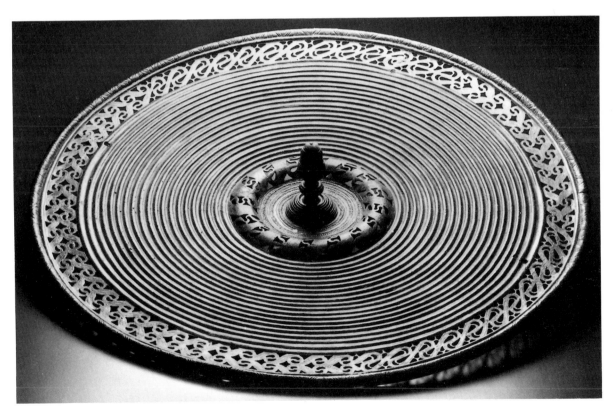

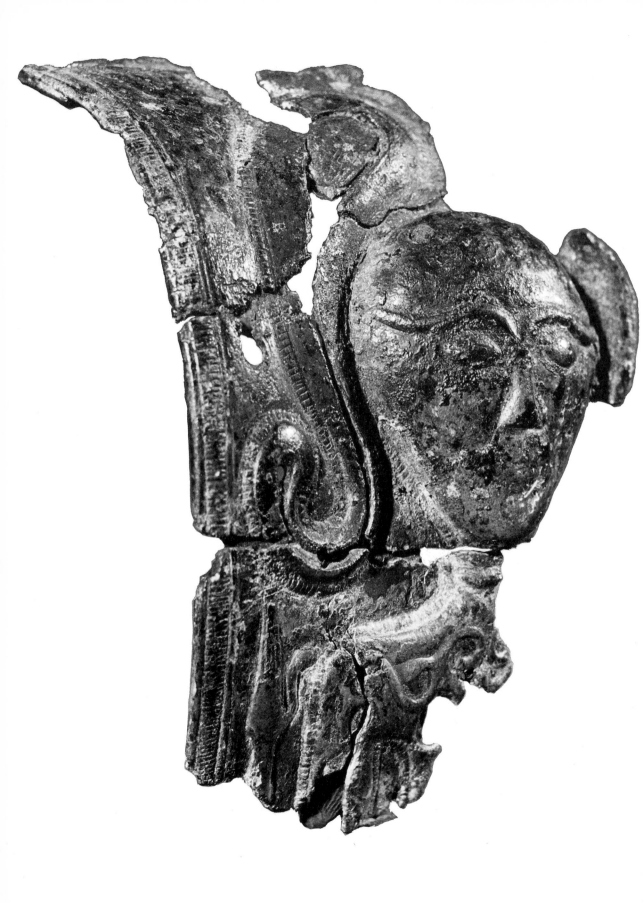

3
The Arts of Expansion

IN THE COURSE OF the fourth and early third centuries BC, the Celts were expanding south and east throughout Europe. Around 387 BC they wakened the geese of Rome and sacked the city, and by 279 they had plundered the treasures of Apollo's sacred Delphi. Classical writers explained these movements as due to overpopulation and consequent land hunger, the direct result of a more efficient exploitation of local economic resources. This expansion is historically and archaeologically attested: except for the region east of Reims, which shows great prosperity, the cemeteries of the Marne and Ardennes were abandoned and there are strong links artistically between the Marne and Italy or eastern Europe.

Expansion brought social change to Celtic society, and the hierarchical and centralized nature of the western Celtic zone apparently gave way to a growth of rural centres. A wider distribution of grave goods in flat cemeteries, rather than the concentration in the rich barrow burials, hints at the growth of a warrior oligarchy in place of a ruling dynasty.

With the decline in the importance of the chieftainly culture of the Rhineland came a shift in the major centres of artistic innovation to the Marne area and to the eastern style province which had earlier been something of an artistic backwater. The art style itself changed with the changes in Celtic society. Though humans and beasts do not vanish entirely from this vegetal art, it becomes essentially a series of variations on classical plant motifs in continuous form; from these, ambiguous faces peer out in the so-called 'Cheshire-cat' style – now you see the face, now only the smile – rather than existing in their own right. The Vegetal Style has a sense of constant motion, a restlessness often lacking in the stricter Early Style.

Material indications of this La Tène B phase are new types of safety-pin brooches which can be used to give relative dates. They are more elongated than earlier forms. One type is named after Münsingen, a flat grave cemetery near Bern: these have disc shaped feet, often inset with coral or enamel. The other type is named after a ritual deposit contained in a big bronze cauldron in a thermal spring at Duchcov in northwest Bohemia: on these brooches a vase-shaped or knobbed terminal finishes the bent-back feet and the spring is wound so that it is inside the curvature of the bow.

147 (Opposite) One of a pair of bronze chariot-mounts from Waldalgesheim, Kr. Mainz-Bingen, Germany. H. 8.9 cm. ?LT B1/B2, later 4th c. BC.

ITALY AND THE ROOTS
OF THE VEGETAL STYLE

Since increased contact with Italy may have been the precipitating cause of
the new style, it is worth examining the evidence available for Celtic
settlement and art south of the Alps in this period. Historical accounts put
Celtic invasion in the first quarter of the fourth century BC, and one account
ascribes it to the Celtic smith Helico: tempted by the riches of Rome and
Etruria where he had worked, on his return home he incited other Celts to
migrate there. Archaeological evidence of the Celtic presence is, however,
distressingly scanty, though it appears that Celts were probably already in
the valley of the Po from the middle of the fifth century BC. From such
writers as Livy and Polybius we know the names of four tribes who settled
south of the Alps. Most southerly were the Senones, who are considered
responsible for the Celtic material found in the cemeteries of the Italian
Marches such as Filottrano and Montefortino – at which latter site, in 1871,
Gabriel de Mortillet first recognized brooches and weapons as evidence of
Celts in Italy. In this region the Celts remained dominant until the Romans
annexed their territory in 283 BC. This is the only Italian group which
apparently practised inhumation regularly. Recent scholars have considered the Senones as particularly important in acting as the agents for the
artistic transformation between Italo-Greek and Celt which resulted in the
developed Vegetal Style. It is, also, the Senones who are credited by Livy
with mounting the sack of Rome in about 387 BC.

Around Bologna was the territory of the Boii, who remained important
in this area till their subjugation by the Romans in 191 BC. The excavations
at Monte Bibele above Monterenzio in the valley of the Idige show both
cremation graves and inhumations. The warrior cremations are interpreted
as evidence of the Celtic newcomers, and certainly the considerable amount
of local and classical material found together in such cemeteries indicates
that we are dealing with a very mixed population.

The Cenomani are represented mostly by later, third-century, material
in the territory round Brescia. The Insubres have left little material
evidence behind in their region south of the Ticino, though they
overlapped territorially with the Golaseccan culture of Liguria, whose own
ethnic identity is a matter for dispute, but who, as already mentioned,
formed an important cultural bridge across the Alps. Hardly surprising,
then, that later Romans termed the area first 'ager gallicus' and
subsequently 'Gallia Cisalpina' – Gaul on the near side of the Alps.

It can be difficult to distinguish Celts archaeologically from those among
whom they settled. They appear to have absorbed Italian material objects
and even social customs almost immediately. Thus even those warriors
buried in typically Celtic fashion with a chariot, also have south Italian
painted pottery and late Etruscan metalwork with them. Celtic weapons in
graves must in turn sometimes indicate no more than the adoption by the
original inhabitants of new military fashions. In the same way, contem-

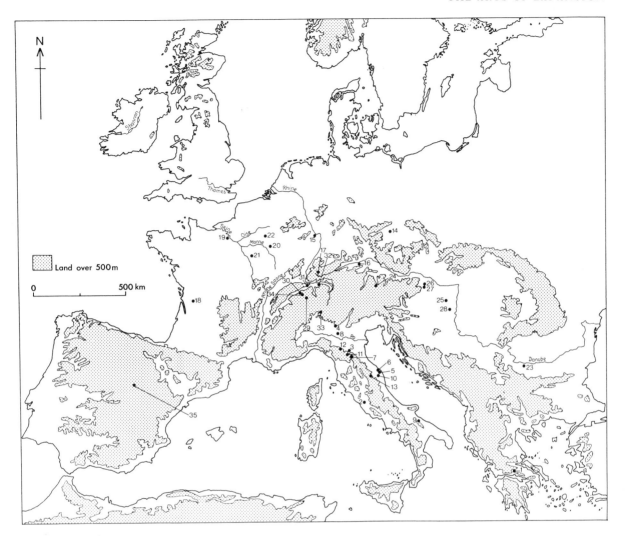

N

Land over 500m

0   500 km

148 *Map of principal sites referred to in Chapter 3.*

porary, non-Celtic, grave markers from northern Italy occasionally depict Celtic warriors.

During the fourth century, it seems that a number of workshops, probably Etruscan, or at least Italian rather than Celtic, were producing helmets of the same hemispherical jockey-cap type already seen on the Hallstatt grave 994 scabbard. Hinged cheek-flaps, a brim – probably to protect the neck – and a fitting to take a central plume are characteristic. The cap was usually made of iron, with decorative bronze panels added.

One of the best preserved of these was found in 1979 in cremation grave 14 on Monte Bibele; there was also a Celtic sword as well as late fourth-century Greek pottery and Italian bronzes. The repoussé bronze band around the helmet brim is formed of a chain of palmettes bordered by a scalloped design: this border is a version of classical tongue-and-groove pattern and is also to be found on Etruscan and south Italian metalwork and pottery.

Another fine example of such a helmet, now in Berlin, is, unfortunately, recorded only as coming from Umbria. Traces of its textile lining can still be seen. The decorative frieze is similar to that from Monte Bibele, but the panels above the cheek-pieces show an elusive face peering out of the swelling leaves of the lyre-shape, a visual trick which can be found on fourth-century Apulian pottery. Another helmet, from Gottolengo in Cenomani territory, turns the ends of similar lyres into birds' heads.

These helmets were almost certainly not made by Celts and possibly not even used by Celts. There are three others which, despite the curious circumstances in which they were found, illustrate the way in which motifs flourishing in the fertile artistic soil of Italy were domesticated and transplanted into almost the whole of the Celtic artistic garden.

In 1895 an underground tomb complex was investigated at Canosa di Puglia (ancient Canusium) in Apulia, far from the northern area of Celtic settlements, though Celtic mercenaries sold their services as far south as Sicily and even north Africa. The warrior here had spears, breastplate and helmet, as well as late fourth-century Apulian painted pottery. The weapons and armour indicated that the dead man was of south Italian origin, but his helmet is of the Italo-Celtic type. In the repoussé bronze frieze over the iron cap are carefully cut coral insets which, following recent restoration, still retain their reddish colour. The lower frieze shows a pattern of lyres, alternately upright and reversed, linked into nearly continuous form by diagonal, fat, S-shaped leaves. On the upper frieze, half-palmettes fill the spaces between highly Celticized lyre-palmettes which show elusive faces peering out, as on the Besançon flagon, the Auvers disc or the Berru helmet. Wheel-turned pottery from the Champagne region also offers a close comparison to the decoration of the Canosa helmet and the Besançon flagon; these pots are dated to the late fourth century by association with brooches related to the Duchcov type. With the Canosa helmet, however, the combination of iron and sheet bronze suggests a place of manufacture south of the Alps, while the artistic influences point to the Marne.

OPPOSITE

149 (Above left) Iron helmet with bronze covering from 'Umbria', Italy. H. (of cap) 19.5 cm. ?LT B1, later 4th c. BC.

150 (Above right) Detail of the linked triskels on the bronze helmet from Amfreville-sous-les-Monts, Eure, France, ill. 154. LT B1, later 4th c. BC.

151 (Centre right) Painted pottery jar with curvilinear design from 'Les Commelles', Prunay, Marne, France. Total H. 35 cm. LT B1/B2, late 4th/3rd c. BC.

152 (Below left) Detail of bronze plates on a helmet from Monte Bibele, Monterenzio, Bologna, Italy, grave 14. H. 19 cm. LT B, mid- to late 4th c. BC.

153 (Below right) Iron helmet with bronze overlay and coral decoration from Canosa di Puglia, Bari, Italy. H. 25 cm. LT B1, second half 4th c. BC.

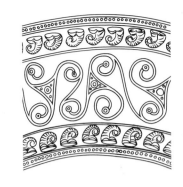

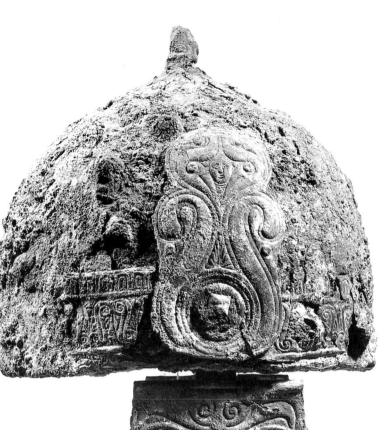

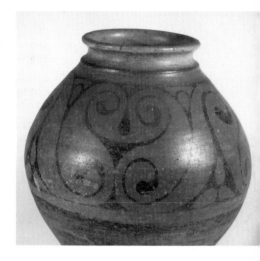

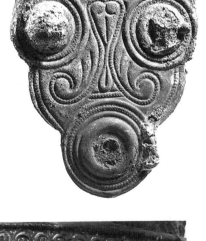

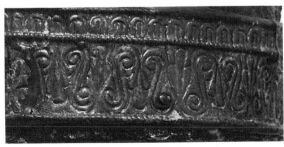

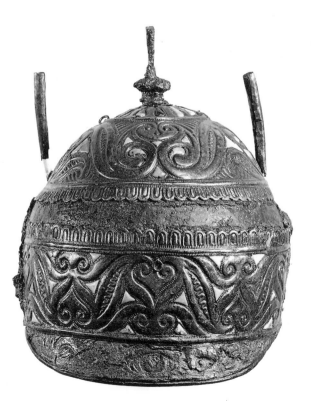

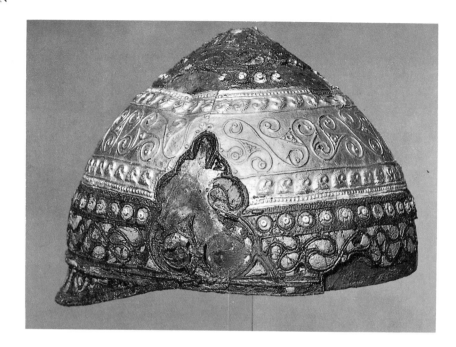

154 Bronze helmet decorated with gold, enamel and iron bands from Amfreville-sous-les-Monts, Eure, France. H. 17.5 cm. LT B1, later 4th c. BC.

From within France itself, though in a region well outside the central Celtic settlement area, a jockey-cap helmet was found in 1981 in a cave at Agris, not far from Angoulême. The iron cap was covered with gold leaf and openwork; coral was inlaid in rosettes as on some of the Münsingen brooches. The palmettes of the main band of decoration are however still in side-by-side, rather than continuous, form.

This helmet has some similarities in construction to one found in an old stream-bed of the Seine. The base cap of the Amfreville-sous-les-Monts helmet is of bronze, with openwork panels, once filled with 'enamel' (more strictly glass) in flat fields, at each side and round the peak and brim. The central gold leaf band has in this case transformed the classical palmette frieze into a linked series of finely drawn triskels or whirligigs. In contrast, however, with Agris and its almost copy-book rendition of Italo-Celtic pattern-making, the iron openwork displays a true 'running dog' continuous pattern formed from fleshy, interlocked S-scrolls. The central gold band is flanked by two rows of hook-shaped and hatched waves – common fill-ins on pottery, metalwork and gravestones in fourth-century Greek, Etruscan and Apulian art. These features are even more evident since recent restoration work on both the Agris and Amfreville helmets.

In their differing ways these helmets, some undoubtedly of Celtic workmanship, some equally clearly not and some where it is impossible to separate Celt from non-Celt, show the incorporation of Celtic features into north Italian regional forms, and in the case of Amfreville, the mainline development taken by Celtic art of its own, distinctive, Vegetal Style.

THE PRINCESS OF WALDALGESHEIM

As we have observed, the fundamental hall-mark of the Vegetal Style is the running tendril or the linked chain of lyre-palmettes. One of the key finds of this style is the rich 'princess's' grave of Waldalgesheim near Bonn, after which the style was originally named. Yet despite this historical accident, the Middle Rhine cannot be regarded as the place of either the origin or the artistic development of this 'new wave' of Celtic art.

The presence of ring jewellery, especially a torc, and the absence of weapons or other specifically male grave goods confirms that this chariot burial is a single woman's grave, and not a double grave as originally thought. Three groups of significant material can be identified among the surviving finds: drinking vessels, gold rings and chariot fittings.

The drinking vessels include the flagon discussed in the previous chapter and an imported situla made in southern Italy in the third quarter of the fourth century. This is the latest of the classical pieces found in rich early Celtic graves and, from this time onwards until the Roman period, imports rarely appear north of the Alps. Its decoration includes a scalloped rim, palmettes and tendril-like roots flanked by a pair of rosettes or star-shaped flowers.

Such tiny rosettes occur on the gold neckring, running around the buffer-shaped terminals which are a common feature in La Tène B. Yet such details are no certain proof that at Waldalgesheim a native goldsmith copied from the situla, since they are found on other locally made Celtic pieces as, for example, in Hungary.

The torc and the two gold bracelets appear to come from the same goldsmith's workshop. The whole find is certainly not, however, from the hand of a single Waldalgesheim master as has been argued, for the spouted flagon, the openwork bronze and the sheet bronze all betray different hands from that responsible for the gold.

Movement, a lack of rigid symmetry and a clear distinction between foreground and background provide a major contrast on these gold rings to the work of the earlier Middle Rhine chieftainly goldsmiths. Palmette chains in two different versions appear on the terminals of all three Waldalgesheim rings. Buried in the tendril foliage of the armrings are pairs of human heads whose scrolled brows, round eyes and tiny down-turned mouths are precisely in the tradition of the mask-decorated brooches seen in the last chapter, evidence of how close in time and space this new vegetal art is to its predecessors. Waves like those on the Amfreville helmet form borders to the decorated zone on the armrings' main curve. Once more it is to Italy that one may trace the tradition of heads sprouting from foliage and one can cite Apulian pottery as providing a more influential model even than occasional bronzes such as the helmet from Umbria.

Humans can be seen among the chariot fittings too. Elusive faces, Janus-fashion back to back, on an openwork strap tag recall the more prosaic forms on the Rodenbach ring. Cross-legged figures with raised hands appear on a pair of curved sheet bronze chariot mounts, their faces again

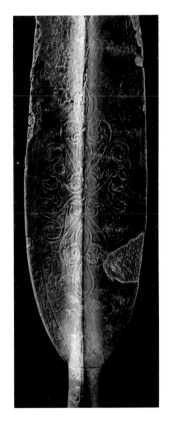

155 *Iron spear head with incised Vegetal Style decoration from an unknown findspot in Hungary. L. 30 cm. ?LT B1/B2, late 4th/early 3rd c. BC.*

113

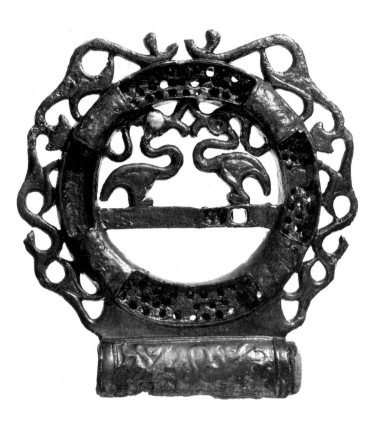

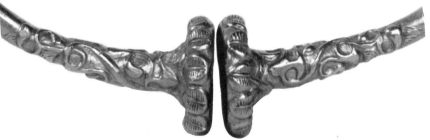

156 (*Above*) *Bronze openwork chariot-mount from Waldalgesheim, Kr. Mainz-Bingen, Germany. H. 7.6 cm. ?LT B1/B2, later 4th c. BC.*

157 (*Right*) *Terminals of gold torc from Filottrano, San Paolino, Italy, grave N 2. D. (of terminals) c. 2.5 cm. LT B1, late 4th c. BC.*

recalling the mask brooches. In the context of a woman's grave, these figures may be female, since they have neckrings and inlay on each breast; they are covered with tendrils which move over them like snakes on a Celtic Laocoön. Such waves appear again on a rectangular zone at the base of another openwork fitting, which contains in the centre two birds, perhaps storks or cranes, whose configuration suggests a relationship to the openwork belt-hooks of Italy and the Marne, described in Chapter 2.

All in all, there is little in the Waldalgesheim grave, save the flagon, which suggests Rhenish manufacture. Nor, in view of the extraordinarily widespread distribution of this new style, can one point with certainty to the region from which its owner must have come. Perhaps the Waldalgesheim princess brought her goods or her craftsmen with her, travelling to an arranged marriage with one of the last of the Rhineland chieftains at a time when the older society – like the older art style – was giving way to the new.

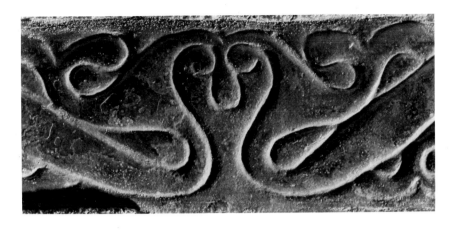

158 *Detail of iron backed bronze scabbard fragment from Filottrano, San Paolino, Italy, grave 22. L. (of fragment) c. 20 cm. LT B1, late 4th c. BC.*

DIFFUSION OF THE VEGETAL STYLE

Italian connections were indubitably influential in the development of the Vegetal Style, and the territory of the Senones has produced material which clearly illustrates this. One such object is the short sword of a warrior found with his horse at Moscano di Fabriano near Ancona. Disastrous earthquakes have delayed the publication of this site, but the dead man's treasures included an Italo-Celtic helmet, Etruscan bronzes and late fourth-century Apulian painted pottery. A brooch shows plant-based continuous decoration, and the wave tendril provides the edging decoration to his sword – decoration which has an intriguing British echo.

From cremation grave 22 of the San Paolino cemetery at Filottrano comes another sword, found only with a spear and two iron rings with which to sling the sword over the shoulder. Sword and scabbard were intentionally bent, or ritually 'killed'. Along the whole length of the bronze scabbard plate runs a complex, intertwined chain of lyre-palmettes, the main lyre elements looking like Celtic heads with bulbous nose and leaf crown. It was this feature which made Jacobsthal refer to a 'Cheshire-cat style' in Celtic art, named after the disappearing cat of Lewis Carroll. Though Jacobsthal rejects the idea of any anthropomorphic intent on Filottrano, it is perhaps worth recalling, for example, those New Guinea woodcarvers who decorate their meeting houses and shields with abstracted – and reversible! – human forms and yet deny any human depictions are intended in their art. So too, beyond theories of an innate human propensity to find natural forms in abstract motifs, it is impossible to be dogmatic on questions of ancient Celtic symbolism, though enticing clues are certainly present.

Pseudo-faces occur again on a gold torc from grave 2 in the same cemetery. This contained a bronze situla, an Etruscan mirror and three red-figure bell-kraters, one from Apulia and two from Attica; these all confirm a late fourth-century date. The neckring itself is made over a core of clay or base metal. The faces appear in the lyre-palmette below each

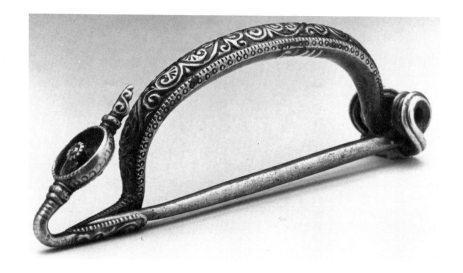

159,160 *Silver brooch (*right*) from Bern-Schosshalde, Kt. Bern, Switzerland, and a drawing of its decoration (*centre right*) and of its possible classical prototype (*centre*). L. 6.3 cm. LT B1, 350–300 BC.*

161 (*Below*) *Bronze mounts from ?Comacchio, Emilia, Italy. L. 12.5 cm. LT B1, later 4th c. BC.*

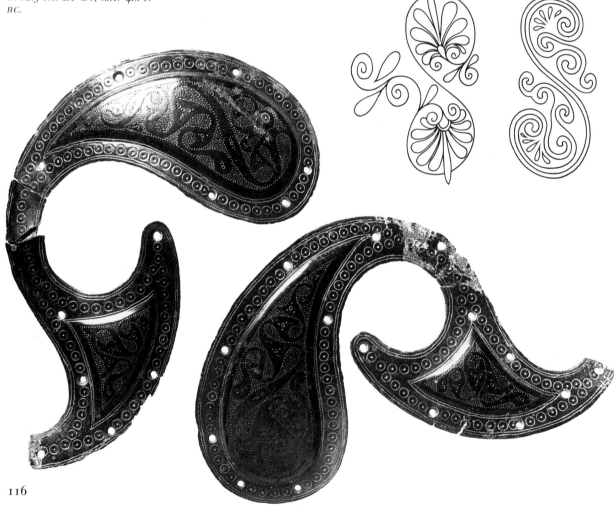

terminal; each terminal is decorated with a hatched version of a scalloped tongue-and-groove design. The tendrils on the main part of the ring end in curved-sided triangles or peltas, and offer one of the closest comparisons for the tendrils on the Waldalgesheim gold rings.

Several bronze mounts, probably from a wooden flagon, are said to come from Comacchio on the Italian Adriatic coast north of Ravenna. Here, even the shape of the mount is curved, and swirls at one end into a pelta or curved-sided triangle; the whole is outlined by stamped dots within circles. The internal writhing tendrils are given prominence by setting them against a punched background. This, and the tiny triple leaves set within peltas on the tendrils, recalls the Besançon flagon and the Marnian painted pottery, and underlines the similar sources behind this regionally distinctive group.

The concentration of objects of the pure Vegetal Style in northern Italy and in areas directly to the north in Switzerland and the Rhine-Danube area suggests that the style may well have been developed in pioneering workshops in Italy or Switzerland.

Many of the Swiss flat grave cemeteries around Berne, including Münsingen itself, show Münsingen brooches bearing the characteristic tendril patterns. Schosshalde, Kt. Bern, produced a silver brooch from a disturbed grave. The classical palmette fronds on its elongated bow are so close to fourth-century classical acanthus ornament as to suggest first-hand acquaintance. This brooch may even be an import from Italy since silver was rarely used north of the Alps, while it was relatively commonly employed in Italy.

The nearby Stettlen-Deisswil cemetery in Kt. Bern produced a silver finger-ring with a vegetal design very closely comparable to the decoration on a pair of cast bronze armlets from the Waldalgesheim grave, possibly the work of the smith who created the openwork mount with its Cheshire-cat face; the ring could even be from the same workshop.

From Dürrnberg grave 28/2 comes another similar finger-ring, this time of gold. The lyre chain round its circumference is typically vegetal, and not dissimilar to that encircling the terminals of the Waldalgesheim neckring.

162 (Below left) Gold finger-ring from the Dürrnberg bei Hallein, Austria, grave 28/2. D. 2.1 cm. LT B1, later 4th c. BC.

163 (Below) Silver finger-ring from Stettlen-Deisswil, Kt. Bern, Switzerland. D. 2.4 cm. LT B1, later 4th c. BC.

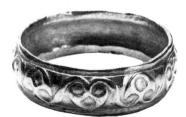
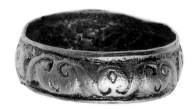

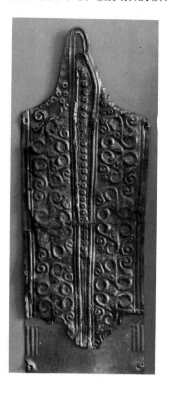

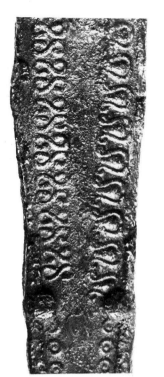

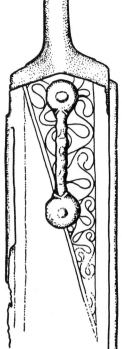

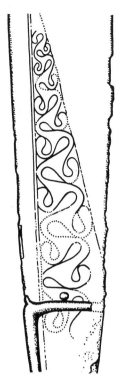

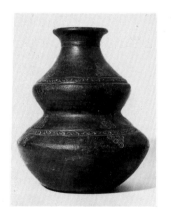

Celtic armourers in widely separated regions quickly adapted the writhing tendril for the embellishment of bronze sword scabbards. Late fourth-century stamped versions come from St Germainmont, Larchant, Epiais-Rhus and the Saône valley in France. Others come from the flat grave cemeteries close to the large Late La Tène site at Manching in Bavaria while it appears too on *Falkata*, or single-edged knives, in Iberia. Of this late fourth-century date, too, is the elegant asymmetric design on a sword from Litér in western Hungary, a key piece in the development of the 'Sword Style' examined below.

In this more easterly zone the designs stamped on pottery also change in La Tène B. The simplified palmettes and lotus-buds died out in the later fourth century, though arcaded ornament continued; and pottery is generally lacking entirely in the extensive flat grave cemeteries of northern Bohemia. Strong interrelationships between pottery and metalwork designs continued to be a feature of this area, which shows its own localized versions of the Vegetal Style, particularly in the areas of western Hungary and of Czechoslovakia into which Celts spread in the fourth century.

Some vegetal designs incorporate more individualistic natural forms. For example, a Münsingen brooch with a tiny human head on its foot was found in the Duchcov hoard. Again, within the four-times repeated lozenge-shaped stamps on a pot from Sopron-Bécsidomb, the vegetal tendril becomes a swimming swan. The Sopron pot also shows the dot-in-circle stamp used as edging on the Comacchio flagon mount.

Much more in local tradition is the sword scabbard from grave 115 at Jenišův Újezd in northern Bohemia. Two versions of the double-S, the simplest form of the lyre-palmette, have been stamped on it. The only close parallel is on a scabbard from Bussy-le-Château in the Marne, and it has been argued that the Bohemian scabbard came from this more westerly region; certainly connections between the Marne and central Europe were close. Yet S-stamps are often a feature of the pottery of this easterly part of the Rhine-Danube province, often in combination with other stamps.

Recent techniques for the analysis of pottery fabric show that late fourth-century pots were being made in local centres and traded within restricted areas, as befits their fragile state and lesser prestige in relation to metalwork. The double pot from Hidegség seems to have been a local type, fired at one of the kilns in the Krautacker settlement to the west of the old Hallstatt fortification and cemeteries near Sopron. It again carries the double-S stamp. Importation of the Jenišův Újezd scabbard thus seems unlikely: one might, indeed, more readily argue that the Bussy piece was imported from further east.

A gold buffer torc with a fourth-century vegetal design was found as far east as Tsibur Varos in Bulgaria, an area which the Celts are not known to have penetrated till the first quarter of the third century. Elements in the design of this torc can once again be paralleled on pottery from Hungary; a

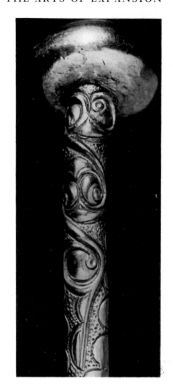

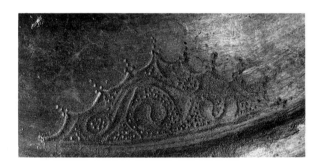

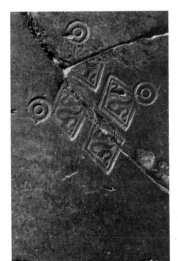

OPPOSITE

164 *(Above, far left) Bronze scabbard-mount with stamped decoration from Manching, Kr. Ingolstadt, Germany. W. 5.4 cm. LT B1, mid-4th c. BC.*

165 *(Above, centre left) Bronze scabbard plate with stamped decoration from Jenišův Újezd, okr. Teplice, Czechoslovakia, grave 115. W. c. 6.3 cm. LT B1, first half 4th c. BC.*

166 *(Above, centre right and right) Vegetal design on the rear of an iron scabbard from Litér, Veszprém, Hungary. W. 4.7 cm. LT B1/B2, late 4th/early 3rd c. BC.*

167 *(Left) Pot with stamped decoration from Hidegség, Györ-Sopron, Hungary. H. 15.5 cm. LT B1, earlier 4th c. BC.*

THIS PAGE

168 *(Top right) Detail of a gold neckring from Tsibur Varos (Gorni Tsibur), Mihailovgrad, Bulgaria. D. 15.2 cm. LT B2, early 3rd c. BC.*

169 *(Above left) Detail of stamped decoration on a pot from Alsópél, Tolna, Hungary. H. (of detail) c. 2 cm. LT B1, late 4th c. BC.*

170 *(Left) Stamped decoration on a pot from Sopron-Bécsidomb, Györ-Sopron, Hungary, grave 1888. H. (of lozenge) c. 1.5 cm. LT B1, 4th-3rd c. BC.*

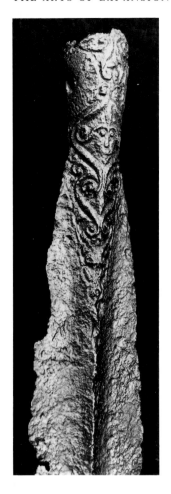

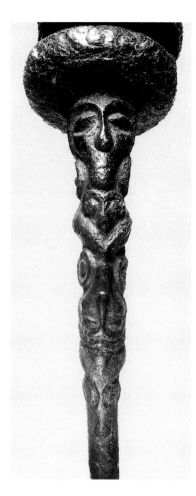

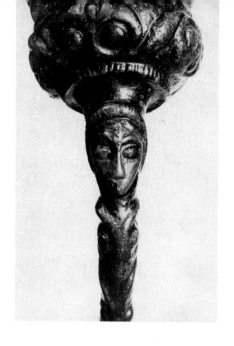

171 (Far left) *Iron spear head from Saunières, Sâone-et-Loire, France. L. 49.1 cm. LT B1/B2, later 4th c. BC.*

172 (Left) *Detail of bronze neckring from Courtisols, Marne, France, grave 11. Total D. 13 cm. LT B1/B2, later 4th c. BC.*

173 (Above) *Detail of bronze neckring from Witry-les-Reims, Champagne, France. D. (of terminals) c. 3.2 cm. LT B1/B2 late 4th/early 3rd c. BC.*

pot from Alsopél shows a similar vegetal tendril surrounded by random dots and stamped arcades or half-moons. Despite the early assimilation of the Vegetal Style in the eastern Celtic province, however, an eastern origin for the Tsibur Varos torc seems unlikely, because of the form of the torc, the use of gold, and the absence of any other similar material in this region. How it arrived so far east must therefore remain yet another unanswered question.

Celtic regions further west also produce examples of regional schools or variants of the Vegetal Style. From the region of the Upper Rhine comes a particular form of woman's neckring, in which the ring and the discs adorning it are generally decorated with red enamel. The vegetal designs in low relief sometimes contain Cheshire-cat human faces. The rosette-like discs and the S-spirals echo the decoration on several Münsingen and Duchcov brooches, with which they are often found. Such rings occur mostly in La Tène B period flat graves, but extend into Middle La Tène (La Tène C) as well; some have even been found in Hungary amongst other evidence of Celtic easterly expansion in the late fourth and early third centuries BC.

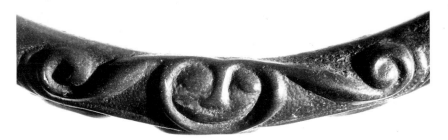

In the Marne region, too, strong local artistic traditions continued to develop. Occasional southern imports do occur, such as the bronze sieve plate with its quadruple writhing tendril, unprovenanced, but recorded as having been found in the Marne. Flat grave cemeteries in the area have produced a series of cast bronze women's neckrings with buffer terminals. Many of these carry vegetal decoration round the terminals or on the ring. Often too, as in the example from Witry-les-Reims in Champagne, human faces support the buffers or appear elsewhere on the rings; these gloomy, lantern-jawed faces are a considerable way from the chinless faces of earlier Middle Rhine metalwork but share the same ultimate Italic origin and general Cheshire-cat formulation which is exhibited by the Waldalgesheim gold armrings.

One further type of French speciality is the *torque ternaire*, or neckring with three separate areas of decoration. The triple knobs round such rings mark as definite French exports fragmentary examples found in Bohemia and in San Polo d'Enzo in Reggio Emilia. The finest example comes from Barbuise, near Troyes. Cheerful Janus faces peer from each lyre-palmette in yet another humanizing of the palmette.

In contrast to the art of the chieftainly period, the Vegetal Style shows a remarkably wide distribution and an extraordinarily rapid spread, including its adaptation to regional forms in both east and west. This in itself is a witness to the mobility of the craftsmen and armourers who served the Celtic warrior oligarchy, as well as to the wanderings of these pillaging expansionist sword bearers, whose art is as restless as their adventurous spirits. It is in fact the art of later Celtic swordsmiths which now demands our attention.

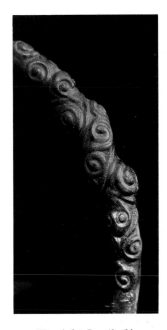

174 (Top left) *Detail of bronze neckring from Barbuise, Aube, France. D. (internal) 12.7 cm. LT B1, 4th c. BC.*

175 (Above) *Detail of bronze neckring from Avon-Fontenay, Aube, France. D. 13 cm. LT B1/B2, later 4th c. BC.*

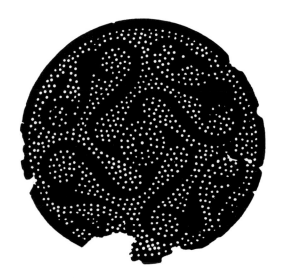

176 *Bronze strainer, found in 'Marne', France. D. 10.2 cm. LT B1, later 4th c. BC.*

121

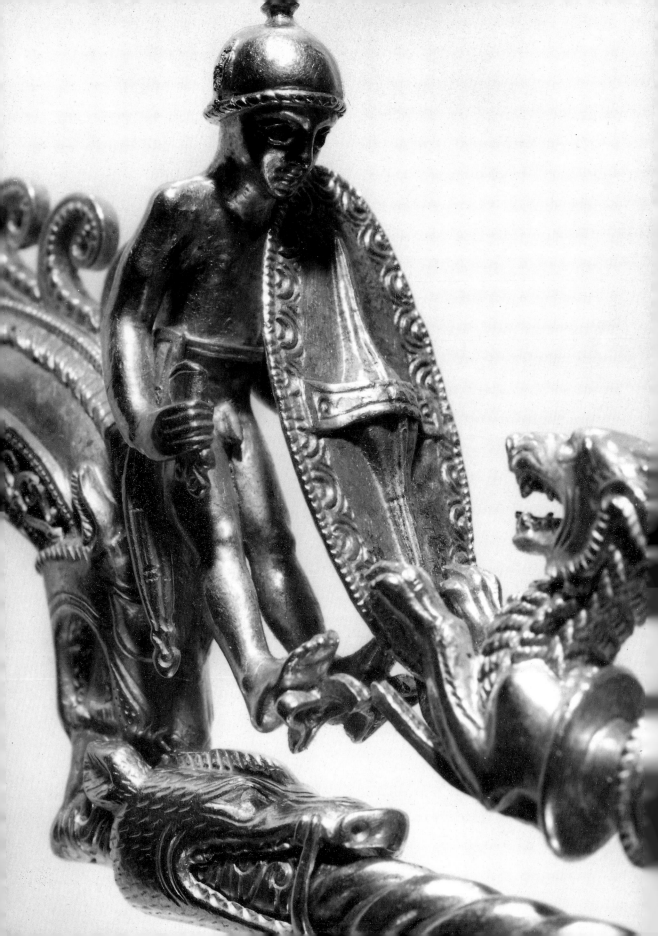

4

The Sword Bearers:
The Celts of the Later
Third and Second Centuries BC

HISTORY

IN THE THIRD AND second centuries BC the expansion and dispersion of the Celts continued across Europe and even into Asia Minor. As Roman power expanded, however, the Celts of northern Italy were gradually subdued, beginning in 295 BC with the defeat of the Senones. Polybius records that the conquest of the Boii in the region of Bologna in 192 BC led to a mass Celtic exodus to the northeast.

Celts were in Bohemia and western Hungary from the fourth century, and the Hellenistic writer Pompeius Trogus indicates their presence in the Balkans in 358 BC, when they came into conflict with the Illyrians to the east of the Adriatic. In 335, Alexander the Great received Celtic envoys on the lower Danube as their warlike penetration eastwards continued. In 298 they had established a kingdom, Tylis, in Bulgaria, while by 279 they had overrun the kingdom of Macedonia, invaded Greece and, as Strabo records, sacked the temple of Apollo at Delphi. The tribe of the Volcae Tectosages is said to have carried off its booty from Delphi to their home at Tolosa, modern Toulouse, in southern France – an indication of the incredible wanderings of these marauding Celts, and an explanation of why near-identical artefacts can be found in this period right across the Celtic world, from Romania to England. By the mid-third century, Celtic power had been consolidated in the Balkans, where the Scordisci are the tribe known to have settled in the area round modern Belgrade, and Celts were on the Great Hungarian Plain, though they had been forced to withdraw from Greece itself.

As mercenaries, Celts fought in Sicily, Greece, Egypt and Asia Minor, though there are only scattered objects in the archaeological record to mark their presence. In Turkey, for example, Middle La Tène, or La Tène C, brooches of the second century are found, while in a third-century Hellenistic chambered tomb called Mal Tepe, at Mezek on the current Bulgarian-Turkish border, were the remains of a Celtic chariot with bronze fittings.

Celts were at first invited to Asia Minor by King Nikomedes of Bithynia, and by 270 BC were settled on the Anatolian plateau near Ankara. These Celts were named Galatae by the Greeks – the Galatians of the New Testament – and among them were members of the Volcae Tectosages, originally from southern France.

177 *(Opposite) Celtic warrior with helmet, shield and sword on a ?Celto-Iberian gold brooch. H. (of figure) 4.5 cm. ?2nd c. BC.*

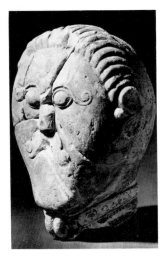

These Galatae proved a constant threat to the established order until they were defeated by a series of campaigns by the Hellenistic rulers of Pergamon, Attalos I (241–197 BC) and his son Eumenes II (197–159 BC). Attalos, in celebration of his victory in *c.* 240 BC, commissioned bronze sculptures with which to decorate the sanctuary of Athene Pallas. These survive only in first-century BC marble copies, including the famous 'Dying Gaul'. Such naturalistic portraiture contrasts markedly with the rare self-representations of the Celts. An example, perhaps contemporary with the Dying Gaul, is a ragstone head from just outside a square enclosure typical of Late La Tène cultic sites at Mšecké Žehrovice near Prague. Its stylized curling eyebrows and moustaches continue the schematization of Early La Tène Middle Rhine mask-faces, while its buffer-terminalled torc recalls the importance of the neckring as a badge of status. The neatly combed hairstyle is typical of Celtic self-portraits and contrasts with the spiky locks of the Dying Gaul.

178 Ragstone head from Mšecké Žehrovice, okr. Rakouník, Czechoslovakia. H. 23.5 cm. LT C, 3rd or 2nd c. BC. See also colour plate XVII.

Polybius wrote of the naked, torc-wearing spearmen defeated by the Romans in 225 BC at the crucial battle of Telamon in Italy. His description can be matched in the warrior with Middle La Tène shield and helmet on an unprovenanced, but possibly Iberian, gold brooch. The standard Celtic weaponry is also clearly portrayed on the balustrade frieze of the Pergamon

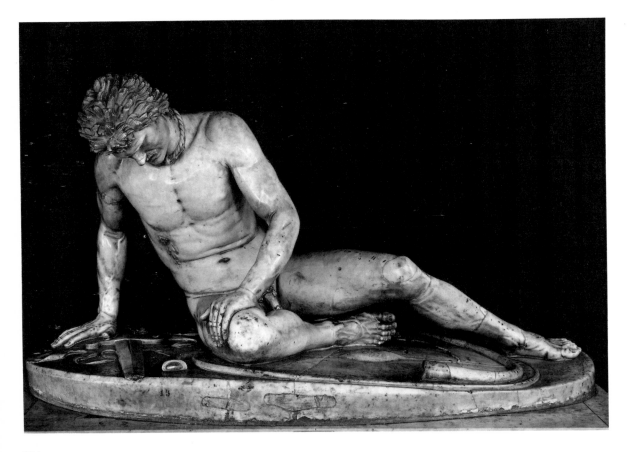

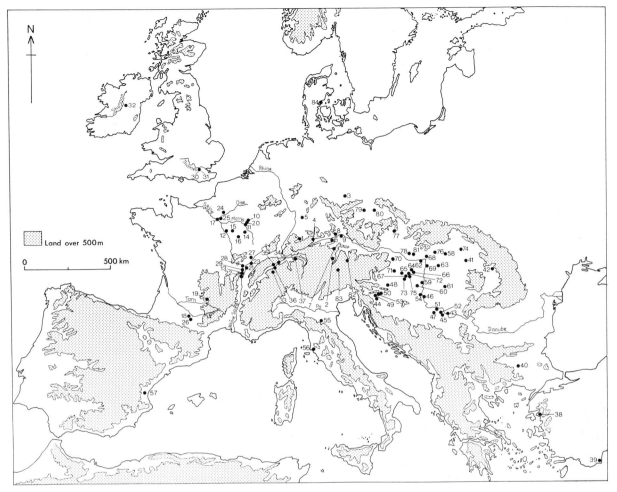

180 *Map of principal sites referred to in Chapter 4.*

179 *(Opposite) Marble statue of the 'Dying Gaul', a Roman copy of an earlier bronze statue from the sanctuary of Athena Nikephoros in Pergamon. H. (of head) 30 cm. Mid-1st c. BC.*

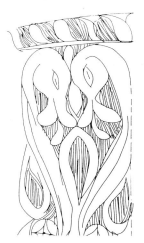

181 *Bronze sheath with incised dragons from Bussy-le-Château, Marne, France. W. 2.8 cm. LT A, 4th c. BC.*

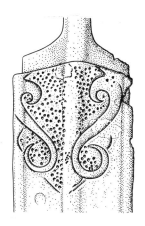

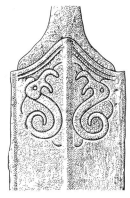

182 *Type II dragon pairs on iron scabbards from Hungary. (Top) Litér, Veszprém. W. 4.7 cm. LT B1/B2, late 4th/early 3rd c. BC. (Above) Taliándörögd, Veszprém. W. 6.8 cm. LT B2, c. 300 BC.*

sanctuary, which was rebuilt by Eumenes, probably for the Panhellenic Games of 181 BC. Some weapons are local 'Galatian' types. Others are of wider distribution. One helmet, for example, is derived from Italo-Celtic types, actual examples of which come from third-century contexts in Slovenia as well as from a disturbed warrior's grave from Ciumeşti in northwest Romania. The shield and chariot yoke of the Pergamon frieze have exact parallels from even further away, at the type-site of La Tène at Marin-Epargnier in Switzerland.

The La Tène C, or Middle La Tène, period begins in the later third century BC and is marked archaeologically by a decrease in the size of burial sites. In contrast to the one or two hundred graves found in La Tène B cemeteries, in La Tène C there are often no more than a dozen. Many of these graves – two-thirds in the old Rhine-Danube area and almost a half in the Middle Rhine and France – contain no grave goods at all. Cremations gradually replace inhumation burials, from Champagne to the Carpathians, though more slowly in the eastern part of the Celtic world than in the west.

Where there are grave goods, they tend to be ring ornaments for women, especially armrings and anklets. In Champagne, women continued to have neckrings, though elsewhere such torcs became a male prerogative. To the east, in women's graves ornamental bronze or iron belt chains replaced earlier organic belts with metal fastenings. Men were buried with iron sword and scabbard and casting spear in the east; in the Middle Rhine shears or a single-edged iron knife are sometimes also found.

The small cemeteries and the absence in central Europe of fortifications in this third- and second-century period suggest a fragmentation into local, family-based communities. These were presumably essentially mobile, though dependent also on mixed farming. The sword seems to have been a symbol of male prowess and also, no doubt, a means of gaining an alternative living as a mercenary. There are few rich graves in any area, but the spread of possessions is nonetheless wider than in the previous La Tène A and B periods. This pattern appears to reflect a more egalitarian society within the tribal system. Celtic expansion was by no means a mass movement of an integrated community, and divisions between the west and the rapidly expanding eastern zone continue to be apparent.

THE ART OF THE SWORDSMITHS

In this period the ironsmiths joined, and even surpassed, the goldsmiths and bronzeworkers as major creators of Celtic art, much of which is found on iron swords and scabbards. Either the smiths or their products were remarkably mobile throughout the expanding Celtic world; certainly there is no evidence for commissioning patrons controlling fixed workshops in this period. It is appropriate that the name 'Sword Style' should be given to a group of the major art styles of this period.

Hungary, especially the Transdanubian area around Lake Balaton, seems to have been the original centre for the development of the

Hungarian Sword Style, or rather of a group of related substyles. Products of these workshops derived their decoration in essence from the sometimes asymmetrical development of the Vegetal Style as visible on the Litér scabbard, sometimes in combination with older motifs or techniques of the eastern area. Hungarian style swords are found widely scattered throughout the areas of Celtic settlement.

Below the mouth of the late fourth-century Litér scabbard is a motif quite distinct from the plant tendrils. This is a lyre, or pair of confronted 'S's with vestiges of dragon heads. This dragon-lyre, possibly an emblem of status or achievement, is found on over two dozen sword scabbards so far known from Romania in the east to England in the west.

Earlier views, based on a smaller known number of scabbards mainly from central or eastern Europe, saw this zoomorphic lyre as developing in eastern Celtic lands under Scythian influences. Opposed animals are, however, as seen in Chapter 2, found in the chieftainly art of the western Celts. It developed further in the Marne in the fourth century BC, as can be seen on the horse-lyre engraved in a combination of freehand and compass layout on a bronze scabbard from Bussy-le-Château. Two dark, burnished, pedestalled urns from around Châlons-sur-Marne also show such animal-headed lyres from a date earlier than the dragon-pair scabbards. The lyre as such was also a motif in use throughout the Celtic world in the Early La Tène period; it takes only the provision of a dot for an eye to turn a lyre into an animal pair. Scythian origins therefore seem both unlikely and unnecessary to explain the appearance of this type of dragon pair.

Sword scabbards with this dragon-lyre are now known in both east and west Europe, with one from England, and several from France and from northern Italy, as well as some fifteen from the east. One, unusually of bronze rather than iron, and with suspension loops subsequently added in local Iberian fashion, comes from Spain. There is a major gap in their distribution between Italy and Lake Balaton in Hungary, yet the scabbards from Csabrendek or Taliándörögd in Hungary, Quintanas de Gormaz in Spain and Montigny-Lencoup in France are so similar as to suggest they are products of the same workshop, as too are the Hungarian-found scabbards from Litér and from Muhi-Koscmadomb. Most of these so-called Type II dragon pairs appear on swords which in date and form belong to the late La Tène B phase.

Of similar earlier third-century date is a variant on the dragon pairs known as Type I. On this the beast's tail is added on to a body which arcs in a C-shape from head to foot. Similar examples again come from widely separated findspots – in the west from England, the Marne and Saône in France and from Switzerland, as well as eastwards from western Hungary. Six swords with dragon pairs came from a mixed cremation and inhumation cemetery unsystematically excavated at Kosd near Budapest. That from grave 15 had been ritually bent then burned in the funeral pyre; its dragon pair and another from the same site are closely comparable to that on a fragmentary scabbard from Marnay, Saône-et-Loire, one of several recovered from the river Saône between Tournus and Chalon. The

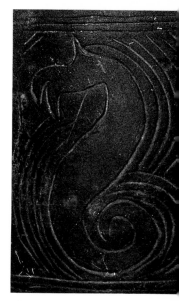

183 'Sea horse' or dragon incised on a dark burnished pot from La Cheppe, Marne. France. H. 34.5 cm. ?LT A, 4th c. BC.

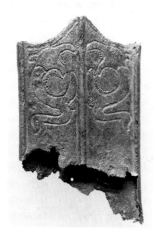

184 Type I dragon pair on an iron scabbard from Marnay, Saône-et-Loire, France. W. 5 cm. LT B2, earlier 3rd c. BC.

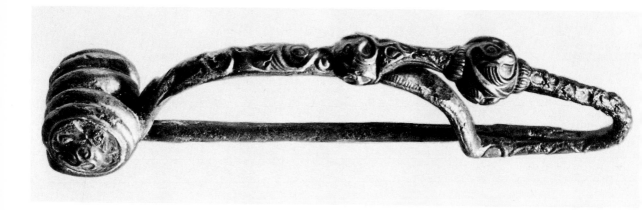

185 *One of a pair of bronze bird-headed brooches from Conflans, Aube, France. L. 12 cm. LT C1, second half 3rd c. BC.*

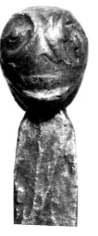

186 *Detail of head on iron sword from Kupinovo, Serbia, Jugoslavia. W. 4.5 cm. LT C1, later 3rd c. BC.*

use of a dotted background to the dragons on the Marnay scabbard can also be seen on Type I dragon pairs from the river Thames at Hammersmith and from a large Swiss river deposit at Port, near La Tène itself. Dragon pairs thus seem to have been a widespread 'inter-Celtic currency' at a time when swordsmen and swordsmiths were constantly on the move throughout Europe.

Other details of readily interchangeable Celtic currencies occur. Hatched half-leaves ending in tight spirals join a Type II dragon pair on a scabbard which probably came from Halimba near Veszprém in Hungary; they reappear on the *inside* of a poorly preserved and probably imported sheath from Montbellet, again in the Saône-et-Loire. These elements also appear on some of the earliest definite Sword Style, though locally made, art in the British Isles. Such leaves and spirals, like the whirligig on a biconical vase from Écs and on other third-century swords from Szob, in Hungary, and from Slovenia indicate the persistence of older motifs alongside the new. Vegetal Style tendrils in low relief, for example, still decorate the suspension loop on an iron scabbard from a warrior's cremation at Cernon-sur-Coole in the Marne and human heads still appear.

Oval-eyed crested birds' heads grow out of the dissected half-palmettes on the Cernon scabbard. Birds' heads appear again on a scabbard from a disturbed cemetery at Drňa in Slovakia, and, in highly abstract form, they are stamped, together with concentric circles and simplified lyres, on a scabbard from Potypuszta, in Hungary. The bird motif recurs on a pair of brooches from Conflans in the Marne area which are probably of cast bronze rather than of iron, as is usually recorded. The shape is characteristic of Middle La Tène, with the bent-over foot encircling the bow; crested birds' heads grow out of low relief tendrils, while a trio of sheep's heads decorate the knob of the birds' heads with a fourth on the bow. Both brooches and the Drňa and Cernon scabbards are all probably products of Middle Danube workshops.

The Hungarian sword scabbards were, by the second century BC, increasingly tending towards a freer and more complex design, using the diagonal layout which was first observed on the Litér scabbard. An early example can be seen on a Jugoslav scabbard from a warrior grave with jockey-cap helmet, spear, shield mounts and sword chains at Batina in Croatia. Here the tendrils and lotus-buds are executed in an assured, swirling style. A similar free translation of lyres occurs in a more symmetrical fashion on an earlier scabbard from Sremska Mitrovica in Serbia. Further west, a fleshy tendril like that on the Serbian scabbard is combined with a rectilinear maze design resembling that on the Alsópél pot or the Basse-Yutz flagons; it is on a spearhead found in the River Broye at Joressant in Switzerland. Even more surprising is the stylistic relationship of these scabbards and the spearhead to the lyre and lotus motifs and rectilinear design on a broken pillar stone from Waldenbuch, in the Forest

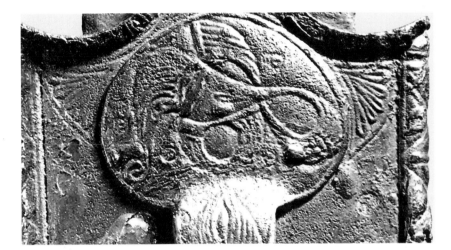

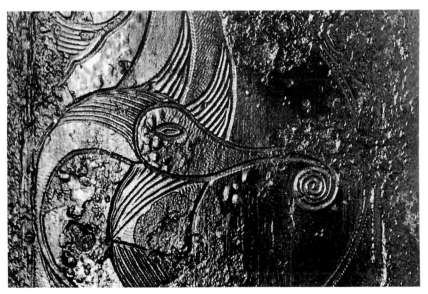

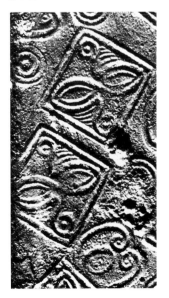

187 (Left) Detail of incised birds' heads on suspension loop of an iron scabbard from Drňa, okr. Rimavská Sobota, Czechoslovakia. W. c. 6.7 cm. Early LT C1, second half 3rd c. BC.

188 (Below left) Detail of birds' heads on an iron scabbard from Cernon-sur-Coole, Marne, France. W. c. 5.2 cm. Early LT C1, second half 3rd c. BC.

189 (Below) 'Swans' and lyres stamped on an iron scabbard from Potypuszta, Vas, Hungary. W. (of sword) 5 cm. LT B1/B2, later 4th/early 3rd c. BC.

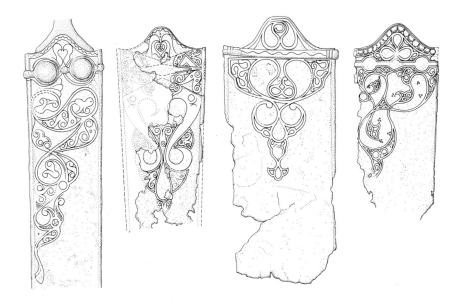

190 *Eastern Sword Style, decoration on iron scabbards, LT B to C, 3rd c. BC.* (Near left) *Batina, Croatia, Jugoslavia (formerly Kisköszeg, Baranya, Hungary). Contains vestigial dragon pair. W. 6 cm.* (Centre left) *?Sremska Mitrovica, Serbia, Jugoslavia. W. c. 5.5 cm.* (Centre right and far right) *Bölcske-Madocsahegy, Tolna, Hungary. W. 5.8 cm and 9.1 cm.*

191 *(Below) Iron spear head with incised geometric and vegetal decoration from Joressant, Vully-le-Haut, Ct. Fribourg, Switzerland. L. 51.5 cm. LT B1/B2, later 4th c. BC.*

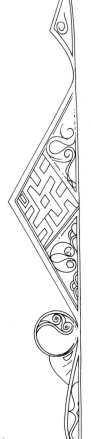

of Greuten – not far from the southwest German findspot of the earlier Holzgerlingen statue discussed in Chapter 2.

The figure-of-eight and triskel fill-ins on two Hungarian scabbards from Bölcske-Madocsahegy continue motifs reflecting the fourth-century beginnings of the Vegetal Style; this time they are used in a delicate design possibly derived from the Hellenistic-inspired acanthus ornament, which was common in Italy in the period of Celtic settlement. Combinations of the older triskel motif with the new 'Free Style' of the latter part of the third century can be seen on scabbards from Szob in Hungary and Formin in Slovenia. The apparent simplicity of the Szob scabbard or of the lyre pattern on that from Mokronog in Slovenia should not be confused with second-rate workmanship; the economy of line and design is a late summation of a long line of experimentations on old themes.

The Free Style decoration on the scabbard of a ritually bent sword from Groitzsch, south of Leipzig, or the asymmetric tendrils on an example from Garlasco, near Pavia in northern Italy, must indicate a trade-network including their Middle Danube place of origin. Poor conservation of iron sword scabbards often means that their decoration is not recognized because of corrosion; only recently has a Hungarian Style scabbard been recognized from a disturbed warrior's grave on the Dürrnberg. Similarly, the earlier Battersea and Hammersmith scabbards, though found a century ago, have only just been recognized as carrying dragon pairs. This, together with the difficulty of ascribing swords to definite stylistic groups, obscures our recognition of the complex system of local workshops and local substyles.

In the eastern Celtic area some late and devolved regional groups can, however, be distinguished. Such are the early second-century variations on

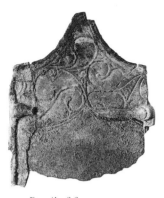

192 *Detail of fragmentary bronze scabbard from Groitzsch, Kr. Borna, Germany. W. 5.3 cm. LT C2, 3rd/2nd c. BC.*

193 *(Right) Stuben sandstone pillar statue from Waldenbuch, Kr. Böblingen, Germany. H. 1.25 m. LT B, 4th–3rd c. BC.*

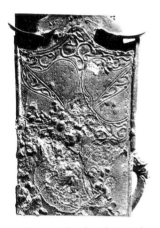

194 *Iron scabbard with incised Vegetal Style decoration from Mokronog, Slovenia, Jugoslavia. W. 5.6 cm. LT B2/C1, 3rd c. BC.*

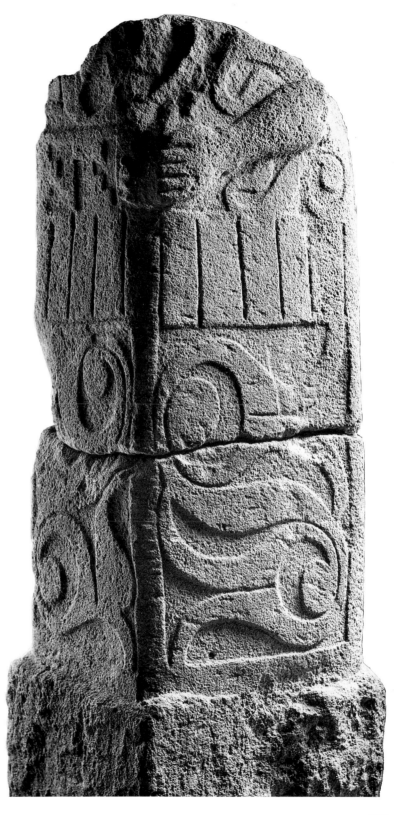

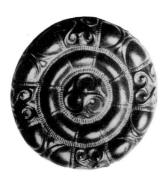

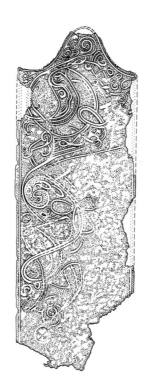

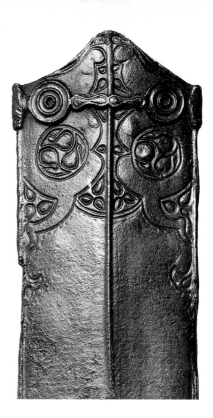

195 (Above) *Bronze rosette on iron chain-mail shirt from Ciumeşti, Maramureş, Romania. D. 6 cm. LT C1, 3rd/2nd c. BC.*

196 (Near right) *Fragmentary iron scabbard with incised diagonal decoration from Šimanovci, Serbia, Jugoslavia. W. 5.6 cm. LT C2, 3rd-2nd c. BC.*

197 (Far right) *Iron scabbard with Type III dragon pair and vegetal designs from Dobova, Slovenia, Jugoslavia, grave 6. W. c. 4.8 cm. LT C2, 2nd c. BC.*

198 (Below) *Iron scabbard from Marin-Epagnier, 'La Tène', Ct, Neuchâtel, Switzerland. W. 5.3 cm. LT C2, 2nd c. BC.*

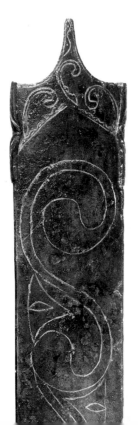

vegetal motifs found on spears and scabbards from Slovene warrior cremations. Long-lived triskels are visible here as on other eastern Celtic metalwork, such as a disc from the chain-mail found in the spectacular warrior grave with eagle-crested helmet at Ciumeşti in northwest Romania. Other Slovene swords, however, look extremely close to products of a much more clearly definable regional school, that of northern Switzerland.

It is clear that in Switzerland, in the Middle La Tène period, yet another distinctive and accomplished group of swordsmiths was at work. By comparison with the Middle Danube workshops, the designs are less elaborate and decoration is usually restricted to the area immediately below the scabbard mouth. The derivation from Hellenistic and Italian floral designs is more explicit than with Hungarian Sword Styles.

Many swords have come from the type-site of La Tène itself and from other sites such as Port on the present Nidau Canal or along the course of the River Broye between Lake Neuchâtel and Lake Murten. The site of La Tène was discovered in November 1857 when Hans Kopp, literally, went fishing for antiquities. Excavations, the most significant of which were carried out by Emil and Paul Vouga, followed the canalization of the Jura waterways in 1874–7. Some three thousand objects were recovered from amongst the remains of buildings, wooden staging and two bridges spanning the old stream bed. Such evidence here and at Port and a number of other locations suggests not so much ritual deposits as local trading posts with attendant armourers and stores, linked perhaps with the local fortified settlement at Mont Vully. Abandonment of the site following flooding, or because of pressure from other Celtic groups, could explain a number of

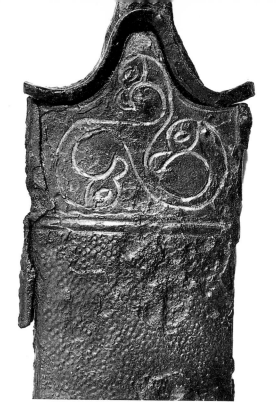

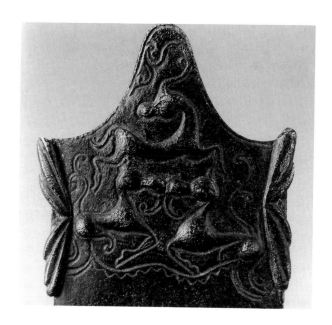

human skeletons found here. Coin evidence indicates that La Tène was forsaken around 60 BC and that the local community were of the Sequani tribe rather than their more powerful neighbours, the Helvetii. Dendrochronological dating of a wooden shield indicates that the site was occupied from early in the third century and dates the major phase of its use to around 200 BC.

More recent discoveries, however, have been used to strengthen the arguments for a religious interpretation for La Tène and similar sites. In 1965 another bridge across the Zihl was discovered at Cornaux, only 3 km from La Tène; beneath the timbers – dated by dendrochronology to between 120 and 116 BC – were found the remains of some eighteen individuals and, once more, a mass of weapons, harness, wagon fittings, pottery, and a single potin coin. Despite the excavator's preference for a catastrophe theory, hydrological research on water levels has largely discounted this in favour of the view that here indeed is evidence of large-scale votive offerings, including human sacrifice as recorded by Caesar.

One is on safer ground with analysis of the art of the Swiss swordsmiths. Motifs on the La Tène sword scabbards are certainly comparable to those found in Hungary and include birds' heads growing out of split palmettes, as on a scabbard from Basadingen, in a fashion similar to the sword sheaths from Drňa and Cernon-sur-Coole. The *chagrinage*, or ring-punched decoration, of the lower part marks the Basadingen scabbard as a Swiss-made piece. Birds' heads sprout from tendrils, or form the ends of whirligig designs, on two scabbards from La Tène itself and on one from grave 7 of a small cemetery at Obermenzing in Bavaria.

199 (Above left) Top of iron scabbard with chagrinage from Obermenzing, Kr. München, Germany, grave 7. W. c. 4.8 cm. LT C1, c. 200 BC.

200 (Above) Iron scabbard from La Tène, Ct. Neuchâtel, Switzerland. W. 4.9 cm. LT C2, 2nd c. BC.

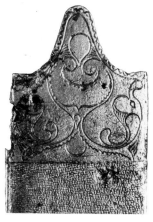

201 Iron scabbard with chagrinage and birds' heads from Basadingen, Kt. Thurgau, Switzerland. W. 5.2 cm. LT C2, 2nd c. BC.

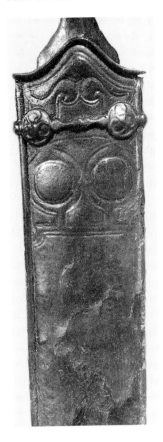

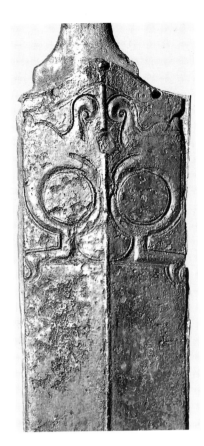

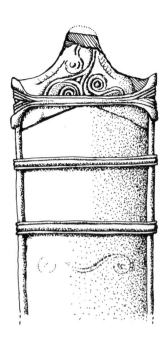

202,203 *Type III dragon pairs on iron scabbards.* (Above left) *Giengen-an-der-Brenz, Kr. Heidenheim, Germany, grave 2. W. 4.4 cm. LT C2, 2nd c. BC.* (Above centre) *La Tène, Kt. Neuchâtel, Switzerland. W. 5.1 cm. LT C1, 2nd c. BC.*

204 (Above right) *Iron scabbard from Gournay-sur-Aronde, Oise, France. W. 5.8 cm. LT C2, 2nd c. BC.*

The ring-punching on this Bavarian piece leaves no doubt that it was a product of the Swiss master-armourers. Its owner was a Celtic surgeon, buried with trephining saw, probe and snare or retractor as well as typical Middle La Tène iron spearhead and shield boss. One may imagine a man whose medical skills were considered as semi-magical powers treating the wounded after battle: the weapons may well have been status symbols rather than evidence of an actual warrior. The Celtic surgical implements are significantly different from those known in the Greek and Roman worlds, though the basic skills are likely once again to have been imported from the Mediterranean.

Another sword from La Tène shows three deer whose bulbous bodies recall much earlier animal figures; the plants hanging from the deer's mouths are descendants of very much earlier elements in the art of the situla.

A third, derivative, and later, version of the dragon pair is known in particular from the site of La Tène. In this Type III the leg and chin join to form a complete circle. This variant is also known far to the east, among the Scordisci, for example, who settled round Belgrade after their return from Delphi, though there they are more likely to be locally produced scabbards than imports. In Slovenia, however, such swords may well be Swiss imports.

Among western groups of Celts with access to the Swiss master-armourers' products were the Middle La Tène warriors buried at Giengen an der Brenz; one of the swords carries the Type III dragon pair.

Yet further to the west, this Type III dragon pair appears on sword scabbards among some two thousand or more metal objects associated with a square sanctuary enclosure adjacent to a fortified settlement or oppidum northeast of Paris, at Gournay-sur-Aronde near Compiègne. Bones of sacrificed cattle, sheep and boar, together with some human bones, were found. The weapons show signs of deliberate destruction, including the ritual 'killing' of swords by bending them double, in contrast to the intact nature of the swords found in the Swiss deposits. The 150 scabbards bridge the Middle and Late La Tène periods. Elements on them can be matched with products of the Swiss school of swordsmiths, but also with more easterly sword decoration.

Yet, despite these similarities, it seems possible that some of the objects may once again represent a regional style of manufacture, rather than the result of complex trading patterns, pilgrims depositing objects from far afield, travelling smiths or locally based craftsmen trained elsewhere, or any combination of these possibilities.

What is certain is that there were several major innovative centres of the ironsmiths' art in eastern Europe, particularly in Hungary. But both to east and west of this region there were other local workshops and artistic variants of the armourers' art, sharing certain motifs such as the dragon pair, the birds' heads and vegetal patterns. These frequently have distributions well beyond their original area of development, though this may be due not so much to trade alone as to the constant journeyings of professional warriors and even craftsmen.

CHESHIRE-CAT TO MICKEY MOUSE

Another distinctive group of material even more widely dispersed than the regional sword scabbards derives from a different element in the preceding Waldalgesheim or Vegetal Style. This is the Cheshire-cat element, where faces peer from the foliage; combined with an increasing tendency to high relief or, in the sculptural sense of the word, 'Plastic' decoration, this produced yet another development in Celtic art. Unlike the sword styles, the designs are sometimes abstract or plant-derived, but some are still based on animal or human representations. Again, this art begins in the first half of the third century BC, or, in typological terms, the end of Early La Tène and the start of Middle La Tène.

Although ostentatious display played a smaller part in the decorative arts of the third and second centuries BC as the social structure altered, the almost standard sets of ring ornaments do exhibit these new developments.

Some pieces still hark back to earlier formulae though in more massive form: a heavy cast bronze bracelet from La Charme has back-to-back human heads.

Typical of this new stage is the neckring – destroyed in World War II – from a cremation grave at Dammelberg, not far from Darmstadt. This is a hybrid of the earlier inlaid disc torcs with torcs ending in buffer-terminals, on which the pop-eyed, bulbous-nosed face on the back of the ring turns the plant-based patterns of the rest of the ring into human form. Such plant-based spirals can also be seen on the gold torc of Middle Rhine type found in a bog at Clonmacnois, Co. Offaly. Low relief spiral ornament appears too on eastern sword scabbards and ornaments.

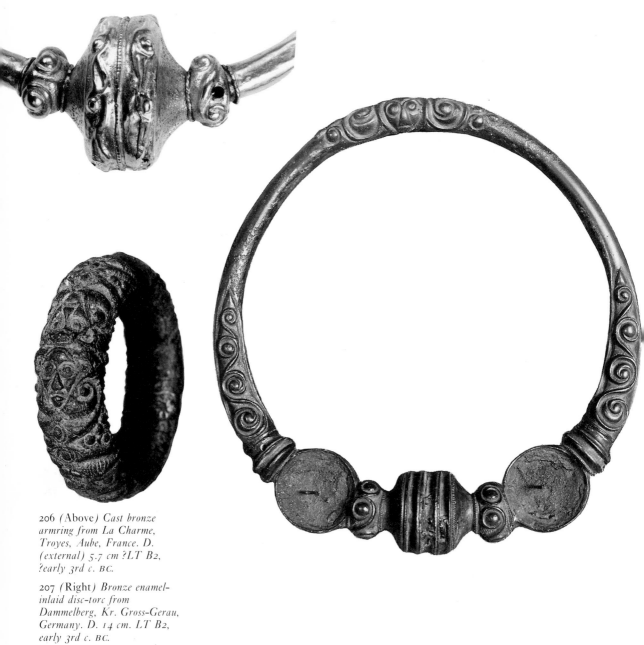

205 (Below) Terminals of a gold neckring from Clonmacnois, Co. Offaly, Ireland. D. (of terminals) 3.8 cm. LT B2, 3rd c. BC.

206 (Above) Cast bronze armring from La Charme, Troyes, Aube, France. D. (external) 5.7 cm ?LT B2, ?early 3rd c. BC.

207 (Right) Bronze enamel-inlaid disc-torc from Dammelberg, Kr. Gross-Gerau, Germany. D. 14 cm. LT B2, early 3rd c. BC.

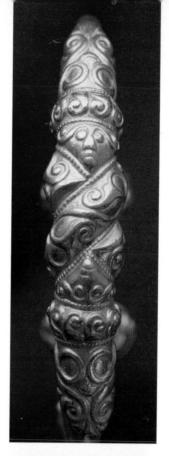

XII–XIV *A gold torc, gold armring and two hollow sheet-gold armrings (*below left*) from Waldalgesheim, Kr. Mainz-Bingen, Germany. The details show decoration on (*below right*) the terminal of the gold torc and (*left*) one of the sheet-gold armrings. D. of torc 18.7 cm. LT B1/B2, later 4th c. BC.*

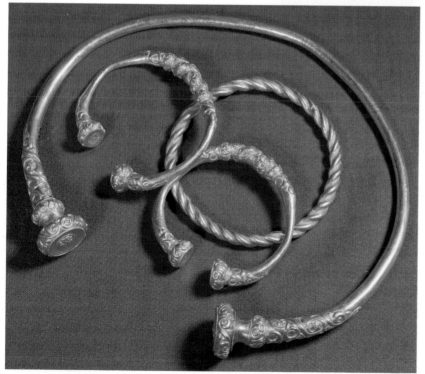

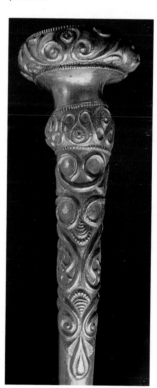

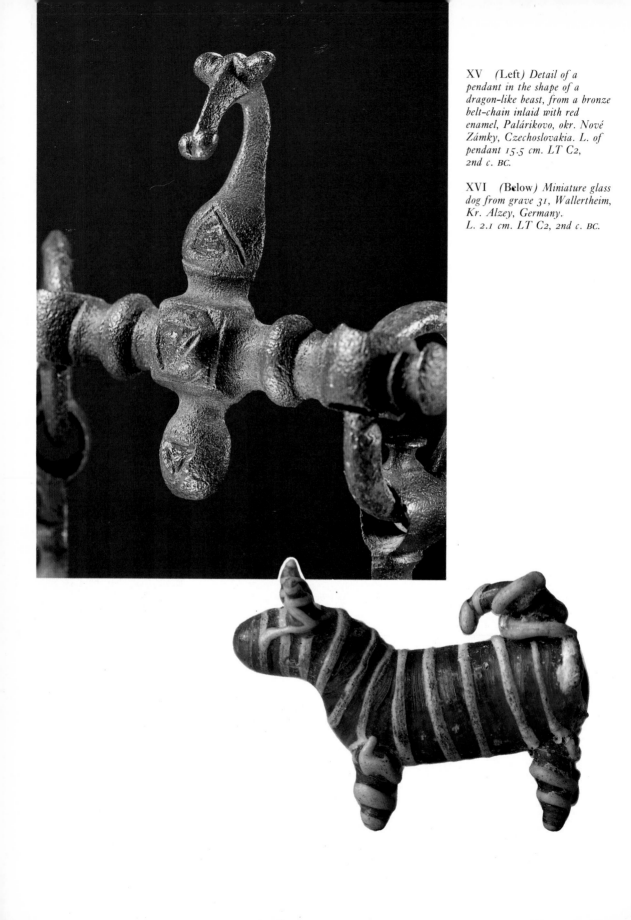

XV (Left) Detail of a pendant in the shape of a dragon-like beast, from a bronze belt-chain inlaid with red enamel, Palárikovo, okr. Nové Zámky, Czechoslovakia. L. of pendant 15.5 cm. LT C2, 2nd c. BC.

XVI (Below) Miniature glass dog from grave 31, Wallertheim, Kr. Alzey, Germany. L. 2.1 cm. LT C2, 2nd c. BC.

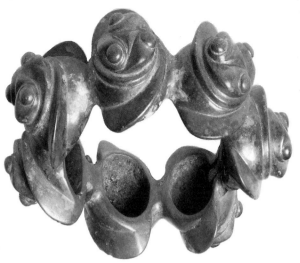

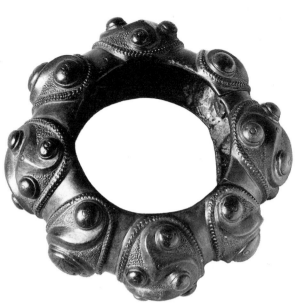

208 (Above) *Bronze hinged anklet from Straubing-Alburg, Stadtkr. Straubing, Germany, grave IV. D. 12 cm. Late LT B2, later 3rd c. BC.*

209 (Right) *Bronze armring from the River Tarn, Tarn, France. D. (internal) 5 cm ?LT B2/C1, late 3rd c. BC.*

Of similar third-century date are knobbed hinged anklets, typical of women's dress. A plain pair – of clearly South German type – from a well near Corinth and a single decorated example from Finike on the southwest coast of Turkey bear witness to the eastern wanderings of Celts from central Europe. In the later third century, these rings show increasingly florid, non-figural, variations in their major region of distribution – western Czechoslovakia, southern Germany and western Hungary. One found in the River Tarn in France shows considerable affinities with those from further east and may well be a third-century import from the eastern Celtic zone.

Another example of markedly protruding, non-representational, relief ornament is a pottery bowl from Bouqueval, Val-d'Oise, in the Paris basin. The region is associated with the Parisii tribe and seems to have been 'Celticized' from east of the Rhine during the third century. Bouqueval itself is a rare example of an excavated Middle La Tène settlement with its associated cemetery. Graves so far discovered contain chariot remains; one warrior burial has a Type II dragon pair sword scabbard. The bowl, handmade of local clay and highly burnished, is a translation into pottery of metal forms; it was, in fact, probably made using a mould. Four fat comma-spirals make up the design, which has some affinities with decorated Breton pots but also looks forward to sheet bronzework from a region of Britain long thought to have been settled by Parisii from the Paris basin.

The most spectacular examples of this style come from very disparate locations. All demonstrate a particular type of abstraction of human and animal heads which, since it shares with modern cartoonists the ability to produce immediately recognizable forms by the economical use of pattern, may be dubbed the 'Walt Disney' style.

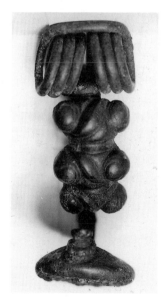

210 *Bronze brooch from Dipşa, Cluj, Romania. L. 9.9 cm. LT C1, c. 200 BC.*

The first example is the glum, chubby-cheeked, mask constructed out of a lyre scroll on a second gold finger-ring, supposedly from Sardinia, from the Waterton collection in the Victoria and Albert Museum. In general form this is close to other, more plant-derived, designs on gold finger-rings from Etoy in Switzerland and from the Dürrnberg.

The second site is the Malkata Mogila near Mezek, close to the present Bulgarian border with Turkey. Chariot fittings found in one of the stone-built tombs here may either be booty seized from Celts by the local Thracian population, or represent a secondary burial, perhaps of some Celtic survivor of the push southwards into Greece in 279–278 BC.

Another group of chariot fittings is supposed to have been discovered in a burial near Paris which included a spear, an iron sword and scabbard but it may well have an east Celtic origin. The Mezek and 'Paris' mounts both display clean-shaven faces with bulbous noses and tiny chins, recalling earlier images based on lyres and spirals. Non-representational protuberances are similar to those on central European sword scabbards and knobbed anklets, also of third-century date, and indicate the artistic origins of the craftsmen who made them. One of the 'Paris' pieces has three identical faces which hold a distorting mirror to more conventional representations. These grotesques, with tiny mouths, one eye half-closed and a prominent wart, may well be intended as a talisman rather than mere satirical whimsy.

The fourth location is at Maloměřice, just outside the present-day Moravian capital of Brno. A number of bronze mounts, perhaps for a wooden flagon, were found in a disturbed grave in a cemetery which spans Early and Middle La Tène periods, and which produced several knobbed anklets. One mount shows a human mask with wing-like lobes which recall earlier leaf crowns; it is impossible, however, to discern whether gripping limbs and body are also intentionally represented.

211 (Below right) *Pottery bowl from Bouqueval, Villiers-le-Bel, Ile-de-France, France, Max.D. 26.8 cm. Late LT C2, early 2nd c. BC.*

OPPOSITE

212 (Above left) *Front view of bronze-covered iron terret (or rein-ring) from Mezek, Bulgaria. W. 7.5 cm. ?LT B2, earlier 3rd c. BC.*

213 (Top right) *Bronze ?flagon-mount from Maloměřice, Brno, Czechoslovakia. 10.5 × 4.6 cm. ?LT B2, earlier 3rd c. BC.*

214 (Above right) *Bronze-covered iron linch-pin from ?Paris, France, W. 8.5 cm. LT B2, earlier 3rd c. BC.*

215 (Below left) *Ring of bronze sheet covering an iron core from ?Paris, France. D. c. 7 cm. LT B2, earlier 3rd c. BC.*

216,217 *Gold finger-rings from: (Centre right) ?Sardinia. D. 2.5 cm. (Below right) Etoy, Kt. Vaud, Switzerland. H. 2 cm. LT B2, first half 3rd c. BC.*

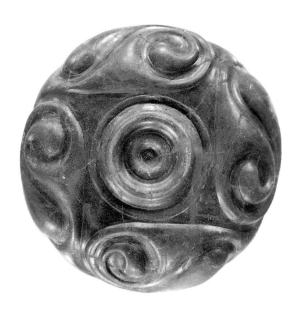

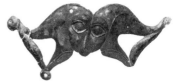

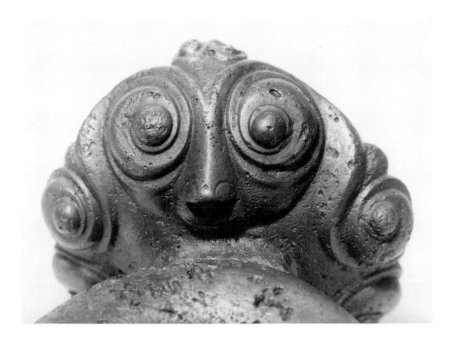

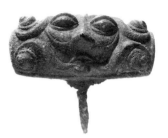

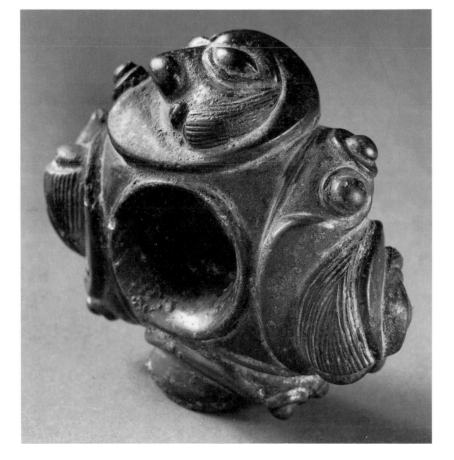

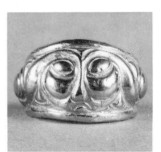

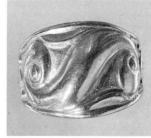

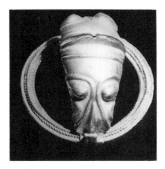

218 *Gold ring fibula from the treasure of Cheste, Valencia, Spain. ?Latter half 3rd c. BC.*

219 *(Right) Bronze openwork ?flagon-mount from Maloměřice, Brno, Czechoslovakia. H. 18 cm. LT B2, early 3rd c. BC.*

The largest of the Maloměřice mounts may have been for a spout. Great upswept horns spring from a clearly bovine head; looked at from above, a second, reversed, horned head is apparent, for which the curved horns serve as open jaws.

Bulls are common in Iron Age iconography, and are often quite naturalistically portrayed. One forms a bronze handle, supposedly from Mâcon in France. Similarly placid beasts appear as cast handle mounts on a dismantled bronze cauldron found in 1952 by a peat bog at Brå in Jutland. Eagle-owls, more precise renditions of those on the Reinheim rings, decorate the three massive suspension rings, each weighing 1 kg. The enormous cauldron was originally 2 m in diameter with a capacity of some 600 litres. Though it comes from the territory of the Germanic Cimbri, and ritual burial of cauldrons is a northern trait, the vessel must have been brought north from Celtic central Europe.

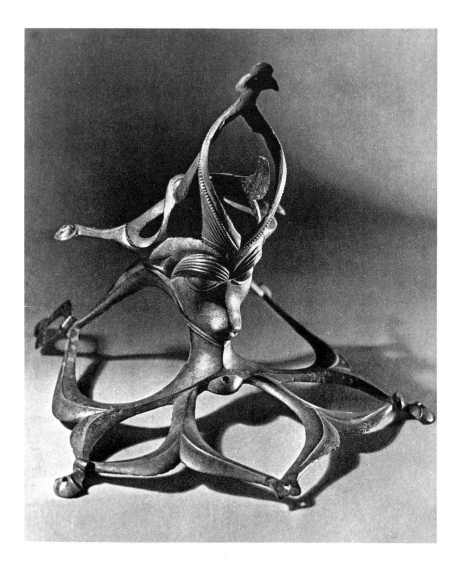

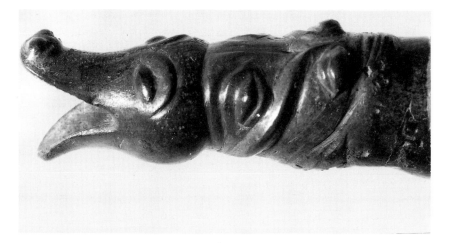

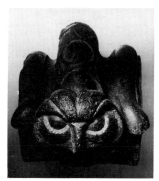

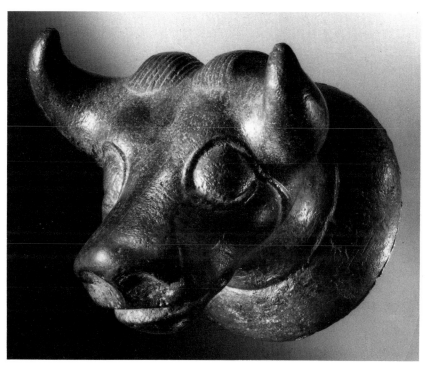

220 (Above left) Bronze
'crocodile' spout of wooden
flagon from the Dürrnberg bei
Hallein, Austria, grave 46/2.
L. (of head) c. 4 cm. LT A/
B1, 4th c. BC.

221,222 Bronze mounts on a
cauldron from Brå, Horsens,
Jutland, Denmark. (Above) W.
of owl 4.2 cm. (Left) W. of
bull's head (between horns)
c. 5.2 cm. ?LT B2, early 3rd c.
BC.

    The Disney Style of central Europe is also represented at the Dürrnberg,
for example in the bronze mounts for a wooden flagon from a warrior's
grave. The spout offers an extraordinary example of shape-changing. It
may represent a crocodile – one must remember that Celts served as
mercenaries in Egypt – or possibly a boar. Behind this open-jawed beast is a
bull with flaring nostrils which, when looked at from the spout end, can be
read as a grotesque, almond-eyed, human face. Possible human faces also
appear, with similar almond eyes, on a gold ring fibula from Cheste, near
Valencia.

Birds too are represented in this style, as in the beaked head, perhaps a flamingo, on the Maloměřice terminal ring. The tail, when reversed, becomes another bird's head with long, upward-curving, knobbed beak. Fearsomely malevolent birds of prey adorn chariot linch-pins from the great defended Celtic centre at Manching, claimed as the tribal centre of the Vindelici, who controlled the region of southern Germany between the Danube and the Alps till they were defeated by the Romans in 15 BC. Despite extensive excavations, objects from Manching have proved difficult to date; these heads, with their traces of red enamel, though without stratigraphic context, probably date from Middle La Tène. Another chariot fitting, perhaps a guide for the reins, was also found without context at Manching, in 1959. It shows two birds' heads supporting a pair of bulls with knobbed horns.

The decorating of animals' horns with knobs is a feature of a range of pendants and other objects extending into the Roman period. Other miniature figures, particularly of deer, come from areas further east where, in the third century, the Celts were an intrusive element. They may reflect in part the iconography of the Scythians, as, for example, the delightful little backward-looking head from Rákos, Kom. Csongrád.

A final point should be made in discussing this Disney Style, or high relief art. Nearly all of it is executed in bronze or gold, and not in the iron which characterizes the sword scabbards. It is cast, rather than using the incised decoration typical of most of the Sword Style art. It also shows a harking back to artistic motifs characteristic not merely of the preceding Vegetal Style, but also of elements found in Early La Tène art, especially in human and animal representations which recall the Erstfeld rings or the human and animal brooches.

There are few occasions where Sword Style and Disney Style art are found together. It seems possible that the Disney Style was produced by bronze- and goldsmiths whose artistic traditions reach back to the earliest Celtic art. Swords however, were primarily the product of a new, widespread, almost professional, class of armourers working in iron, a metal apparently little used for art, as opposed to utility, in the earlier periods of the Celtic Iron Age.

EAST MEETS WEST IN LATER CELTIC ART

More east-west links can be seen in a remarkable collection of six gold neckrings, found during canal construction in 1841 at Fenouillet in the Haute-Garonne. They share decorative features, metallic analysis and fastening mechanism with other French pieces, with an ornate version of a buffer-terminalled torc from Gajić in the Vojvodina (formerly Hercegmárok, Kom. Baranya) and with a set of beads from the Mezek chariot burial. Opinion is divided as to where this goldwork developed; a local origin in the south of France could be linked with the historic eastern movements of the Volcae Tectosages.

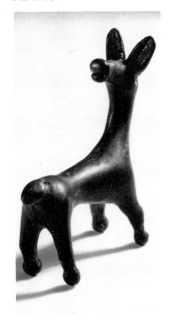

223 Bronze deer figurine from Rákos, Csongrád, Hungary. H. 3.7 cm. ?Celto-Scythian. ?3rd/2nd c. BC.

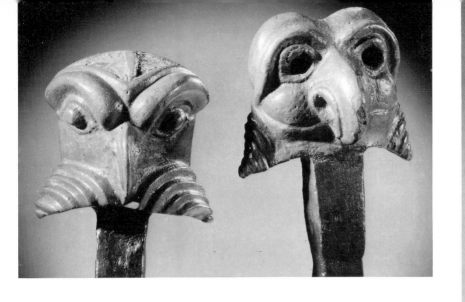

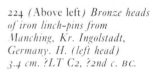

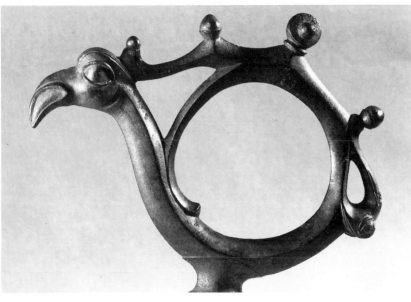

224 (Above left) Bronze heads of iron linch-pins from Manching, Kr. Ingolstadt, Germany. H. (left head) 3.4 cm. ?LT C2, ?2nd c. BC.

225 (Above) Bronze rein-ring or yoke-mount from Manching, Kr. Ingolstadt, Germany. H. 9 cm. LT D, 2nd/1st c. BC.

226 (Left) Bronze ?flagon-mount from Maloměřice, Brno, Czechoslovakia. Max. D. (of ring) 11.8 cm. ?LT B2, early 3rd c. BC.

227 (Below) Cast bronze 'dragon' head from drinking-horn from Jászberény-Cseröhalom, Szolnok, Hungary, grave 17. L. 20.3 cm. LT C2, 2nd c. BC.

Again the result of Celtic contact with the different technology and stylistic fashions of the Balkans is a slightly later group of cast bronze rings and brooches ornamented in 'pseudo-filigree' manner – that is, in imitation of the use of droplets of gold and gold wire in the production of jewellery perfected by the Etruscans, but also used by the Greeks. From southern Moravia through Slovakia, Hungary and Jugoslavia to Romania the Celtic flat grave cemeteries contain examples of this imitation filigree work; such pieces as the hinged armring from grave 15 at Palárikovo, okr. Nové Zámky, are local variants of the central European knobbed arm- and foot-rings previously described, but their decoration is in a definitely eastern manner.

One of the most obvious examples of the stylistic meeting of east and west is the incised and stamped decoration of a biconical urn from grave 1 of a flat grave cemetery at Lábatlan, Kom. Komáron, Hungary. The profile is typical of east Celtic pottery, but the scene of fighting animals, including a pair of (probable) wolves attacking with open jaws a backward-looking deer, seems an echo of the art of the Caucasus region whence originally came the Sigynnae, one of the non-Celtic components of the Hungarian population of the third century.

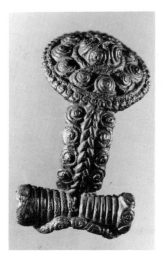

228 (Above) Cast bronze brooch from Bölcske, Tolna, Hungary. L. 6 cm. LT C1, 2nd c. BC.

229 (Right) Cast bronze armring from Palárikovo, okr. Nové Zámky, Czechoslovakia, grave 15. D. 8 cm. LT C1, 3rd/2nd c. BC.

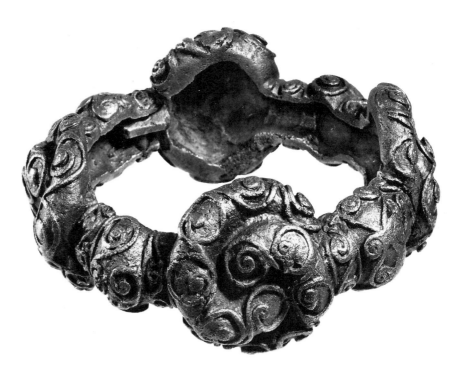

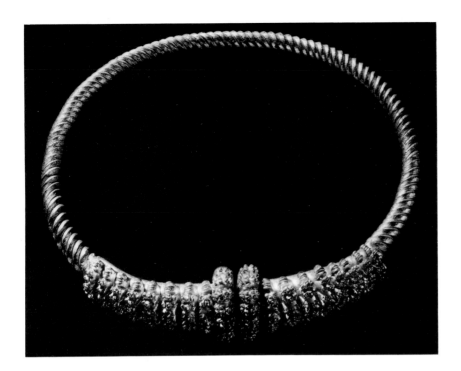

230 *Gold neckring from Fenouillet, Haute-Garonne, France. D. 13.5 cm. LT B2, 3rd c. BC.*

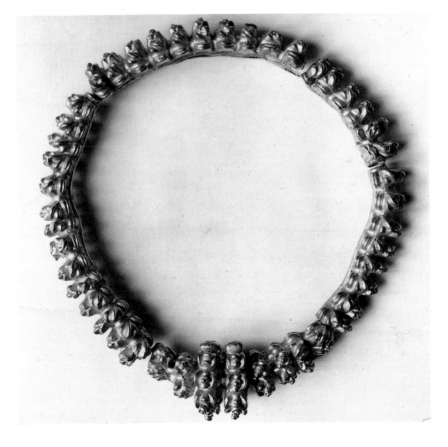

231 *Gold neckring from Gajič, Vojvodina, Jugoslavia (formerly Hercegmárok, Baranya, Hungary). D.(surviving) 10 cm. ?LT B2/C1, later 3rd/2nd c. BC.*

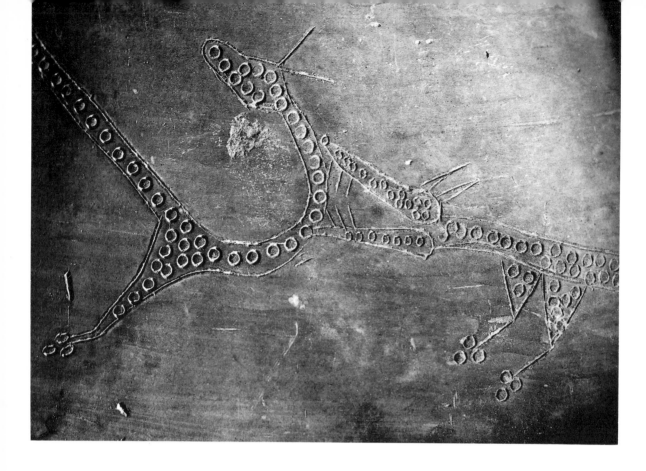

232 *Detail of stamped and incised pot from Lábatlan, Komáron, Hungary, grave 1. H. (of pot) 40.2 cm. LT C1, 3rd/ 2nd c. BC.*

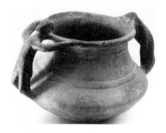

233 *Pottery vessel with one handle in human form and one plaited, from Kakasd, Tolna, Hungary. H. 14.3 cm. LT C2, 2nd c. BC.*

Celtic and non-Celtic can be observed in material from another Hungarian cemetery, grave 17 at Jászberény-Cserőhalom, Kom. Szolnok. A single-edged knife decorated in developed Hungarian Sword Style suggests a second-century date for the cremation burial, which was accompanied also by the remains of a drinking-horn with bronze fittings. The form of such horns, as noted in earlier contexts, has been claimed as an eastern introduction; certainly the open-mouthed 'sea horse' dragon, or perhaps griffon, despite its wearing of a Celtic torc, is suggestive not so much of nomadic as of Hellenistic Greek influence. Strange animal heads – in the company of the familiar stylized waterbirds – form the clasp on another later La Tène form to be found particularly in the Carpathian area. From Slovakia through Hungary to Romania one finds in women's graves complex girdle-chains made of cast bronze links and often embellished with enamel or other inlay; typical of these is the chain illustrated here from the Palárikovo cemetery (colour plate XV), whose infill patterns reflect contemporary Celtic curvilinear motifs. Such girdle-chains continue into the second century.

A final group of east Celtic material suggests the influence of the Mediterranean at the time when the first local coinage was being adapted from that same region. This is handled pottery from Middle La Tène third-century contexts, mainly in northwestern Jugoslavia and western Hungary.

There are some forms of two-handled vessels from what has been termed the 'Illyrian-Pannonian' region which strongly suggest local copying of contemporary Hellenistic kantharoi; the wheel-made vessels illustrated here, however, while all from Celtic contexts, relate in their general forms to the indigenous, non-Celtic, pottery tradition. In contrast to this, though, their decoration is quite different. The use of human heads in relief, or occasionally of a complete human body as a handle, suggests classical influence; an example is a pot from Kakasd, Kom. Tolna, in Hungary. More individual is the moustached head forming the handle terminal on a vessel from Balatonederics, Kom. Veszprém. Other pots, though, with their use of stamped decoration and such standard animal supporters as the ram, must reflect the effect of intrusive Celtic traditions as represented in several vessels from the Kosd, Kom. Nógrád, cemetery.

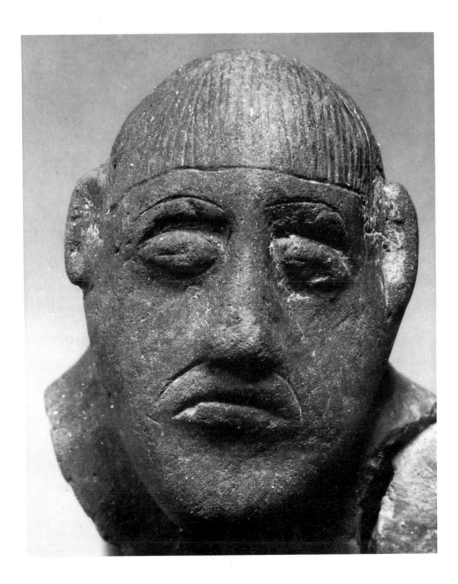

234 *Upper end of handle on a pot from Balatonederics, Veszprém, Hungary. H. (of head) c. 4.2 cm. LT C1, 3rd c. BC.*

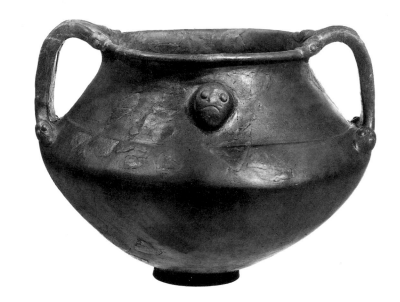

235–237 *Pot with animal-terminal handles and human faces from Novo mesto-Kandija, Slovenia, Jugoslavia, grave 40. H. 27.7 cm. H. (of faces) 4.9 cm. H. (of animal heads) 4.5 cm. LT C1, 3rd/2nd c. BC.*

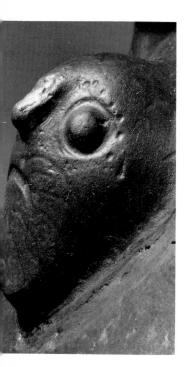

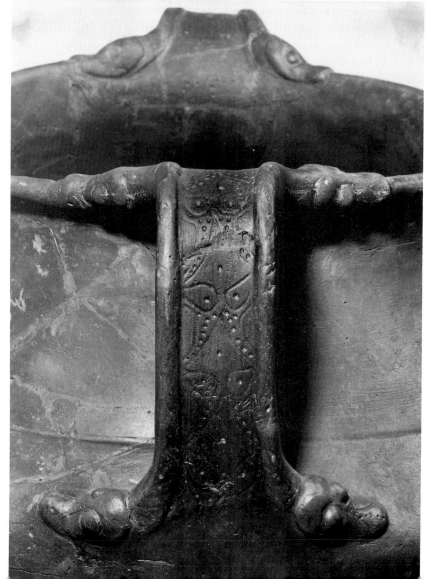

It is, however, a two-handled pot from one of the later Celtic graves of the Novo mesto settlement which most clearly demonstrates this admixture of traditions. Grave 40, in the Kandija complex of more than sixty cremation burials, produced a vessel decorated in a combination of low relief and incised ornament. The latter, though crudely executed, is really nothing more or less than a version of classical vine scrolls. The human heads one may consider as apotropaic emblems suitable to a funerary offering, while the handles are embellished with what have been taken to be ram-headed serpents, creatures of the Celtic underworld, to judge from later contexts. One literal footnote may be added to these notes on later eastern Celtic pottery. In central Europe in the pre-Celtic later Bronze Age, or late second millennium, there was a tradition of making pots in the form of shoes, particularly in the Carpathian basin, Poland and Romania. In the later La Tène phase one finds a number of vessels in Celtic contexts which continue this tradition, with the upper part of the vessel often in the form of a miniature bowl and decorated with stamped designs. Examples can be cited from the Dürrnberg in the west to such Hungarian examples as that from Gáva, Kom. Szabolce in the east. Although there is no firm evidence, some have claimed that such novel forms as the shoe-vessels indicate the new impact on central Europe brought about at the end of the second century by the migration of certain, non-Celtic, Germanic groups from northern Europe. Notable among these were the Cimbri, whose southern and eastern movement into the client kingdom of Noricum (ancient Austria) was to threaten not only the Celts, but also the growing power of Rome.

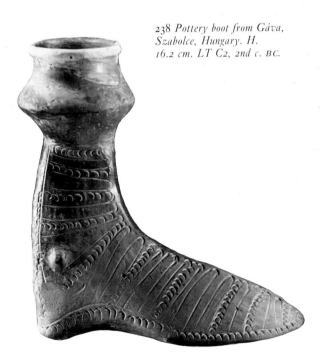

238 Pottery boot from Gáva, Szabolce, Hungary. H. 16.2 cm. LT C2, 2nd c. BC.

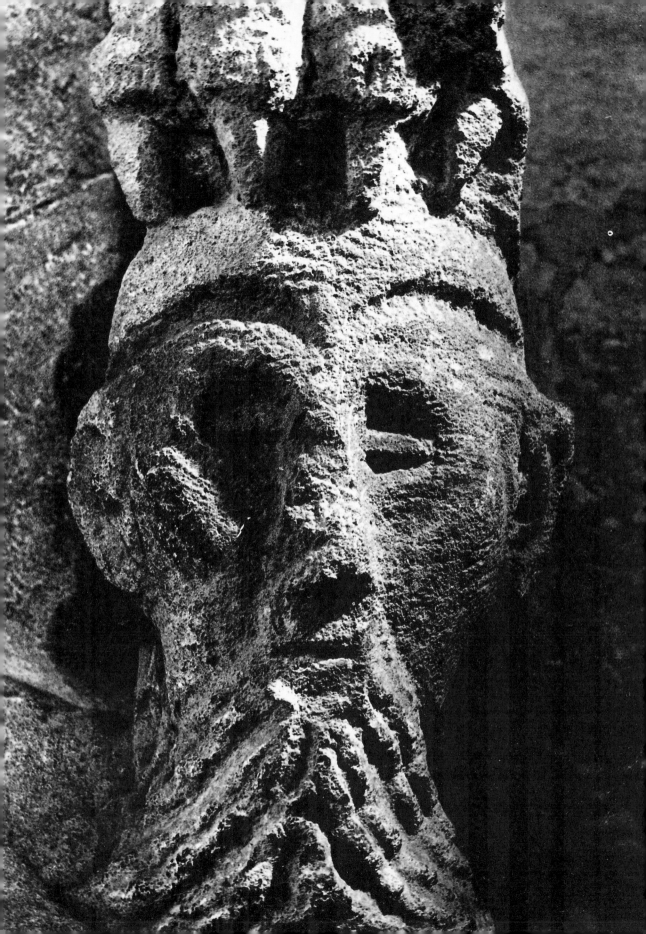

5
Cities, Centralization and Coinage

IN THE SECOND AND first centuries BC, there were further major changes in Celtic society. One was a reversal of Celtic expansion, the other the emergence of large settlements, mostly enclosed and defended, containing up to two thousand inhabitants. Julius Caesar called them *oppida*, or towns; some are certainly close in size to 2,500 inhabitants, which was the figure used to distinguish urban from rural settlement in nineteenth-century America. These oppida are in marked contrast to the small-scale scattered settlements of the Celtic age of expansion. Though a few were expanded from earlier hillforts, many are apparently new creations, suggesting the economic, political and social amalgamation of smaller groups.

Oppida appear first in the east of the Celtic zone in the second century BC, and by a generation or two later are to be found throughout the Celtic world. In the east, as at Zemplín, in eastern Slovakia, a small defended hilltop area was surrounded by areas of settlement, and the area enclosed was smaller than further west – about 80 ha at Stradonice in Bohemia, for example. To the west, residential quarters and barns or even farms were included within fortifications and the enclosed area ranges up to the 1000 ha of Camulodunum (modern Colchester).

Two major causes appear to be intertwined in these developments. One of these is pressure from outside, which checked and even reversed Celtic expansion. In eastern Hungary, Jugoslavia, Romania and Slovakia, this threat was from the revival of the Dacians under Burebista, who in the first half of the first century BC first attacked and defeated the Scordisci around modern Belgrade and in southern Hungary, then turned northwards against the Boii and Taurisci, so that many Boii were forced to flee into Switzerland. In central and western Europe, Germanic tribes from the northern European plain pressed southwards. Cimbri leaving Jutland because of land hunger, caused by loss of land to sea encroachment, were joined by Celtic groups; Teutones may well have been northerly Celts. From about 120 to 113 BC the Cimbri swept through areas of modern Czechoslovakia and Austria, before moving through Switzerland to France, where Cimbri and Teutones defeated Roman armies in 109, 107 and, most humiliatingly, at Orange in 105 BC. The Teutones were defeated in 102 BC at Aix-en-Provence by the Romans, but the Cimbri remained unconquered until they had crossed the Alps into the Po Valley. Many Celtic tribes were forced to move – the Helvetii southwards into Switzerland, for example – and in Gaul only the Belgae of the northeast were strong enough to hold off the invaders.

239 (Opposite) 'Severed' head under the paw of the limestone 'Tarasque de Noves', ill. 274, Bouches-du-Rhône, France. Celto-Ligurian. ?3rd c. BC.

153

Above all, the expansion of Rome pressed on and absorbed areas of Celtic Europe; southern France, later *Gallia Narbonensis*, was annexed in 125–124 BC. In the following century the attempted migration in 58 BC of over 300,000 Helvetii and other groups westwards from Switzerland through Roman territory gave Julius Caesar a reason to invade Gaul. His conquest of it was completed in 51 BC. Caesar records a number of tribal centres, oligarchic, increasingly centralized, but frequently at war with each other; the centralization of political and military power can perhaps be seen in the fact that the taking of a tribe's oppidum usually resulted in the surrender of the whole tribe.

Rome moved on to establish a major frontier on the Rhine; the passes from Italy into Switzerland were secured, and in 16–15 BC the Celtic kingdom of Noricum, in southern Austria – already, for a century or more, under Roman influence – was formally annexed. In central Europe it was not just the Romans who presented a threat; around 10 BC a Germanic tribe, the Marcomanni from the region of the Elbe, invaded central and northern Bohemia under their leader Maroboduus.

One major scholarly explanation for the emergence of the oppida thus stresses the need for defence. Another explains their creation – though not the need to defend them – as the result of the re-emergence of Mediterranean trade with Celtic Europe. From the second century onwards, wine, oil and luxury metalwork make their appearance in Celtic areas, evidenced most commonly by pottery fragments. At the Magdalensberg in Noricum (Austria), Roman written records show the presence of Roman traders and the control of trade by the Italians; southern merchants were also present throughout Gaul. The last desperate Gaulish revolt under Vercingetorix, a chief of the Arverni, was signalled by the massacre of Roman traders, at Cenabum, centre of the Carnutes at present-day Orléans.

Romans imported iron in finished and unfinished forms from the Magdalensberg. Leather and slaves were also important trade commodities; Strabo records the importing from Gaul of salt pork and woollen textiles shortly after the Roman conquest. The need to increase and concentrate surplus production for trade has been seen as the major cause for the creation of the craft centres which can be recognized at oppida such as Manching, and for an increase in the volume and specialization of production. Noricum was a major centre for the production of iron and even steel. The Dürrnberg, Bad Nauheim and Schwäbisch Hall produced salt, while concentrations of glass were found at Manching, Staré Hradisko, the Dürrnberg and Breisach-Hochstetten. Special graphitic clays for fine pottery production were imported to sites such as Manching from at least 200 km away. Wood, leather, bone and metals other than iron were also worked in the oppida. The need for external trade may have led to increasing social stratification and greater exactions on the agricultural production which still provided the basis of Celtic society. There is certainly evidence of production for trade, and many oppida are well situated for raw materials or trade routes. Trade in slaves could well have

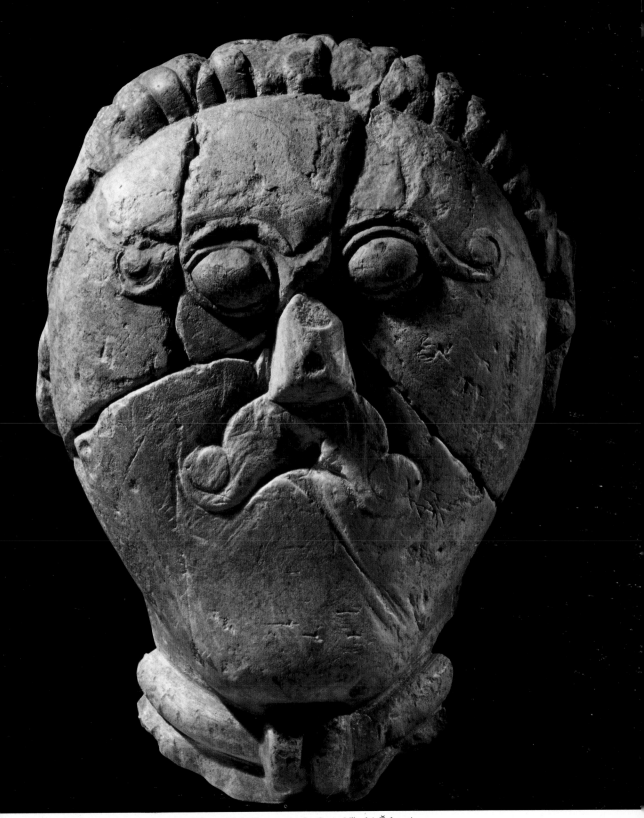

XVII   *Ragstone head wearing a neckring with buffer terminals, from Mšecké Žehrovice,
okr. Rakounik, Czechoslovakia. H. 23.5 cm. LT C, 3rd or 2nd c. BC.*

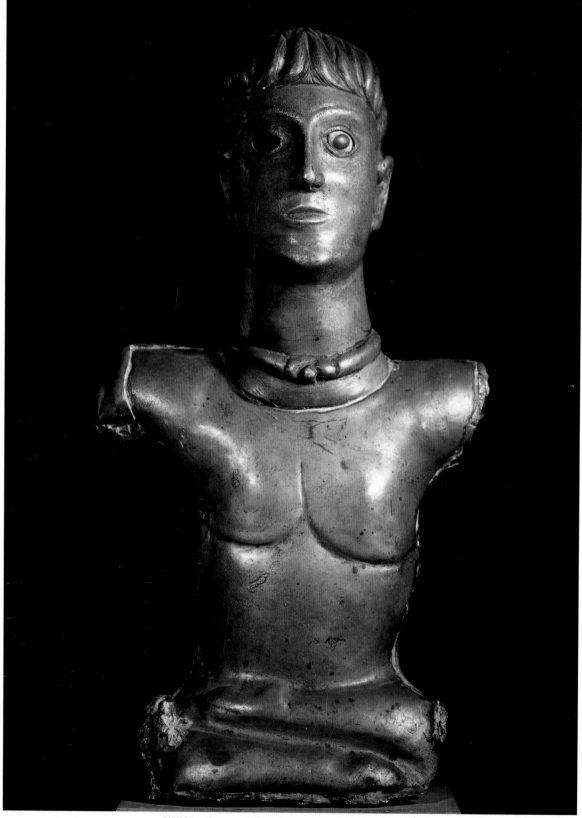

XVIII Cast- and sheet-bronze cross-legged, animal-hoofed figure with one remaining
blue-and-white glass eye, from Bouray, Essonne, France. H. 42 cm. 1st c BC or 1st c. AD.

led to aggression to seize slaves; in general, however, though trade may have encouraged the growth of oppida, it does not alone provide a reason for their defence.

Population increase, in lands recorded as rich in plant and animal resources by classical writers, may have contributed to the capacity to support concentrated settlements; improvement in tools probably increased the efficiency of agriculture at this time. Oppida also acted as focuses for political authority; in Gaul, Caesar records forms of elected government, as well as the emergence of tyrants from time to time. Evidence for the production of weights and minting of coinage at several oppida implies not only standardized values but the existence of some centralized authority to determine and validate them.

From Caesar's first-hand observations in Gaul we also have some of the best evidence of Celtic religion, though it must be emphasized that this applies only to France and Britain and cannot safely be generalized to all Celts. Caesar was also attempting in *De Bello Gallico* to justify his risky and nearly disastrous conquest to his own people, hence his emphasis on human sacrifice, which was indubitably practised by Celts, usually on criminals, and banned in Roman domains by a Senatorial decree not so very many years earlier, in 97 BC. Druids, according to Caesar, were clearly lawyers, judges, educators, healers, philosophers and astronomers as well as priests; they were the oral repository of historical and legal knowledge as well as of myth and religion. Celts apparently believed in personal immortality, in an afterworld like the world they lived in already, not, as Caesar incorrectly recorded, in transmigration of souls. No names of Celtic deities were recorded in *De Bello Gallico*; Celtic gods and goddesses were simply and simplistically equated with Roman ones. Most known names of Celtic deities come from later Gallo-Roman inscriptions, written in what was a foreign language for Celts; of around four hundred, three-quarters are only mentioned once, including the stag-antlered god Cernunnos, which suggests that attempts to generalize these names are not soundly based; sixty-nine separate Celtic god-names have been associated with Mars, the Roman god of war. Of detailed Celtic beliefs and practices, we still know very little indeed.

Most of the archaeological evidence in this period comes from settlement sites, and shows considerable similarity in form and decoration throughout the Celtic world. Very few burials, with or without grave goods, are known from the late second or the first century BC, indicating not only the increasing use of cremation but a different attitude to the afterworld and to death. Only in northeastern France and the Middle Rhine did vehicle burials continue into Roman times. Grave goods tend to be carefully chosen and even especially made; finds from settlements are rubbish, or the result of chance loss. This contrast in part explains why, though there is a marked increase in the quantity of finds, there is an apparent decrease in the quality of artistic skill and innovation. Other important finds of this period are probably the result of ritual deposition; carefully selected though these objects were, they are often very hard to date accurately.

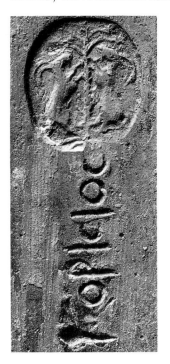

Another factor at work was also the renewed trade in classical goods which led to increased copying of classical models. Unlike Early La Tène art, the art of the oppida period seems to have been less selective, less able to transform imported ideas and imagery. Continuity of Celtic animal and human iconography is clear, but the presentation is increasingly naturalistic, less elusive, while plant-based decoration becomes increasingly rare.

Much of the characteristic pottery of the oppida, for example, was either plain, or painted in simple bands of colour often applied in slapdash fashion. On one pot from the oppidum at Basel, unearthed during the construction of gas works, a plant tendril is still apparent: it has been split down the middle, and the two halves of the pattern reversed. More geometric painted patterns survived into the Roman period on pots from cemeteries in the Loire valley, and from other sites in Switzerland, Hungary and Germany.

Sword stamps, which had made their appearance in the Sword Style of the Celtic age of expansion, continue into this Late La Tène period. Most remarkable is that found on a ritually 'killed' sword from Port in Switzerland. Greek characters alongside the stamped boar spell the Celtic name KORISIOS. Evidence of writing at Manching, together with classical references – such as Caesar's to the use of Greek by the Helvetii in drawing up the census lists taken on their migration – make it clear that Celts could write; here then may be the only name of a Swiss master swordsmith that we know. That the Celts had standard weights and measures is clearly evidenced by their coinage; an actual lead weight of some 125 g from Manching bears either writing or tally-marks and depicts a torc-wearing god whose attribute, carried in his arms, may be intended as a plough.

240 *Stamp showing name* KORISIOS *on an iron sword from Port, Kt. Bern, Switzerland. L. (of inscription and stamp) 2.7 cm. LT D, 1st c. BC.*

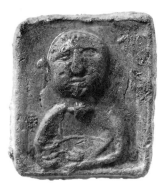

241 *(Above) Lead weight showing figure holding ?plough from Manching, Kr. Ingolstadt, Germany. H. c. 4.6 cm. Wt c. 125g. ?LT D, 1st c. BC.*

242 *(Right) Painted pot from Basel Gasworks site, Kt. Basel, Switzerland. H. c. 37 cm. LT D1, 2nd c. BC.*

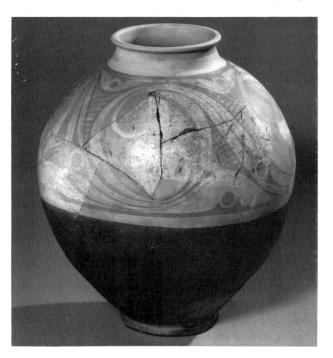

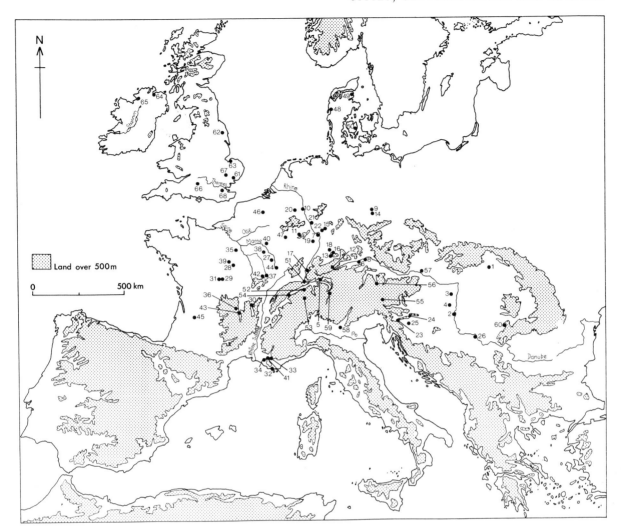

Alesia 42	Châtillon-sur-Indre 31
Altenburg 14	Cologne 10
Altenburg-Rheinau 5	Corent 43
Aylesford 68	Dinnyés 3
Bad Nauheim 15	Dejbjerg 48
Baldock 67	Donnersberg 19
Ballyshannon Bay 65	Dürrnberg bei Hallein 56
Balzers 59	Eggendorf 57
Basel 51	Entremont 33
Báta 2	Euffigneix 27
Bouray 35	Fellbach-Schmiden 13
Breisach-Hochstetten 17	Frasnes-lez-Buissenal 46
Broighter 64	Goeblingen-Nospelt 47
Camulodunum 61	Grabenstetten 18
Cenabum 39	Gundestrup 49
Chamalières 36	Heidetränktal 22
Châtenay-Macheron 44	Leipzig-Connewitz 9

Levroux 29	Roanne 30
Luncani 60	Rynkeby 50
Magdalensburg 55	Roquepertuse 34
Mailly-le-Camp 38	Salon 40
Manching 6	Schwäbisch Hall 16
Manerbio 58	Šmarjeta 24
Marlborough 66	Snettisham 63
Massalia 32	Sources-de-la-Seine 37
Mihovo 23	Surduk 26
Neuvy-en-Sullias 28	Szárazd-Regöly 4
Neuwied 21	Tayac 45
Niederzier 20	Trichtingen 12
North Grimston 62	Trier 11
Noves 41	Wallertheim 7
Novo mesto 25	Weltenburg 8
Oberhofen 53	Yverdon 54
Port 52	Zemplin 1

243 *Map of principal sites referred to in Chapter 5.*

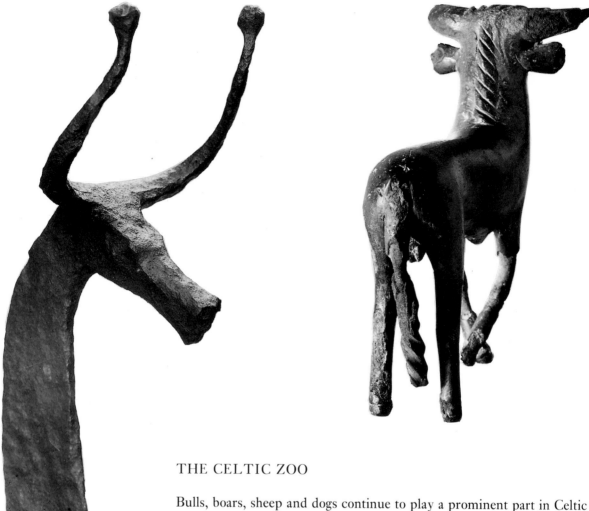

244 (Above left) *Terminal of iron fire-dog from Lord's Bridge, Barton, Cambridgeshire, England. H. 71 cm. LT D, 1st c. BC.*

245 (Above right) *Bronze figurine from Weltenburg, Kr. Kelheim, Germany. H. 9.5 cm. ?LT C/D, 2nd/1st c. BC.*

THE CELTIC ZOO

Bulls, boars, sheep and dogs continue to play a prominent part in Celtic iconography, though the all-important horse was increasingly confined to coins. Bones of these animals are also found in the domestic debris of settlements.

One young bull in cast bronze comes from Weltenburg, near the 650 ha Michelsberg oppidum in Bavaria. Other bull figurines have knobbed horns, as do the bulls' heads on the late iron fire-dogs found from Britain in the west to the Hradiště at Stradonice in Bohemia. The knobs may reflect stock-management practices rather than ritual significance.

Boars still occur everywhere in the Celtic regions, as figurines, as helmet crests, as sword stamps and on coinage, confirming their particular associations with warfare or power. In France the boar-god was sometimes Baco or Moccus; a deity can be seen with a boar on the fragmentary pillar stone from Euffigneix in the Haute-Marne, a region which still has the boar as emblem. The form probably reflects wood-carving techniques: archaic Celtic features such as the stylized boar's crest and shoulder curl contrast with the apotropaic eye on the side of the figure. Among the figures from

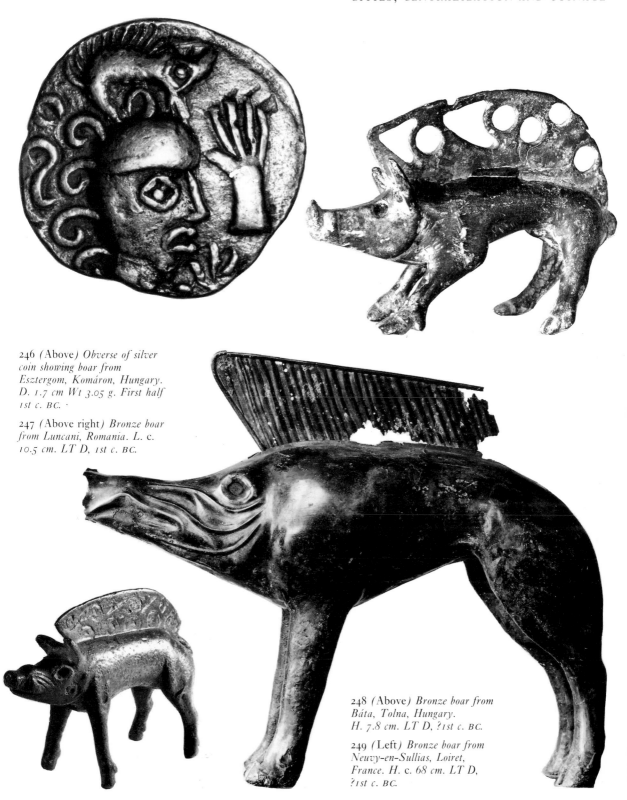

246 (Above) *Obverse of silver coin showing boar from Esztergom, Komáron, Hungary. D. 1.7 cm Wt 3.05 g. First half 1st c. BC.*

247 (Above right) *Bronze boar from Luncani, Romania. L. c. 10.5 cm. LT D, 1st c. BC.*

248 (Above) *Bronze boar from Báta, Tolna, Hungary. H. 7.8 cm. LT D, ?1st c. BC.*

249 (Left) *Bronze boar from Neuvy-en-Sullias, Loiret, France. H. c. 68 cm. LT D, ?1st c. BC.*

Neuvy-en-Sullias, opposite a Celtic sanctuary of the Carnutes dating from Roman times, at Fleury on the river Loire, came three nearly lifesize bronze boars.

Dog figurines, including this delightful glass terrier from a second- or first-century BC warrior's grave, appear in Middle and Late La Tène cremation graves from the Middle Rhine. The body is of blue spiral-moulded glass with additional yellow and white piping; the technique used was one of spinning semi-molten ribbons of variously coloured glass on a rod. More than half the known finds of Celtic glass date from the oppida period, though glass had been known to the Celts since late Hallstatt times. Dogs or wolves appear in less appealing guise on the cheek-flaps of a helmet from Novo mesto in Jugoslavia. Similar bronze or iron helmets, with wide neckguards and hinged cheek-pieces, are found from France and Italy in the west as well. Helmets from Mihovo and Šmarjeta have cranes on their cheek-flaps; birds are rarely portrayed except on coins (usually eagles) in the Late La Tène period on the continent. The scoring of the rivet heads to hold enamel is characteristic of metalwork of this period.

Stylized deer, together with horses, appear in friezes on some painted pots from near Roanne in the Haute-Marne. A stag, together with rams or goats, possibly supporting a missing human figure, are among oak carvings recently recovered, together with domestic rubbish, from a well in a square ritual enclosure at Fellbach-Schmiden near Stuttgart. Dendrochronology suggests the oak was felled in 123 BC. A much more easterly example of antithetically placed goats occurs on the bronze appliqué for a first-century BC iron sword also from Mihovo; here they support a 'tree of life', a long-lasting eastern motif, and are surmounted by a bull with a bird on its back. The tree of life motif recurs on the Swiss 'Korisios' sword from Port, in this case most probably copied from a classical gemstone.

250,251 Bronze helmet (below left) with cranes on the cheek-pieces (below right) from Šmarjeta, Slovenia, Jugoslavia. H. of detail c. 11 cm. LT D, 1st c. BC.

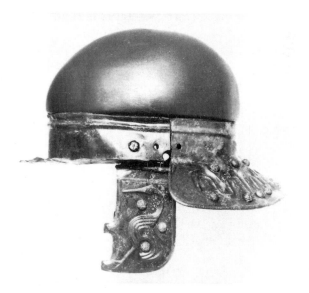
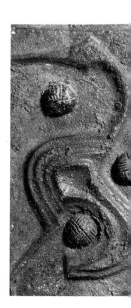

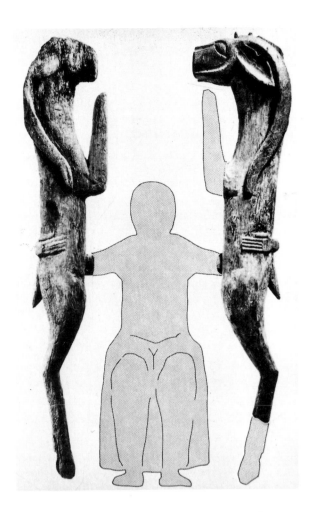

252,253 *Wooden carvings from Fellbach-Schmiden, Kr. Rems-Murr, Germany. (Left) Reconstruction of scene with seated figure and ?goats. H. 87 cm. (Below) Stag. H. 77 cm. LT D1, last quarter 2nd c. BC.*

254,255 *(Below left) Bronze plate for iron scabbard from Mihovo, Slovenia, Jugoslavia, grave 1846/5. W. 5 cm. LT D, first half 1st c. BC.*

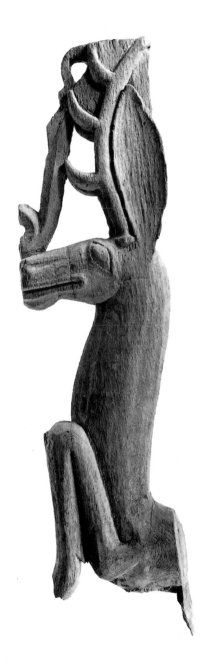

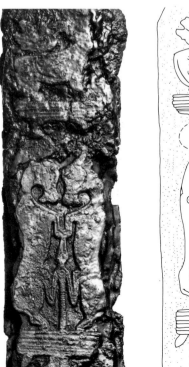

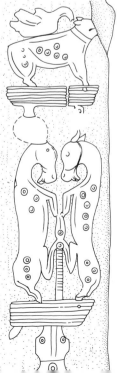

163

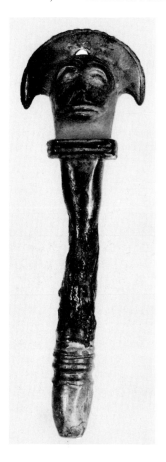

THE HUMAN HEAD

Human heads are of continuing importance and increasing frequency and realism in the art of the late Iron Age. More archaic versions are visible in the axle linch-pin from the huge Donnersberg oppidum in the Rhine Palatinate with its hint of the Hathor crown of Early La Tène chieftainly art; or the menacing head of another linch-pin from Urach near Stuttgart, near the 1600 ha Heidengraben, largest of all the German oppida.

Heads on weapons are probably of talismanic significance, and are often found as finial decoration: examples are a knife handle from Zemplín, the Slovakian defended settlement, and the torc-wearing head on the replacement bronze hilt brazed on to a late Bronze Age knife handle found at the Basel oppidum, centre of the Helvetii. A belt-hook from Leipzig-Connewitz also has a human head.

Hilts of Middle to Late La Tène swords become truly anthropomorphic, with the figure's body as sword grip and the arms and legs as cross bars. Such Middle La Tène or late second-century BC swords have been found, for example, at Dinnyés in Hungary, in northern Italy and Switzerland, from Les Jacquemâtres, Salon, in the Aube and from Châtenay-Macheron, in the Haute-Marne. One example comes from North Grimston in Yorkshire and another was found in 1916 at Ballyshannon Bay in Ireland; these two were certainly imported from the European mainland. The more regular features and hairstyle of the Ballyshannon example are closely matched on the Middle La Tène sword from Châtenay-Macheron, found in a boat-coffin warrior burial.

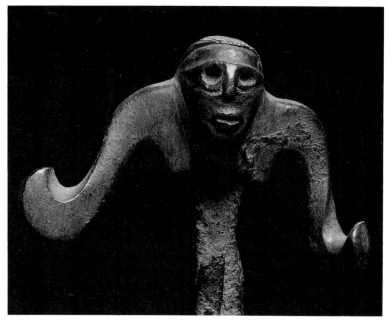

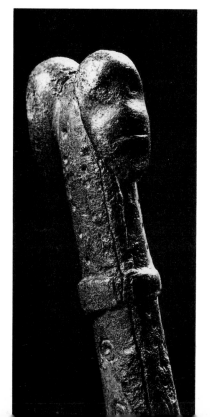

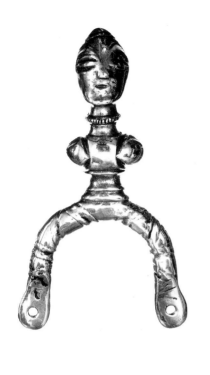

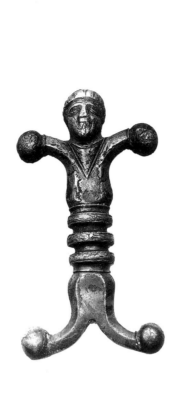

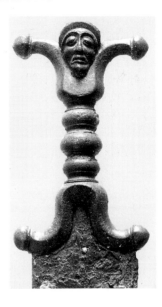

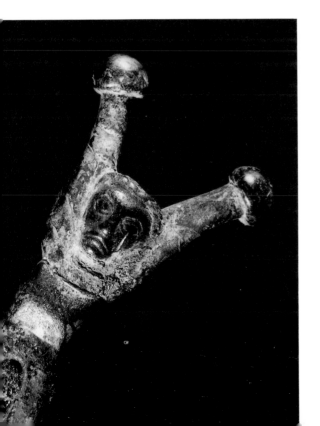

OPPOSITE

256 (Above left) *Bronze and iron linch-pin from Donnersberg, Donnersbergkr., Germany. W. 3.9 cm. LT D, 2nd/1st c. BC.*

257 (Below left) *Detail of iron and bronze linch-pin from Urach, Kr. Reutlingen, Germany. W. 7.8 cm.?LT D, 1st c. BC.*

258 (Below right) *Bronze knife-handle from Zemplín, okr. Trebišov, Czechoslovakia. H. (of head) 1.8 cm. LT D, 1st c. BC.*

THIS PAGE

259 (Above left) *Bronze belt-hook from Leipzig-Connewitz, Germany. L. 7.9 cm. LT D, 1st c. BC.*

260 (Above centre) *Bronze anthropoid sword-hilt from Ballyshannon Bay, off Co. Donegal, Ireland. H. (of head) c. 2.5 cm. LT D1, 1st c. BC.*

261 (Above right) *Bronze anthropoid sword-hilt from Châtenay-Macheron, Chaumont, Haute-Marne, France. H. (of head) c. 3 cm. LT D1, 1st c. BC.*

262 (Left) *Bronze anthropoid hilt of iron sword from Salon, Aube, France. W. (across arms) 4.5 cm. LT C, 2nd c. BC.*

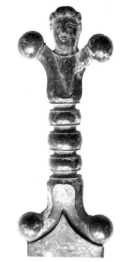

263 Bronze sword-hilt from Châtillon-sur-Indre, Indre, France. H. (of hilt) c. 14 cm. LT D, ?30–20 BC.

Later first-century anthropomorphic swords demonstrate the increasing influence of provincial Roman art in their representation of the human head; examples include the sword hilt from Châtillon-sur-Indre and the hilt-mount which was found at the Staré Hradisko defended settlement in Moravia, but was almost certainly imported from France.

Widely separated examples of moustached faces with carefully fringed hair appear on first-century BC coins of the Taurisci in Austria and Hungary. Very similar heads appear on a group of silver discs and other objects from a grave at Manerbio sul Mella in the area of Brescia, once Cenomani territory. The two largest Manerbio discs have central triskels, as do some other *phalerae*, or discs, from north of the Alps. Analogies have been claimed between the Manerbio discs and the Gundestrup cauldron, or the Entremont sculptures, both discussed later in this chapter. Other Manerbio fragments show the typically Celtic combination of torc-wearing humans with highly stylized rams. Since classical sources attest the use of silver by north Italian Celts, it is unnecessary to look for their source of manufacture further east in the territory of the Taurisci or Boii.

Moustached heads occur, more surprisingly, on a pair of first-century BC four-wheeled wagons found as a votive deposit in a bog at Dejbjerg in Jutland, booty perhaps from the wanderings of the Cimbri. The wagons have been considered as Celtic products, most probably from the Middle Rhine area, but there is also evidence to suggest that they may belong to a local, North European, group.

Further east a different type of influence can be seen. Gold and silver ornaments were found at the turn of the century between Szárazd and Regöly in southern Hungary. Clearly Celtic motifs of human heads or miniature wheels are executed in the filigree technique already borrowed by eastern Celts, in Middle La Tène times, from the Balkans, especially from the Hellenistic-influenced culture of the Thracian-Illyrian communities adjoining Greece. Buried in the first century BC, though probably made in the second, these gold pieces could come either from an Illyrian workshop producing for the Celts in the territory of the Scordisci near Belgrade, or from the area of Transdanubia where they were found.

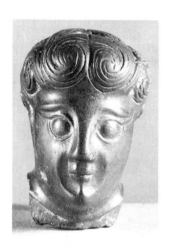

264 Bronze mount from sword-hilt from Staré Hradisko, okr. Prostějov, Czechoslovakia. H. 2.6 cm. LT D, 1st c. BC.

SCULPTURE

Interaction between classical culture and non-classical communities of Iron Age Europe can be clearly demonstrated in the Celto-Ligurian culture in the hinterland of the French Mediterranean coast. Influence from Massalia and other Greek trading colonies can be seen from the sixth century onwards in the adoption of coinage, of grid-plan layout and stone defences, and even in the use of mosaic within the small hilltop settlements which developed. The attempted seizure of Massalia by these communities provoked the Roman takeover of Provence (Roman Provincia).

Around the Rhône delta are a number of Celtic shrines associated with the cult of the severed head. Classical influence is clearly apparent in the

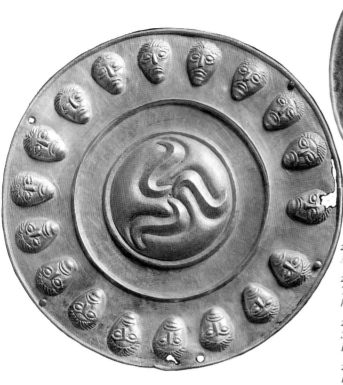

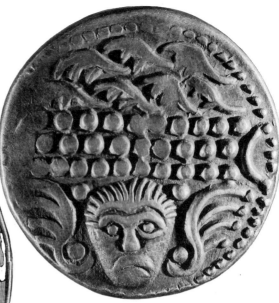

265 *(Left) Silver disc from Villa Vecchia, Manerbio sul Mella, Italy. D. 19.2 cm. ?LT D, 1st c. BC.*

266 *(Above) Obverse of a silver coin of the ?Taurisci from Trifail, Steiermark, Austria. D. 2.4 cm. Wt 10.17 g. 1st half 1st c. BC.*

267 *(Below left) Gold beads with filigree ornament from Szárazd-Regöly, Tolna, Hungary. D. 1.4 mm–3.8 cm. ?LT D, 1st c. BC.*

268 *(Below right) Bronze hand-grip of 'ritual' wagon from Dejbjerg Mose, Ringkobing, W. Jutland, Denmark. Mask 6.5 × 7.6 cm. LT D, 1st c. BC.*

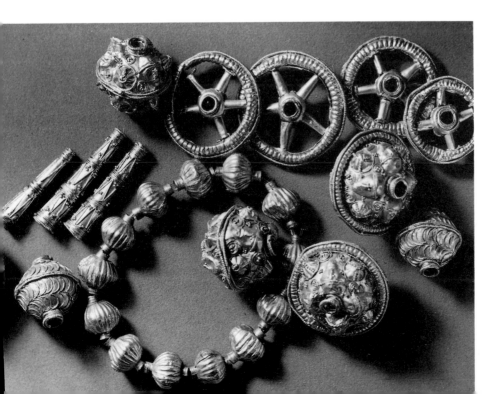

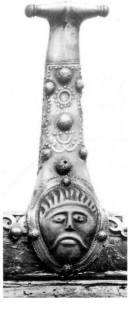

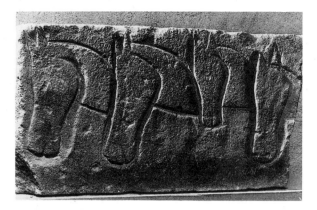

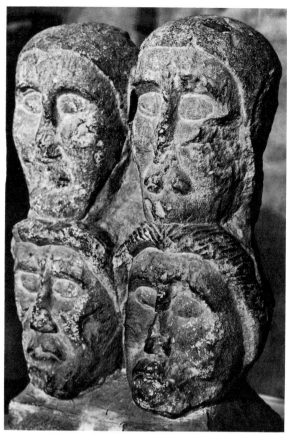

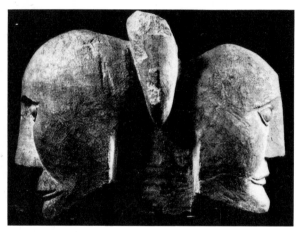

269,271 *Limestone carvings from Roquepertuse, Bouches-du-Rhône, France. Celto-Ligurian. ?3rd–2nd c. BC. (Top) Frieze of horses with traces of paint. L. 63 cm. (Above) Janus heads. H. 34 cm.*

270 *(Above right) Limestone 'severed' heads from Entremont, Bouches-du-Rhône, France. H. 43 cm. Celto-Ligurian. ?3rd/2nd c. BC.*

272 *(Opposite) Limestone statue from Roquepertuse, Bouches-du-Rhône, France. H. 1.05 m. Celto-Ligurian. ?3rd/2nd c. BC.*

use of limestone statues, rather than the more ambiguous pillar stones or portrayals on metalwork common elsewhere.

At Entremont, near Aix-en-Provence, the shrine of the Celto-Ligurian Salivii was destroyed by the Romans in 123–122 BC. Human heads here were carved in stone, and there is provision for the display of skulls. At nearby Roquepertuse there are carved stone friezes of horses' heads, sufficiently Greek in style to lead Jacobsthal to write of craftsmen trained in Massalia. The entrance to the sanctuary, however, has totally non-classical niches for real human heads with, above the skull racks, twin Janus heads divided by the beak of a bird of prey. Other, freestanding, statues from Roquepertuse, such as the pair of cross-legged figures, strongly recall the coinage of northern France with its torc-wearing, cross-legged gods, though the armour of the Roquepertuse figures has a very classical look about it.

These Roquepertuse figures may have supported severed heads, as did the 'Tarasque' of Noves in the Bouches-du-Rhône. This monster is usually interpreted as a lion, though it might be a wolf; as in much situla art, it has a

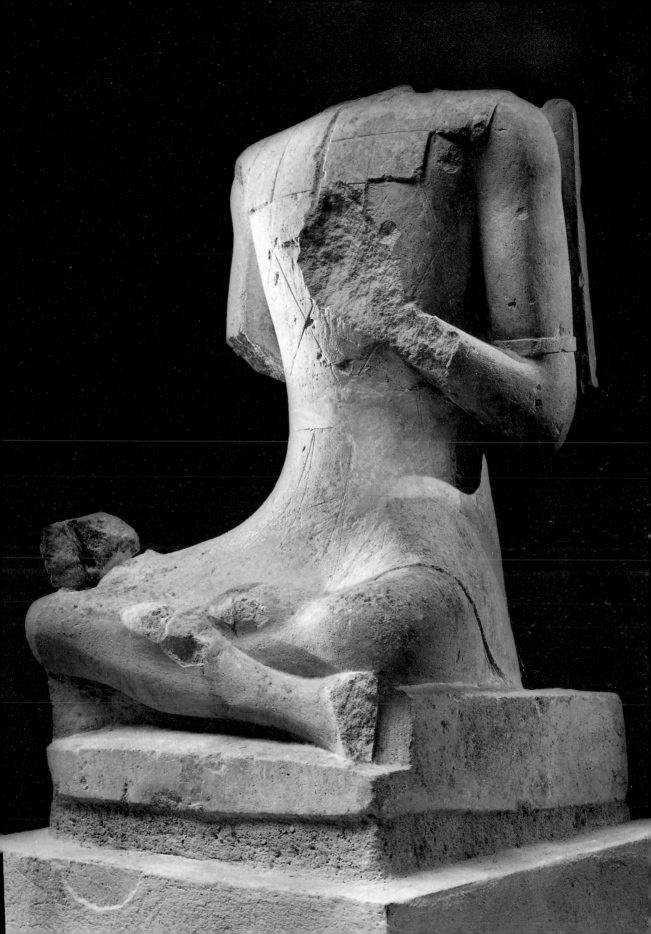

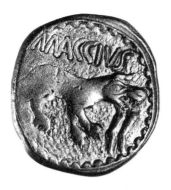

dismembered limb hanging from its snarling mouth, as too do images on first-century BC silver coinage of the Bratislava region, which shows influence from western Celtic areas. Beneath each front paw is a human head with long forked beard, recalling the much earlier Dürrnberg flagon handle. Most of these sculptures were probably carved in the third or early second century BC, long before Roman occupation.

Another limestone monster is said to have been found at Linsdorf in Alsace; this beast supports itself on two clean-shaven heads between which there is space for a skull. If this is indeed Celtic workmanship, it has clear points of comparison with Roman funerary sculpture.

Clear evidence of the transformation in Celtic style under advancing Roman influence can be seen by comparing the Euffigneix pillar stone with the sheet bronze figure dredged in 1845 from the river Juine at Bouray,

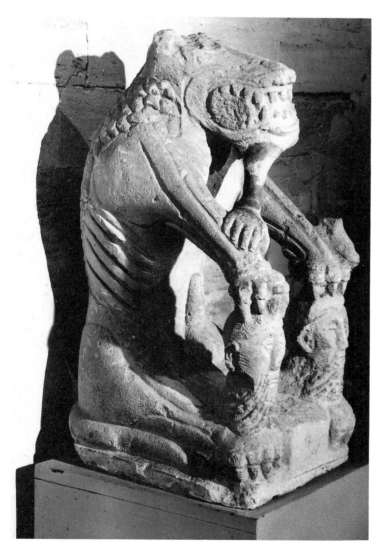

273 (Above left) Reverse of a 'Bratislava' type silver coin from Bratislava, Czechoslovakia, showing devouring beast. D. 2.9 cm, Wt 16.75 g. 1st half 1st c. BC.

274 (Left) The limestone 'Tarasque de Noves' from Noves, Bouches-du-Rhône, France. H. 1.12 m. Celto-Ligurian. ?3rd c. BC.

275 (Right) Carved stone monster from Linsdorf, Alsace, France. H. 55 cm. ?3rd/2nd c. BC.

276 (Below) Limestone pillar statue from Euffigneix, Haute-Marne, France. H. c. 30 cm. LT D, 1st c. BC.

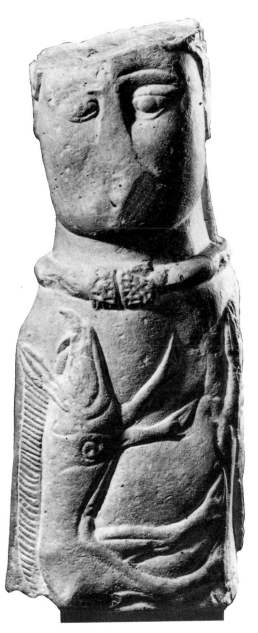

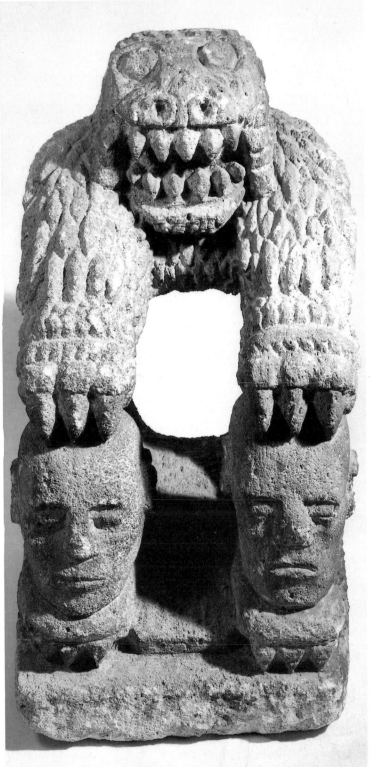

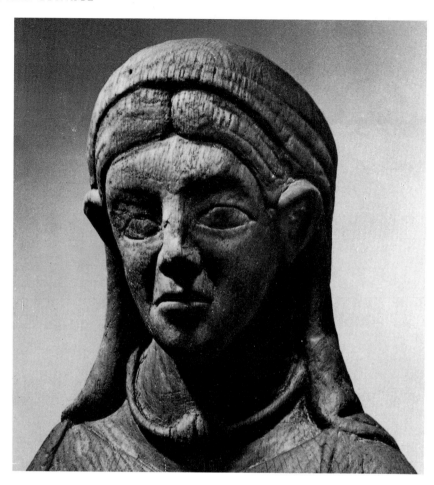

277 *Wooden carving of a woman with a neckring from Source-de-la-Roche, Chamalières, Puy-de-Dôme, France. H. 41 cm. 1st c. AD.*

OPPOSITE

278 *(Left) Bronze 'dancer' from Neuvy-en-Sullias, Loiret, France. H. 14 cm. Late 1st c. BC/1st c. AD.*

279 *(Centre above) Bronze figurine from Kunjic, Hercegovina, Jugoslavia. H. 11 cm. LT C/D, 2nd/1st c. BC.*

280 *(Far right) Oak 'pilgrim' from Sources-de-la-Seine, Côte d'Or, France. H. 47 cm. ?1st c. AD.*

281 *(Centre below) Bronze figurine holding war-trumpet from Hradiště, Stradonice, okr. Beroun, Czechoslovakia. H. 4.5 cm. LT D1, 1st c. BC.*

south of Paris. One glass eye remains in the head of this torc-wearing, cross-legged, animal-hoofed deity, but stylistically it shows Roman influence in its realism. Even more in the style of the Roman provinces are the bronze statuettes of nude dancers found in a cache on the left bank of the Loire at Neuvy-en-Sullias. The female figure is stamped with the name S(CO)UTO and was probably buried at the time of Caesar's conquest in the mid-first century BC.

A great deal of wooden sculpture has survived in France, especially at two votive deposits at sacred springs. At Source-de-la-Roche at Chamalières, in the territory of the powerful Arverni in the Massif Central, several thousand wooden statues and *ex voto* representations of parts of the body were found in a thermal spring. The female figure shown wears a torc and has characteristically Celtic oval eyes, but her realism is classical in style.

Three hundred or so wooden *ex voto* offerings, in various styles and less Romanized than those at Chamalières, were discovered at Sources-de-la-Seine, northwest of Dijon. Ribcages, viscera and even a recognizable hernia are among them, as well as carved human heads, which echo the severed heads of the south. These come from the pool of a Gallo-Roman sanctuary which was probably created in the first century AD, but the carvings themselves are probably much older, since they show no sign of Mediterranean influence.

More enigmatic human figures, more reminiscent of earlier Celtic portrayals, can be found in areas further removed from Roman influence as in the curious little bronze females from Aust Cliff in Gloucestershire and Kunjic in Jugoslavia, or the ithyphallic Celtic warrior brandishing his war-trumpet from Stradonice in Czechoslovakia.

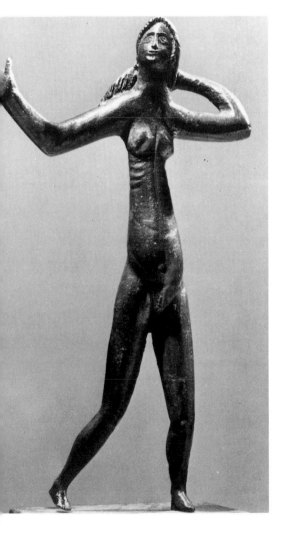

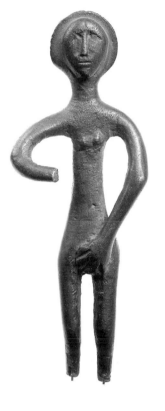

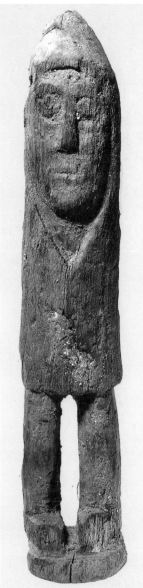

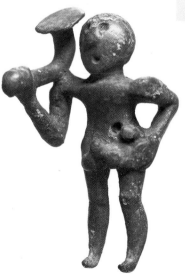

CAULDRONS OF PLENTY

Torc-wearing, cross-legged gods, like those from Roquepertuse and Bouray, are visible again on two extraordinary cauldrons deposited in Danish peat-bogs. Fragments only remain of the bronze example found at Rynkeby, on the island of Funen. A broad, Romanized face with glass eyes is flanked by bulls' heads; the torc shown is a buffer-terminalled type known mostly from France. The inner plate shows two wild beasts flanking a triskel. The symbolism is Celtic and the metalworking techniques (probably from more than one hand) recall the sheet metalwork of central Gaul. Trade, or the warlike wanderings of the Cimbri, may have brought this cauldron north to Denmark.

The other, frequently published, gilded silver cauldron was found in 1891 dismantled on the surface of a peat-bog at Raevemosen near Gundestrup in northern Jutland. Five internal plaques and a basal disc survive, together with seven out of eight square external plates. Their combined weight is almost 9 kg. There has been much discussion of the iconography and geographical origins of the Gundestrup cauldron. Some of the iconography is clearly Celtic, for example, the torc-wearing, cross-legged, antlered god with another twisted torc in his hand. The warriors with their jockey-cap helmets, with crests of boars or birds of prey, their use of spurs, their animal-headed war trumpets, their circular harness mounts and their shield-bosses of Late La Tène type, are also clearly Celtic. Similar helmet crests occur at Ciumeşti and perhaps Luncani in Romania. The bestiary includes Celtic dogs or wolves, but also more exotic animals such as lions, dragons or griffons, even elephants, together with a boy on a dolphin. The base plate depicts a bull, possibly in its death agonies, with a huntsman and two hounds.

282,283 General view (below left) and base-plate (below right) of the silver-gilt cauldron from Gundestrup, Rævemosen, Aars, Denmark. D. (whole) 69 cm; (base-plate) 25.6 cm.

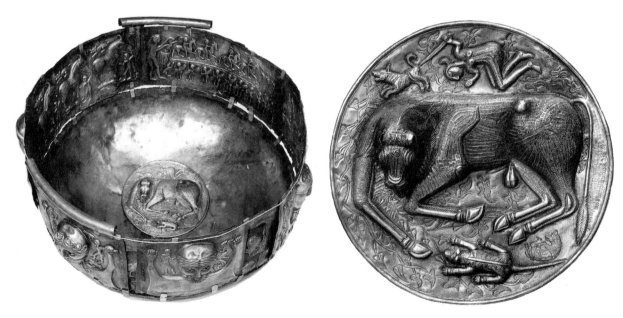

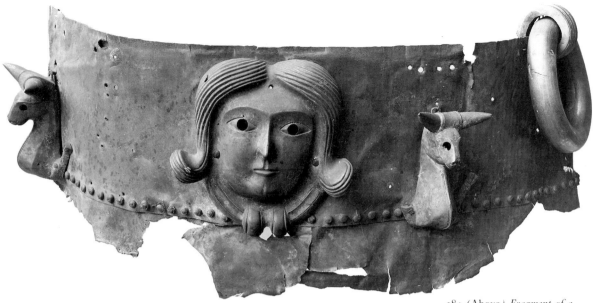

284 (Above) Fragment of a bronze cauldron from Rynkeby, Funen, Denmark. H. 20 cm. LT D, 1st c. BC.

285,286 Inner plates C (left) and A (below left) of the Gundestrup cauldron (ill. 282). Both 40 × 20 cm. ?Thraco-Getic. ?Late 2nd/early 1st c. BC.

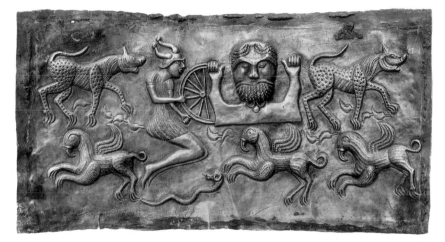

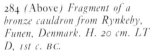

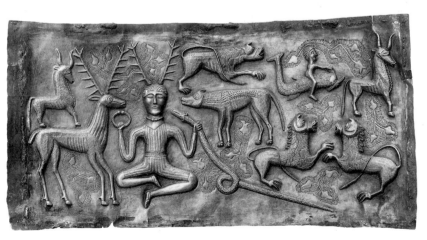

287 (Above) Obverse of a potin coin from the Somme basin, France. D. 2 cm. Wt 3.55 g. 1st c. BC.

Attempts to identify the cross-legged god or the other male and female torc-wearing heads as specific Celtic deities can only be conjectural at best. Similarly conjectural are interpretations of the outsize figure holding other, smaller, humans upside-down as a god of war offering sacrifice, or as a representation of the restoration to life of a dead hero by immersion in the 'cauldron of plenty' mentioned in much later Celtic written sources.

Stylistically, however, the cauldron suggests a non-Celtic origin. The ivy-leaf fill-ins, the punch-dotting and ridging of human clothing and animal pelts strongly recall the Istro-Pontic or Thraco-Getic metalwork of Dacians and Thracians in Romania, Bulgaria and eastern Hungary, a style first developed under Hellenistic influence in the fourth century BC. Silver, rarely used by Celts except for coins, was also commonly employed to the east of the Celtic zones. The most likely area of manufacture is thus eastern Europe, rather than – as has been suggested – northwestern Gaul, even using captive Thracian silversmiths. Before ravaging Gaul from 113 BC onwards, the Cimbri apparently raided deep into eastern Europe. This raid may well have provided the opportunity to commission or loot this cauldron, with its Celtic iconography and very un-Celtic style.

Recent study has shown technically what was earlier suggested stylistically, that the plates were made by several different hands, perhaps by second-century Thracians for eastern Celts, Scordisci or Boii; silver coinage around Bratislava, a centre of the Boii until Burebista, king of Dacia, overran it in about 60 BC, carries much the same heraldic bestiary as the cauldron.

Another silver piece showing apparently eastern influence is the great silver torc found in drainage operations in 1928 on the eastern bank of the Neckar, at Trichtingen near Stuttgart. It weighs 6 kg, though much of the mass is accounted for by its iron core. The bulls' heads of the torc terminals

288 Inner plate E of the Gundestrup cauldron, ill. 282. 40 × 20 cm.

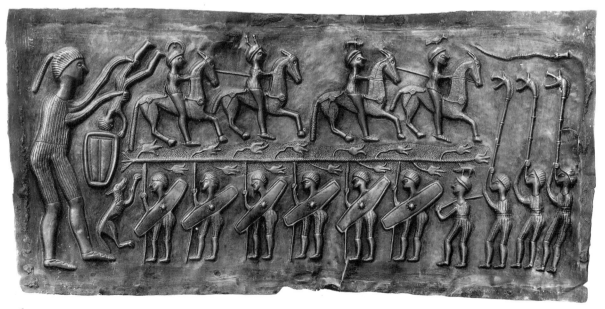

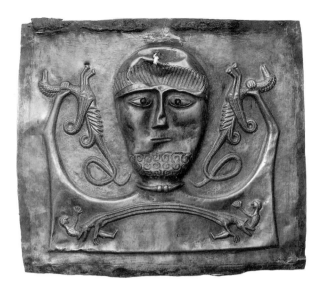

289 *Outer plate b of the Gundestrup cauldron, ill. 282. 25 × 20 cm.*

themselves wear torcs, with buffer terminals; these, together with the undulating punched and ridged decoration and the iron core, suggest a late second-century BC date, and an origin once again in the silver-using Thraco-Getic area.

CELTIC COINS

Coinage was first used in the East Greek cities of Asia Minor in the latter part of the seventh century BC, and was adopted in Greece itself during the sixth century. In temperate Europe, Dacians and Celts from Romania to France began striking their own silver or gold coins in the course of the fourth and third centuries BC. Republican Rome, by contrast, did not mint its own gold coinage until the third century; low value bronze coins for everyday transactions were not struck in Rome until about 30 BC.

Celts must have encountered coinage in Hellenistic lands as they moved eastwards as mercenaries and invaders, since early Greek and Celtic coins were employed as tribute, taxes and military payments, rather than in trade. Occasional early Celtic coins are found in graves – as at Giengen-an-der-Brenz near Manching or in the boat-coffin burial of Châtenay-Macheron – suggesting their use to purchase services in the afterworld as well. Celtic coins were based on Hellenistic prototypes in form as well as function, though the specific models varied, as did the metal used in different areas.

Silver was used in an arc from the Danube mouth through northern Italy and into southern France. In the Middle Danube, tetradrachms of Philip II of Macedon (359–336 BC) were imitated; these show Zeus on one side and a victorious rider on the other. In Italy north of the Po river drachms of the Greek colony of Massalia were copied, and in the Garonne basin in France the didrachms of Rhoda, another western Greek colony in Spain.

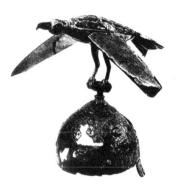

290 *Iron helmet with bronze crest from Ciumeşti, Maramureş, Romania. H. 25 cm. LT C, 3rd–2nd c. BC.*

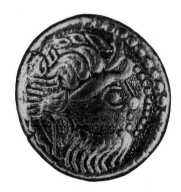

291 *Copy of the wreathed head of Zeus on a silver 'Kaposthal' type coin from Velemszentvid, Vas, Hungary. D. 2.2 cm. Wt 12.5 g. 2nd c. BC.*

North of the silver-using belt, gold was employed from France to Bohemia. In the eastern part, a common model was the gold stater of Alexander III (336–323 BC), with the helmeted head of Athene on one side and a winged victory on the other. Further west, the commonest prototype was the gold stater of Philip II, struck to commemorate Philip's victory of the Olympic Games of 356 BC, with a beardless and wreathed head of Apollo on one side, and a charioteer drawn by twin horses on the other side.

Gold and silver coins were first cast as blank flans, then struck between engraved metal dies, whose production needed a skill possessed only by metalsmiths such as those who produced sword stamps. Later bronze or potin (bronze with a high proportion of tin) coins were often cast in strips; the occurrence of such low denomination coins from the late second century onwards at many oppida suggests a move towards the use of money in market transactions. Traces of minting have also been found at oppida such as Manching, though coin production was not necessarily confined to oppida nor, in many cases, produced solely under the aegis of local chieftains.

The political importance of coins as symbols of power and identity or evidence of state formation is a matter too complex to deal with here. Celtic coins, however, illustrate the transformation of borrowed forms by introducing Celtic symbols to Hellenistic prototypes and by a complex disintegration of naturalistic Hellenistic portrayals into more characteristically abstract and ambiguous Celtic forms.

Late fourth-century BC Dacian coins are probably the earliest securely dated imitations of Hellenistic coins. They are still recognizably close to their Hellenistic prototypes, as too are the third- and second-century silver coins of much of Hungary, Jugoslavia and northwestern Romania. Even on the first-century BC silver Boiian coin from Slovakia the derivation is still clear, though the figure is altogether livelier, the palm frond has become a bough and ivy leaves, like those on the Gundestrup cauldron, are visible. These fine 'BIATEC' coins (named after the inscription borne by many of them), minted in the Boiian oppidum where Bratislava now stands, already, however, owe something to Roman Republican denarii and to the coins of Syracuse and of more westerly Celts.

The riderless horse on a coin of the Taurisci of the first half of the first century BC is much more stylized and abstract; the mane becomes pattern only. A similarly sway-backed horse appears on a Middle La Tène silver-gilt die-stamped finger-ring from a grave at Oberhofen in Switzerland. This latter horse also has the very Celtic three-armed whirligig, or triskel, both above and below it. Similar transference of motifs between coins and other forms of Celtic art can be seen in the comparison of a third-century BC silver coin from the lower Danube – showing the seated figure of Zeus – with a pottery stamp on a sherd from a Middle and Late La Tène settlement at Eggendorf in Lower Austria. Further west, within the silver-using belt, the Insubres in northern Italy reduced the lion of Massalia to a curious disjointed scorpion shape on their coins.

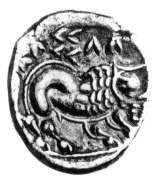

292 Reverse of a silver coin of the Insubres from the Po Valley in northern Italy, showing scorpion-like imitation of the lion of Massalia. D. 1.5 cm. Wt 6 g. ?3rd c. BC.

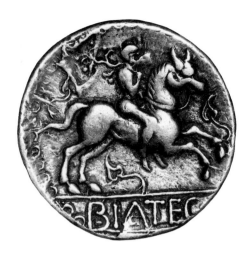

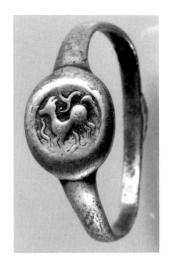

293 (Left) Reverse of a silver coin of the Boii from near Bratislava, Czechoslovakia. D. 2.6 cm. Wt 17.1 g. 1st half 1st c. BC.

294 (Right) Silver gilt finger-ring from Oberhofen am Thunersee, Kt. Bern, Switzerland, inhumation grave 1. D. (internal) 1.9 cm. LT C, ?late 2nd c. BC.

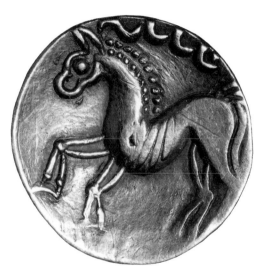

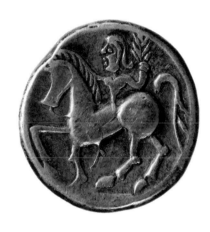

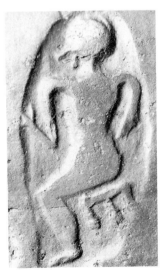

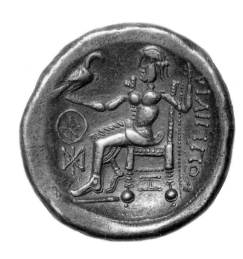

295 (Above left) Reverse of a silver coin of the ?Taurisci from Trifail, Steiermark, Austria. D. 2.4 cm. Wt 10.17 g. 1st half 1st c. BC.

296 (Above) Reverse of a silver coin from ?Northern Romania. D. c. 2.5 cm. Wt 12.12 g. 3rd c. BC.

297 (Far left) Detail of seated figure on a pot from Eggendorf, Niederösterreich, Austria. H. 2.3 cm. LT C2/D, late 2nd/1st c. BC.

298 (Left) Reverse of a silver coin from the Lower Danube area. D. c. 2.8 cm. Wt 16 g. 3rd c. BC.

179

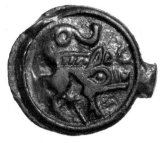

299 (Above) Reverse of a potin coin from the Somme basin, France. D. 2 cm. Wt 3.55 g. 1st c. BC.

300 (Right) Gold coin of the Redones from France. D. c. 2 cm. Wt 7.6 g.

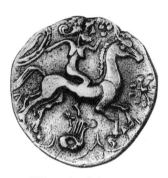

301 Billon coin of the Coriosolites from northwest France. D. 2.2 cm. Wt 6.09 g. 1st half 1st c. BC.

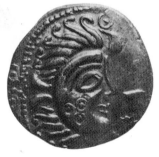

302 Gold stater of the Aulerci Diablintes (formerly attributed to the Redones) from northwest France. D. 2.2 cm. Wt 6.7 g. 1st c. BC.

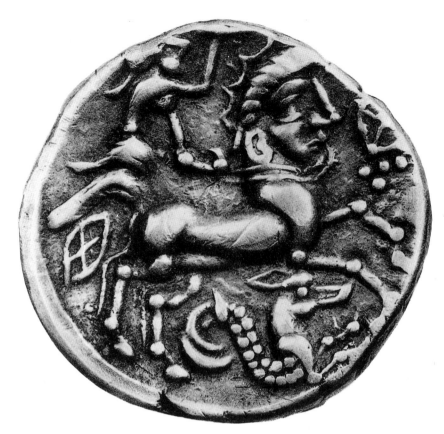

In the gold-using Celtic belt the processes of disintegration and Celticization of Hellenistic prototypes are, if anything, even more marked. A late second- or early first-century gold coin from northwestern France has moved a long way from its two-horse chariot prototype. The single horse is human-headed, the rider and chariot almost abstract, while below is a curious dog-headed beast. Another type ascribed to the Redones of Brittany has a naked woman on a horse, with an apparently classical lyre below. As gold became rarer, this region adopted a debased silver or 'billon' coinage, on which the wreathed head of Apollo is still recognizable.

Later cast potin coins of the mid-first century BC from the Somme basin show on one side a cross-legged Celtic deity, and on the other a boar, with, above, what looks like a war trumpet.

In southern Germany, gold coins of the Vindelici display the extremes to which Celtic abstraction could be carried. Many of these have been found in hoards, as at Irsching, Gaggers and Manching. An eagle's head, or sometimes three birds' heads formed into a triskel, often decorate one side while Apollo's wreath becomes a border; the concave reverse in some cases shows a torc. In the Middle Ages these coins were regarded as having magical properties and they were called 'rainbow cups' (*Regenbogenschüsselchen*).

Increased Roman influence can be seen as Gaul fell to the Romans, for instance, in a Roman eagle surmounting the very Celtic horse on the usually inscribed gold coins of the Bituriges Cubi of central France. A bronze coin of the Remi in Belgic northeast France dates from the mid-first century BC: on one side it shows a Belgic chariot of around the time of Julius Caesar, while the other shows a trinity of heads probably based on the triumvirs Octavian, Antony and Lepidus. Other Gallo-Belgic coins, such as those of the Ambiani, with the Celticized head of Apollo, were among the first to be exported in significant numbers across the Channel; some were apparently struck as payment for aid by Belgic groups during the war against Caesar. The head of Vercingetorix, 'Great King of Warriors', last and greatest of Caesar's Gaulish opponents, appears on gold and bronze coins of the Arverni, to the west of the Rhône valley in the Puy-de-Dôme; many such coins come from mass grave deposits at Mont Auxois, Alise-Ste-Reine, regarded as the site of the oppidum of Alesia, where Vercingetorix fought his last battle against Caesar. Rome, too, recorded the Gallic wars on her coins; a silver denarius struck in 50 BC depicts a trophy of Celtic arms and armour, and the bowed figure of a Celtic warrior, presumed to be Vercingetorix himself. This telling depiction of Roman pressure on the Celts shows too that coins frequently portray not just symbols of power but specific events in history.

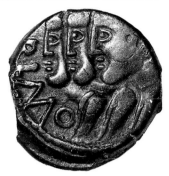

303 Bronze coin of the Remi from northeast France. D. 1.5 cm. Wt 3.16 g. Mid-1st c. BC.

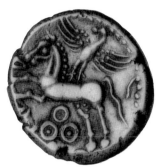

304 Gold coin of the Bituriges Cubi from Berry, France. D. c. 1.7 cm. Wt 6.78 g. 1st c. BC.

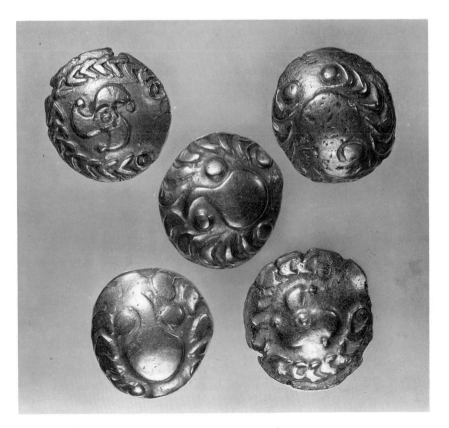

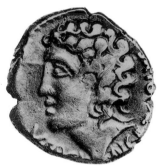

305 (Left) Gold 'rainbow cup' coins of the Vindelici from the Goldberg bei Mardorf, Hesse, Germany. D. c. 1.8 cm. Wt c. 7.5 g. 1st c. BC.

306 (Above) Gold coin of the Arverni: obverse, with inscription VERCINGETORIXS. D. 1.9 cm. Wt 7.43 g. c. 52 BC.

THE SACRED RING

Particularly in the Celtic west, coins are found in several areas in hoards associated with gold torcs of such weight as to suggest only the most occasional wear. One such find was made in 1893 at Tayac in the Gironde. The massive, twisted, buffer-terminalled, locally made gold torc weighs 0.75 kg and was intentionally broken in three. The five hundred and more coins include some blank flans, as well as coins from northern, eastern and central Gaul and 'rainbow cups' from the Arverni, directly to the east of Tayac. Some may be as late as 98–90 BC, so they are unlikely to be the result of a panic burial during the raids of the Cimbri and Teutones in Aquitaine in 113–105 BC. That this was a scrap metal hoard is obviously a possibility but there are other interpretations.

Three neckrings and some fifty coins were found in a cloth bag near a rubbish pit in the fortified settlement of Niederzier, in the Rhineland. Some of the coins are early rainbow cups with a star on one side; others are those of the Belgic Ambiani.

The 'Saint-Louis' gold hoard found in 1883 on the banks of the Rhine near the Basel Gasworks site and the nearby Münsterhügel oppidum contains fragments of two hollow neckrings of sheet gold together with coins of the Boii, rainbow cups and local Swiss coins. The torcs themselves are made on a core of iron with beeswax and resin coating, and are of a type known mostly from northern France, Belgium and from Snettisham in East Anglia. One chance find of such a torc at Mailly-le-Camp in Champagne bears an inscription in Greek letters. It indicates that the Mailly torc was part of a large dedicated offering of treasure by Nitrobriges of southwestern Gaul. This, together with classical references to the Celtic use of gold for religious offerings, makes clear the possibility that all these hoards may be ritual offerings, not scrap or panic hoards. With the torcs depicted on the Trichtingen ring and on such pillar statues as Euffigneix in mind, one might envisage these torcs being used to adorn the necks of cult figures rather than actual men and women. Another such find, containing two torcs together in a pot with fifty coins of the local Nervii, was actually found near a local spring, at Frasnes-lez-Buissenal in Belgian Hainault. Both the Frasnes torcs are formed of sheet gold over an iron core, and have pseudo-buffer terminals. One is plain, but the larger is highly decorated in repoussé technique. The animals under the terminals are probably rams rather than bulls. These beasts and the supporting S-lyres, with outward-looking birds below, belong to a tradition which goes back to Early La Tène art, though the torc itself is not earlier than late second century BC, and the coins indicate that the hoard as a whole must have been deposited around the time of the Caesarian subjugation of the area in 53 BC. Other possible associations of torcs of this general type with water deposits are an example from La Tène and two from a river find, together with tools and weapons, from Pommereuil, again in Belgian Hainault.

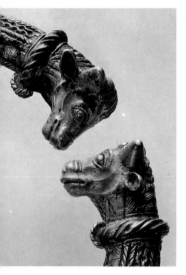

307 *Terminals of massive silver neckring with iron core from Trichtingen, Kr. Rottweil, Germany. L. (of heads)* c. *6 cm. ?LT C, ?2nd c. BC.*

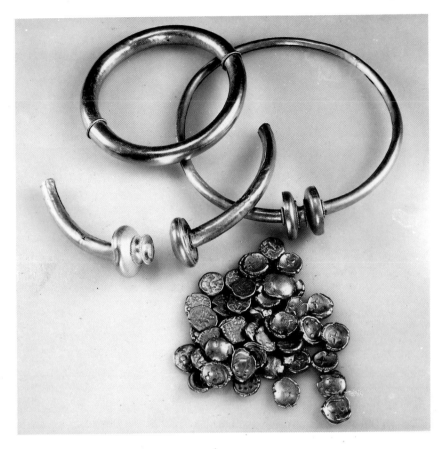

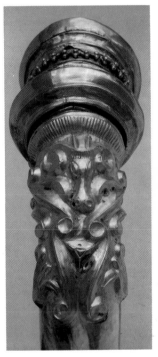

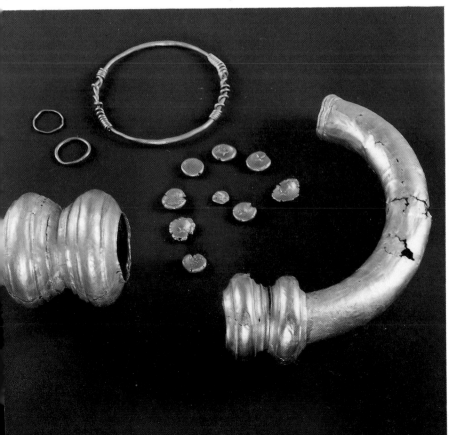

308 (Above left) Sheet gold neckrings, armring and coins from Niederzier, Kr. Düren, Germany. D. (of neckrings) 15 cm. LT D, 1st c. BC.

309 (Left) The 'Saint-Louis' treasure of gold neckring fragments, armring, finger-rings and gold coins from the Basel Gasworks site, Kt. Basel, Switzerland. D. (of armring) 8.6 cm. LT D, 1st c. BC.

310 (Above) Detail of gold neckring from Frasnes-lez-Buissenal, Hainault, Belgium. D. (of tube) 2.7 cm. LT C2/D1, ?2nd/1st c. BC.

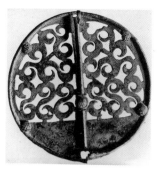

311 *Enamelled bronze harness-disc from 'Altenburg', Niederstein, Kr. Fritzlar-Homberg, Germany. D. 10.6 cm. LT D, 1st c. BC/1st c. AD.*

The terminals of the Frasnes torc cover a tenon catch and there is a small decorated area opposite. This is also the case on the largest of the three tubular torcs from Snettisham in East Anglia, though the decoration on the Norfolk neckring looks insular rather than continental. One final neckring of this type comes from a find of gold near the old shoreline of Lough Foyle at Broighter, Co. Londonderry, a spot again suggesting ritual deposition. The terminals of the Broighter torc closely resemble those of the decorated Frasnes neckring in form and decoration; the design of the rest of the ring is, by contrast, certainly first-century BC Irish, as we shall see in the next chapter.

THE BELGAE AND THE FRENCH CONNECTION

In the Late La Tène phase, graves in the Rhineland and Champagne or in Belgium, the core areas of Early La Tène art, continue to produce some of the more striking pieces of this period. A cremation cemetery at Goeblingen-Nospelt in Luxembourg contains four rich warrior graves of the Treveri, whose tribal centre became Roman Trier. These graves are dated to the last years of the first century BC by the imported Roman bronze drinking vessels and pottery, including urns and amphorae. Two Celtic iron swords from these graves have openwork ornament on their scabbards. This work is thoroughly Romanized, and shows little sign of the earlier Celtic adaptation. Other such scabbards are found throughout the Celtic world: in the Middle Rhine, the southwest Alpine region and as far east as Jugoslavia, while a dagger with similar openwork sheath was found in the nineteenth century in the Thames at Hammersmith. Several come from the Magdalensberg in Austria, which may well suggest some link with that region's famed and traded iron industry, though several other workshops may also have been involved. Slightly less classicized, but scarcely more inventive, openwork can be seen on a bronze harness mount from the Altenburg at Niederstein, and among the wagon fittings of a cremation grave at Neuwied near Bonn.

Goeblingen-Nospelt grave B also produced the sheet bronze coverings for two four-footed wooden stave buckets. One bears a geometric design, while the other has a typically late Celtic curvilinear pattern. Across the Channel in southeastern Britain a parallel culture to that of northeastern Gaul seems to have developed at about the time of Caesar's Gallic conquests. Here Gallo-Belgic coins of groups such as the Ambiani are common and versions of the stave buckets of Belgic Gaul are also found. The first to come to light was that discovered in 1807, possibly from a cremation burial, at St Margaret's Mead, Marlborough, in Wiltshire. The reconstruction is far from certain, but certain artistic features such as the pair of horses with tendrils hanging from their mouths, or the classicized full-frontal faces with provision for inset eyes recall continental coinage and the classicized faces of the Rynkeby cauldron or the Châtillon-sur-Indre

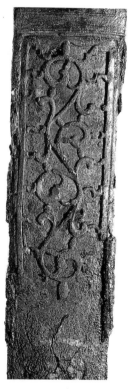

312 *Bronze scabbard-plate from Goeblingen-Nospelt, Luxembourg, grave C2. W. (of decoration) 3.5 cm. LT D, 1st c. BC.*

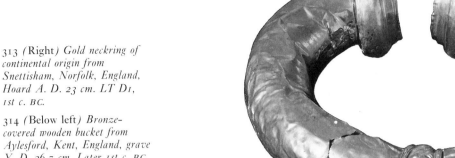

313 (Right) Gold neckring of continental origin from Snettisham, Norfolk, England, Hoard A. D. 23 cm. LT D1, 1st c. BC.

314 (Below left) Bronze-covered wooden bucket from Aylesford, Kent, England, grave Y. D. 26.7 cm. Later 1st c. BC.

315 (Below right) Bronze-covered yew stave bucket from Goeblingen-Nospelt, Luxembourg. D. 32 cm. LT D, 1st c. BC.

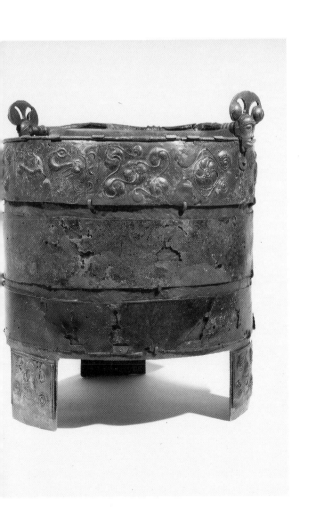

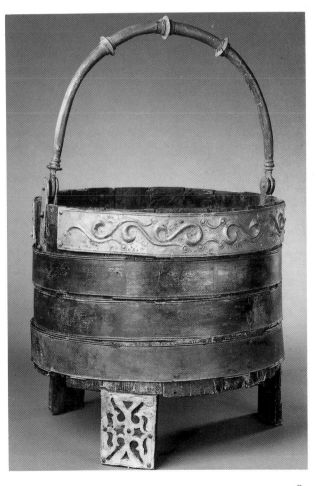

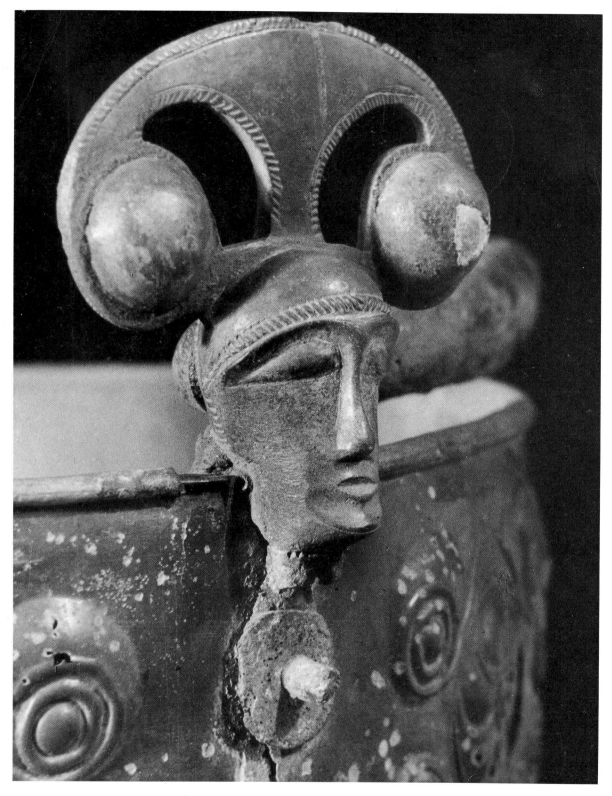

sword. The Marlborough bucket may well be an import from the region of Gaul between Seine and Loire, the region where, perhaps, the Belgic settlers in southeastern England originated.

More recently, two three-footed buckets were recovered in 1967 from a burial at The Tene, Baldock, Hertfordshire, together with iron firedogs and imported bronzes and amphorae. These buckets have human-head handle-mounts with down-curved knobbed horns. Such horns recall a three-horned bronze head from the Roman docks at Cologne on the Rhine. Stylized horns may thus have been intended as the crown for a pair of lantern-jawed human heads on the finest of all late Celtic stave buckets. This was found in 1886, by Arthur Evans and his father Sir John Evans, in a Belgic cremation cemetery, once more with imported Italian bronze drinking vessels, at Aylesford in Kent. The sheet bronze panels appear to have been made by beating the metal on bronze or iron formers. The backward-looking griffon-like horses – recently interpreted as Celtic hobby horses – have a long Celtic pedigree and may be compared with the animals on the Rynkeby fragments, though the disjointed tendril designs and spirals bring to mind continental coinage. Arthur Evans also drew attention to the horses of the Swiss Sword Style 'stable', notably those on the fine scabbard from La Tène itself; the view has more recently been advanced that here could be a continental heirloom made as early as about 100 BC. But by the first century BC, Celtic craftsmen in the British Isles had already long developed their own individual styles and it is to the detailed examination of such insular art that we must now turn.

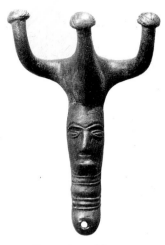

317 *Bronze horned face-mount from Cologne Docks, Germany. W. 5.5 cm. LT D, 1st c. BC/1st c. AD.*

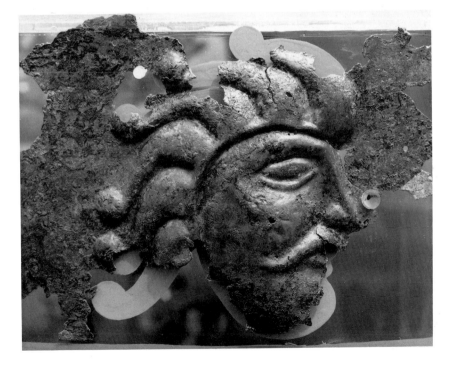

318 (Left) *Bronze mount for wooden stave bucket from Marlborough, Wilts. H. 8.4 cm. 1st c. BC/1st c. AD*

316 (Opposite) *Head from handle-mount of the Aylesford bucket, ill. 314. H. c. 4 cm. Later 1st c. BC.*

187

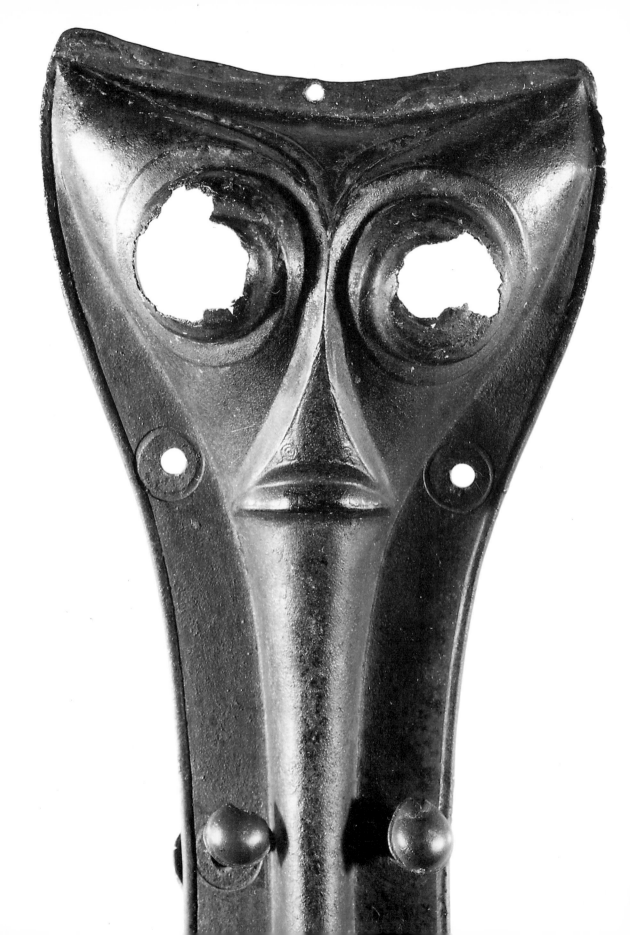

6

Insular Pre-Roman Celtic Art

ORIGINS

SCOTLAND, WALES, IRELAND and Cornwall are often popularly thought of as the surviving insular Celtic regions. Most of the stereotyped, romantic images of the Celts come from Britain – the small, dark-haired, individualistic, romantic warrior peoples, heroic and proud, given to poetry and song. Or, as Stuart Piggott less flatteringly describes them, 'swaggering, belching, touchy chieftains and their equally impossible warrior crew, hands twitching to the sword-hilt at the imagined hint of an insult'. Yet the hard fact of the matter is that archaeological and historical sources cannot prove definitively when or whence the Celts reached Britain. Our only certainty is that both Celtic 'P' (Welsh) and the earlier 'Q' language (Gaelic) groups are known there, so that probably two separate groups of Celts must at some stage have reached Europe's offshore islands from the continent.

Traditional views of the British Iron Age saw it as created by waves of conquerors or settlers from the continent, like the later period from the Roman Conquest to that of the Normans. A phase of late Hallstatt settlement in the eighth century was thought to be followed by Early La Tène invasions of Sussex from the Marne region about 250 BC, which were associated with the construction of hillforts to repel the foreigners.

More recently scholars have tended to think that, though goods, technology and ideas crossed the sea-barriers, large-scale movements of people did not take place. Despite a flurry of new hypotheses and excavations since the 1960s, no cohesive reinterpretation of the insular Iron Age has yet emerged. The process of Celticization may well have been cumulative, with Bronze Age Hallstatt settlers being the first Celts, their 'Celticity' reinforced by trade and other contacts with the continent of Europe and perhaps the arrival of small groups of settlers from time to time.

One major candidate for continental settlement connections is the Arras culture of Yorkshire, with dates going back perhaps to about 300 BC. This is the only area of Britain where chariot burial was practised, but direct connections with any of the Marne or Champagne areas of France is impossible to prove from the art or the material remains of this small group. 'Marnian' invasion of Sussex around 250 BC causing the construction of hillforts to repel the invaders is now generally discounted. Hillfort construction in Britain is now known to go back to 1000 BC in the earliest

319 (Opposite) *Detail of bronze shield-mount no. 2 from the River Thames at Wandsworth, Middlesex, London. (See also ill. 1). W. 5 cm. ?2nd/1st c. BC.*

instances, and their spread and later destruction is better explained by political and economic developments within Britain.

In the first century BC Julius Caesar claimed that Belgae from northeastern Gaul had invaded Britain some twenty-five years before his invasions of 55 and 54 BC. Archaeological material from Britain has failed to produce conclusive supporting evidence from earlier than the middle of the first century BC, though, as we saw at the end of the previous chapter, there are signs of definite cross-Channel connections.

Continental links with Britain appear to have been strong in the early Iron Age between about the seventh and fifth centuries; in the middle period the evidence shows an apparent weakening in such links, which revive again in the first century BC. This is also the position in Ireland, where areas of Celtic settlement in the north and centre appear for a long time to have co-existed with non-Celtic settlement elsewhere.

Our knowledge of the Iron Age in the British Isles is also hampered by the nature of the evidence. Burials with clearly datable grave goods are rare; most weapons come from hoards or single finds deposited in or near water, and many ornaments such as brooches are scattered finds. Even that commonest of artefacts, pottery, rarely comes from securely dated sources and attempts to translate relative pottery sequences into absolute dates are largely useless before the first century BC. Few sites produce evidence for radiocarbon or dendrochronological (tree-ring) dating. How much the archaeological evidence can tell us about invasion is also dubious. Those momentous events in early history, the two campaigns of Caesar or, later, the Norman Conquest, have left virtually no traces in the archaeological record, and it is possible that archaeologists have detected too few rather than too many invasions.

ECONOMY AND SOCIETY

Most Iron Age inhabitants of Britain and Ireland were farmers, as on the European mainland. Arable and pastoral areas were expanded and new, winter-sown strains of barley and wheat introduced. Cattle, sheep, pig, horse and dog bones are found on most settlement sites; few signs of fish, poultry or game animals have been recovered.

Evidence for the introduction of ironworking dates at latest to the seventh century BC; it was mostly smelted in small bowl furnaces with the aid of simple bellows. Bronze was used, however, for ornaments and horse-harness and for shield covers and sword scabbards at a time when the continental armourers, from the third century BC, were using iron. Native gold and silver were also mined and worked. Pottery was handmade until the first century BC, when the potter's wheel was introduced, and some regional specialization is probable. Woodworking and textile production have left us the evidence of the tools used, but little trace of their finished products. Glass and enamel production is evident, and reached a degree of considerable skill and sophistication from the first century BC.

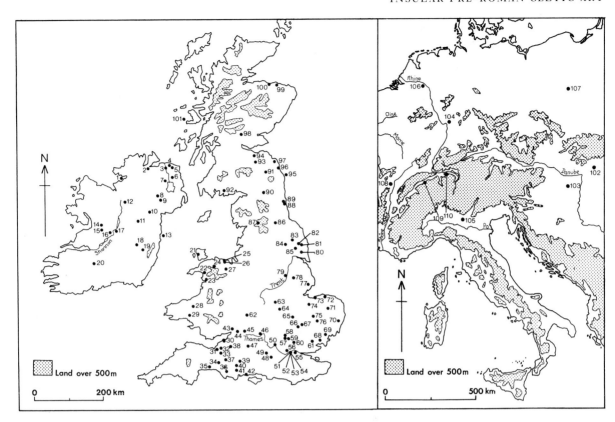

320 *Map of principal sites referred to in Chapter 6.*

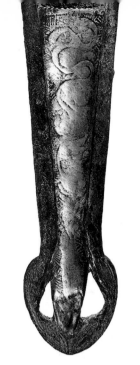

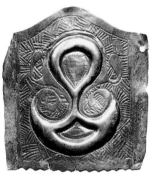

321,322 *Bronze scabbard-mounts from the River Thames at Standlake, Oxfordshire, England. W. of lower mount 5 cm. ?c. 300 BC.*

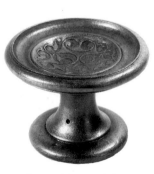

323 *Bronze 'horn-cap' from the Thames at Brentford, England. H. 6.2 cm. ?2nd/1st c. BC.*

Religion in Britain appears to have been similar to that of Gaul. Continental veneration for springs seems to have been extended to rivers and lakes as well. Deposits such as that in the former lake at Llyn Cerrig were in use over a considerable period of time, with people throwing in votive offerings as requests or thanks – as is still done for example at sites of Christian pilgrimage. It is close to the Druidic centre of Mona on Anglesey, where the victorious Romans, as described by Tacitus, hacked down groves devoted to savage rites and drenched with blood of prisoners. Other sacred sites may have been in woodland groves. It is not until the fourth century AD, during the Roman occupation, that we find definite structures in Britain associated with worship, in the form of Romano-Celtic temples on previous Iron Age sites such as that dedicated to the god Nodens at Lydney Park on the banks of the Severn in Gloucestershire. There are other reoccupied sites from this period, such as Maiden Castle or the site of Heathrow Airport.

Druids were as important in the British Isles as in Gaul, and Caesar records: 'It is thought that the doctrine of the Druids was invented in Britain and was brought from there into Gaul; even today those who want to study the doctrine in greater detail usually go to Britain to learn there.' Determined Roman attempts to stamp out the Druids and Celtic religion in Gaul in the latter half of the first century BC, and in Britain after the Roman Conquest may have been due in part to fear of the use of that religion as a rallying point against the Romans.

If one cannot be certain of the accuracy of contemporary or near-contemporary classical sources on the subject of Celtic religion, the insular vernacular writings, though clearly based on older oral traditions, are much overlain with Christian interpolations and interpretations. Certainly for the Roman period and that part of Britain which was under military rule one may identify certain deities – bull- or ram-horned war gods, and goddesses associated with water. Elsewhere we find references to smith-gods and to the great Taranis himself, the god who was equated in Gaul with Jupiter and whose symbol was the wheel. Rarely, however, can one do more than begin to identify individual representations in stone or metal.

THE SWORD-BEARERS AND THE EARLIEST CELTIC ART IN BRITAIN AND IRELAND

No imported or native Celtic art of the chieftainly Early Style is known from the British Isles. Of the succeeding, later fourth-century and third-century classic Waldalgesheim or Vegetal Style is the hanging bowl (more probably lid fragments) from Cerrig-y-Drudion with its strong resemblance to Breton material but its non-Breton hatching. Other pieces, sometimes regarded as Vegetal Style imports, are the bronze armring from a possible chariot burial at Newnham Croft in Cambridgeshire or the so-called Brentford so-called horn cap. These were more probably made rather later in England itself: the near-symmetry of the Brentford piece, for example, is not very characteristic of the Vegetal Style on the European mainland. The bronze scabbard collected in the last century by 'Philosopher' Smith of Wisbech in Cambridgeshire shows a stack of poorly incised lyre-palmettes in the Vegetal Style and may well be one of the earliest examples of British-made Celtic art. These pieces, like the indubitably imported Clonmacnois torc from Co. Offaly in Ireland, are so dubious in date, so scattered and isolated, that they cannot be used as proof of a native Vegetal Style in the British Isles contemporary with that of the European mainland.

Closest in form to continental Vegetal Style are the two bronze scabbard plates, probably from a leather scabbard, found in the upper Thames at Standlake. The lower plate shows a flowing vegetal tendril design set against basketry hatching. The chape is a ring type of Early La Tène date, but shows signs of remodelling in antiquity and the iron cross bridge holding the chape to the leather scabbard is modelled on those of scabbards of the Swiss Sword Style of the late third century BC. The better preserved upper plate shows a repoussé palmette enclosing a pelta, with tendrils depending from it; this design has similarities to that engraved on the Swiss sword from Basadingen, and on some swords from La Tène. It too has a hatched basketry background. The worn condition of the lower plate and the remodelling of the chape make it possible that the lower plate, at least, is earlier than late third-century, possibly around 300 BC. Continental influence is clear and the inclusion of elements of Vegetal Style on a sword of such a date echoes the evolution of continental developed sword sub-styles as seen in chapter 4.

A recent find from Chertsey is an iron sword with similar asymmetric bronze mounts and open ring chape to those on Standlake. Here the decoration on the plates is in higher relief, more 'plastic' and closer in fact to the tendril-based decoration of the shield mounts shortly to be discussed. Chertsey, then, tends to confirm the insular origin of the Standlake mounts.

Definite imports of the Celtic age of expansion do occur in Britain, as on the two iron scabbards with Type I and Type II dragon pairs of around 300 BC found in the Thames at Hammersmith and Battersea. A descendant of these occurs on an iron scabbard from Fovant in Wiltshire, British in execution to judge from its hatching, and reverting in form towards the lyre shape from which the continental dragons may well have originally grown.

Other Sword Style elements can also be seen on British swords. 'Laddering', which is a feature of the Swiss swordsmiths' workshops, can be seen on a bronze scabbard from Sutton-on-Trent in Nottinghamshire, and on sword blades from Little Wittenham and the River Lea at Walthamstow. This last one, however, is the only possible import; the others must have been locally made.

It is noticeable how much of the earliest Celtic art in the British Isles is to be found on weapons and horse-accessories, and how many of these pieces were found in circumstances which suggest ritual deposit. It is not found on

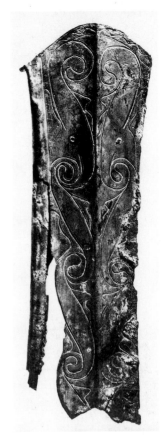

324 *Bronze scabbard from Wisbech, Cambridgeshire, England. W. c. 4 cm. 3rd c. BC.*

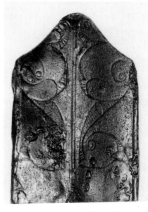

325 *Iron scabbard from Fovant, Wiltshire, England. W. 4.5 cm. 2nd c. BC.*

metal objects for domestic use or on objects of personal adornment. The earliest surviving Celtic art is a high-status warrior art, a noble technology which is at odds with the otherwise unspectacular evidence for everyday life in the British Iron Age. The patchy and unsatisfactory picture of its earliest emergence in the British Isles reflects the still fragmentary state of our knowledge.

Weapons and horse-trappings again predominate in the material which offers us the first picture of the emergence of recognizable, and perhaps regional, schools of Celtic art in the British Isles. Basically, these are a group of eight sword scabbards from Northern Ireland, the pony cap found at Torrs in Scotland, the group of swords and shield bosses found in the Rivers Witham and Thames, material from Wetwang Slack in Yorkshire and at least one piece from Llyn Cerrig Bach in Wales.

These show various elements which link them closely to both Swiss and Middle Danubian Sword Styles, including the use of birds' heads as on swords such as Drňa, Cernon-sur-Coole and Basadingen, hatched comma-leaves ending in hair-spring spirals as on some continental swords; the diagonal layout of the Witham scabbard recalls that of the developed Hungarian Sword Style. Some features are, however, distinctive. These include the all-over designs on the Irish scabbards, the use of compasses on some of the Irish scabbards, the frequent assured combination of repoussé work with engraving on the British material, and the cross-hatching which was often used. All, save the Arras culture material from Wetwang Slack, come from in or near water, suggesting ritual deposition, and offering little help for precise dating.

Eight Northern Irish bronze scabbards are known from in or near the River Bann, all closely related stylistically, even if perhaps produced over a period of time with varying degrees of skill. For example, despite sophisticated use of compasses and engraving tools, in at least one case the graver has slipped. Six have engraved decoration covering the whole length of the scabbard plates, based on tendril motifs or running S-curves and in two cases on large comma-shapes stacked on top of each other. Hair-spring spirals are noticeable on five, much tighter than those on Wisbech, for example, as is the hatching used as infill, though in only one case is there basketry cross-hatching. Triangles or scallops edging the design on four scabbards recall the edging on the Wisbech and Standlake scabbards. Birds' heads can be distinguished in the curvilinear design at the top left of one of the scabbards, with a hair-spring spiral as an eye, and pseudo-birds' heads can be discerned on at least one other. The hatched areas on one of the River Bann scabbards can also be closely matched on the iron scabbard from Fovant.

Recent excavations at the Arras culture site of Wetwang Slack in Yorkshire have produced decorated scabbards similar in design to those of Northern Ireland as well as a bronze container with chain attachment. This strengthens the case for a connection between Northern Ireland and Yorkshire, and suggests that even if the Irish scabbards were not imports from there, there were considerable connections with Britain which were

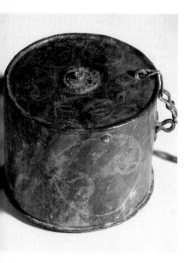

326 Bronze canister with chain from Wetwang Slack, N. Humberside, England. D. 9 cm. 2nd c. BC.

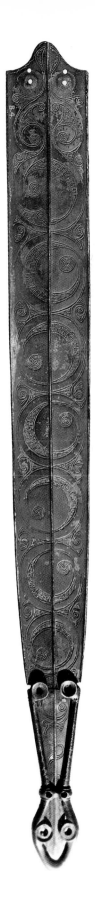

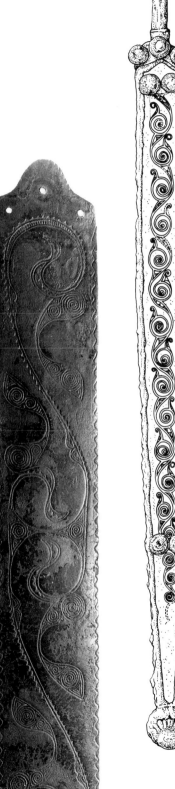

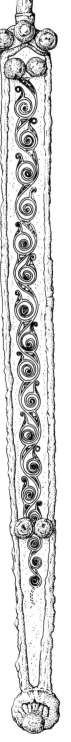

327,328 *Bronze scabbard plates from Lisnacrogher, Co. Antrim, N. Ireland. (Far left) no.3. L. c. 42.8 cm. (Centre) no.1. W. 4.2 cm. ?2nd c. BC.*

329 *(Left) Iron sword and scabbard from Wetwang Slack, N. Humberside, England. L. 73 cm. 2nd c. BC.*

330 *(Below) Bronze scabbard-plate no.2 from Lisnacrogher, Co. Antrim, N. Ireland. W. 4.1 cm. ?2nd c. BC.*

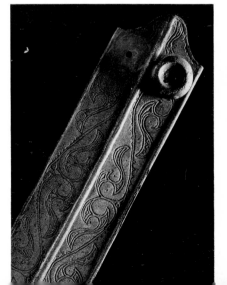

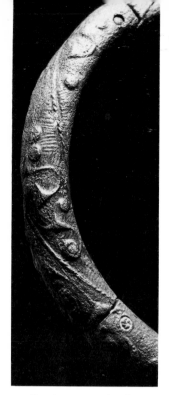

331 *Cast bronze armring from Newnham Croft, Cambridgeshire, England. W. 8 cm. ?2nd/1st c. BC.*

332 *?Gilt bronze scabbard-mount from the River Witham, near Lincoln, England. L. 13 cm. ?2nd/1st c. BC.*

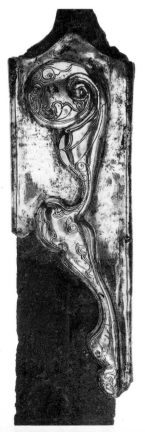

much closer than those which can be demonstrated between Ireland and the continental Sword Styles.

Closely associated in form and design with the Irish scabbards is the Torrs 'chamfrain' or pony cap. This unique piece of horse-trapping was found in a Scottish peat bog and came into the hands of James Train, an excise man acting also as agent for the collection of antiquities by Sir Walter Scott, who purchased it in 1829. The piece has clearly been modified several times in the distant as well as the more recent past. The cap itself is made of two sheets of bronze riveted together; the two openings low on the sides (possibly for a pony's ears) are original, but those to which the horns are now attached are not. The main design on the cap is repoussé, balanced symmetrically round the centre line. It shows an open looped pelta which ends in trumpet spirals forming pseudo-birds' heads. The horns are made of sheet bronze tapering in thickness as well as shape. Repair strips are visible on horns and cap. Each horn originally ended in a cast bird's head, echoing the design on the cap itself and reminiscent of the design on the Newnham Croft armlet. Birds' heads and a tiny but explicit human face are also visible within the asymmetric plant-derived design on the horns, the outer lines of which were executed by the rocked tracer technique.

Various places of manufacture in Scotland, England and Ireland have been suggested. The engraved decoration on the horns with its hatching and its tight spirals is remarkably close to that on the Wetwang Slack container and the Northern Irish scabbards. A compromise view is that the cap, and less certainly the horns, were made somewhere in central eastern England, though the design on the horns especially has a considerable ancestry on the continent.

While the horns' closest stylistic affinities are with the Wetwang Slack material and the Irish scabbards, those of the cap are with other material. Its looped repoussé pelta is like that on the upper Standlake scabbard plate. The tendrils and trumpet coils on the Newnham Croft armlet and the bell from the mouth of a horn found at Loughnashade in Northern Ireland are also basically similar, though more finely drawn. The armlet was found with a coral-inlaid brooch, a British version of continental La Tène C forms; hatching again appears as part of the background. The Loughnashade horn was found in 1794 in a peat bog together with three others; like the horns of the Torrs cap they were made by hammering sheet bronze into a tubular shape and covering the joins with riveted bronze strips. The symmetrical repoussé design on the horn bell with its pseudo-birds' heads again echoes that of the Torrs cap though in spindlier form. The horn is generally taken as an early piece from Ireland, but it is possible that it was in fact an import from Britain.

A bronze scabbard plate found in 1926 in the River Witham combines, like Torrs, asymmetrical repoussé work with engraved decoration of partial lyre-palmettes. Such asymmetric plates are rare in Britain, and reminiscent of the Danubian swordsmiths. It is possible to read the repoussé form as a bird, with the head at the lowest point, leading into the body, and perhaps a ribbed leg or wing attached.

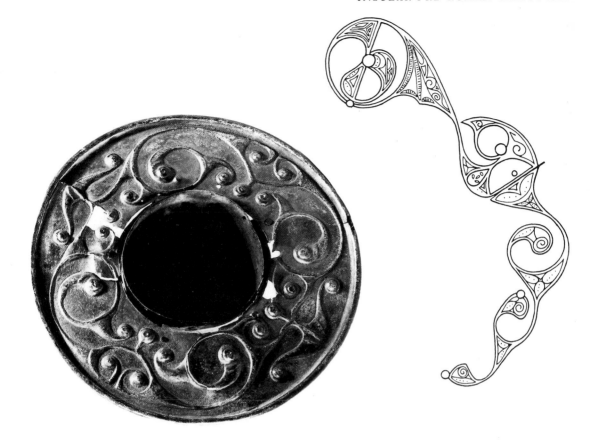

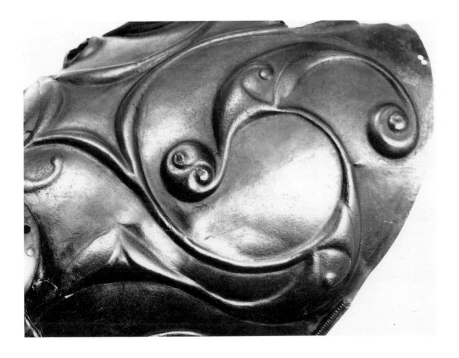

333 (Above left) Bronze mount from the mouth of a horn from Loughnashade, Co. Antrim, N. Ireland. D. 20.3 cm. ? 2nd/1st c. BC.

334,335 Drawing of the decoration on one of the horns (above) and detail of sheet bronze pony cap (left) from Torrs Farm, Kelton, Dumfries and Galloway, Scotland. L. (of horn) 25 cm. L. (of bird's head spiral) 3 cm. ?2nd c. BC.

The combination of repoussé relief work with line engraving of birds is also to be found on one of two shield bosses from the River Thames at Wandsworth. Here the circular plate displays two birds in flight with outstretched wings and long tail-feathers executed in repoussé around the circumference. On the wing of each repoussé bird is engraved another bird, while additional crested birds' heads appear in the engraved decoration of the central boss.

A more elongated shield boss was found with the first one in the Thames at Wandsworth. It is beaten out in high relief repoussé from a single sheet of bronze. The oval central portion once more displays a pair of birds, this time the heads only springing from triangles, from which also emerge lobed leaves with hair-spring spirals clearly visible in the original 1863 publication. The surviving extremity of the mid-rib bears a glum, if toothy, human face with a tiny spiral engraved on its nose.

The River Witham also produced, in 1826, the bronze facing for a shield probably originally made of wood or leather. This shows signs of very considerable remodelling in antiquity. The outline of an emaciated boar, which had originally been riveted on separately and was later removed, can still be seen. The clearest representation of the boar figure now available is in Orlando Jewitt's illustration for the *Horae Ferales* of 1863, which makes it obvious that any connection with continental material, such as the possible north Italian shield now in Stuttgart, is tenuous in the extreme. The Witham shield was subsequently cut down and the central, coral-inlaid, high domed boss added to make room for a handgrip at the rear. Artistically, too, the shield is something of a ragbag of styles and motifs found elsewhere. The circles of each end roundel finish in birds' heads yet again, and pseudo-birds' heads are incised inside. The engraved decoration within the end circles shows hair-spring spirals and split palmettes which recall both the Witham scabbard and the decoration of the Irish scabbards, though transferred on to a circular rather than a longitudinal shape. A horse's head, formed from a lyre-palmette, supports the end roundels, its repoussé shape emphasized by engraved palmettes and recalling continental parallels. The edging ornament around the central boss and rib is similar to that on the edge of the Torrs cap. The wing-like fill-ins on the horse's ears, repeated on the central boss, are found both on much earlier gold torcs from Waldalgesheim and on later ones from Snettisham, and are thus a motif of no particular chronological significance. The shield has such widespread British affinities that its continental connections must be echoes, rather than close relatives.

A puzzle piece is another animal-headed trumpet or carnyx recently identified from sheet bronze fragments and decorated with low relief repoussé birds' heads. This was found in 1914 in a disturbed grave at Castiglione delle Stiviere near Mantua in Lombardy. Like Wandsworth the bird's head is executed in low relief and one could just as well suggest that this was a British export, as claim, as has been done on the strength of this piece, that Italy south of the Alps was the immediate source of inspiration for the Torrs-Witham group!

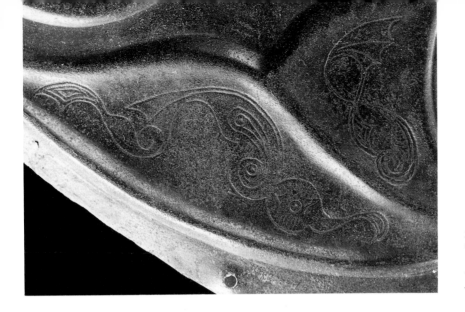

336 *Detail of bronze shield-boss no. 1 from the River Thames at Wandsworth, Middlesex, England, see ill. 1. D. (of boss) 33 cm. ?2nd/1st c. BC.*

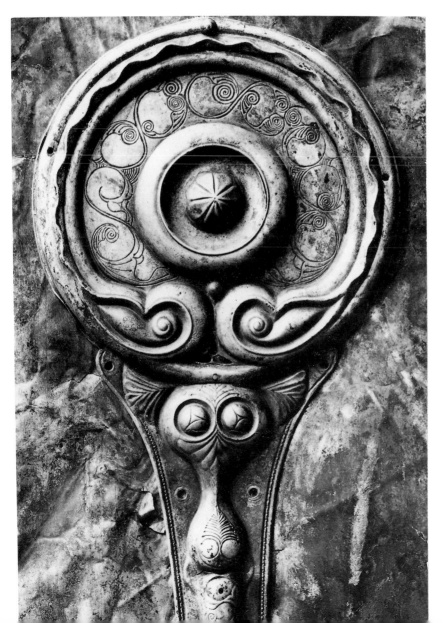

337 *One of the two end-roundels of a bronze shield cover from the River Witham near Washingborough, Lincolnshire, England. D. (of roundel) 14 cm. ?2nd c. BC.*

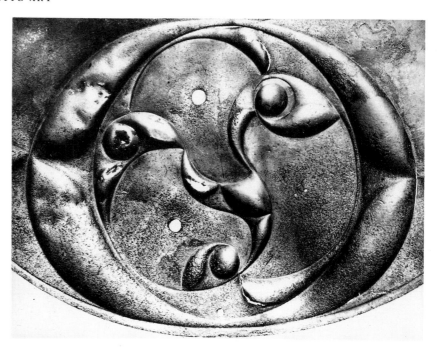

The Battersea shield, which has been assembled and disassembled several times, may also be included here, despite continuing debate about its date and its stylistic affinities. As with Witham, it is the bronze cover of a shield made of leather or wood. Its total symmetry around both vertical and horizontal axes, its 'waisted' shape, the form of the outer roundels and the particular use of glass inlay have led a number of observers to suggest a date during the Roman occupation of Britain. The high relief repoussé work has few close continental parallels, but the layout is similar to that of the Wandsworth round shield boss. The three-roundel form is shared with the Witham shield and presumably with the long boss from Wandsworth before it was broken. Like Witham and Wandsworth there are heads between centre and outer roundels. The malevolent Battersea heads are reversible faces: one way with a crown, the other flowing moustaches.

The final piece in this survey of the earliest insular Celtic art comes from Llyn Cerrig Bach, Anglesey. It is a bronze repoussé disc which may have decorated a chariot at the point where the pole meets the chariot. It was found in 1942–3, during the construction of an aerodrome, with some 150 other objects in what seems to have been a ritual deposit over a long period of time, in the bed of what, at the time of deposition, was a lake. The other objects appear to range in date from the second century BC to the first century AD and to have originated in Ireland, southwest and southeast England as well as Wales. The latest date of deposition could coincide with the attack in AD 60–1 by Suetonius Paulinus on the Druid-controlled stronghold of Mona, ancient Anglesey.

The plaque is a culmination of the Early La Tène art style of the British Isles. On it the ubiquitous birds' heads have become comma-leafed or

339 *(Opposite) Bronze shield with glass or enamel inlay from the River Thames at Battersea, Middlesex, England. L. 77.5 cm. ?2nd/1st c. BC.*

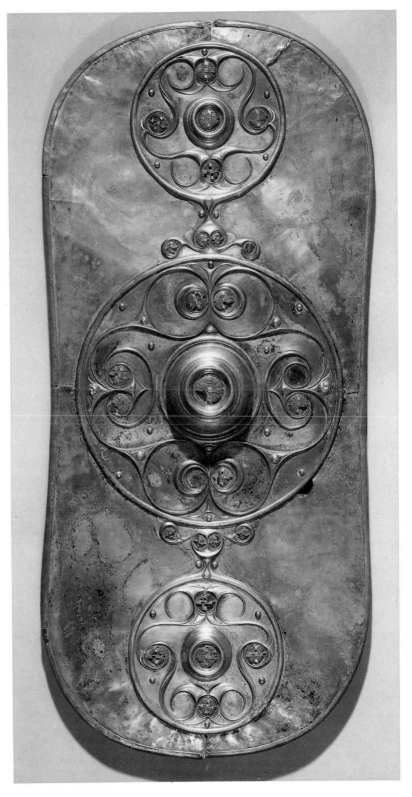

lobed elements. Two birds' heads share a crest; together with a third comma they form a triskel, an old motif in the Celtic repertoire, but one of enormous importance in later insular art, for Llyn Cerrig Bach is a key piece for the later mainstream of British art as well as a summary of the preceding phase. It uses compass-drawn designs, although it is not symmetrical. Furthermore, it makes use of voids in the design – here peltas or curved-sided triangles – which is a feature of great significance in the mirrors from southern England examined below.

In this early period there are at least two major concentrations of art, one centred on Northern Ireland, and the other somewhere in eastern England. But there are obvious, strong, connections stylistically between these two areas and they clearly shared major technical and iconographical traits which certainly suggest at the very least a common origin and continuing contacts between Britain and Ireland.

BRITISH SOCIETY
AND ROMAN EXPANSION

The continuing expansion of the Roman Empire caused major changes for British society well before the Claudian conquest in AD 43. In the first century BC the area round the Isle of Wight became one focus for the renewed and widespread trade with the continent which was the result of changes in trade routes now largely controlled by the Romans. The port of Hengistbury Head received wine amphorae, central Italian pottery and metal goods which came overland to the Bordeaux region and thence by sea to Britain, a route attested to by the historian Strabo. As the Romans moved into Germany to establish their frontier on the Rhine at the end of the first century BC, a further trade developed with southeastern England, probably along a route via the Rhône, Saône and Rhine to the Thames. This is evidenced archaeologically by the presence in graves and elsewhere of amphorae and of Gallo-Belgic pottery from northeastern Gaul. Around the same time cremation cemeteries appear in southeast England as does wheel-turned Celtic pottery; as we have seen, however, none of these can definitely be dated before about 55 BC. This southeastern area is that generally identified as the region of the Belgic settlement in Britain of which Caesar writes, though Barry Cunliffe has recently suggested the Belgic area could be in Wessex, in the hinterland of Hengistbury Head.

Two separate types of society in southern Britain have been postulated, both based on agriculture. In the western region were communities whose outside wealth was won by exchange and which were not primarily warlike nor highly stratified, though they had a military nobility and military capacity. Further east in the 'Belgic' area of England and in Belgic Gaul were warrior societies which gained external wealth through conquest and plunder (including trade in slaves) or by hiring themselves out as mercenaries.

Such warrior areas were apparently better able to mobilize on a large scale against invasion and this distinction could explain why Caesar and, later, Claudius faced mass opposition (four thousand chariots according to the former) in the areas of Kent and East Anglia, where military opposition collapsed after major decisive battles. Further west it appears that Vespasian's legions in AD 43 met opposition at each successive hillfort which they reduced inexorably one after another.

In prehistoric times, as later, the bulk of Britain's wealth and population was situated south of the Severn-Wash line. In Wales, Scotland, northern England and Ireland were other distinctive regional communities; in the period before the Roman arrival, however, much of the most spectacular art comes from southern England – with distinctions visible between eastern and western areas – and from Ireland.

COINS

The use of iron currency bars and of stone weights in Britain before coins appear in the first century BC suggests that the British were used to the idea of fixed units of value. More than 13,000 coins are recorded from Iron Age Britain but only about half of them now survive. Of these only some 1100 came from excavations as opposed to buried hoards, mostly from Camulodunum (Colchester), Braughing and Harlow.

The discovery within southeast England of Gallo-Belgic coins has also been used to support the idea of insular warrior societies being paid to provide aid to the Gauls in their last major battles against Caesar between 58 and 51 BC. It was indeed such support which Caesar himself cites as a major reason for his invasions in 55 and 54 BC.

Two main types of continental Celtic coins are found in Britain. There is a scattering of Armorican coins found at Hengistbury Head and in its hinterland, supporting the other evidence for trade; half of them come from Hengistbury Head itself. Here, however, the insular Celtic coinage did not develop from the Armorican coins, but from the Gallo-Belgic coins found further east, and there is no evidence that coins were used as part of normal exchange patterns.

The so-called 'Gallo-Belgic B' coins were, as we have seen, most probably payment to mercenaries. Although it is now thought by some that they were circulating only just before Caesar's invasion, like all the imported Gallo-Belgic coins, they were concentrated in the Thames valley, in northern Kent and in East Anglia; typical are Gallo-Belgic imitations of a gold stater of the Ambiani, which could indicate settlement around 75 BC.

As well as locally struck and imported gold coins, smaller potin coins were in use in the southeast; they were cast rather than die-stamped out of a bronze with a high proportion of tin. They have often been found in settlements and oppida such as Colchester rather than in hoards and burials, which suggests that they may have functioned more like modern money as a means of exchange. Unlike other coinage, however, the potin coins show little standardization of size, weight or of the metal alloy used.

340 (Right) Soldier and the inscription TASCIIOVANTIS on the reverse of a bronze coin of Cunobelin from southeast England. D. 1.7 cm. Wt 2.21 g. Early 1st c. AD.

341 (Centre) Obverse of gold coin of the Ambiani (Gallo-Belgic AB1) showing wreathed head. D. 2.6 cm. Wt 7.45 g.

342 (Below right) Obverse of gold coin of Tasciovanus from north of the Thames showing 'Apollo wreath'. D. 1.7 cm. Wt 5.45 g.

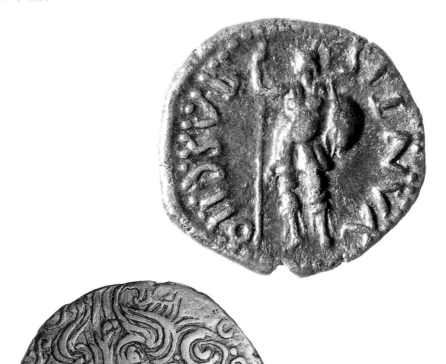

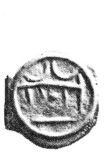

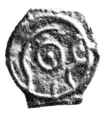

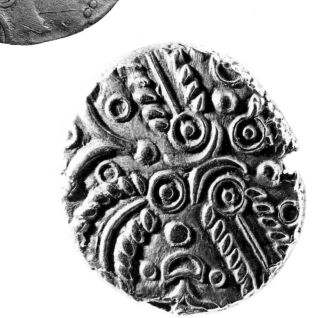

343 Tin-rich bronze coin from lower Thames Valley, England, with head of Apollo on one side and charging bull derived from the bull of Massalia on the other. D. 1.7 cm. Wt 1.52 g. 1st c. BC/1st c. AD.

They were cast in rows and copy Gaulish imitations of the bull on the reverse of the bronze coins of Massalia.

The earliest development of British gold coins imitated Gallo-Belgic coins in typology, weight and fineness. Coins were soon widely minted, from the late first century BC, throughout southern and central Britain, in an area which overlaps but is more extensive than that of the known circulation of imported Gallo-Belgic coins: different groups such as the Iceni in Norfolk or the Coritani round Leicester seem to have produced coins which circulated exclusively within their own territory.

Since locally minted coins frequently bore inscriptions they have been used to trace the emergence of royal dynasties, as can be seen in the gold coins of the Catuvellauni, centred north of the Thames in the area of rich, Welwyn-type, burials. Coins of Tasciovanus are followed by those of his son Cunobelin (Shakespeare's Cymbeline); both refer to themselves as kings on their Latin-inscribed coins. The name TASCIIOVANTIS can be seen on late coins of Cunobelin, a Celtic misreading of the Latin Tasciovani(i) (F) (son of Tasciovanus); the standing soldier is also a Roman from head to toe save for his Celtic trousers. The reverse bears the inscription CUNOB and shows a naked horseman with a throwing spear and a Celtic shield.

In artistic terms early British coins, like continental ones, show classical lineage: the potin coins derive from Massalia (Marseilles) and show the highly stylized head of Apollo on one side and a bull on the other. The 'ears of barley' from an early, uninscribed coin of Cunobelin struck at Colchester is an adaptation for corn-rich Britain of the Apollo-wreath on fourth-century Hellenistic prototypes. Other coins show the characteristic tendency to disarticulate representational designs into their component parts, leaving them near-abstract, as with the horse and rider on the coins of the Coritani or the early coins of Tasciovanus.

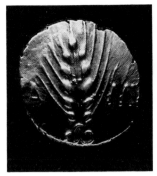

344 *Obverse of 'ear of barley' gold coin of Cunobelin, king of the Catuvellauni, based on the wreathed head of Apollo from the mint at Colchester, Essex, England. D. 1.7 cm. Wt 5.42 g. Early 1st c. AD.*

METALWORKING

The study of coinage raises many questions as to the nature of Celtic metalworking and trade. In this first-century BC period we have rare evidence of a bronzesmith at work. It comes from pit 209 at Gussage All Saints in Dorset, and consists of moulds for *cire perdue*, or lost wax casting, for what has been calculated as fifty matched sets of chariot- and horse-fittings. Such a concentration is eloquent evidence for the degree of military preparation, the number of horses kept and the land required to feed them, and the forces which Celts could put in the field. The four thousand chariots mentioned by Caesar become a real possibility. Gussage does not, however, solve the vexed problem of whether metalworkers were based in fixed workshops or were itinerant, if highly skilled, 'tinkers'.

Gussage also provides a warning to the archaeologist of the dangers of typological and stylistic analysis. It was earlier generally assumed that relative chronology for horse- and chariot-fittings could be deduced from the types of decoration used. Three out of the five types considered chronologically distinct were found among the moulds at Gussage, apparently deposited over a short period late in the site's occupation, in the first century BC.

THE FLOWERING OF INSULAR CELTIC ART

While Celtic art on the European mainland faltered in the first century BC, that of Celtic Britain and Ireland entered a period of remarkable flowering – developing and rediscovering elements of earlier Celtic styles. Compass design, largely abandoned in the fourth century on the continent, was widely used in both Britain and Ireland. In England and Wales extensive use was made of basketry cross-hatching on bronze mirrors, scabbards and gold torcs; in the southeast and in East Anglia enamelling was more widely and inventively used. Birds' heads continued in Ireland, though they became a rare motif in Britain, and the Celtic zoo in England has strong echoes of the three-dimensional Plastic Style of the Celtic age of expansion. All in all the continuity of insular art from the earlier metalwork of Torrs, Witham and the River Bann is more apparent in Ireland than in Britain.

The importance of compasses in the layout of Irish art can be seen in the Lough Crew, Co. Meath, 'trial pieces'. Over a period of some eighty years from 1863, a large number of bone flakes was recovered from the Iron Age squatters' occupation of a Neolithic passage-grave cemetery, together with beads of glass, bone and amber, bone combs and pins, bronze and iron rings, and 'an iron object described as the leg of a compass': this last, however, is of dubious antiquity. A small fraction of the 500–600 bone flakes bears decoration, mostly of compass-drawn motifs, though other techniques such as stippling, hatching and cross-hatching are also present. These bone flakes have been interpreted as trial pieces for a bronzesmith, but no sign of bronzeworking was found. There are parallels to the designs on a wide variety of Irish material in gold, bone, bronze and stone; for example the bronze 'spoons' whose suggested uses range 'from castanets to christenings' and for which that old archaeological let-out description 'ritual object' may be appropriate, a quernstone from Clonmacnois, Co. Offaly and the bone 'gaming pieces' from Cush, Co. Limerick and Mentrim Lough, Co. Meath. Parallels further afield in Scotland, Yorkshire, and south Wales can be found, while the pottery and woodwork of

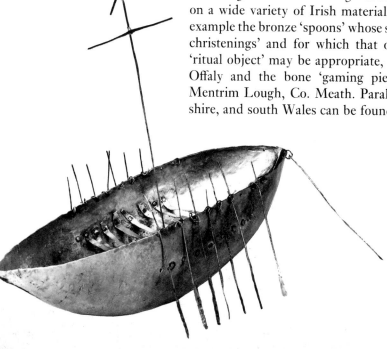

345 (Opposite below) Gold model boat from Broighter, Limavady, Co. Londonderry, N. Ireland. H. 5 cm. LT D, late 1st c. BC.

346 (Below) Detail of the gold neckring from Broighter, Limavady, Co. Londonderry N. Ireland. D. (of tubes) 3 cm. LT D, late 1st c. BC.

347 (Right) Bone 'trial' pieces from Lough Crew, Co. Meath, Ireland, Cairn 'H'. L. (of largest) 14 cm. ?Late 1st c. BC/1st c. AD.

348 (Below right) Top of one of a pair of bronze 'scoops' from an unknown findspot in Ireland. W. 6.8 cm. ?1st c. AD.

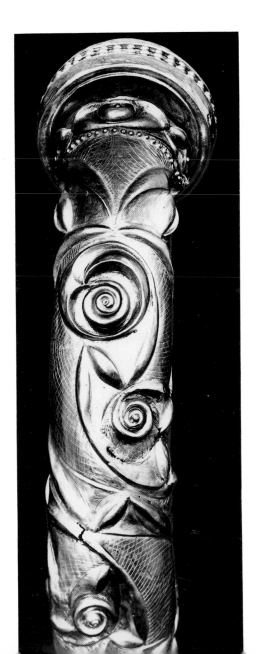

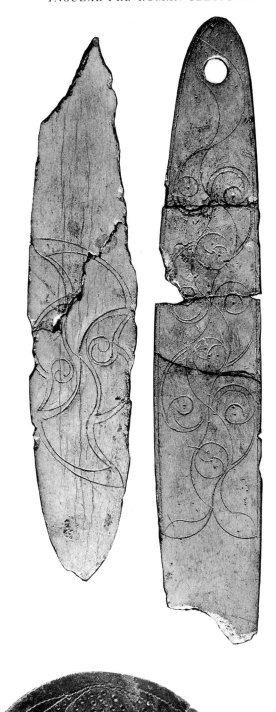

Meare and Glastonbury in Somerset also uses similar motifs, visible too on some of the Irish carved stones.

Five decorated standing stones with abstract Celtic designs, used presumably for religious or ritual purposes, have been found in Ireland: three are illustrated here. That from Turoe, Co. Galway, found in 1902 close to a ringfort, is the best-known and most discussed. Since Brittany contains carved standing stones, which are unknown elsewhere in the British Isles, it was first thought that Turoe might show evidence of the third-century BC presence in Ireland of a Breton stonecarver. The style of decoration on the stone, however, is so unlike that on Breton examples and so closely similar to other, later, Irish and British art, that such a contention now seems unlikely in the extreme. The idea of carved stones may possibly have reached Ireland from Brittany by way of areas such as Somerset. Until Caesar destroyed their fleet in 56 BC, the Veneti of Brittany are known to have traded with southern and southwestern Britain. Like the Derrykeighan stone, Turoe shows motifs near identical to some of those on the Lough Crew flakes, with similar pelta shapes and swirling voids. On the Turoe stone the background was cut away, leaving the main designs standing out in low relief, while the step pattern beneath was incised into the stone. Though the Turoe stone is not four-sided, unlike some Breton stones, the design is divided into four carefully laid-out panels.

The stone from Mullaghmast, Co. Kildare, again has its decoration divided into four distinct panels, with separate designs on each area. One has incised curves, drawn so precisely as to suggest the use of compasses or a template. Another has thick-lobed spirals contained in an oval, with a zig-zag and x-design below on the edging border: this x-design is visible on a Breton stone from Kermaria and both zig-zag and x-design are present on the pots from Meare in Somerset. Two reversed spirals of fat commas appear within a further panel and the fourth is composed of trumpet

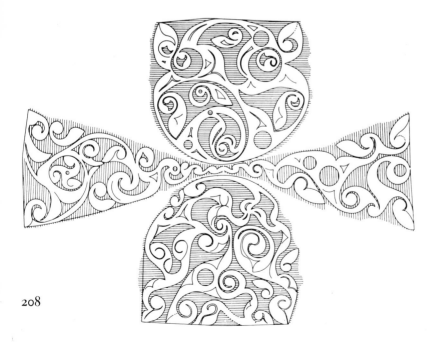

349,350 *Drawing of the decoration (left) and (right above) view from the southwest of the carved granite pillar at Turoe, Co. Galway, Ireland. H. 1.20 m. ?1st c. BC/1st c. AD.*

351 *(Near right) Carved stone from Derrykeighan Old Church, Co. Antrim, N. Ireland. H. (of ornamented section) 34 cm. ?2nd/1st c. BC.*

352 *(Far right) Carved stone from Mullaghmast, Co. Kildare, Ireland. H. 91 cm. 3rd c. BC or 4th/5th c. AD.*

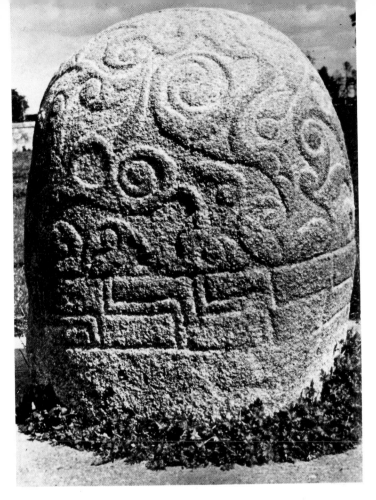

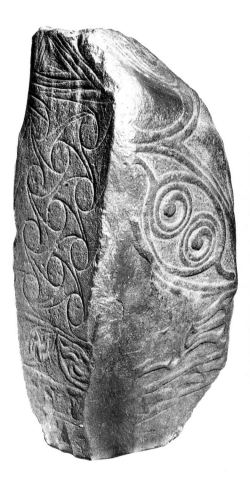

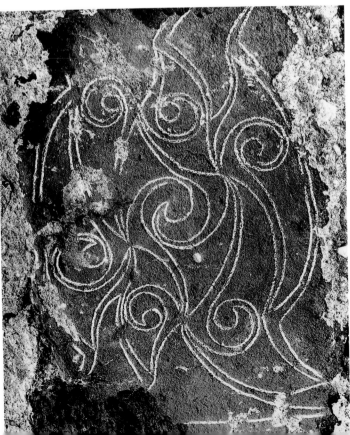

209

curves. All these designs can be found on Irish metalwork, but a firm date is difficult since one can argue either that this stone with its anthology of Celtic designs is very early (third century BC) or very late (fourth or fifth century AD). The other stones are most probably first century BC or AD, roughly contemporary with the Lough Crew flakes: the design on Turoe also has parallels on first-century BC Armorican coins of the Coriosolites, as well as on British mirrors and horse-harness of the first century BC or AD.

The great tubular gold torc from Broighter was first mentioned in Chapter 5 as a possible continental import, locally decorated in Ireland. This was part of a hoard of gold objects found in 1896 near the old shoreline of Lough Foyle, in Co. Derry. As well as the large torc there were two necklaces, a complete and a fragmentary bar torc, a hemispherical bowl and a unique model ship with oars, mast, rowers' benches and yardarm, possibly representing a contemporary skin boat. The relief ornament on the torc is slightly asymmetrical, composed of characteristically Irish slender trumpet curves with lentoid ends and deep snail-shell spirals set against an elegant background of compass-drawn 'engine-turned' matting. The layout is strikingly similar to one of the Lough Crew flakes and there are likenesses also to one facet of the Turoe stone. The engine-turned design is also found on other Irish pieces including a second Lough Crew bone flake.

Broighter has been compared to the gold torcs from Snettisham and Ipswich in East Anglia, but closer examination will show that it has little in common with, for example, the Snettisham or Cairnmuir terminals except for the beaded edging and the fact that both are gold, decorated torcs; even the voids enclosed by the designs differ between the Irish and English examples. Nor are there any real parallels on the continent for the decoration of this, the most beautifully conceived and executed of all torcs from the British Isles. Equally there can be no dispute as to its date of manufacture; it comes from the later first century BC.

HOLDING MIRRORS UP TO ART

Compass layout, together with extensive use of basketry hatching, characterizes the 'Mirror Style' of southern England, found on scabbards and spears as well as on the three dozen known mirrors found from Cornwall to East Anglia.

Mirrors were widespread in the Roman world, though rarely found among Celts on the European mainland or in Ireland. About fifteen of them have been found associated with burials in England, cremations in the Belgic areas of Hertfordshire and Essex, and inhumation elsewhere. Where the sex can be identified, the graves are those of adult females.

With the exception of the earliest iron mirrors from the Arras group of Yorkshire and Humberside barrows, the mirrors are of bronze and are decorated on the back, usually with hatched basketry and often in a three-part design based on a looped lyre shape. The enclosed voids are of importance to the design, as is the changing interplay in the light and shade of smooth and matted areas. The cast handles bear loops ranging from one to four in number, a trait which has been used, not entirely successfully, to try to order the mirrors stylistically and chronologically. When not in use, the mirrors must have been hung upside-down by the handles since only in this position can one see the elusive Cheshire-cat faces on the handles of the Old Warden, Bedfordshire, and the Holcombe, Devon, examples. Celtic mirrors contain much more copper and lead than the bronze of Roman mirrors.

While the mirrors themselves are generally competently made, the standard of design and execution is more variable. This is particularly the case with the southeastern mirrors. On that from Great Chesterford in Essex, the lyre design has slipped sideways and the execution of the irregular oblong hatching is somewhat slapdash. The pattern on that from Old Warden, Bedfordshire, has been described as 'frighteningly mad disintegration'; this is an asymmetrical basketry pattern produced from zig-zag lines grouped in oblong blocks and enclosing curved-sided

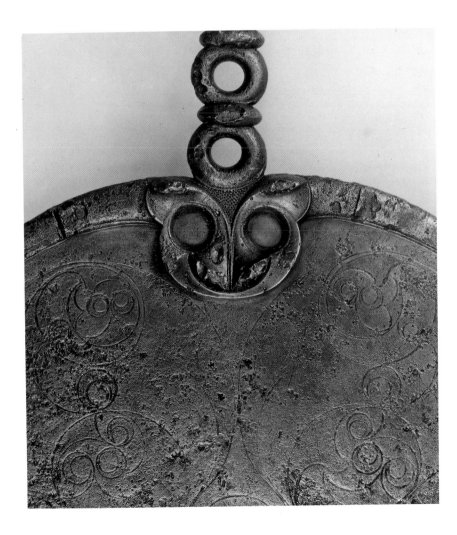

353 *Detail of bronze mirror from Holcombe, Devon, England. H. 37.2 cm. ?Late 1st c. BC/early 1st c. AD.*

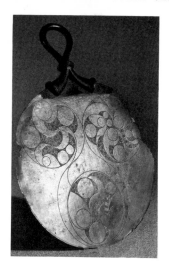

triangles, from which almost all trace of the lyre pattern has vanished. More symmetrical lyre designs appear on the mirrors from Aston, in Hertfordshire and Dorton in Buckinghamshire. Upside-down, the slight, simple design on that from Aston suggests yet again a Cheshire-cat face; it was produced by using a straight-edged engraving tool at an angle as a punch, with the mostly irregular oblong basketry added subsequently. The workmanship indicates a 'craftsman of limited technical ability – and perhaps with unsatisfactory tools – whose chief aim in this piece was to achieve the greatest economy of time consistent with his powers'. The Aston mirror was a surface find made in 1979, perhaps associated with a nearby cremation burial containing two pottery vessels, tentatively dated to early in the first century A D, a date confirmed by the Dorton find. All these four mirrors come from East Anglia or the Chilterns and have similar plate areas and handles.

The craftsmanship on the so-called 'Mayer' mirror, yet another piece

354 *(Above) The 'Mayer' bronze mirror from ?southeast England. H. 22.5 cm. Later 1st c. BC.*

355 *(Right) Bronze mirror from Great Chesterford, Essex, England. H. 23.5 cm. Early 1st c. AD.*

356 *(Below right) Bronze mirror from Aston, Hertfordshire, England. D. 19.4 cm. Late 1st c. BC/early 1st c. AD.*

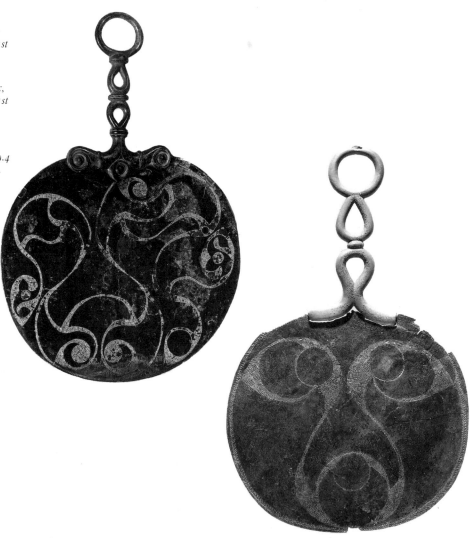

supposed to come from the Thames, is, however, of a much higher standard. There are traces of freehand guidelines under its tripartite lyre pattern, executed with superbly economical skill and with no errors; the oblong basketry is regular; the patterns contained within each roundel are different from each other and asymmetrical internally. While design, shape and plate are similar to those of the four mirrors described above, this is a much more accomplished piece. Basketry and other design elements very like those on the Mayer mirror appear again on the four decorated bronze plates attached to an iron spearhead also found in the River Thames.

Other mirrors have a geographic distribution along the Jurassic ridge, running from southwestern England to Yorkshire. These include some of the most accomplished, such as those from Holcombe in Devon, Birdlip in Gloucestershire, and Desborough in Northamptonshire. These share certain technical and artistic features with those found in a mirror from Nijmegen in the Netherlands, which is clearly British in origin.

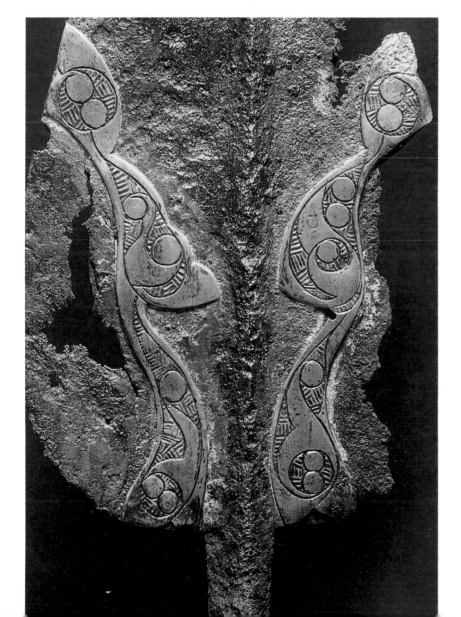

357 *Iron spear with bronze decorated plates from the River Thames, England. L. (of right hand bronze ornament) 9 cm. Later 1st c. BC/early 1st c. AD.*

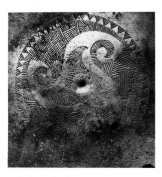

358 *Detail of compass-created decoration on bronze shield-mount no. 1 from Tal-y-Llyn, Gwynedd, Wales. D. (of decorated area) 8.5 cm. ?Early 1st c. BC.*

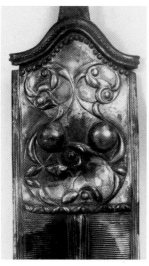

359 *Top of a bronze scabbard from Little Wittenham, Oxfordshire, England. W. 5.3 cm. 2nd/1st c. BC.*

The kidney-shaped Desborough mirror was found in 1908 near a hillfort during digging operations for ironstone. The square basketry of the complex lyre design is carefully executed with three strokes in each direction, unlike the more irregular work on the Mayer or Great Chesterford mirrors which use up to six or seven strokes at a time. The hatched, curved-sided triangle shapes which, linked together, form much of the enclosing design, are echoed in the larger smooth areas enclosed. Similarly enclosed are comma-shapes with eared ends, reflecting the hatched shapes in which the lyre ends at left and right. These contain two tiny motifs of a triangle in a circle, found also on the Birdlip mirror and possibly 'a good luck sign or a craftsman's mark'.

Reversal of shapes between hatched and plain areas is also visible on the closely related and equally accomplished Holcombe mirror found in 1970, apparently buried deliberately in a pit on a late Iron Age settlement. The cat or owl face of the handle appears again within the lyre design. This is similar in basketry, plate size and handle to the Desborough and Birdlip mirrors.

Other objects stylistically related to the mirrors again come from southern England. These include two bronze scabbards from Oxfordshire – one from Little Wittenham, and one from the Thames at Henley. The Little Wittenham scabbard was found in the course of drainage works not far from the hillfort of Wittenham Clumps. It has low relief repoussé work on its upper plate. The lyre-shaped ornament, formed from three roundels linked by lobes, is similar to incised ornament on other scabbards but it also reflects in inverted form the design on the Mayer mirror and the Llyn Cerrig Bach plaque. The chape is British, with three-dimensional treatment similar to the contemporary mirror handles. The most unusual feature of this scabbard is the lateral lines, or 'laddering', rare in Britain, except on the 'Swiss' scabbard from the Trent at Sutton Reach. The lower plate of the Henley sword scabbard shows not only a cut-out version of the Llyn Cerrig Bach triskel but, once again, birds' heads in the decoration, a detail paralleled by two tiny birds' heads on the reverse side at the top of the chape frame.

These scabbards, like Swiss Middle La Tène examples are decorated only at top and bottom, showing some surviving European influence on indubitably British work. By contrast, the iron and bronze scabbard from Bugthorpe in Northamptonshire has all-over decoration, though it is quite different from the all-over designs on the earlier Northern Irish scabbards. Viewed sideways, the great cast chape looks somewhat like a pouting fish-mouth. The irregular basketry recalls that of some of the mirrors, but also resembles that on the gold torcs discussed below.

The art generally assigned to this period often has no precise find-associations and thus no precise dates. Stylistic dating on the basis of decorative features such as cross-hatching or basketry fill-in or of technical features such as the use of compasses has led to considerable controversy. Basketry not unlike that of the Mirror Style appears on the shield disc from Tal-y-Llyn, Gwynedd, where the voids, as in so much of the later insular metalwork, are of enormous importance to the design as a whole. Here, despite the use of engraving rather than repoussé, the triskel design echoes that of Llyn Cerrig Bach. The Tal-y-Llyn disc was part of a hoard of objects found under a boulder some 230 m above sea-level; the date of deposition, if not of manufacture, must be no earlier than the first century AD, since the hoard contains a Roman lock-plate. The disc itself was well-worn and, because of the triskel motif and the cross-hatching, a date in the third century BC has been suggested. Triskels and hatching are, however, long-lasting features of Celtic art; the triskel is often found on other more recent pieces and is repeated on another, repoussé, shield mount from Tal-y-Llyn itself. The engraved disc, moreover, is based on a complex design laid out with compasses, which suggests a date very much later in the pre-Roman Iron Age and more probably contemporary with the mirrors of the first centuries BC and AD.

THE GOLDEN NECKLACES OF BOUDICA

Between 1948 and 1950, in the course of ploughing at Ken Hill, Snettisham, Norfolk, one of the richest treasures of British prehistory was uncovered. The great ring-terminalled torc from Hoard E has been compared to crown jewels of later eras. Dio Cassius, indeed, records that Boudica, queen of the Iceni, who in AD 60–1 led her people into battle in their doomed revolt against the Romans, invariably wore a 'great twisted golden necklace'.

The Snettisham treasure was discovered close to the Wash within the area of the Iceni. Like the later continental gold torc hoards, the Snettisham torc was associated with first-century BC coins of both gold and potin. Also found was a bracelet and a large number of other less ornate torcs of gold alloy, bronze and tin. The fragmentary nature of some of the Snettisham torcs together with the presence of ingots and signs of 'cake' of gold alloy and tin, suggest the stock-in-trade of an itinerant metalsmith, an alternative explanation for the continental finds of torcs associated with coins, and of similar British finds at Weybourne in Norfolk and Netherurd, in the Borders region of Scotland.

When found, the torc from Hoard E was undamaged, but threaded through one of its terminal rings was a second, damaged, buffer-terminalled torc. The 20 cm diameter hoop of the larger torc consists of eight separate strands, each in turn formed from eight twisted wires, soldered into the separately hollow-cast and chased rings. Properly speaking, the material is electrum, not gold, since it contains 38% of silver and 3% of copper: the torc weighs 1085 g.

The decoration on the torc terminals and on the accompanying bracelet is so similar as to suggest the work of the same metalsmith. The highly organized terminal design again shows basketry work, shaped to fit the areas of decoration, together with small raised dots with three or four punched indentations and larger raised concentric circles. There is a raised

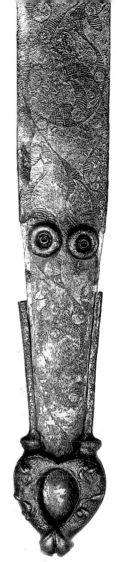

360 *Lower part of a bronze scabbard from Bugthorpe, N. Humberside, England. W. 4.3 cm. 2nd/1st c. BC.*

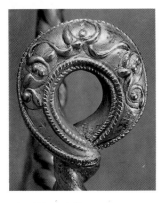

361 (Above) Decoration on one of the terminals of electrum neckring no. 4 from Ipswich, Suffolk, England. Max. D. c. 4 cm. Mid-1st c. BC.

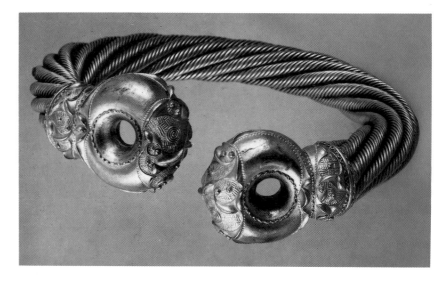

362 (Above right) Electrum neckring from Ken Hill, Snettisham, Norfolk, England, Hoard 'E'. D. 20 cm. Mid-1st c. BC.

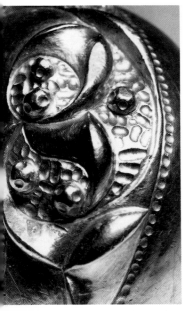

363 Detail of the terminal of a gold neckring from New Cairnmuir, Netherurd, Borders, Scotland. D. 5.5 cm. Mid-1st c. BC.

sinuous edging to the decorated areas, while punched dots provide an edging to defined areas within the design. The spindly raised ridge curves have concave endings, and form slender commas or trumpet coils. These are the key features of the Snettisham torc, and of the 'Snettisham-Ipswich' style in general, so named since similar decorative features can be seen on the loop terminals of two of the six gold torcs found during building operations near Ipswich in 1968. These are thought in some cases to be unfinished and to show a craftsman's style in progress. The terminals, like those on the Snettisham torc, have been cast by the *cire perdue* method. Their decorative layout shows a similar design of trumpet coils and commas, with raised dots, but the chased ornament added after casting to the great torc is missing.

All the details on the Snettisham torc terminals can be matched, however, on the surviving single torc terminal from Shaw Hill, Netherurd – an undoubted stray from the south found with a group of continental 'emergency issue' electrum coins. The Llyn Cerrig voids are present on Netherurd though they are here filled with hatching and thus not so obvious as on the plain Ipswich rings. We have already largely dismissed claims for a relationship between the torcs from Snettisham and Ipswich and those from Broighter, and before one accepts too readily a source for the gold of the eastern torcs as being in Ireland or Wales, one should look again at the upper mount of the Little Wittenham scabbard and the high probability that gold coinage, most probably of continental origin, is likely to have provided much of the raw material in areas distant from local ore bodies. It is also surely significant that another of the Snettisham hoards contained a hollow buffer-terminalled torc of continental Late La Tène type – the type represented of course by Broighter itself. As so frequently noted in these pages one must not underestimate the ability for forms and motifs to be freely exchanged across disparate parts of the Celtic world.

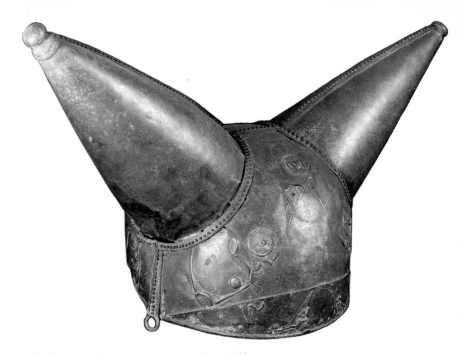

The Snettisham-Ipswich school of decoration can at least be dated by a well-worn coin found actually enclosed inside one of the ring terminals of the Hoard E torc. This is a Gallo-Belgic quarter-stater of type Dc struck during the wars against Caesar. Thus the torc was not made before the coinage had circulated for some time after 58 BC. Comparisons with known historical events and the fact that Gallo-Belgic coins circulated in Britain in Kent and not in the more northerly Icenic territory, have led to claims that the Snettisham objects were deposited in 54 BC by a smith fleeing the second of Caesar's incursions, or that it may be associated with the flight of Addeomarus, king of the Trinovantes in Essex, after his overthrow by the Catuvellauni in 10 BC. Neither of these explanations is wholly convincing. Snettisham is well north of the area Caesar invaded and the need for the burial due to flight would apply within the Kent area rather than in the relative safety of the Wash. Addeomarus came from a region where the Gallo-Belgic coins did not circulate. If the British hoards, like those on the continent, may be considered as votive deposits rather than as panic burials, then a date as late as the first century AD may be possible for the burial of the hoards, if not for their manufacture. Apart from the Scottish example, electrum torcs are known mainly from East Anglia; none comes from the southeastern area where the Gallo-Belgic coins mainly circulated. It seems possible therefore that the rings were actually manufactured in the territory of the Iceni.

Similar decoration to that found on Snettisham-Ipswich torcs, employing long, slender, curved ridges and punched matting, also occurs on other types of objects made of different materials. One is the bronze helmet with enamel inlay found in the Thames at Waterloo Bridge in the last century; the other is the surviving bronze-covered iron horse-bit side-ring of a pair found at Ulceby-on-Humber. The Waterloo helmet is probably a ceremonial rather than a war piece; it is both very small and very thin. Its asymmetrical decoration recalls that of the Snettisham terminals, pulled out to cover a much larger area, and thus less compact and more spindly in appearance: the matting within curved-sided triangle, the tiny raised knobs with punched marks on them recall Snettisham though the cross-ridged backing to the enamel studs is like continental examples. The Ulceby bit-ring has matting-filled curved-sided triangles and shows a double-knob pair, while the 'frilling' of the outer margin again recalls the Snettisham-Ipswich decoration.

These pieces are sufficiently closely connected stylistically to suggest itinerant smiths, or at least related workshops, operating in eastern England north of the Thames, producing goods for local use and for trading as far north as Scotland. The date, in view of Snettisham, must be in the second half of the first century BC, or the first decades AD.

HORSE-HARNESS

Horses and the necessary accoutrements for riding and the use of chariots were of great importance in Celtic society. Something has been said above about the specialization shown in this by the smiths' debris from Gussage All Saints. In the same area as the torcs, there is also evidence of another school of metalwork producing richly decorated enamelled harness mounts, possibly around the middle of the first century AD. The quadrilobe mount or strap-link from Santon, Norfolk (or possibly Santon Downham, Suffolk), dated to around AD 50–60 was found by a labourer in 1897. With it, in a cauldron, were a number of other pieces including a second mount, a two-piece bridle bit, tools and other fittings as well as 'thistle' type brooches common in Gaul between AD 25 and 50.

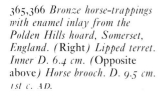

*365,366 Bronze horse-trappings with enamel inlay from the Polden Hills hoard, Somerset, England. (*Right*) Lipped terret. Inner D. 6.4 cm. (*Opposite above*) Horse brooch. D. 9.5 cm. 1st c. AD.*

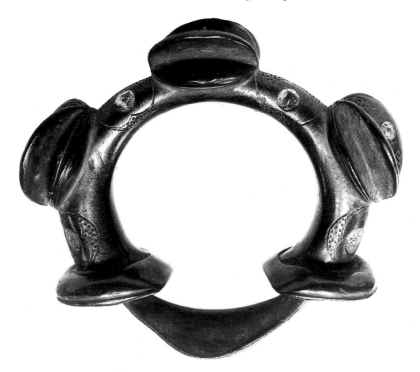

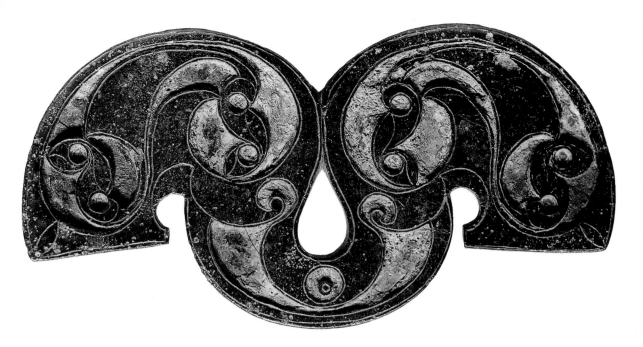

The remaining mounts of this general form come mostly from other findspots in East Anglia, or the London area, though two exports have been found in France and in the Faiyum in north Egypt. One pair was found as part of a hoard in ploughing operations in 1803 in the Polden Hills in Somerset. This large Polden Hills collection of horse-fittings and shield bosses – probably the stock of a scrap merchant – shows some decorative influence from western Britain, including the Llyn Cerrig Bach plate and a group of late southwestern neckrings. Despite the view put forward that such trappings were the result of Roman commissioning of native workmanship, it seems unnecessary to regard this material as anything other than local work made for local use. The enamelling on these pieces – red only in Santon and Polden Hills, but including green, blue and yellow as well in examples from London and from Westhall in Suffolk – is a particularly non-Mediterranean use of colour and one which seems to have been much in vogue in the territory of the Iceni. The swirling tendril designs contrast with pelta-shaped spaces, ending in fat commas; occasionally these can be 'read' as insular descendants of the continental lyre-palmette 'Cheshire-cats'. The Polden example has palmettes on the two side-pieces; edges are bordered with rows of triangles inlaid with coloured glass; the four lobes carry fat S's. Punched background decoration also frequently survives in non-enamelled portions of these quadrilobe harness mounts.

Such punched background is visible too on the bronze scabbard plates of the sword from Isleham, Cambridgeshire, found in 1976 during the harrowing of a field. The upper front plate has opposing comma-eared spirals within semi-circular arcs; the stippled coils form trumpets. The lower front plate shows a freehand drawn tendril design with pseudo-birds' heads and variously shaped stippled peltas.

367 (Below) *Top of the bronze front plate of a scabbard from Isleham, Cambridgeshire, England (with the binding strip at the top of the scabbard removed). W. c. 4.1 cm. ?Early 1st c. AD.*

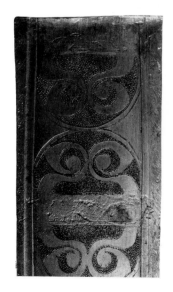

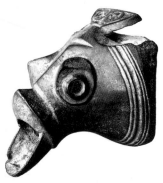

368 *Boar-shaped spout of a bronze bowl with enamel inlay from Łęg Piekarski, Turek, Poland, grave I. L. (of spout) 7.5 cm. Mid-1st c. AD.*

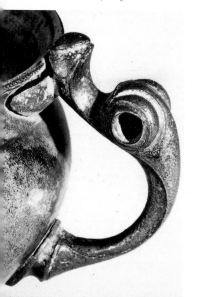

369 *Fish-shaped spout on a bronze bowl from Felmersham-on-Ouse, Bedfordshire, England. L. (of spout) c. 11 cm. 1st c. AD.*

370 *(Below) Duck-shaped handle on a bronze cup from the River Shannon at Keshcarrigan, Co. Leitrim, Ireland. H. 7.2 cm. Late 1st c. BC/early 1st c. AD.*

REPRESENTATIONS OF MEN AND BEASTS

While the art of Iron Age Britain is usually uncompromisingly abstract, with occasional tantalizing, shape-changing, hints of faces and animal forms, there are some less ambiguous representations, particularly from bowls and buckets in Belgic contexts, and bird portrayals continue in Ireland.

So-called Colchester-Keshcarrigan bowls with animal spouts or handles have been found from contexts as widely separated as Keshcarrigan in Ireland and in non-Celtic Poland, as well as in Britain itself. The technique of forming the bowls from sheet metal with the use of a slow turning lathe appears wholly west Celtic. On the Łęg Piekarski bowl from Poland the spout is in the form of a boar with broken crest and enamel inlay; Roman provincial metalwork found with it in the cremation grave date the burial to the late first century or second century AD. The Keshcarrigan bowl was found in the River Shannon; its beautifully modelled shoveller or sheldrake duck's head is a handle rather than a spout. Attempts to claim the Keshcarrigan bowl as of Irish manufacture seem unconvincing and it, like the Polish bowl, must be an import from Britain, though the handle could possibly be Irish-made. Yet another beast from a probable Aylesford-Welwyn grave at Felmersham Bridge on the River Ouse is a spout in the form of a pouting, open-mouthed fish, a creature rarely portrayed by Celts.

Boars, cattle and sheep are among the animals portrayed in Britain as on the European mainland. Three boar figurines came from Hounslow in Middlesex, together with two model dogs and a model wheel. Domestic sheep and cattle were frequently mounts for wooden stave buckets from the first century BC until late Roman times. Knobbed bull's head mounts, with

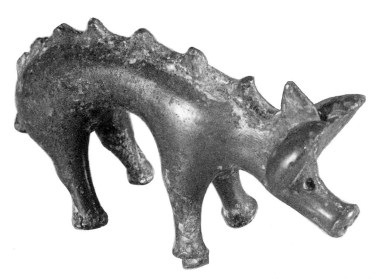

371 *(Above) Bronze boar from Hounslow, Middlesex, England. L. 8 cm. 1st c. BC/1st c. AD.*

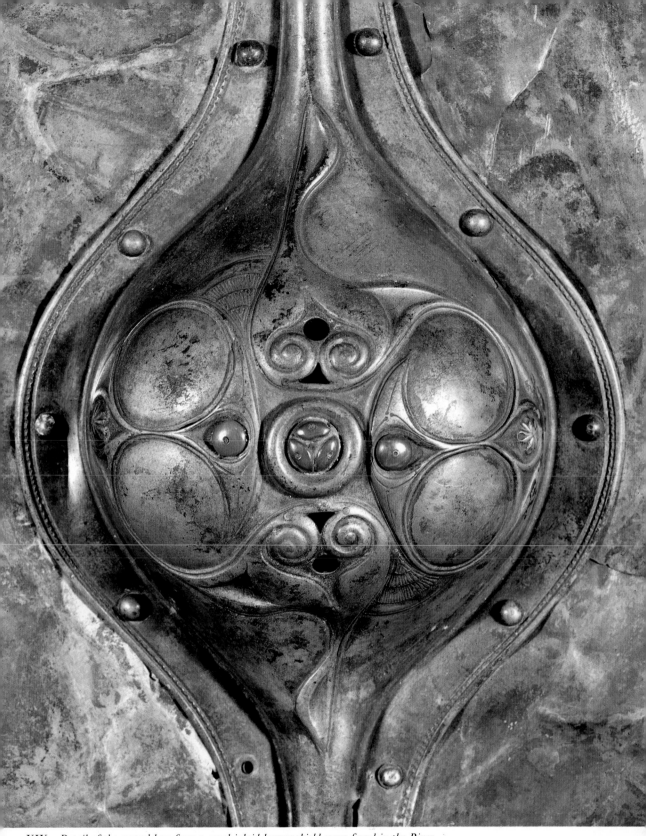

XIX   *Detail of the central boss from a coral-inlaid bronze shield cover found in the River Witham, Lincolnshire, England. Total L. 1.13 m. ?2nd c.* BC.

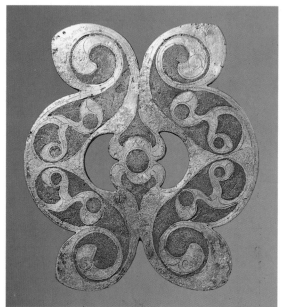

XX *Enamelled bronze harness-mount in the form of a double lyre from Santon, Norfolk, or Santon Downham, Suffolk, England. H. 7.9 cm. AD 40–60.*

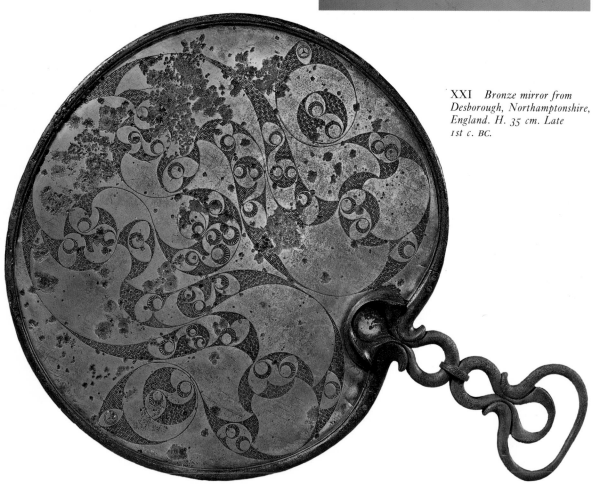

XXI *Bronze mirror from Desborough, Northamptonshire, England. H. 35 cm. Late 1st c. BC.*

hour-glass shaped head and huge scrolled nostrils above a smiling mouth, come from a hillfort at Ham Hill in Somerset. The bovine head from Dinorben near Abergele in Clwyd decorated a stave bucket found in 1912 and probably dates to a century and a half after the Roman occupation. Though it still shows three-dimensional modelling, oval eyes and flared muzzle, it is a more placid and less lively beast than that from Ham Hill.

To return to a slightly earlier period, a hillfort at Bulbury in Dorset produced a pair of precursors to Ferdinand the Bull, with their petalled tails visible when they are viewed from the front as was obviously intended. Their splay-legged stance is probably functional as well as expressive, since each leg is pierced by two holes for attachment to wood, possibly to a cart or chariot yoke with the curved tails acting as guides for the reins. These delightful creatures came from a collection of metalwork including a mirror, tools, an anchor and at least one bowl of Keshcarrigan type; it was probably deposited in the first century AD.

Birds' heads continued to feature in Irish metalwork. Ambiguous birds' heads appear on the side-piece of an incomplete, unprovenanced, cast bronze three-link horse-bit and on the cast bronze mirror handle from Ballybogey Bog, Ballymoney, Co. Antrim.

More obviously bird-like are the heads on the horse-bit in the National Museum of Ireland. The bit itself is typologically early in the Irish

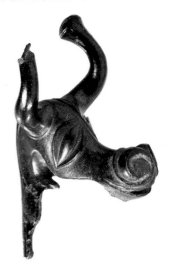

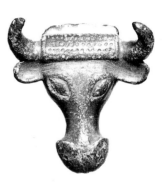

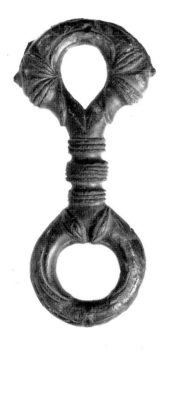

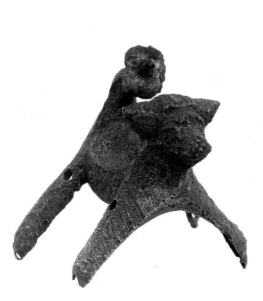

372 (Top) Bronze ?bucket-mount from Ham Hill, Somerset, England. H. 4 cm. 1st c. AD.

373 (Above) Bronze mount on wooden stave bucket from Dinorben, Clwyd, Wales. L. 3.8 cm. Late 1st c. AD.

374 (Far left) Bronze mirror handle from Ballymoney, Co. Antrim, N. Ireland. W. 5.6 cm. ?Late 1st c. AD.

375 (Left) Bronze chariot-mount from Bulbury, Dorset, England. L. 6.4 cm. 1st c. BC.

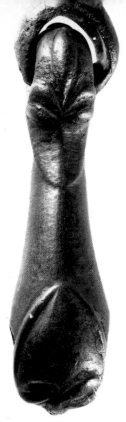

376 *Outer link of a bronze horse-bit from Ireland, showing bird's head at top and human face at outer end. L. (of link) c. 7 cm. ?2nd c. BC to 1st c. AD.*

sequence – first century AD – and belongs to the most common type found in Ireland; this extraordinary piece can be 'read' several ways. Crested ducks' heads adjoin the central ring of the bit; if turned upside-down they can also be seen as a Pinocchio-nosed, mouthless human face, another example of the upside-down faces seen on the continent from the beginning of Celtic art onwards. At the other end of the bit is one further surviving, asymmetrical face, which has no known close parallels. Its mournful, twisted visage is formed with masterly simplicity from four slightly curved ridges. Altogether this is one of the most shifting of the shape-changing figures found in Celtic art since, if the piece is viewed sideways, a yet larger bird's head can be seen, incorporating part of the central loop and using the loop of the outer piece as the bird's eye. Though we lack information as to where it was found or its date, this horse-bit is as clear a demonstration of the abstracting ambiguity of Celtic art over the centuries as anything illustrated in these pages.

Most of these animals are reminiscent of the much earlier continental three-dimensional style of the third century BC with its exaggerated modelling in high relief. Yet they are certainly Irish or British, showing survival or revival of the earlier style. They reflect, too, continuing Celtic preoccupations with the herd animals which symbolized wealth and with birds and boars, dwellers both in this world and the Celtic otherworld.

Horses are rarely portrayed, except on coins. One exception is a splendidly assured equine face from the great stronghold of the Brigantes at Melsonby, near Stanwick, in North Yorkshire. Here the tranquil but mournful visage is created, by contrast to the beasts above, from a minimum of lines executed in sharply keeled repoussé bronze. This mount comes from a large hoard discovered some time before 1846 and consisting mainly of horse-and-chariot gear, some of which is related to that of the more three-dimensional pieces above. The hoard may have been hastily buried at the time of Roman attacks on the Brigantes under Petilius Cerialis between AD 71 and 74. The horse-face may have been a chariot-fitting; most certainly it is the work of a highly skilled artist, long familiar with horses and able to convey the essence rather than the precise likeness of his model.

Human heads are also present on Celtic metalwork, though frequently only in elusive form, scarcely visible as they peer, Cheshire-cat-like, out of the mirrors or harness mounts or from the vegetal designs on the Torrs horns. Sometimes, more definite heads appear, as on this bronze-coated iron terret or rein-ring, from the area of Roman Aldborough, North Yorkshire, also in Brigantian territory. The horns would originally have curved into rings for the reins. The oval eyes of this melancholy face were once inlaid with enamel; its nose has, unfortunately, been broken. The ears beneath the horns recall bulls' ears and the figure as a whole may represent a horned deity. Much more elusive is the repoussé face on another object from the Melsonby hoard. Its huge baleful oval eyes were originally inlaid with enamel, and its flowing moustaches, or forked beard, are like the shoulder curls on the god-figure above.

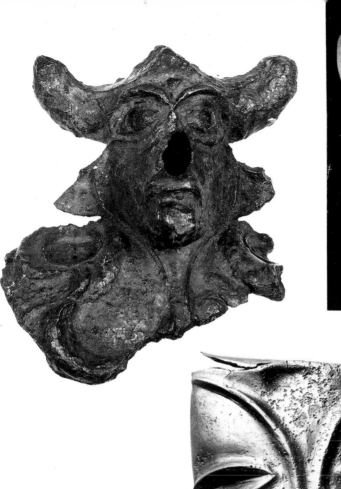

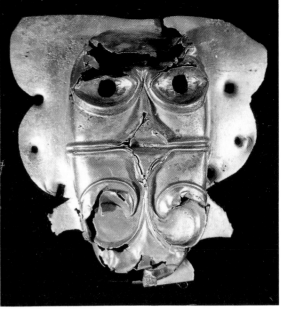

377 (Above left) Bronze-coated iron terret from Aldborough, N. Yorkshire, England. H. 12.8 cm. 1st c. AD.

378,379 Bronze mounts from Melsonby, N. Yorkshire, England. (Above) showing human face. H. 7.5 cm. (Left) showing horse. H. 10.9 cm. 1st c. AD.

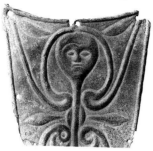

380 *Detail of copper-zinc ?shield-mount from Tal-y-Llyn, Gwynedd, Wales. W. 10.4 cm. ?Late 1st c. BC/early 1st c. AD.*

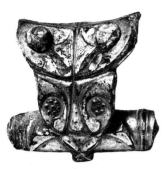

381 *Gilt-bronze brooch from Tre'r Ceiri, Gwynedd, Wales. W. 3.2 cm. Later 1st c. AD.*

The large Welsh hoard at Tal-y-Llyn mentioned above also produced a trapezoid brass plaque with a human representation. It is one of a pair, possibly used as shield-mounts. A central stem ends in matching clean-shaven faces like severed heads. The hair is *en brosse*. Surrounding the human heads is a loose tendril pattern with two pseudo-birds' heads, visible at the bottom of the illustration. This piece is almost certainly of Roman date, since brass is rarely found in pre-Roman contexts. Copper deposits in Wales do contain unusually high proportions of zinc, and this has been suggested to be the reason that the piece is brass and not the usual bronze, but zinc is very easily lost in smelting so its presence in the finished product is probably intentional. It is therefore unlikely that this object dates, as has been claimed, to 200 BC. Stylistically, too, the piece shows the less free-flowing use of vegetal ornament which is a feature of later insular art, so that a first-century AD date seems most likely.

From Wales once again comes the cast gilt-bronze brooch found inside a hut in the great defended settlement of Tre'r Ceiri, high in the mountains in Gwynedd. Like the better-known Aesica example, it is a native copy of a Roman fan-tail brooch form which developed in the period AD 60–100. Its berried eyes are a late feature in British metalwork; its angled eyebrows sweep down to form comma-shaped moustaches. Altogether its decoration is that of the casket ornament motifs found in material from the Melsonby hoard.

As well as the elusive faces in metalwork there are some human representations in wood and stone. A carved yew figure from Ralaghan, Co. Cavan, is generally regarded as male (possibly with a detachable penis affixed to the hole). It is one of the few full-length figures known in Britain, standing some 1.14 m tall. Without radiocarbon analysis it is almost impossible to date its creation and some of its possible parallels go back to the Bronze Age, but there are similarities in form and treatment to the later Gallo-Roman figures from Les Sources-de-la-Seine and it is more probably of the first or second century AD.

Stone heads are also widely known in Britain, and provide the most plentiful illustrations of the human form in Ireland. The menacing bust from Tanderagee came from near a pre-Christian shrine in Co. Armagh. It wears a conical helmet or cap, with vestigial horns: possibly a horned helmet, or perhaps antlers in the style of other horned deities. Its absolute age is again a matter of conjecture.

More benign are the stone heads like the 'tricephalos' or three-faced granite head from Sutherlandshire (Highland region, Scotland). The triple- or double-faced head is not uncommon in British contexts; the magic of the number three is widespread in the western Celtic world and is emphasized in later Welsh and Irish literature. Triple heads also occur on Breton and Icenian coins. The granite is not local and may in fact come from the continent, but the rounded form and drooping Celtic moustaches appear on triple-faced heads from Bron-y-Garth, Shropshire, and Ross-on-Wye, Gloucestershire, while similar heads, though minus moustaches, are found in Corleck, Co. Cavan and from as far away as the Iberian

382 (Right) *Granite three-faced head from ?Sutherlandshire, Highland region, Scotland. H. 12 cm. ?1st c. AD.*

383 (Far right) *Carved yew figure from Ralaghan, Co. Cavan, Ireland. H. 1.4 m. ?1st c. AD.*

384 (Below) *Stone figure from Tanderagee, Co. Armagh, N. Ireland. H. c. 60 cm. ?1st/2nd c. AD.*

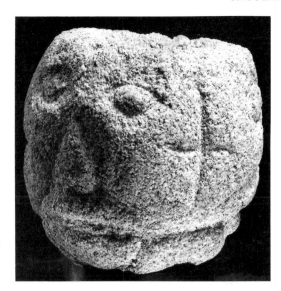

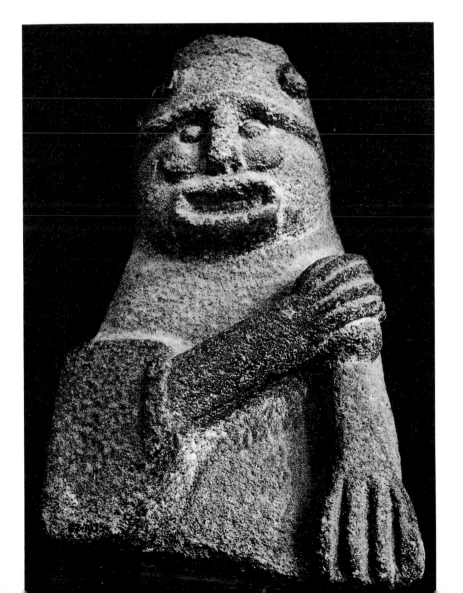

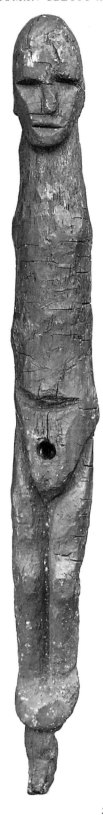

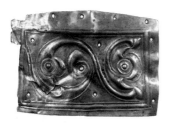

385 *Bronze plaque from the Dowgate, London, England. W. 10 cm. Later 1st c. AD.*

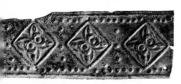

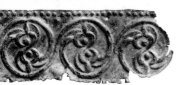

386 *Die-stamped bronze casket strips from Rodborough Common, Gloucestershire, England. W. 2.7 and 2.6 cm. Later 1st c. AD.*

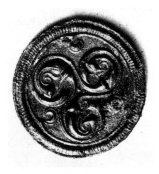

387 *Bronze disc brooch from Silchester, Hampshire, England. D. 5 cm. Later 1st c. AD.*

peninsula. The hollow on top of the Sutherland head suggests use for libations, and the date may be around the time of the Roman conquest. However, such is the proven continuity of insular carving traditions, as in the case of the stone heads from Lough Erne – some of which are undoubtedly of the nineteenth century – that only the most foolhardy would categorically claim a fixed date for such pieces.

LATER CELTIC ART IN BRITAIN WITHIN AND BEYOND THE IMPERIAL FRONTIERS

After the Romans occupied Britain, Celtic art there sometimes took on a more mechanical, provincial appearance, particularly in the south. Yet conquest was also a stimulus to production; the area of Brigantia, stretching from present-day southern Yorkshire and Lancashire into lowland Scotland, began producing large quantities of decorated metalwork, where before it had made little. The destruction of native power by the Romans, and the conquerors' understandable lack of enthusiasm for sustaining Celtic military might, may well have displaced metalsmiths in both location and function, for much of Celtic art had been devoted to display and to the potential of waging war. Destruction in battle or the slower attrition of power and wealth through Romanization of the economy and political structure, especially in southern Britain, means that much of the surviving art production comes from the Celtic fringes where Roman power was less.

In Wales and Brigantia refugees from southern Britain appear to have introduced new techniques and forms. Four major northern artistic schools have been tentatively identified. The first is a south Brigantian, traditionally inclined, school, with roots in the repertoire of Llyn Cerrig Bach but employing new techniques such as die-stamping. Second is a group based on the traditions of the Iceni and the Belgic southeast and making extensive use of polychrome enamel. A third, lowland Scots, school produced a 'poor man's substitute' for enamel, with raised bosses replacing the colour and variety of the first two schools. A fourth, the only one north of the Forth-Clyde line, produced a series of massive armrings and horse-trappings.

Characteristics of later Celtic metalwork include the adoption or imitation of Roman forms, sometimes combined with Celtic forms. Stylistically late features include 'berried' rosettes, an increasing use of straight lines, and the use of die-stamped repetitive ornament rather than the once-only cast and repoussé work. Only in Ireland did the Celtic tradition continue with relatively little interruption or major alteration.

Some pieces, such as a late first-century AD bronze repoussé plaque for a box, do continue to appear from southern England; this was found in black mud in the angle between the rivers Thames and Walbrook at Dowgate in the City of London. Organic salts in the flood silt had not only scoured the plaque, but etched a latent thumbprint on it. The plaque is not symmetrical, but would have been one of several. The left-hand trumpet

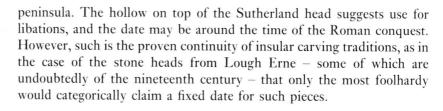

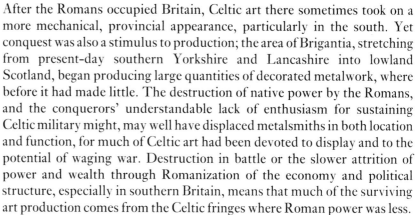

ends in knobbed tails recalling Llyn Cerrig Bach, while the right-hand element, if turned through ninety degrees, is a squashed lyre. As well as these earlier features, Dowgate shows such motifs as the scroll and trumpet of late die-stamped casket ornament, as on the cruder strip from Rodborough Common, Gloucestershire. The embossed repoussé disc for a brooch cover from Silchester also shows clearly, in its triskel motif, the half-moons which are an integral part of the Dowgate plaque's right-hand element.

TRINKETS, TRUMPETS AND TRISKELS

Moving further north, the 11.5 cm long Aesica brooch was found in 1894 in an uncontrolled dig at the Hadrian's Wall fort of Great Chesters. Its date is uncertain, but like the Tre'r Ceiri brooch it is a variation on a Romano-British type which developed out of thistle brooches imported from Gaul in the Julio-Claudian period, and should probably be assigned to the latter half of the first century AD. Suspension loops suggest it was meant to be worn tail upwards, with a safety chain linking it to a twin. Despite its form, its use of beading edging and its long slender trumpets – all of which are late features – its decoration is in the age-old tradition of Celtic art in the lyre and tendril forms and in the figural allusions within them: the pseudo-birds' heads on the fan, the muzzle shape of an equine on the bow and the face at the bottom. Though a southern origin has been suggested, it was probably manufactured in northern England.

Another example of the later Celtic metalsmith's concentration on brooches of ultimately provincial Roman type is the splendidly cheerful and colourful dragonesque form. Some seventy of these are known, the majority found in Brigantia and southern Scotland but with a few from Belgium, France, Germany and as far east as Hungary, testifying to the mobility of civil and military personnel within the Roman Empire. Basically, the design is the ubiquitous Celtic S-curve, to which the Celtic artist has, as so frequently, added a head at the top of the curve. The earliest, from Lakenheath in Suffolk, has a probable date of AD 40–60 and an Icenian context, pointing once again to the close connection between refugee Iceni and the Brigantian region; the rest of the brooches continue probably into the third century AD.

The particular specimen illustrated has no recorded findspot, but two nearly identical specimens come from York and Corbridge. Together with several other examples, it has been assigned on stylistic grounds to an 'East Brigantian' School. The neck joins the top of the head, and to balance this the crest is enlarged and divided in two. These brooches all have champlevé enamel in the central portion. Our current example has a lozenge pattern, while others have squares or more 'Celtic' roundels flanked by the curves.

Other Roman forms turned to Celtic ends can be seen in trumpet brooches. One from Carmarthen, Dyfed, was cast in silver and then gilded by means of applying a mixture of gold dust and mercury, a technique

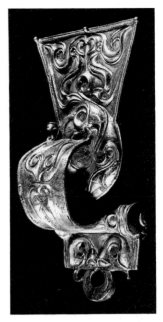

388 *Gilt bronze 'Aesica' brooch from Great Chesters, Northumberland, England. L. 10.3 cm. Late 1st c. AD.*

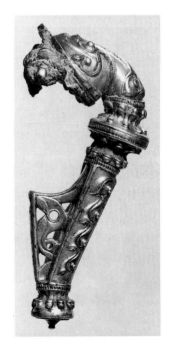

389 *Silver-gilt trumpet brooch from Carmarthen, Wales. L. 6.2 cm. Second half 1st c. AD.*

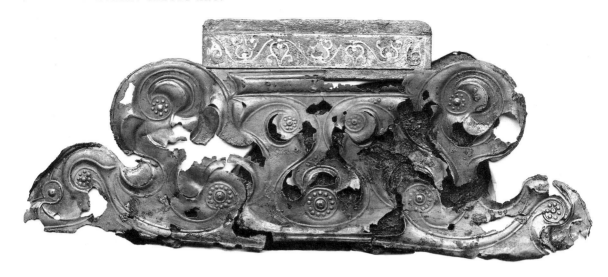

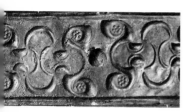

390 (Top) Enamelled bronze casket-mount on iron base from Elmswell, Humberside, England. W. 24 cm. Late 1st c. AD.

391 (Above) Die-stamped bronze casket strip from Santon Downham, Suffolk, or Santon, Norfolk, England. W. c. 3 cm. Later 1st c. AD.

probably introduced by the Romans. Very few safety-pin brooches of any kind occur in the north of England before the second century AD, and their appearance there and in Wales at that period is perhaps connected with the presence of the Roman legions. The brooches again combine Celtic and Roman features.

The very elaborate Carmarthen brooch has been claimed to date to AD 25–50, thus preceding the Roman occupation, and to be ancestral to two divergent types of trumpet brooches centred on Wales and southwest England. The acanthus petals echo the open flower of its head loop and the closed petal form of its head. The catchplate is of open fretwork and, when reversed, looks like a bird, with the smaller circle as eye and the two lobed leaves as wings. On the body is a series of S-curves recalling the Llandysul and Wraxall collars. The high relief bosses which, whether intentionally or because of wear, stand out in silver against the gold background, and the beaded edges which define the decorative zones, suggest some slight echoes of the Snettisham-Ipswich torcs. The brooch was, however, found in spoil from a workman's trench within what was the Romano-British walled town of Moridunum and the type, the use of silver rather than bronze or gold and the technique of gilding are almost certainly from the later part of the first century AD.

It is noticeable how much decoration after the Roman Conquest is on trinkets – brooches and boxes, for example – and how little on the scabbards, shields, spears, torcs and armrings of the pre-Roman period. The Romans, who had their own armourers, obviously provided a significantly different source of patronage for Celtic metalworkers, who, like all craftsmen, needed a viable market. In the areas of Roman military occupation, one can see the Celts turning to a form of 'tourist' art, as have more modern indigenous peoples conquered by an outside power. A significant proportion of the continued Celtic metalwork comes from in or near Roman forts, and provides telling evidence of a culture in transition.

A casket mount from Elmswell in North Yorkshire shows, like Aesica, an elusive face and combines Celtic features with Roman. The basic lyre-palmette is still present, but the enamel-inlaid edging strip displays a definite Augustan vine pattern. Like the die-stamped casket strips from the Santon tinker's hoard it shows berried rosettes. Most of these first-to-second-century-AD strips come from south of the Severn-Wash line, and an iron mould for producing them comes from Viroconium (Roman Wroxeter), further evidence for continuing, if limited, Celtic craft production in the Roman province. While the Santon strip shows a curvilinear acanthus pattern, those from Rodborough Common show the increasing use of straight-sided forms new to the Celtic repertory.

The bronze collar from Stichill, in Borders region, Scotland, which is in two parts, hinged together and fastened with a pin, also uses straight-sided forms. Two front panels, which combine tooled and stamped decoration, are attached to the collar with rivets, contrasting with the rest of the engraved design. These plates carry an exaggerated 'swash N' design. This variation on the trumpet scroll, or a contraction of a triskel to suit a rectangular space, was commonly used by Celtic metalworkers to fill these unfamiliar voids acquired through Roman influence. The rest of the Stichill collar shows sinuous spirals and slender trumpet shapes as on the Deskford carnyx or the late Irish Petrie Crown and Bann disc. The collar suggests the involvement of two separate craftsmen; it may originate

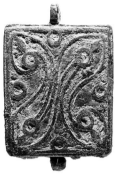

392 *(Above) Enamelled bronze seal-box from Lincoln, England. W. 2.9 cm. ?Late 1st c. AD.*

393 *(Below) Bronze neck-collar with pin fastening from Stichill, Roxburghshire, Borders, Scotland. D. (outer) 19 cm. Late 1st c. AD.*

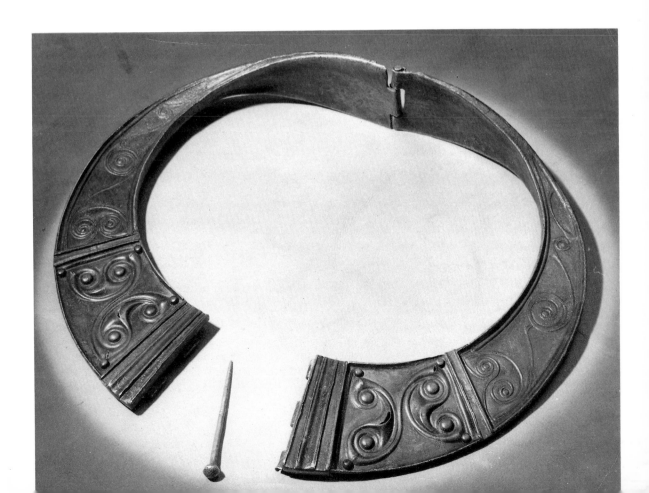

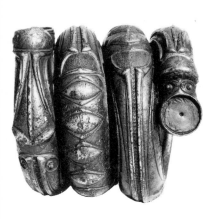

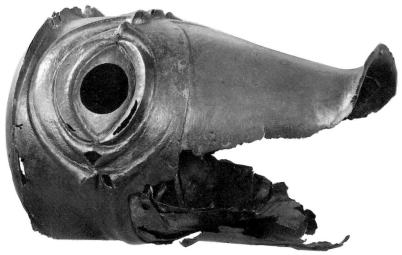

394 (Above left) Cast bronze armlet from Culbin Sands, Grampian, Scotland. D. c. 8 cm. ?1st c. AD.

395 (Above right) Boar's head on the end of a bronze carnyx (war-trumpet) from Deskford, Grampian, Scotland. L. 21.5 cm. Mid-1st c. AD.

396 (Below) Lower part of a bronze scabbard from Mortonhall, Edinburgh, Scotland. W. (of chape) 5.5 cm. Late 1st c. AD.

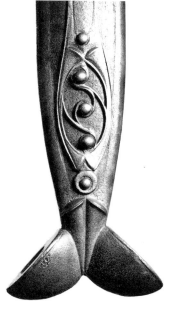

further south, in the Midlands, since its form has some parallels in a southwestern group of hinged neckrings.

Thinner swash Ns, rather than the fat ones on Stichill, appear to have originated in Midlands workshops, as on the enamelled seal-box from Lincoln. Such boxes were used by the Romans: sealed with cord to a package they were intended to provide security in days when the delivery of letters and parcels was entrusted to slaves.

Three further pieces from Scotland share a major characteristic of late northern British and Irish metalwork: the use of slender, curving trumpets to outline major features. On the mouthpiece of a beaten bronze carnyx, or animal-headed war trumpet, found in 1874 during peat-cutting at Deskford in Grampian, these form the eyebrows of a boar's head; joined end to end they also outline its eyes. When found, the head contained 'a wooden tongue, movable by springs' and it still displays a pig's palate in bronze inside the mouth. The enamelled eyes were still in place, and the lower jaw was movable. The boar's ears, like its eyes, have been lost, though its crest is still visible. One inspired flight of fancy sees this warhorn sounding against the Roman legions at the (possibly nearby) battle of Mons Graupius in AD 84–5.

Long, slender trumpets appear again on the bronze scabbard from Mortonhall, Lothian, flanking broken-backed S-curves on its lower half. The tip of the chape is formed of two adjoining trumpet shapes; the upper plate is decorated with a saltire.

Similar slender trumpets outline the eyes of the two gaping faces which form the terminals of a cast bronze spiral armlet found on the Culbin Sands in Grampian. Back to back trumpets also characterize the main body; the spirals flanking the trumpets here recall Welsh parallels such as Moel Hiraddug. This bracelet has a stylistic predecessor in a find from a Belgic cremation burial of around AD 43 at Snailwell in Cambridgeshire, the only one in a long-lasting type with terminals in the form of ram's-headed serpents found outside Scotland. Culbin Sands is possibly another Brigantian product influenced by refugees. It can also be seen as a precursor to the later 'massive' armlets from northern Scotland.

THE WEST OF BRITAIN

In Wales and southwest England, the impact of the Romans on Celtic society and art was less immediate. Regional traditions of metalworking continued. The bronze plaque from a 'tinker's' hoard at Moel Hiraddug in Clwyd with its broken-backed triskel, may perhaps be from Brigantia, but is more probably of Welsh manufacture. It shows the slender trumpets seen on the Deskford carnyx or the Culbin Sands armlet, but the triskel was also found on earlier Welsh mounts from Tal-y-Llyn.

Wales in the Roman period also produced a superb piece of late Celtic craftsmanship in the bronze fittings of a wooden tankard found at Trawsfynydd, Gwynedd. The curved yew tankard is covered in sheet bronze, which is folded over the rim, and has an openwork handle of great elegance and simplicity. The ancestors to this tankard are the Belgic wooden stave buckets at Aylesford and Marlborough, but its immediate artistic inspiration owes much to Celticized provincial Roman harness mounts and brooches. Wooden tankards, as opposed to pottery ones, appear in Wales about AD 43–75 and may be due to craftsmen or owners moving west with the retinue of the fleeing Caratacus.

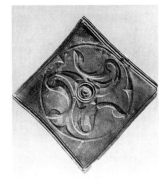

397 *Broken-backed triskel on a tin-plated bronze plaque from Moel Hiraddug, Dyserth, Clwyd, Wales. L. (of side) 15.3 cm. 1st c. AD.*

398 *Yew stave tankard with bronze covering and handle from Trawsfynydd, Gwynedd, Wales. H. 14.3 cm. Late 1st c. AD.*

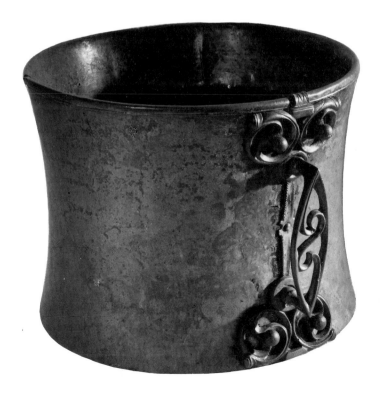

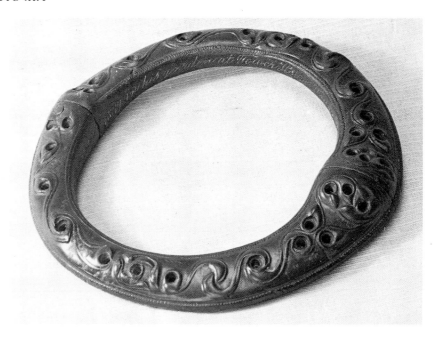

399 *Cast bronze neck-collar with provision for insets, probably of glass, from Wraxall, Avon, England. D. (internal) 12.5 cm. Late 1st c. AD.*

Such a supposition is strengthened by the Capel Garmon imitations of the wrought-iron fire-dogs found in earlier Belgic graves and the appearance of enamelling in Welsh metalwork. The broken-backed scrolls of the Trawsfynydd handle can also be compared with those on more northerly material such as the Mortonhall scabbard or on the southern Birdcombe Court collar and Birdlip mirror, showing again how widespread are some design features in late Celtic art.

The hinged bronze collar from Birdcombe Court, Wraxall, Avon, seems to be the earliest and most accomplished of a group of very similar, but rather undistinguished, late first- and second-century AD neckrings found mostly westwards from Dorset and sharing so many features of design and manufacture that one can see the products of a single craftsman or workshop. It carries a series of eared trumpet shapes forming a running S-scroll and has provision for glass inlay in fifteen sockets. The design has similarities to the S-scrolls on the Carmarthen brooch and to a half of a collar or beaded torc found at Llandysul, Dyfed, where the sockets for inlay are replaced by raised bosses.

IRELAND

Across the Irish sea, by contrast, Roman influence produced only faint and indirect echoes in Celtic art, whether in the imitation of Roman forms or in the visible influence of southern British refugees. An essential conservatism is apparent, though there are very clear connections with the more conservative elements of the art of north Britain and Wales.

Britain proper produces little evidence for Celtic horse-riding from the late first century AD onwards, but Ireland continues to do so for several centuries. From Attymon, Co. Galway, come a matching pair of horse-bits and a pair of the mysterious Y- or U-shaped objects generally described as pendants, found some 7.6 m down on the base of a bog, without datable associations. The bit is of the so-called type E, and has been placed by various commentators at dates ranging from the second to the sixth century AD. Like many other horse-bits, Attymon is extremely worn, but the side-ring still shows its version of the long-lived lyre with scrolls. The pendant has opposing palmette spirals on the two prong terminals and a broken-backed triskel enclosing three 'Llyn Cerrig' curved-sided triangles on its stem terminal.

Horse-trappings, it is worth noting, comprise about 250 objects, or about a quarter of all surviving non-pottery Iron Age objects from Ireland. Despite the later evidence of the Old Irish hero tales for the use of chariots well into the first millennium AD, much later than in Britain, archaeological proof for horse-drawn chariots or even carts is very sparse: indeed only four are known, as well as two other pairs of matching horse-bits and one of matching pendants which imply paired draught. The popular image of the Irish Celt as always at war gains little support from archaeology.

A collection of objects from Lambay Island, Co. Dublin, which does include sword scabbards and local versions of Late La Tène brooches, has most recently been regarded as the equipment of Brigantian refugees. Such an incursion would certainly explain the presence in Ireland of the one massive armlet found outside Scotland, that from Newry, Co. Down. Also a foreigner is the Lambay sheet bronze disc, with repoussé decoration in the form of a rather meagre triskel with outward curling S-scrolls and a separately riveted-on central rosette. This is no Irish piece; its parallels are to be found rather in the Moel Hiraddug plaque or English casket ornament.

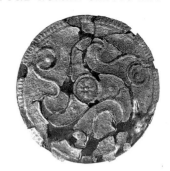

400 Bronze disc from Lambay Island, Co. Dublin, Ireland. D. 17.6 cm. Late 1st c. AD.

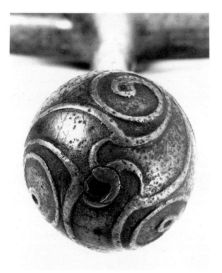 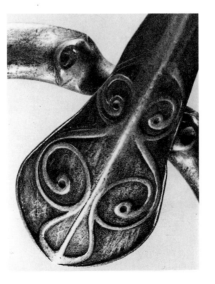

401,402 Details of horse-trappings from Attymon, Co. Galway, Ireland. (Far left) Stem terminal of one of a pair of matching bronze horse-pendants. D. c. 2.4 cm. (Left) One of a pair of three-ring bronze horse-bits. Max. W. c. 2.4 cm. ?1st/2nd c. AD.

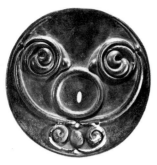

403 *Bronze disc from Monasterevin, Co. Kildare, Ireland. D. 30.5 cm. ?1st/2nd c. AD.*

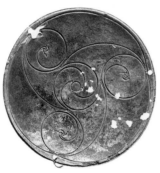

404 *(Above) Bronze disc from Loughan Island, River Bann, Co. Londonderry, N. Ireland. D. 10.5 cm. ?1st/2nd c. AD.*

405 *Silver plaque from Norries Law, Fife, Scotland. W. 12.6 cm. 2nd–6th c. AD.*

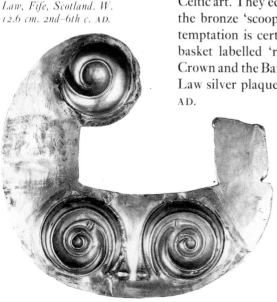

The birds' heads found in early insular metalwork still display a vigorous life of their own in late Iron Age Ireland. Crested and uncrested ducks' heads can be seen on the bronze disc from Loughan Island in the River Bann and on the discs, frieze and horns of the so-called Petrie Crown. These pieces were apparently made by a most unusual technique, paring away the surface of the bronze to leave the relief elements standing out. Once again as on north British metalwork from Deskford, Culbin Sands, Mortonhall, Drummond Castle and Melsonby, these Irish pieces display long, flowing, pencil-point-thin trumpet curves. The Bann disc has a triskel laid out with a compass: it is slightly convex and tiny bronze loops, one of which survives, were threaded through the holes in its circumference in order to hang it perhaps as a scale pan. Even more enigmatic is the function of the incomplete 'crown' from the collection of George Petrie, the nineteenth-century antiquarian. The crested heads on frieze and horns may be great tufted ducks: they certainly look remarkably like the heads of the dragonesque brooches. These Irish pieces, together with three horns found at Cork in 1909, show such close correspondence in design and technique that they must surely be from the same hand. Outside Ireland, their closest relations are north British and of the first and second centuries AD rather than the very much later dates sometimes suggested for these assured and restrained Irish objects.

Within Ireland, the closest parallels are the repoussé bronze discs sometimes referred to as offering bowls because of their dished shape, though again their use can only be guessed at. Seven have been discovered, but only the two from Monasterevin, Co. Kildare, have a known findspot. Diameters vary from 24 to 30 cm, and the design and technique used to produce the raised curves are not quite identical. One shown here has beautifully executed keeled curves set against voids matted with short stabbing marks except on the dish, which is always left plain. This piece lacks the triple motif opposite the eyebrows which was shared by all the others and consists of a central boss with two flanking snail commas. The Monasterevin discs look like great staring faces, enigmatic as so often in Celtic art. They echo the layout of one of the Petrie Crown discs or some of the bronze 'scoops'. With all these similar objects of unknown use, the temptation is certainly to put them into that well-known archaeological basket labelled 'ritual use'. To other analogies shared with the Petrie Crown and the Bann discs one can add the snail-shell spirals on the Norries Law silver plaque from a hoard deposited in Fife in the seventh century AD.

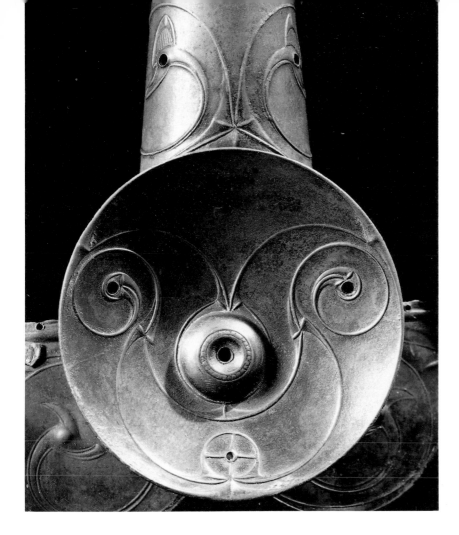

406 *Detail of 'Petrie Crown' from Ireland. D. (of disc) 6 cm. ?1st/2nd c.* AD.

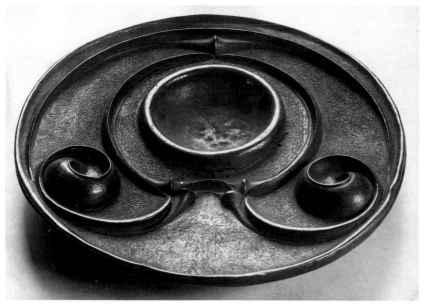

407 *Bronze disc of Monasterevin type from Ireland. D. 27.2 cm. ?1st/2nd c.* AD.

CELTIC ART AND THE ROMAN LEGIONS

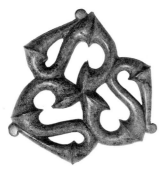

408 *Bronze harness-mount from Heddernheim-Nida, Frankfurt, Germany. D. 14 cm. ?2nd c. AD.*

409 *Bronze harness-mount from South Shields, Tyne and Wear, England. W. 6.4 cm. ?2nd c. AD.*

We have already seen Celtic art applied to Roman forms with brooches and boxes, but occasionally the Celts seem to have produced items specifically for the Roman legions and such products are found throughout the Roman world. An example of this tourist art, embellishing objects of Roman type, is provided by the second-century AD *paterae* or skillets. A complete one found in 1865 somewhere in west Lothian is one of the most splendidly decorated, the outside bearing red, blue and green enamel. Inscriptions on two other examples of these skillets, one found at Amiens in northern France, and the other at Rudge in Wiltshire, between them carry the names of six of the forts on the western part of Hadrian's Wall and a crenellated design which probably represents the Wall itself.

A different type of influence and diffusion is shown in the development of *Trompetenmuster* (trumpet-pattern) openwork harness mounts. These are found throughout the Roman Empire as far east as Dura-Europos in Mesopotamia, as far south as Volubilis in North Africa and as far west as the British Isles. Typical examples illustrated here come from the Roman military and civilian town of Nida, at Heddernheim north of Frankfurt, and from South Shields, Tyne and Wear. They seem to have originated in the products of a 'factory' established at Baden-Argau (Roman Aquae Helveticae) in Switzerland, which, during the first century AD, produced scabbard ornaments and chapes as well as the round discs. Their spread into Germany, Gaul, Austria, northern Italy and Britain closely follows the frontier posts of the Roman army.

These discs were copied locally, and British producers were particularly influenced by the versions from the Rhine such as that shown here with its trumpet-based design. In the South Shields version the design has, however, been converted into the persistent Celtic broken-backed triskel. Each triskel arm itself is made of three elements; the innermost is a two-domed trumpet, the central an S-shaped trumpet curve, and the outer a trumpet ending in a 'snout'. This piece could be British, though the snout shows it may well be a Rhenish import.

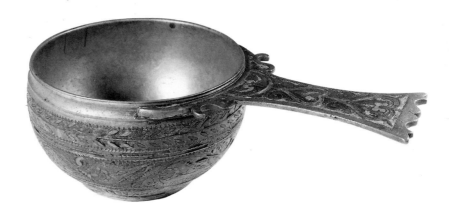

410 *Red, blue and green enamelled bronze* patera *from West Lothian, Scotland. D. 10.8 cm. 2nd c. AD.*

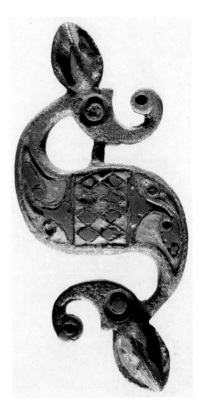

XXII   *Enamelled bronze dragonesque brooch from ?England. L. 4.9 cm. Late 1st c.* AD.

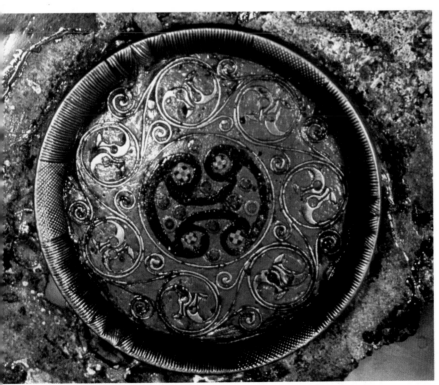

XXIII   *Enamelled bronze escutcheon from the outside of the base of bronze hanging bowl no. 2 from Sutton Hoo, Suffolk, England. D. 5.5 cm. Early 7th c.* AD.

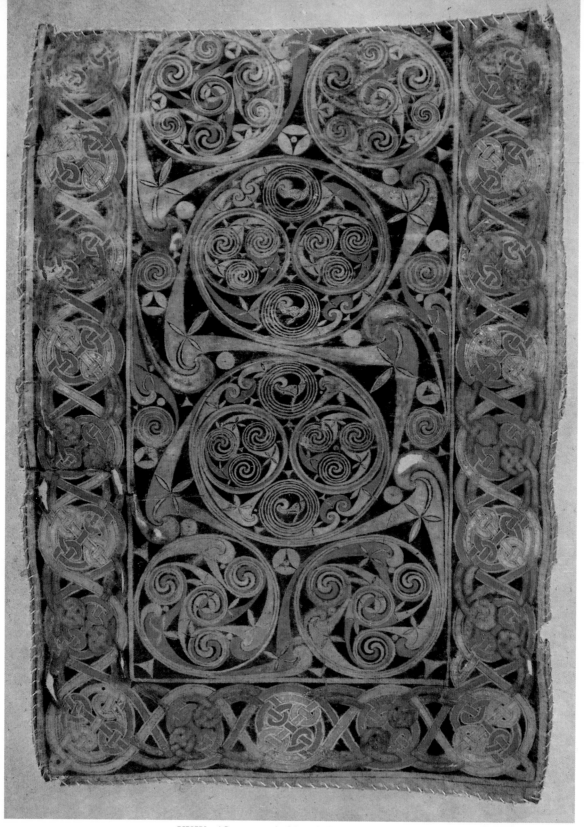

XXIV *'Carpet page', folio 3v, from the Book of Durrow. 24.5 × 14.5 cm. About* AD *675.*

CELTS IN THE SHADOW OF ROME

Roman influence on human portrayal is clear in the first century AD. From a well at Kelvedon, Essex, comes a wreathed, tunic-wearing figure – more probably Roman than Celt as has been suggested. He is mounted on a horse with a remarkably dog-like head, and carries a shield in his left hand. This appears, not on metalwork, but on a pot imitating Roman bronze, possibly a local *terra nigra* copy; the decorative frieze was apparently stamped into the clay from metal dies, a technique which at present has no known parallels. This figure recalls mounted figures on Celtic coins. It is not clear whether it is carrying, as suggested, a 'crook' or whether it may even be a spear with a severed head. The date is set from other finds in the first half of the first century AD.

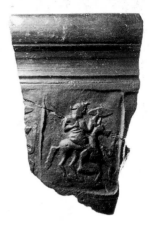

411 *Die-stamped pottery fragment from Kelvedon, Essex, England. H. (of mounted figure) c. 2.3 cm. 1st half 1st c. AD.*

War and transformation, the uneasy transition from independent Celtic society to Roman rule and the influence of Romanization on most aspects of life can be illustrated from one final human face. It comes from Cadbury Castle in Dorset, one of the hillforts of the more westerly region of Britain. Cadbury was destroyed by the Romans, not in AD 43 in the inexorable sweep westwards of Vespasian's legions, but at a period a little more than thirty years later, in what Leslie Alcock, the excavator of Cadbury-Camelot, has described as a brutal police action rather than a full-scale military campaign. Despite attempts to improve the defences, the native inhabitants fell to superior Roman might and some of the bodies were simply left to rot at the gate where they had died. In the massacre level of the southwest gate on the floor of the guardchamber and under the burned and collapsed roof was a bronze repoussé plaque. It may be a god, or the goddess Medusa, rather than a mere mortal and it very clearly shows Roman stylistic influence and Roman self-confidence in its definite, determined realism, in the modelling of nose, brows and chin. Yet there are still Celtic aspects to it: the oval ridged eyes, the straight mouth and the stylized curls. It may be the product of a Celtic craftsman, influenced by Roman models, seeking Roman patronage. It symbolizes the forced emergence of the Celts from the swirling, ambiguous, shape-changing world of their ancestors, where the otherworld was as accessible as this one, into the ordered, straight-edged, rational and disciplined world of the Romans. But is was to take more than Roman might and Roman *mores* totally to subdue the art of so resilient a culture as that of the early Celts.

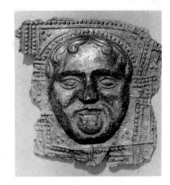

412 *Bronze mask from Cadbury-Camelot, Somerset, England. H. 13.3 cm. Mid-1st c. AD.*

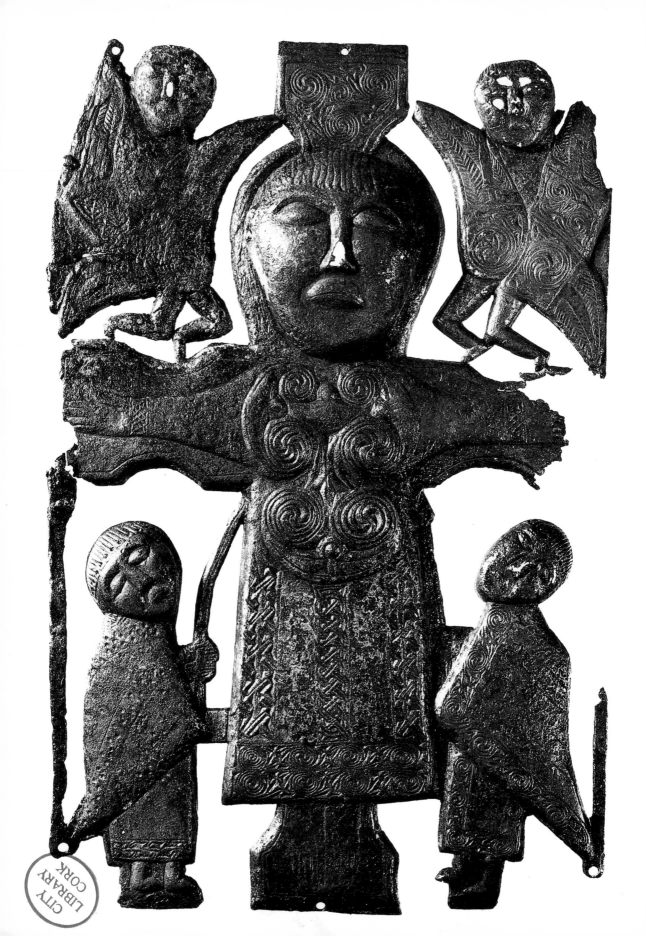

Epilogue: Into the Christian Era

SOME HISTORIANS OF Roman Britain and of its art have tended to misunderstand the nature of Celtic art and to underestimate its tenacity. Thus R.G. Collingwood wrote in 1936 that Celtic art was 'interrupted' or that the artists 'throughout the Roman period were ... working under what may be described as a permanent strain'. More recently Sheppard Frere has claimed that the Celts produced 'a narrow art ... completely divorced from nature and the observation of reality', without 'broad popular foundations' and 'with the Roman conquest the whole basis of society and its aspirations changed very quickly and they became more civilised' or that 'the Celtic craftsmen who worked in the west and north during the third and fourth centuries were tinkers rather than artists and practised a peasant craft.'

The idea of an inevitable decline in Celtic art was even put back to the pre-Roman period by E.T. Leeds in 1933 who stated that it 'contained within it all the seeds of rapid and complete decay; it was breaking up on the rock of petty detail.' This is echoed in Jocelyn Toynbee's 1964 survey of art in Roman Britain: 'the time had in fact come when Britain needed the stimulus of new ideas.'

Even more sympathetic observers have sometimes apologized for Celtic art, claiming that it adapts rather than innovates, or expressing (like De Navarro) surprise that a barbaric people living in squalid conditions should be capable of producing art. Given such ideas, the reflorescence of Celtic art in the post-Roman period becomes a major puzzle.

In fact, as we have seen, Celtic craftsmanship neither vanished nor went underground in Roman Britain and was little affected in Ireland. Adaptable indeed, metalworkers turned to practising forms new to them, and for a transformed Roman market where necessary. They had been the specialist artist/artisans of the pre-Roman period and their skills and techniques were sufficiently developed to enable them to master, assimilate and transform alien ideas as Celts had for centuries past; early Celtic art, while owing much to Etruria and Greece, is still completely distinctive. Tinkers they may have been in Roman Britain but it is probable that some smiths had always been itinerants, and the pejorative sense of the word is modern, post-dating the Industrial Revolution. As for squalor, as anyone who has watched the development of a 'transitional' style of art among Australian Aborigines in the last few years can testify, dirt, disease and social disruption are no necessary bar to the production of art of the highest quality: here too new forms and techniques have been pressed into the

413 (Opposite) Gilt-bronze crucifixion plaque from St John's, Rinnagan, Co. Roscommon, Ireland. 21.1 × 13.9 cm. ?Late 7th c. AD.

243

service of old beliefs and ways of representing the world, as well as providing material means of survival in a new market economy. Thus the swirling, mystical, curvilinear world of Celtic art and belief was able to meet the four-square, rational, naturalistic world of the Romans, and survive.

Celts seem to have been less adept and enthusiastic at adapting to Roman ideas of three-dimensional sculpture in wood or stone, or to fresco painting and mosaic design, and none of these media long survived the departure of the Romans. But this was a rejection of forms inimical to Celtic artistic language rather than an inability to master new techniques, as is shown by the remarkable Celtic incorporation of more compatible Germanic and eastern Mediterranean elements in the post-Roman period to produce an outstanding new art style.

Given the tenacity and flexibility of Celtic art, it is not surprising that in the centuries following the formal withdrawal of Roman power in AD 410, it enjoyed a major renaissance, despite the disruptive effects of the Anglo-Saxon invasions of east and southeast England in the fifth century. The decline of Roman influence and the Germanic advance were more gradual than one might suppose from the pin-pointing by history books of the arrival in AD 447 of Hengist and Horsa. Saxon mercenaries had already served on British soil in the fourth century and the authority of Rome had been slowly eroded long before AD 410. The northern frontier had rarely been very secure, and Hadrian's Wall had never completely recovered from the massive, Germanic-aided, native revolt of AD 367–9. Irish raiders too were harassing British coasts and later settled in parts of Wales, Cornwall, the English southwest and Galloway. Our sources for this period are, however, either later monastic accounts or the Anglo-Saxon Chronicle, neither reflecting contemporary British viewpoints nor unbiased on the subject of Vortigern, the local ruler who invited Germanic aid against the Picts and Scots and thus allegedly opened the floodgates to Anglo-Saxon invasion. Vortigern is accused of tyranny, Pelagian heresy and marital infidelity by these sources. Sources on the legendary King Arthur, the last military champion of the British against the pagan invaders, are even more imprecise. The great battle of Mons Badonicus where Arthur was finally defeated after temporary successes probably did take place but where or when cannot be definitely demonstrated, and Arthur himself cannot be identified except as a heroic idea.

Germanic settlement did not reach Ireland, where the later narratives give a picture of quarrelsome heroic societies based on agriculture and pastoralism, heavily stratified, reliant on slaves and much given to inter-tribal raids, a picture little different from that given by classical sources of the pre-Roman Celts. Yet Ireland seems to have provided a tolerant home for the spread of Christianity, and, unlike Rome, Ireland produced no martyrs for the faith but rather a symbiosis where many monasteries were closely associated with local defended settlements or raths. In the fifth century the precarious balance of the four Irish provinces of Ulster, Connaught, Leinster and Munster was upset by the emergence of an

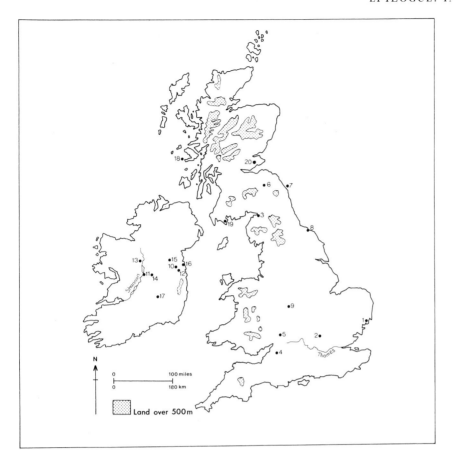

414 *Map of principal sites referred to in the Epilogue.*

expansionist dynasty in Meath, centred on royal Tara and led by the Uí Néill. The Uí Néill dismembered Ulster and by constant harassment of Leinster, allowed the Munster dynasty of Eogananacht to become dominant in southern Ireland. Munster was the most prosperous and civilized area, partly because of the Mediterranean trade connections. It was here that the old hero tales were probably first written down in the late sixth century.

In Britain by this date the Saxons had pushed west as far as Bath, Cirencester and Gloucester, on the borders of Wales and Cornwall where the original Celts had already fallen increasingly under the sway of Irish settlers. In Scotland, though Anglo-Saxon settlement had penetrated into the lowlands, to the north of the old Antonine Wall the Picts (the surviving pre-Celtic population) still remained, while the Irish had established themselves in some western areas. As the ethnic map of Britain altered, some Celts had left the southwest for Brittany early in the fifth century, leaving areas of Devon and Cornwall stripped of population, and in Brittany replacing the Gallo-Roman language there with a form of Celtic, thus drawing the region back into the Celtic world, aloof from the rest of France, an isolationist position still maintained in the 1980s.

In this post-Roman period one major transformational force on both Celtic society and Celtic art was Christianity. Introduced to Britain by the Romans in the earlier part of the third century as one of a number of religions of eastern origin, it was the only one to strike permanent root. At first it was concentrated in urban areas within the Roman province, but by the fifth century there were pockets of Christian influence in Galloway, Wales, Cornwall, northwest England and perhaps Ireland. Roman Christianity was apparently wiped out in lowland Britain by the pagan Saxons and revived only by St Augustine's mission in AD 597 which began in Kent and spread northwards, but it survived in the Celtic west.

Christianity was strengthened in Ireland by the apostleship of St Patrick, traditionally regarded as having been born in a Romano-British family near Carlisle and kidnapped in his youth by Ulster slave-raiders. After escaping to the continent, he returned to Ireland after a decade or so in AD 432 as a consecrated bishop (in the Irish Church's official version) and died in AD 461, though later dates such as AD 495 have been suggested. St Ninian, bishop of Whithorn in Galloway, possibly also came from the Carlisle area, slightly earlier, and in both cases it seems probable that they were ministering to established Christian communities rather than converting the heathen from scratch. Thus, while Christianity lost ground in Saxon England, it was being strengthened in Celtic areas, which also demonstrably maintained direct trade links with the Mediterranean, including the eastern part of it. Ascetic monasticism, with its roots in North Africa, appeared in the Celtic area, with the first datable monastery late in the fifth century at Tintagel. By the sixth century it had spread to Wales and Ireland, where it gradually superseded the episcopal form of Christianity, practised by Saints Patrick and Ninian, with localized monasteries which had close links to the lay communities in which they lived. In AD 563 St Columba sailed from Ireland to the Irish colony in Argyll and established the monastery of Iona. Then, in AD 634–5, the Northumbrian prince Oswald brought Aidan of Iona to Northumberland with him when he returned from exile in Scotland. Celtic Christianity converted Northumbria and led to the establishment there of the great monasteries such as Jarrow, Old Melrose, Whitby and Lindisfarne. From Northumbria the monks spread Christianity into the pagan Saxon kingdoms of Wessex, East Anglia and Mercia, and thence in a re-transference of Celtic traditions to the continent, the Germanic homelands, to France, to Switzerland and to Italy itself at the monastery of Bobbio.

These widespread Celtic monasteries, established in settlements almost indistinguishable from the stone huts of the pre-Roman Iron Age, produced some of the greatest treasures of Early Christian art. Christianity was a spur to the revival of Celtic art, providing new patronage, new subject-matter and new techniques. In the end, however, this monastic tradition was seen as inimical to the episcopal, centrally organized, hierarchy of the Church of Rome, and in the final test of strength at the Synod of Whitby in AD 664, the Roman model prevailed – absorbing the fire and passion of the Celtic church.

THE ART OF THE CELTIC RENAISSANCE

Within Britain one of the main sources for the survival of Celtic art is in the 'hanging bowls', of which over 150 survive. The bowls themselves are of very thin beaten or spun bronze of roughly hemispherical shape and shouldered at the top. On the outside, below the shoulder, they generally have three or four escutcheons, often enamelled, which hold the rings by which the bowls were hung. Some bowls, such as the largest one from Sutton Hoo, carry further enamelled plaques on the base, both inside and out. Many come from Saxon burials, and some from domestic or ecclesiastical contexts; some carry Christian symbols as does the largest Sutton Hoo bowl, which contained a bronze fish on a pedestal. The thin bowls themselves have often perished, leaving only the escutcheons.

Frustratingly we do not know their function, though votive chalices, lamps, handbasins, serving bowls or drinking vessels have all been suggested. It seems probable that they originated from Roman prototypes and continued to be made until at least as late as the seventh century by craftsmen in Northumbria, Scotland and western England; Ireland was long considered the major source of production but it is now obvious that it was not the only one. Since they were apparently produced for both Anglo-Saxon and Celtic users it is not clear whether this particular group of objects was stimulated by Christianity or paganism.

The escutcheons from Hitchin in Hertfordshire and Middleton Moor in Derbyshire are both enamelled in red and yellow. The fragmentary piece from Middleton Moor shows a massive pair of spirals with a mushroom shape, or pelta, between them; part of a lyre shape sitting on another pelta is visible at the broken end. The design is similar to that shown on the more commonly shaped complete circular escutcheon from the same bowl (not illustrated). The superb Hitchin disc uses a more complex technique which juxtaposes the two colours without a separating division of metal. It shows an even more elaborate design than Middleton Moor: the triskel formed of the four large spirals linked to each other by trumpet shapes can also be read as three interlocking palmette coils, each incorporating the central spiral. Each spiral is itself a yin-yang comma; also of significance are the little trefoil and leaf motifs. These designs can be seen again in the Rinnagan bronze crucifixion plaque and in the seventh century illumination of the Book of Durrow.

Sutton Hoo, near Woodbridge in Suffolk, produced three Celtic hanging bowls from among the spectacular treasures found in this ship burial. It was first excavated shortly before World War II, and is dated to shortly after AD 625 by the eighty Merovingian coins and blanks which it contained. This regal burial in a 30-metre-long ship contained some Christian objects and symbols, yet had obviously not abandoned the pagan custom of burial with grave goods. The ship itself is longer than any other surviving from this or the later Viking period. Together with some of the grave goods, it points towards a Swedish connection; there are also a bronze Coptic bowl, a silver dish from the Byzantine Empire and goods from the Rhineland as well as the Merovingian coins. Among the far-flung English and foreign treasures were the three bronze Celtic hanging bowls. They were obviously old when buried, for the largest had been lovingly repaired with silver patches by Germanic metalsmiths. The enamelled disc shown here comes from the outside of the base. It shows a running pattern of interlocked S-curves; within the circles thus produced are pairs of birds' heads. In the centre of the disc, two linked mushroom or pelta shapes form

415 Enamelled bronze hanging bowl escutcheon from Middleton Moor, Derbyshire, England. 3.8 × 3.5 cm. ?6th/7th c. AD.

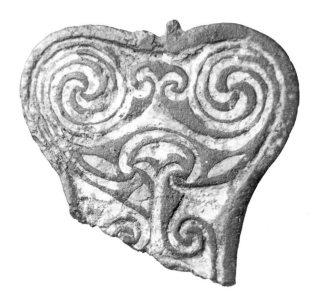

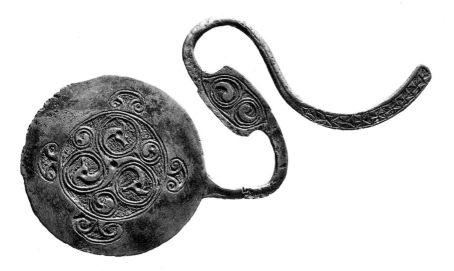

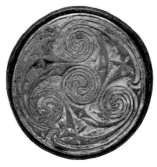

416 (Left) *Enamelled cast bronze dress-fastener or latchet from Ireland. L. 13 cm. 6th c. AD.*

417 (Above) *Enamelled bronze hanging bowl escutcheon from Hitchin, Hertfordshire, England. D. 5.1 cm ?6th/7th c. AD.*

the framework for the insertion of millefiori enamel. This is a technique whereby bundles of glass rods of different colours are heated together and pulled out; the resulting multicoloured pieces are then sliced off and inserted in the metalwork. Similar millefiori designs were used in some of the Saxon jewellery from Sutton Hoo in a cloisonné technique (insertion into cells raised on the surface of the metal) rather than the Celtic champlevé (in spaces cut into the metal). This is the first time such enamelling is found in Germanic jewellery and it suggests a close interchange of ideas and techniques between Germanic and Celtic craftsmen, who had used millefiori probably since Roman times. The disc, like the red-enamelled escutcheon from the smallest Sutton Hoo bowl has a heavily milled metal frame.

The Sutton Hoo hanging bowls may be imports from Ireland, like the silver openwork and repoussé brooch from Swallowcliffe Down in Wiltshire, which was found in a rich female burial probably also from the earlier part of the seventh century. This is a strangely eclectic piece reflecting Celtic, Germanic and Mediterranean elements.

It is certainly possible to produce Irish parallels for these hanging bowls. Similar birds' heads and triskels can be seen on a poorly cast enamelled unprovenanced Irish latchet (or dress-fastener) attributed to the sixth century. Two penannular (or open ring) brooches, one from the River Shannon near Athlone, Co. Westmeath, and one unprovenanced, bear a considerable resemblance, with their triskels and double spirals, to the Hitchin and Middleton Moor escutcheons, as does an enamelled disc from Lagore crannog, Co. Meath. Penannular brooches probably originated from provincial Roman prototypes, but are also found from the second century AD onwards in Ireland, where they had a long and increasingly

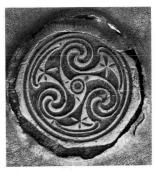

418 *Enamelled bronze disc from Lagore, Co. Meath, Ireland. D. 7.2 cm. 8th c. AD.*

419 *Silver brooch from Swallowcliffe Down, Wiltshire, England. D. 8.6 cm. ?Early 7th c. AD.*

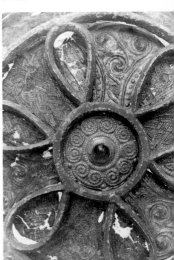

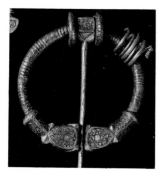

420 *Penannular bronze brooch with millefiori enamel from Ballinderry, Co. Offaly, Ireland, crannóg no. 2. D. 8.6 cm. ?Later 7th c. AD.*

elaborate life. These examples are probably seventh-century and have animal heads on their terminals facing away from the open ends. A penannular brooch, whose heavy milled ring shows fine-ribbed, criss-cross and fish-bone patterns, provides a precise parallel for the frames of the Sutton Hoo discs. This comes from Ballinderry crannog 2, Co. Offaly. This brooch is again animal-headed, the creature's muzzle being covered with interlace ornament. Only the pin is undecorated; even the sides and back of the terminals are covered with decoration. On the back of the terminals are separately attached engraved plaques, a feature found again on the Tara brooch, described later. The Ballinderry brooch is usually dated to the early seventh century because of its Sutton Hoo connections, but it shows the Germanic-derived tendency to decorate every possible surface, characteristic of later works of developed Hiberno-Saxon art such as the Books of Durrow and Lichfield, the Tara brooch or the buckle from Lagore crannog, Co. Meath.

These comparisons do not of course prove that the Sutton Hoo and other hanging bowls necessarily come from Ireland. Françoise Henry has, however, suggested that the Irish mission of St Fursa to East Anglia, which began in AD 635 and which, since it was by invitation, may have been preceded by friendly contacts, could show how Irish metalwork reached East Anglia. Alternatively, the similarities could merely show how widely motifs in Celtic art were shared in various parts of the British Isles in the sixth and seventh centuries, as in earlier times.

CELTS AND THE WORD OF GOD

Whatever may be the case with Celtic hanging bowls, the origins of the manuscript tradition in the British Isles are most certainly Irish.

The so-called Cathach (Battler) of St Columba derives its curious name from being carried as a talisman in front of the army of O'Donnell in AD 1497 before a battle. It is in fact a copy of the Psalms written in an early Irish version of the majuscule script. Tradition has it that it was transcribed by Columba himself, who died in AD 597. So early a date is possible, but the motifs of dots and fish inside some initial letters suggest Coptic manuscripts: such manuscripts could most probably have reached Ireland through the Celtic monastery of Bobbio, in Italy, which was not founded till AD 613, so that a seventh-century date may be more probable. The decoration is sparse, limited to the enlarged initial letters of each psalm, and colour is used very sparingly with red dots and possible yellow painting originally inside the initials.

The initials shown here are respectively a capital 'M' and 'ds'. The 'ds' comes from folio 19a 'D(eu)s In nomine tuo saluum me fac'. The 'd' is composed of trumpet forms with elaborate pelta-shaped ends, and contains small wavy lines and dots. The 's' has elaborate coiled ends decorated with curved-sided triangles or peltas. The 'M' comes from folio 21a and begins

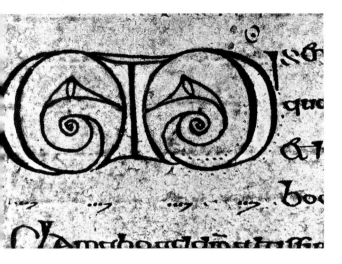
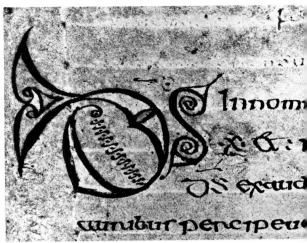

the line 'Miserere mei d(eu)s miserere mei'. It too is composed of swelling trumpet forms and massive spirals forming a shape which has echoes as an early Christian stone *stele* from North Inishkea, Co. Mayo.

The Cathach is important because its decorated initials give the first hint of the elaboration characteristic of later illuminated manuscripts, and most unlike Coptic or other holy books. It uses Celtic designs to illustrate an artefact of a non-Celtic religion, in a non-Celtic language, and in a medium of writing with ink on vellum alien to Celtic visual and oral tradition.

Whether or not Columba himself copied this Psalter, there is a tradition that his clandestine copying of a Gospel book belonging to one of his Irish colleagues led to a series of violent disputes which culminated in his precipitate departure to Iona in AD 563, thus starting the spread of Celtic Christianity and the Irish manuscript tradition to Britain and Europe. The Cathach itself shows the tentative beginnings of this decorative tradition before its fusion with other elements such as those incorporated in the Book of Durrow.

The splendid 'carpet' page, folio 3v of the Book of Durrow, is incomplete; it has lost one part of its border and has come loose from its place. The decoration is painted in red, yellow, green and deep brown, either, as here, against a black background or against the vellum page itself. The central panel of this page echoes the Middleton Moor and Hitchin hanging bowl escutcheons in its four corner elements, and includes the trefoil motifs of Hitchin in the six similar elements of the ribbon interlace and in the top of each roundel. The broad ribbon interlace most probably comes from Coptic manuscripts, again perhaps via Bobbio. One famous page (folio 192v), not illustrated here, shows for the first time the introduction to Celtic art of the quite different type of interlaced animals found in Germanic art. Once introduced, these two types of interlace become a major feature of Celtic metalwork and manuscripts alike. Durrow marks a crucial point in the development of the so-called Hiberno-Saxon style, exhibiting as it does the four essential elements: the Celtic motifs, ribbon

421,422 Decorated initials from the Cathach of St Columba. (Above left) 'M' from folio 21 (beginning of Psalm 55). (Above) 'ds' from folio 19 (beginning of Psalm 53). Complete page 20 × 13 cm. ?Later 6th/early 7th c. AD.

251

interlace, animal interlace and rectilinear patterns (check, step and key patterns and diagonal fretwork). These are combined into extraordinary, restless and enigmatic compositions totally at odds with classical art, but also contrasting with the spare restraint of such late pagan Celtic creations as the Petrie Crown and the Monasterevin discs.

Durrow also exhibits a number of other key features. It employs the suede-surfaced insular vellum so different from that in use on the continent and quite remarkably receptive to colours or to ink. This is due to the method of processing animal skins and not, as used to be thought, to the use of calf rather than sheepskin; both at times are used in the same manuscript. It is much more richly decorated than the Cathach and the illumination extends not just to increasingly elaborate initials but to the use of 'carpet' pages of overall decoration facing the beginning of each Gospel, an idea apparently borrowed from eastern Christian manuscripts. Durrow also displays representational designs: one page carries the symbols or personifications of all four Evangelists and each Gospel is preceded by such a page with a single such illustration. These are quite remarkably non-naturalistic; animals and men are reduced to flat two-dimensional designs. Saints lack conventional haloes or wings. St Matthew, for example, lacks arms, and only his head and feet poke out from the bell-shaped body decorated with a chequered pattern derived from millefiori enamel – yet further testimony that at least one of the painters, like that of the carpet page, was familiar with metalwork designs and may even have been a metalsmith. As in the pre-Christian period, naturalistic representations were still foreign to the Early Christian Celtic artistic style and syntax suggesting, in Kendrick's words applied to a pagan Celtic mask, that it was 'a sublimation of human countenance, as though it were the supernatural aspect of man's form ... that the artist sought to portray'.

The precise location within the Celtic monastic world which produced this magnificent use of pagan tradition in the service of Christ is still in dispute. Iona, one of the Northumbrian monasteries or Durrow itself have all been claimed as possible sources; a date around AD 675 seems correct.

Some Early Christian manuscripts may also have contained crucifixion scenes as well as representations of the Evangelists. It seems likely that the artist who created this gilt-bronze openwork plaque (possibly the cover for a holy book) which comes from a long-occupied settlement at Rinnagan, Co. Roscommon, may have seen such a portrayal. The backward-turning heads of Stephaton and Longinus, who proffer lance and sponge, recall those of manuscript paintings. The Christ-figure is much larger than the humans and the slightly awkward angels, and Christ's head is also large in proportion to His body so that it becomes the focus of our attention. All five heads are schematic, the oval eyes and stylized hair recalling earlier Celtic faces. This is a clothed Celt, not an eastern semi-naked Messiah; his long-sleeved garment has borders which display at the hem a design of linked spirals, derived from late pagan La Tène art. The sides and centre carry panels of rounded or angular interlace. On his breast the massive spirals recall those on the Middleton Moor and Hitchin escutcheons. Spirals, triskels and saltires with a plaited basketry background cover the bodies and wings of the angels. On the Cross, above Christ's head, is a triskel with three six-petalled peltas separating the three outer spirals. This piece is probably roughly contemporary with the Book of Durrow, a date in the late seventh century seeming more likely than one in the eighth.

Christianity thus provided not only new patronage for the Celtic artist, but a new *raison d'être*, which for the first time demanded the use of narrative art. The monasteries also provided a focus for written learning which increasingly replaced that of the oral traditions and law nourished by the Druids, though not those of the poetry and song centred on the local chieftainly centres.

Secular metalwork also shows the changes in art styles. A brooch from Ardakillin, Co. Roscommon combines simple interlace ribbon design, like that on the borders of the Book of Durrow, with raised spirals strongly reminiscent of the keeled curves of the repoussé silver plaque from Norries Law in Scotland. This plaque has been set by some writers at a relatively early date, but could well be a much later (seventh-century) import from Ireland. Such interlace can also be seen on the Rinnagan cover and the numerous carved stone crosses of the later eighth to tenth centuries.

The increasing tendency to decorate all available space is seen too on the buckle from the 'royal' crannog of Lagore in Co. Meath. The fat triskel nearest the belt reflects the increasing use on metalwork of the chip-carving technique derived from woodworking: a V-shaped edge is cut into a casting mould or chiselled into the metal to produce a vivid, faceted interplay of light and shade. The yin-yang commas in the second roundel are another long-lasting Celtic motif. At the narrowest part of the decoration is a tiny, backward-turned dog's head, derived from Germanic art. The crannog itself is an artificial island in a lake only some 9 km from the fabled Tara, centre of the High Kings of Ireland; Lagore was apparently occupied as a royal residence after Tara was destroyed.

Tara was not, however, the origin of the elaborate silver-gilt pseudo-penannular Tara brooch (this term being used because there is no gap in the ring). It comes in fact from a wooden box found on the beach near Bettystown, Co. Meath. The jeweller seems to have applied every technique he knew, including casting, engraving, intaglio, filigree, and the insertion of enamel, moulded glass and amber. The back is as elaborately decorated as the front, although it would only have been seen by the wearer in putting it on and taking it off. On the back were attached two separate plaques of which one is illustrated. Against a background of writhing, interlaced birds and animals executed in gold in chip-carved false relief are silver foil plates with an intaglio design cut through to underlying copper. Each plate, like Lagore, bears two triskels of unequal size. Like so much Early Christian metalwork this brooch cannot be precisely dated, but it has been suggested that it can be compared with the decoration of the Lindisfarne Gospels which are placed half way between the Books of Durrow and St Chad, early in the eighth century, though the style of the animals on the back points to a date much later in the eighth century.

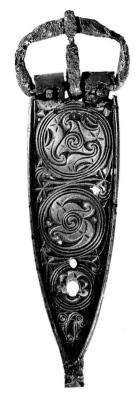

423 *Bronze belt-buckle from Lagore, Co. Meath, Ireland. L. 15.8 cm. 8th c. AD.*

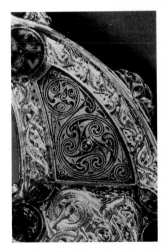

424 *Detail of the underside of the silver-gilt 'Tara' brooch found at Bettystown, Co. Meath, Ireland. W. (of terminals) 4.6 cm. 8th c. AD.*

THE MIRACULOUS FUSION

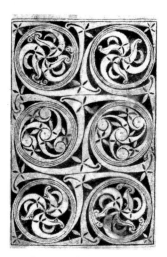

The fusion of Celtic, Germanic and Mediterranean elements first seen in the Book of Durrow reached almost perfect flowering in the Lindisfarne Gospels, the Book of St Chad (the Lichfield Gospels) and the Book of Kells. The detail shows the head of the letter Q(uoniam) from folio 121r, the opening of St Luke's gospel, in the Book of St Chad. On this page the letters take an angular, runic form, copied possibly from stonecarving, and the borders show a vivid Germanic pattern of interlaced birds. Yet the interior of the 'Q' shows Celtic triskels formed from chip-carved trumpet

425 *Interior of the head of initial 'Q' (*quoniam*) from the beginning of St Luke's Gospel in the Lichfield Gospels or Book of St Chad, folio 221. Complete page 30.8 × 23.5 cm. W. (of detail) c. 5.2 cm. ?Second quarter 8th c. AD.*

426 *The Chi-Rho page of the Book of Kells, folio 34R. Complete page 33 × 25 cm. Late 8th/early 9th c. AD.*

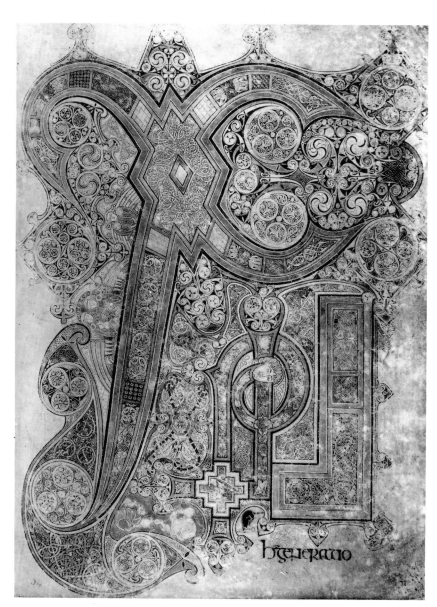

scrolls; the four at the corners are of broken-backed form. The ribbon surrounds of the spirals are a simplified version of those surrounding the roundels on the carpet page of the Book of Durrow, right down to the little trefoil motifs. There are major points of similarity between Lichfield and the Lindisfarne Gospels as well as with the Book of Durrow, including the use of compasses to lay out the design. On the carpet page preceding St Mark's Gospel in Lindisfarne the design has been carefully set out on the blank back of the page with compasses and ruler in a fashion typical of earlier insular design such as the Lough Crew flakes or the English mirrors. Then it was carefully pricked through to the other side to guide the painter.

The Lichfield gospels lack most of the pages after the beginning of St Luke's Gospel, and the surviving portions are damaged. Violet or mauve is the main colour used, with the addition of brown, yellow, blue and green. In the ninth century, it was traded to the Church of Llandello Fawr, Dyfed, in exchange for 'a good horse' and may have reached Lichfield Cathedral in the tenth century; it is probably the oldest manuscript still in liturgical use in Europe. Where and when it was originally created is, however, still a matter of dispute; Iona, Northumbria and Mercia have all been suggested. An origin in Northumbria and a date in the second quarter of the eighth century, after Lindisfarne, but before Kells, seems probable.

The Book of Kells is the most ornate of all these gospels. The illustration shown here is of the so-called 'Chi-Rho' page (folio 34R, Matthew ch. 1, 18) bearing the Greek initials 'XP', the first two letters of the Greek word *Christos*. The intricacy of the design, barely fully discernible without a magnifying glass – an aid perhaps provided in the scriptoria by a natural crystal – bears witness to the extraordinary patience and skill of the several scribes and painters who devoted decades of their lives to its creation.

Within the Chi itself are panels of various types of interlace; some rectilinear and some of animals. Each of the four points of the Chi swirls into triskel forms. Clearly visible at several points of the design are triskels, themselves formed out of smaller triskels, while on the right-hand side are two adjoining lyre-palmettes set sideways. The palmettes are made up of trumpet scrolls, the outer ends of which whirl into comma-spirals and yet more triskels. In the largest of these triskels, the main arms (black on yellow) are shadowed by a further series of three arms formed out of the trefoil (three leaves and a stem). Elsewhere on the page there are tiny heads or busts and animals appearing out of the riot of motifs. Along the outer side of the left-hand border of the Chi are, from top to bottom, two moths which also become a single moth outlined with red dots, a small human shape, and a pair of angels. Just to the right of the bottom of this arm of the Chi are two cats and four mice playing together like some naïve depiction of Christ's peaceable kingdom. The mice have been described as kittens, but their ears and pointed noses are clearly distinguished from those of the cats. Further right again is an otter swallowing a fish, symbol of Christianity. It is noticeable that the Celtic ritual zoo of boar, cattle, horse and sheep has made way for a more playful and less fearsome range of animals, used to illustrate Christian symbolism: the otter with the Christian symbol of the fish, and the mice playing with a tiny disc which may be intended as symbolizing the Host or Eucharist. The human or angelic elements (a head forms a terminal for the Rho, and in the topmost point of the Chi is yet another) are less ambiguous than those of earlier insular Celtic art, but scarcely more realistic.

At least three scribes, and three illustrators (who may or may not have been the scribes themselves) have been identified at work, one more archaic in style than the others. One painter was responsible for the portraits of the Evangelists, one for the dramatic scenes such as the Temptation of Christ and one, named by Françoise Henry 'the Goldsmith', for the ornamental pages such as that shown here. The Goldsmith at least was thoroughly familiar with metalworking design and technique. No other Early Christian manuscript from the British Isles is so lavishly produced; only two of its 680 pages have no colour, a fitting coda to the increasingly polychromatic Celtic art of the British Isles.

Its recent history is clear: following the twelfth century reform, the monastery was dissolved but its church continued to serve the parish of Kells. In 1661 the Bishop of Meath presented the Book, previously kept in the church, to the Library of Trinity College, Dublin. The place of origin for the Book of Kells, as with all the early manuscripts save Lindisfarne, is still, however, a matter for debate. Obviously only one of the major monastic centres could have provided all the skills and talent needed. This precludes Kells itself until after the monks of Iona took refuge there following the first devastating Viking raid of AD 806; Lindisfarne, Durrow or Iona or others of the Northumbrian scriptoria are also possible candidates. In trying to solve these questions, there are four main areas for investigation: the form of the handwriting (basically Irish majuscule); the text(s), mistakes and all, from which the scribes apparently copied (here the closest correspondences are with the Book of Durrow, though other texts were also used); the style of decoration; and, finally, the new features such as the depiction of the Madonna and Child. The weight of recent opinion seems to be that the manuscript was begun in Iona, but transferred, with the remnants of the Iona community to Kells, and possibly completed there.

If the Llyn Cerrig Bach plaque was, in Ian Finlay's telling phrase, 'a trumpet blast in bronze' the Book of Kells can perhaps be seen as the orchestration of a triumphant Mass, combining features from Celtic, Saxon and wider European sources to the greater glory of God.

ENVOI

The coming of the Vikings is not the end of the story of Celtic art; the Romanesque and Gothic periods in Ireland saw another virtual renaissance, less contrived and more culturally integrated than the visual expressions of the romantic Celtic Revival of the late nineteenth and twentieth centuries. But even if the International Style has set the tone for much of the recent arts and crafts of the Celtic Far West, the traditions of the past can still be perceived today. The design by Art O'Murnaghan in 1922 for an illuminated Irish Republican Memorial includes an 'Éire page' which is a veritable anthology of Early Christian motifs; the text is from the 'Vision of St Brigid', the sixth-century abbess of Kildare. The project, like the history of Celtic art, has never been completed . . .

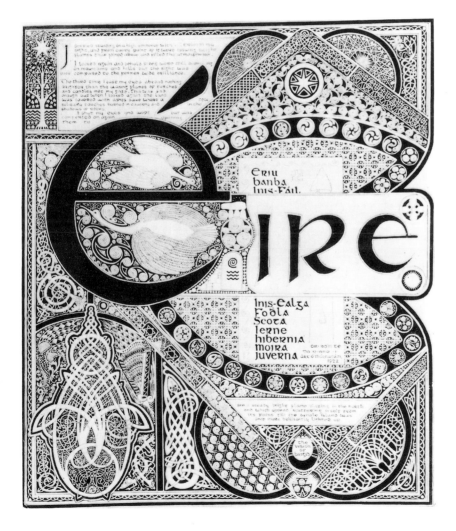

427 'Éire page' from an unrealized project for an Irish Republican Memorial, designed by Art O'Murnaghan. The text is from the 'Vision of St Brigid'; the names in bold script are various synonyms for 'Ireland'. AD 1922.

	Eastern France	S.Germany / Switzerland	N.Italy	Jugoslavia	Dendro-chronology	Historical Events	Early Celtic Art Styles
BC	Bronze final III	Hallstatt B3 (Late Urnfields) — Ha I / Ha C1	Villanova III (Benacci II) — Este II			Steppe nomads in Assyria	
700	Hallstatt I (Early Hallstatt)	Long swords / Hill-forts — Ha C2	Vill IVa	Slovenia: Podzemelj 'Thraco-Cimmerian' influence			
600	Ha IIa	Ha II / Ha D1 — Daggers / Princely graves	Vill IVb (Arnoaldi) — Situlae	Stična I / Novo mesto Italian influence / Stična II		Etruscans at Rome / c.600 Foundation of Massalia	
500	Ha IIb / Les Jogasses (Late Hallstatt)	Ha D2 / Ha D3	Certosa — Este III — Etruscans	Horizon with double ridged helmets / Scythian influence		c.520 Foundation of Spina / 513 Persians in Balkans / 508 End of Etruscan rule in Rome	
		LT Ia Chieftains' graves / LT A			Altrier 464	Etruria Padana	Early style
400	(Early La Tène)		Celts	Hallstatt graves with 'Negau' helmets / La Tène influence		Gaulish invasion of Italy/Pannonia / 387 Sack of Rome	
	La Tène I	LT Ib / LT B1 — Duchcov & Münsingen brooches	West group: Mokronog 1 / East group: Belgrade 1		335 Celtic embassy to Alexander the Great	'Waldalgesheim' or 'Vegetal'
300		LT Ic / LT B2	Romans			279-7 Celts in Balkans Sack of Delphi / 270 Settlement of Asia Minor / 240/30 War of Attalos I against Galatae	'Sword' styles — Early 'plastic' / Late 'plastic'
200	LT II (Middle La Tène)	LT II / LT C1 — LT C2	Mokronog 2-4 / Belgrade 2	La Tène shields 229 / Wederath 208	233/2 Ager gallicus / 225 Battle of Telamon / 222 Defeat of Insubres / 191 Defeat of Boii / 190/81 Pergamene reliefs	Early insular style (Torrs-Witham)
100		Oppida — LT III / LT D1			Fellbach 123 / Cornaux 120-16 / Manching 105	124/3 Roman conquest of Gallia Narbonensis / 113/101 Invasion of Cimbri & Teutones	
	LT III (Late La Tène)	LT D2 — Nauheim brooches / LT D3	Mokronog 5-6 / Belgrade 3	Ehrang 70	58 Defeat of Helvetii / 58/50 Gallic wars / 52 Fall of Alesia End of Oppida / 15 Alpine campaign	Later insular style (mirrors/ harness mounts)
AD						AD43 Claudian invasion of Britain	
100							Ultimate or Late N. British/Irish

Bibliography

As with the main text it is impossible to do justice to the bibliography of the art of the early Celts without also offering some pointers to the literature on the general social and economic context of that art – insofar as this has been reconstructed from the available archaeological and historical evidence. The annotated lists follow the order of chapters and topics contained therein; though English texts are quoted wherever possible, of necessity reference is made to non-English language sources.

References published since 1969 – the date of the completion of J.V.S. Megaw *Art of the European Iron Age* (Adams and Dart, Bath 1970) – general works on a class of objects or those giving additional full bibliographical details have been preferred to earlier publications and therefore not every individual piece has been provided with a specific reference. In the works that are cited further reference to earlier material can, we hope, be readily found. The end date for materials cited is usually April 1987.

ABBREVIATIONS

AK Archäologisches Korrespondenzblatt.

APAS F. Moosleitner *Arte Protoceltica a Salisburgo: Mostra della Regione di Salisburgo, Museo degli Argenti, Palazzo Pitti, Firenze, 10 May–31 October 1987* (Salzburger Landesregierung 1987).

ATS Ancient Treasures of Scotland: loan exhibition from the National Museum of Antiquities of Scotland Feb.–Apr. 1978. (City of Aberdeen Art Gallery and Museum Dept., 1978).

BAR British Archaeological Reports

Brailsford John Brailsford *Early Celtic Masterpieces from Britain in the Collections of the British Museum* (British Museum Publications, London 1975).

Castriota D.R. Castriota *Continuity and Innovation in Celtic and Mediterranean Ornament: a grammatical-syntactical analysis of the processes of reception and innovation in the decorative arts of antiquity* Ph.D. thesis, Columbia University, 1981 (University Microfilms Ltd., Ann Arbor 1982).

Champion and Megaw T.C. Champion and J.V.S. Megaw (eds.) *Settlement and Society: aspects of West European prehistory in the first millennium B.C.* (Leicester U.P. 1985).

Daoulas *Au temps des Celtes: V^e au Ier siècle avant J.-C.; exhibition catalogue Abbaye de Daoulas 13 June–14 September 1986* (Association Abbaye de Daoulas 1986).

Duval P.-M. Duval *Les Celtes* (Gallimard, Paris 1977).

Duval and Hawkes P.-M. Duval and C.F.C. Hawkes (eds.) *Celtic Art in Ancient Europe: Five protohistoric centuries* (Seminar Press, London 1976).

Duval and Kruta 1979 P.-M. Duval and V. Kruta (eds.) *Les Mouvements celtiques du Ve au Ier siècle avant notre ère* (CNRS, Paris 1979).

Duval and Kruta 1982 P.-M. Duval and V. Kruta (eds.) *L'Art celtique de la période d'expansion: IVe et IIIe siècles avant notre ère* (Librairie Droz, Geneva/Paris 1982).

EC Etudes Celtiques.

FIK Frühe Irische Kunst (Berlin, Munich, Hamburg 1959).

Fitz J. Fitz (ed.) *The Celts in Central Europe = Papers of the II Pannonia Conference = Bull. du Musée Roi Saint-Etienne* A20 (Székesfehérvár 1975).

Fox Sir Cyril Fox *Pattern and Purpose: a survey of Early Celtic Art in Britain* (National Museum of Wales, Cardiff 1958).

Gauls Provincial *L'Art celtique en Gaule 1983–4: Collections des Musées de Province: catalogue* (Ministère de la Culture: Direction des Musées de France, 1983).

Hallstattkultur Catalogue *Die Hallstattkultur; Frühform europäischer Einheit* (Schloss Lamberg, Steyr 1980). Exhibition catalogue.

Hallstattkultur Symposium *Die Hallstattkultur: Symposium Steyr 1980* (Linz 1981): a collection of papers in connection with the Hallstatt exhibition.

HBA Hamburger Beiträge zur Archäologie.

Henry F. Henry *Irish Art in the Early Christian Period to A.D. 800* (Methuen, London 1965).

I Galli *I Galli e l'Italia: catalogue* (Soprintendenza Archeologica di Roma, Rome 1978).

IK *Irische Kunst aus drei Jahrtausenden: Thesaurus Hiberniae* (Römisch-Germanisches Museum, Köln 1983).

Jacobsthal ECA P. Jacobsthal *Early Celtic Art* 2 vols. (Clarendon Press, Oxford 1944; reprinted 1969).

Keltoi *KEATOI: Kelti in njihovi sobobniki na ozemljn Jugoslavije* Catalogue (Narodni Muzej Ljubljana, 1983).

Kilbride-Jones H.E. Kilbride-Jones *Celtic Craftsmanship in Bronze* (Croom Helm, London 1980).

KKM M. Szabó and E.F. Petres *A Keleti Kelta Müvészet – Eastern Celtic Art* Catalogue (Istvan Király Múzeum, Székesfehérvár 1974). Hungarian and English text.

KM L. Pauli (ed.) *Die Kelten in Mitteleuropa: Kultur-Kunst-Wissenschaft* (Salzburger Landesregierung, 1980).

Leeds E.T. Leeds *Celtic ornament in the British Isles down to A.D. 700* (Clarendon Press, Oxford 1933).

Lessing E. Lessing *Hallstatt: Bilder aus der Frühzeit Europas* (Jugend und Volk, Vienna and Munich 1980).

MacGregor M. MacGregor *Early Celtic Art in North Britain* 2 vols. (Leicester U.P. 1976).

Megaw AEIA J.V.S. Megaw *Art of the European Iron Age* (Adams and Dart, Bath 1970).

Megaw 1986 R. and V. Megaw *Early Celtic Art in Britain and Ireland* (Shire Publications, Princes Risborough 1986).

Popoli e Facies *Popoli e facies culturali celtiche a nord e a sud delle Alpi. Atti del Colloquio Intern., Milano 1980* (Museo Civico, Milan 1983).

PPS Proceedings of the Prehistoric Society.

Raftery 1 B. Raftery *A Catalogue of Irish Iron Age Antiquities = Veröffentlichungen des Vorgeschichtlichen Seminars Marburg Sonderband 1 (1983) 2 vols.*

Raftery 2 B. Raftery *La Tène in Ireland: Problems of Origin and Chronology = Veröffentlichungen des Vorgeschichtlichen Seminars Marburg Sonderband 2 (1984).*

RGK Römisch-Germanische Kommission.

RGZM Römisch-Germanisches Zentralmuseum.

Savory H.N. Savory *Early Iron Age Art in Wales* (National Museum of Wales, Cardiff 1968).

Stead I.M. Stead *Celtic Art in Britain Before the Roman Conquest* (British Museum Publications, London 1985).

Szabó M. Szabó *The Celtic Heritage in Hungary* (Corvina, Budapest 1971).

TEIA *Treasures of Early Irish Art 1500 BC to 1500 AD from the collections of the National Museum of Ireland, Royal Irish Academy, Trinity College Dublin, exhibited at the Metropolitan Museum* (New York 1977).

Toynbee 1962 J.M.C. Toynbee *Art in Roman Britain* (Phaidon, London 1962).

Toynbee 1964 J.M.C. Toynbee *Art in Britain under the Romans* (Clarendon Press, Oxford 1964).

INTRODUCTION

Iron Age Europe

John Collis *The European Iron Age* (Batsford, London 1984) provides an introduction to the Celts and their neighbours, strongest on the Hallstatt and oppida periods. On the Celts useful and lucid introductions include two older books, T.G.E. Powell *The Celts* (Thames and Hudson, London 1958) reissued unchanged save for further illustrations in 1980, and J. Filip *Celtic Civilization and its Heritage* 2nd rev. ed. (Collets, Wellingborough and Academia, Prague 1977), first published in 1962. V. Kruta *Les Celtes* 3rd ed. (Presses Universitaires de France, Paris 1983) is a brief study without illustrations.

For sober and authoritative surveys of the problems of bringing linguistic and archaeological evidence together in search of origins, D. Ellis Evans 'Celts and Germans' *Bull. Board of Celtic Studies* 29:2 (1981) 230–55; J.P. Mallory 'The Origins of the Irish' *J. Irish Arch.* 2 (1984) 65–69; J.P. Mallory *In Search of the Indo-Europeans* (Thames and Hudson, London and New York 1989).

Other more popular books, frequently lavishly illustrated, include A. Ross *The Pagan Celts: Creators of Europe* (Batsford, London 1986); J.-J. Hatt *The Ancient Civilization of Celts and Gallo-Romans* (Barrie and Jenkins, London 1970); D. Norton-Taylor et al. *The Celts* (Time-Life Books, New York 1974); B. Cunliffe *The Celtic World* (Bodley Head, London 1979), a thematic treatment which comes up to the present; J. Moreau *Die Welt der Kelten* (Klipper, Stuttgart 1979); F. Schlette *Kelten zwischen Alesia und Pergamon* (Urania, Leipzig 1979); V. Kruta with M. Szabó *Les Celtes* (Hatier, Paris 1978) with spectacular photography by E. Lessing. Some books, such as N. Chadwick and M. Dillon *The Celtic Realms* (Weidenfeld and Nicolson, London 1967) or N. Chadwick *The Celts* (Penguin, Harmondsworth 1970) deal almost exclusively with the British Isles, despite the wider implications of their titles. V. Kruta and W. Forman *The Celts of the West* (Orbis, London 1985) deals with Brittany and the British Isles. The latest overview, Frank Delaney *The Celts* (Hodder, London 1986) cannot be recommended here despite its attractive illustrations.

Scholarly pan-European surveys include Fitz, Duval and Kruta 1979, and the still invaluable J. Déchelette *Manuel d'archéologie préhistorique, celtique et gallo-romaine* 2nd ed. III–IV (Picard, Paris 1927) and *Manuel . . .* II: *Appendices* (1910).

Some books or articles dealing with specific regions or countries are also very useful, especially in areas of central and eastern Europe where recent research to disentangle Celts from other peoples is still complex.

Western Europe

FRANCE: There is no general treatment of Iron Age France. Some recent regional studies include J.-P. Mohen *L'Age du Fer en Aquitaine = Mémoires de la Société Préhistorique Française* 14 (1980); M. Willaume *Le Berry à l'âge du fer: HaC-La Tène II = BAR Suppl. Series* 247 (1985); P.-R. Giot et al. *Protohistoire de la Bretagne* (Ouest France, Rennes 1979). GERMANY: K. Bittel et al. *Die Kelten in Baden-Württemberg* (Konrad Theiss Verlag, Stuttgart 1981). Two series of regional archaeological guides are of major value: *Führer zu vor- und frühgeschichtlichen Denkmälern* published by Philipp von Zabern, Mainz, for the RGZM 1–50 (1964–82) and *Führer zu archäologischen Denkmälern in Deutschland* published by Konrad Theiss Verlag, Stuttgart, for Nordwestdeutscher und West- und Sudwestdeutscher Verband für Altertumsforschung 1– (1982–). AUSTRIA: R.

Pittioni, *Geschichte Österreichs* I: 1–2, *Urzeit* (Verlag der Österr. Akad. der Wiss., Vienna 1980), for a survey and literature review 1954–1978. SWITZERLAND: W. Drack *Ur- und Frühgeschichtliche Archäologie der Schweiz* IV: *Die Eisenzeit* (Schweizerische Gesellschaft für Ur- und Frühgeschichte, Basel 1974). ALPS: L. Pauli *The Alps: archaeology and early history* (Thames and Hudson, London 1984). SPAIN: M. Lenerz-de Wilde 'Keltische Funden aus Spanien' *AK* 11 (1981) 315–9; and personal information from the author, who is working on a major study of Iberian Celts. See also M. Almagro. *Ars Hispaniae* I: *Arte Prehistorico* (Editorial Plus-Ultra, Madrid 1947), 301–338; J. Maluquer de Motes 'Pueblas celtas' in R. Menendez Pidal *Historia de España* I: III (Espasa-Calpe SA, Madrid 1963) 5–194; W. Schüle 'Probleme der Eisenzeit auf der iberischen Halbinsel *Jahrbuch d. RGZM Mainz* 7 (1960) 59–125. BRITISH ISLES: see under Chapters 6 and Epilogue.

Central/Eastern Europe

Many valuable essays in Fitz. CZECHOSLOVAKIA: J. Filip *Keltové ve středni Evropě = Monumenta Archeologica* 5 (ČSAV, Prague 1956). His interpretations, and in particular his absolute chronology, have been modified recently by younger scholars in the light of new excavations, but the volume remains of value as an overview. HUNGARY: Szabó is brief, readable, in English, and well-illustrated. JUGOSLAVIA: M. Guštin 'Die Kelten in Jugoslavien; Übersicht über das archäologische Fundgut *Jahrb. RGZM* 31 (1984) 305–63; J. Todorovič *Kelti in jugostocnoj Europi = Dissertationes* 7 (Belgrade 1968); R. Vasić *The Chronology of the Early Iron Age in Serbia = BAR Suppl. Series* 3 (1977) gives an account of Serbia up to the period of Celtic settlement in the third century BC. ROMANIA: in English, V. Zirra 'The eastern Celts of Romania' *J. of Indo-European Studies* 4 (1976) 1–42. BULGARIA: Z. Woźniak 'Die Kelten und die Latènekultur auf den thrakischen Gebieten' in Fitz, 177–83. LOWER DANUBE (ROMANIA/BULGARIA): Z. Woźniak 'Die Östliche Randzone der Latènekultur' *Germania* 54 (1976) 382–402 is a summary of Z. Woźniak *Wschodnie prograniczе kultury laténskiej* (Ossolineum, Wroclaw–Warsaw–Cracow 1974). M. Domaradski *Keltite na Balkanskiya Poluostrov* (Nauka i Iskustvo, Sofia 1984) is the most recent regional survey.

Journals

The two most essential are *Etudes Celtiques* 1– (1944–) and *Hambürger Beiträge zur Archäologie* 1– (1971–). The former regularly includes regional bibliographies on the Celts, especially from vol. 14 on. Another useful bibliographical tool is H. Lorenz and O.-H. Frey (eds.) *Kommentierte Bibliographie zur Archäologie der Kelten* (Vorgeschichtliches Seminar, Philipps-Universität, Marburg) 1– (1976–), preceded by *Informationen zur Laténezeit* (1974–6). The much enlarged second edition of Johannes Hoops *Reallexikon der germanischen Altertumskunde* edited by H. Beck et al. (Walter de Gruyter, Berlin/New York 1973–), has lengthy entries on most aspects of the Celts, all fully referenced.

Horses and Chariots

S. Piggott *The Earliest Wheeled Transport* (Thames and Hudson, London 1983). ch. 5–6; L. Pauli and M. Guštin (eds.) *Keltski Voz* (Posavski Muzej, Brežice 1984); *Les tombes à char des princes et guerriers celtes = Histoire et archéologie: les dossiers*: 98 (October 1985); O.-H. Frey 'The chariot tomb from Adria: some notes on Celtic horsemanship and chariots' in J.V.S. Megaw (ed.) *To Illustrate the Monuments* (Thames and Hudson, London 1976) 172–9.

Technology and Crafts

There are useful summaries in B. Cunliffe *The Celtic World* (Bodley Head, London 1979) 112–25; H. Drescher 'Zur Technik der Hallstatt- zeit' in *Hallstattkultur Catalogue*, 54–66; F. Moosleitner 'Handwerk und Handel' *KM* 93–100; R. Wyss 'Technik, Wirtschaft, Handel und Kriegswesen der Eisenzeit' in W. Drack (ed.) *Ur- und Frühgeschichtliche Archäologie der Schweiz* IV: *Die Eizenzeit* (Schweiz. Gesellschaft für Ur- und Frühgeschichte, Basel 1974), 105–38.

Sources

Though it deals with the classical world, M, Crawford (ed.) *Sources for Ancient History* (Cambridge U.P. 1983) discusses in general the use of classical written sources and of archaeology respectively. T.C. Champion 'Written sources and the study of the European Iron Age' in Champion and Megaw 9–22 has recently discussed the problem in relation to the Celts. K.H. Jackson *The Oldest Irish Tradition: a window on the Iron Age* (Cambridge U.P. 1964) has strongly argued that later Irish literature may be used as a source for the structure of earlier Celtic societies, a challenge accepted by C. Gosden 'Gifts and Kin in Early Iron Age Europe' *Man* 20 (1985) 475–93, while C.L. Crumley *Celtic Social Structure: the generation of archaeologically testable hypotheses from literary evidence = Mus. Anthropology Univ. of Michigan Anthropological Papers* 54 (1974) has attempted to use classical sources for Gaul.

Major attempts to disentangle the classical sources on Celts include J.J. Tierney 'The Celtic Ethnography of Posidonius' *Procs. Royal Irish Acad.* 60C (1960) 189–275; F. Fischer 'Die Kelten bei Herodot' *Madrider Mitteilungen* 13 (1972) 109–24; C.F.C. Hawkes 'Britain and Julius Caesar' *Procs. British Acad.* 63 (1977), 125–92; C.F.C. Hawkes *Pytheas: Europe and the Greek Explorers = 8th J.L. Myres Memorial Lecture* (Oxford 1977).

A survey listing of relevant classical sources can be found in Crumley above and a discussion of Celtic ones in N. Chadwick *The Celts* (Penguin, Harmondsworth 1970) 255–91 and N. Chadwick and M. Dillon *The Celtic Realms* (Weidenfeld and Nicolson, London 1967) 159–286. An introductory anthology of later Celtic literature is K.H. Jackson *A Celtic Miscellany* rev. ed. (Penguin, Harmondsworth 1971).

History of Celtic Archaeology

A pioneer study is J.M. de Navarro 'A Survey of Research on an Early Phase of Celtic Culture' *Procs. British Acad.* 22 (1936) 297–344. For central Europe from Germany to Transylvania K. Sklenář *Archaeology in Central Europe: the First 500 Years* tr. I. Lewitová (Leicester U.P. 1983) deals with Celts among others. On Britain an elegant summary is S. Piggott *Celts, Saxons and the Early Antiquaries = The O'Donnell Lecture 1966* (Edinburgh U.P. 1966) and his *The Druids* (Thames and Hudson, London and New York 1975) also deals with the uses of words such as 'Celt' as well as being an object lesson in how to combine various types of sources, written or archaeological. On contemporary views concerning the chronology of the Iron Age (summarized in the Table on p. 258) see the various contributors to the article 'Chronologie' in J. Hoops *Reallexikon der Germanischen Altertumskunde* 4:5 (Walter de Gruyter, Berlin 1981), esp. 648 ff.

Ways of Seeing

On the psychology of perception see the writings of E.H. Gombrich esp. *Art and Illusion* 5th ed. (Phaidon, London 1977) and *The Sense of Order* (Phaidon, London 1979) on pictorial representation and ornament respectively; John M. Kennedy *A Psychology of Picture Perception* (Jossey-Bass, Washington and London 1974); R. Arnheim *Art and Visual Perception* 2nd ed. (University of California Press, Berkeley 1974). The debate on aesthetic versus social context theories of art has never been a real one in the study of prehistoric or non-Western art, though the tendency used to be to lump 'Primitive' art with material culture.

On non-western art see e.g. A. Forge (ed.) *Primitive Art and Society* (Oxford 1973); N.H.H. Graburn (ed.) *Ethnic and Tourist Arts* (University of California Press, Berkeley 1976); R. Layton *The Anthropology of Art* (Elek, London 1981); M. Greenhalgh and J.V.S. Megaw (eds.) *Art in Society* (Duckworth, London 1978). Satisfactory definitions are rare but a range may be found in D. Brook 'A New Theory of Art' *British Journal of Aesthetics* 20 (1980) 305–21; P. Canaday *What is Art?* (Knopf, New York 1981). On the nature of Western art R. Wollheim *Painting as an Art* (Thames and Hudson, London 1987).

Lively and iconoclastic views of art in prehistoric societies including the rejection of art as FIF (something that produces a Funny Inner Feeling) in J. Clegg *Notes Towards Mathesis Art* rev. ed. (Clegg Calendars, Sydney 1981); C. Chippindale 'What is "Prehistoric Art"?: a Definition and Its Consequences' *Arch. Review from Cambridge* 4 (1985) 141–58, though some other views in these works are more disputable. Attempts to 'objectify' the study of such art are generally less satisfactory since new models and 'information' do not always fit happily together, especially since prehistoric data cannot always be a representative sample. Compare Clegg *Notes . . .* (above), 3–199, on theory with Clegg *Notes . . .*, 200–384, on Australian Prehistoric Art, or D.K. Washburn 'Towards a theory of Structural styles in art' with her 'Symmetry analysis of pottery design: two tests of the method on Neolithic material from Greece and the Aegean', both in D.K. Washburn (ed.) *Structure and Cognition in Art* (Cambridge U.P. 1983) 1–7 and 138–164, an attempt to apply systems theory to problems in prehistoric style analysis.

Most books defining art also attempt to define style. Studies of individual stylistic variability within archaeological cultures include S. Plog *Stylistic Variability in Prehistoric Ceramics* (Cambridge U.P. 1980); J.N. Hill and J. Gunn (eds.) *Individual in Prehistory: Studies of Variability of Style in Prehistoric Technologies* (Academic Press, New York/San Francisco/London 1977).

Method and Technique

On Iron Age artistic techniques of decorating sheet metal see P.R. Lowery, R.D.A. Savage and R.L. Wilkins 'Scriber, Graver, Scorper, Tracer: notes on Experiments in Bronzeworking Technique' *PPS* 37 (1971) 167–82. Useful also is A. Steines *Metall – Treiben: Arbeitstechniken – Beispiele – Oberflächenbehandlung* (Coleman, Lübeck 1984). An interesting discussion of craft and workmanship – from a contemporary point of view – is D. Pye *The Nature and Art of Workmanship* (Cambridge U.P. 1968).

On the long-debated question of workshop versus itinerant metalwork production see J.V.S. Megaw 'Celtic art – product of travelling craftsmen or chieftainly vassals?' in Duval and Kruta 1979, 49–54; J.V.S. Megaw 'Meditations on a Celtic hobby-horse: notes towards a social archaeology of Iron Age art' in Champion and Megaw 161–91; S. Champion 'Production and exchange in Early Iron Age central Europe' in Champion and Megaw 133–60 addresses the questions of production of coral-decorated objects as well as their exchange.

Importance of the Head to Celts

P. Lambrechts *L'exaltation de la tête dans la pensée et dans l'art des Celtes = Dissertationes Archaeologicae Gandenses* 2 (1954); Megaw *AEIA passim*. For the 'religious' quality of Celtic art see esp. L. Pauli *Keltische Volksglaube: Amulette und Sonderbestattungen am Dürrnberg bei Hallein und im eisenzeitlichen Mitteleuropa = Münchner Beiträge zur Vor- und Frühgeschichte* 28 (1975). F. Maier 'Bronzes animaliers des Celtes' in Duval and Kruta 1982, 85–99, has some general observations on Celtic three-dimensional animal representations. See further on Celtic religion below.

Celtic Art

The starting point for all scholars is Jacobsthal *ECA* which is essential, though complex to use, and, since it was published early in 1944, contains no material discovered in the last forty years. The time and conditions of its production have also given it a Western European bias.

N.K. Sandars *Prehistoric Art in Ancient Europe* 2nd. ed. (Penguin, Harmondsworth 1985) is an overview, expressed with near-poetic insight and based on wide scholarship, of all prehistoric Europe. Ian Finlay *Celtic Art* (Faber, London 1973) and Kilbride-Jones, despite their titles, deal mainly with the British Isles. Megaw *AEIA* includes the British Isles; it contains an introductory essay together with illustrations, detailed catalogue entries and bibliographies on over 300 objects. This detail is why, when no more recent specific publication is available, bibliographical references are made to this book. Duval with its interesting and scholarly views and its wonderful photography, does not supply such information. Two sets of edited essays are also essential reading matter: Duval and Hawkes, and Duval and Kruta

1982. A. Varagnac et al. *L'Art gaulois* (Zodiaque, Abbaye Sainte Marie de la Pierre-qui-Vire, Yvonne 1956) is useful on France, as are K. Pieta *Umenie doby železnej = Ars Slovaca Antiqua* 15 (Tatran 1982) with English summary and catalogue and splendid photographs in colour on Slovakia, and Szabó again on Hungary; V. Kruta *L'Art celtique en Bohême: les parures métalliques du Ve au IIe siècle avant notre ère* (Honoré Champion, Paris 1975) on Bohemia.

Catalogues

Much material of importance, and sometimes the only publication of newer material, is in various museum or exhibition catalogues. R.A. Smith *Guide to the Antiquities of the early Iron Age in the Department of British and Mediaeval Antiquities* 2nd ed. (British Museum, London 1935). S. Piggott with D.F. Allen *Early Celtic Art* (Arts Council/Edinburgh U.P. 1971). I.M. Stead with V. Rigby *The Gauls: Celtic Antiquities from France* (British Museum Publications, London 1981) contains the same French material as *I Galli*, with some British. The illustrations are, however, poor. Based on the same lean material from France, *I Galli* has a great deal more on Italy than on Gaul, including essays of value. *Gauls Provincial* is in many ways the fullest catalogue on French Celtic material. For Central Europe, *KM* is absolutely essential, providing detailed entries with bibliography, many colour photographs and valuable introductory essays. Further east, *KKM* is very valuable especially on Hungary, as is *Keltoi* on Jugoslavia. Most recently *Au Temps des Celtes: V^e–Ier siècle avant J.-C. Catalogue of exhibition Abbaye de Daoulas 13 June–14 Sept 1986* has superb colour photographs but thin introductions and no bibliographical data for its catalogue. Too recent to cite extensively is *Trésors des princes celtes* (Musées nationeaux, Paris 1987).

Celtic Art and Religion in General

O.-H. Frey 'Die keltische Kunst' in *KM* 76–92. P.-M. Duval *Découverte et nature de l'art celtique ancien* public lecture to the Institut de France: Académie des Inscriptions et Belles-Lettres 25 Nov. 1977 (Paris 1977). P.-M. Duval 'Comment analyser, reproduire et expliquer les formes d'art celtique' in Duval and Kruta 1982, 3–24 deals with the vexed question of drawing and photographing Celtic art. J.V.S. Megaw 'Finding purposeful patterns: further notes towards a methodology of pre-Roman Celtic art' in Duval and Kruta 1982, 213–29; J.V.S. Megaw 'Meditations on a Celtic hobby-horse; notes towards a social archaeology of Iron Age art' in Champion and Megaw 161–91.

Some classical sources on religion are collected in J. Zwicken *Fontes Historiae Religionis Celticae = Fontes Hist. Relig. ex Auctoribus Graecis et Latinis* 5:1 (Walter de Gruyter, Berlin 1934); see also P.-M. Duval *Les dieux de la Gaule* (Presses Universitaires Françaises, Paris 1957); J.-L. Brunaux *Les Gaulois; sanctuaires et rites* (Errance, Paris 1986); J. de Vries *Keltische Religion* (Kohlhammer, Stuttgart 1961); Proinsias MacCana, *Celtic Mythology* rev. ed. (Newnes, Feltham 1983); Miranda Green, *The Gods of the Celts* (Alan Sutton, Gloucester 1986); W. Kimmig 'Götter-Druiden-Heiligtümer: Zeugnisse keltischer Religionsübung' *Jahrb. der Wittheit zu Bremen* 20 (1976) 43–72; J.-J. Hatt 'Die keltische Götterwelt und ihre bildliche Darstellung in vorrömischer Zeit', *KM* 52–67.

CHAPTER 1

Hallstatt Iron Age

Essential, especially for eastern and central Europe, are *Hallstattkultur Catalogue* and *Hallstattkultur Symposium*. An earlier catalogue *Kreiger und Salzherren: Hallstattkultur im Ostalpenraum* (RGZM, Mainz 1970) also has useful essays. Lessing has superb illustrations as well as some useful essays; collections of essays of value on central and eastern Europe are B. Chropovský (ed.) *Symposium zu Problemen der jüngeren Hallstattzeit in Mitteleuropa* (Verlag der Slowakischen Akademia der Wissenschaften, Bratislava 1974), and E. Jerem (ed.) *Hallstatt Kolloquium Veszprém 1984 = Mitt. Arch. Inst. d. Ungarischen Akad. d. Wiss.* Beiheft 3 (1986).

HALLSTATT: the basic publication, despite many errors, often due to

earlier faulty excavation, is still K. Kromer *Das Gräberfeld von Hallstatt* (Firenze 1959). On population composition see A. Häusler 'Kritische Bemerkungen zum Versuch Soziologischer Deutungen ur- and frühgeschichtlicher Gräberfelder' *Ethnographisch-Archäologische Zeitschrift* 9 (1968) 1–30. Recent summaries appear in F.E. Barth 'Das prähistorische Hallstatt; Bergbau und Gräberfeld' *Hallstattkultur Catalogue* 67–79; Lessing, 72–94; F.E. Barth 'Prehistoric Saltmining at Hallstatt' *Bull. Institute of Archaeology* 19 (1982) 31–43; F.R. Hodson 'Hallstatt: dry bones and flesh *Proc. British Acad.* 71 (1985) 187–202.

SPEIKERN FIGURINE: F. Vollrath 'Das Reiterlein von Speikern' *Vorzeit* 1/2 (1964) 3–8; H.-P. Uenze and J. Gregor 'Das Gräberfeld von Speikern im Landkreis Lauf-an-der-Pegnitz' *Jahresbericht Bayerischer Denkmalpflege* 11/12 (1970/1) 97–115.

BYČÍ SKÁLA: *Hallstatt a Byčí skála* (exhibition catalogue) Brno, Bratislava, Praha (Československa Akademie Ved, 1969); J. Nekvasil 'Die Byčí skála Höhle' Lessing 95–99; W. Angeli 'Zur Deutung der Funde aus der Byčí skála Höhle' in *Krieger und Salzherren* (Mainz 1970) 139–50; J. Nekvasil 'Revisions of Wankel's observations in the cave of Byčí skála, cadastral Territory of Habrůvka, District of Blansko' *Nouvelles Archéologiques dans la République Socialiste Tchèque = Archaeological News in the Czech Socialist Republic* (Archaeological Institute, Czechoslovak Academy of Sciences, Prague 1981) 75–81.

SWORDS: see briefly W. Kimmig 'Bewaffnung – Hallstattzeit' in *Reallexikon der Germanischen Altertumskunde* Bd. 2 (De Gruyter, Berlin/New York 1976) 388ff. and O.-H. Frey 'Bewaffnung im Hallstattkreis' *EC* 20, 1983, 7–21; more fully H. Gerdsen *Studien zu den Schwertgräbern der älteren Hallstattzeit* (Philipp von Zabern, Mainz 1986).

POTTERY – EASTERN: in general see C. Dobiat 'Menschen-darstellungen auf ostalpiner Hallstattkeramik'. *Acta Archaeologica Academiae Scientarum Hungaricae* 34 (1984) 279–322; A. Reichenberger 'Figürliche Darstellungen der Hallstattzeit' in S. Rieckhoff-Pauli and W. Torbrügge *Regensburg-Kelheim-Straubing* I = *Führer zu archäologischen Denkmälern in Deutschland* 5 (Theiss, Stuttgart 1984) 190–7. On music-players A. Reichenberg 'Der Leierspieler im Bild der Hallstattzeit' *AK* 15 (1985) 325–33; A. Eibner 'Musikleben in der Hallstattzeit', in M. von Albrecht (ed.) *Quellen und Studien zur Musikgeschichte von der Antike bis in die Gegenwart* 1 (Frankfurt) 271–318.

SOPRON: E. Patek 'Die Gruppe der Hallstattkultur in der Umgebung von Sopron' *Archaeologiai Értesitö* 103 (1976) 3–28; E. Patek 'Über die neueren Ausgrabungen in Sopron-Varhély (Burgstall) und die Probleme der östlichen Beziehungen' *Mitteilungen des Arch. Inst. der Ungarischen Akademie der Wissenschaften* 6 (1976) 39ff.; A. Eibner-Persy *Hallstattzeitliche Grabhügel von Sopron (Ödenburg) = Wissenschaftliche Arbeiten aus dem Burgenland* 62 (Eisenstadt 1980); E. Patek 'Neue Untersuchungen auf dem Burgstall bei Sopron' *63 Ber. d. RGK Mainz* (1982) 105–77. Still useful is Sandor Gallus 'Die figuralverzierten Urnen vom Soproner Burgstall' *Arch. Hungarica* XIII (1934).

DUNAJSKÁ LUŽNÁ: M. Pichlerová *Nové Košariská* (Slovenské Narodné Múzeum, Bratislava 1969).

POTTERY – BAVARIA: W. Torbrügge 'Figürliche Zeichnungen der Hallstattzeit aus Nordostbayern und ihre Beziehungen zur antiken Welt' *Festschrift für Max Spindler zum 75. Geburtstag* (Munich 1979) 1–24; H.P. Uenze 'Zu einigen bildlichen Darstellungen der Hallstattzeit aus Nordostbayern' *Hallstattkultur Symposium* 375–88.

FISCHBACH: W. Torbrügge 'Hallstattzeitliche Terrakotten von Fischbach-Schirndorf in der Oberpfalz' *Studien zur vor- und frühgeschichtlichen Archäologie = Festschrift für Joachim Werner zum 65. Geburtstag* I (1974) 57–72; A. Strob *Die hallstattzeitliche Gräberfeld von Schirndorf, Ldkr. Regensburg* I = *Materialhefte bayerischer Vorgeschichte* Reihe A, 35 (1979).

STRETTWEG CULT WAGON: W. Schmid *Der Kultwagen von Strettweg = Führer zur Urgeschichte* 12 (Curt Kabitsch, Leipzig 1934); W. Modrijan *Der Kultwagen von Strettweg* (Steiermärkisches Landesmuseum Joanneum, Graz, Section 5, 3.1.1., 1973); W. Modrijan 'Der Kultwagen von Strettweg' *IPEK* 24 (1974–7) 91–7.

Situula Art

GENERAL: O.-H. Frey *Die Entstehung der Situlenkunst: Studien zur figürlich verzierten Toreutik von Este = Römisch-Germanische Forschungen* 31 (De Gruyter, Berlin 1969); O.-H. Frey 'Die Kunst der Situlen: Metallarbeiten der Vorzeit im Sudostalpinenraum' *IPEK* 23 (1970–73) 41–45; O.-H. Frey 'Situlenkunst' in Lessing 126–34; O.-H. Frey 'Werke der Situlenkunst' in *Hallstattkultur Catalogue* 138–49; W. Lücke and O.-H. Frey *Die Situla in Providence (Rhode Island) = Römisch-Germanische Forschungen* 26 (1962); *Situlenkunst zwischen Po und Donau*: exhibition catalogue Padua, Ljubljana, Vienna (1962).

SLOVENIA: summary in T. Knez 'Denkmäler der Situlenkunst in Slowenien: Fundkatalog und Bibliographie' *Archeološki Vestnik* 34 (1983) 85–105. MAGDALENSKA GORA: H. Hencken with P.S. Wells *The Iron Age Cemetery of Magdalenska gora in Slovenia: Mecklenburg Collection Part II* (Peabody Museum Harvard, Cambridge Mass. 1978). VAČE: F. Stare *Vače = Arkeološki Katalogi Slovenije I* (Ljubljana 1985); on the situlae J. Kastelic *Die Situla aus Vače Jugoslavia* (Belgrade 1956). NOVO MESTO: T. Knez *Novo mesto v antiki: razstavni Katalog* (Novo mesto 1974); T. Knez 'Novo mesto in der Hallstattzeit' in *Hallstattkultur Symposium* 241–60; on the situlae T. Knez 'Novo mesto: figuralverzierte Situlen aus Novo mesto' *Antike Welt* 7 (1976) 32–8; T. Knez 'Figurale Situlen aus Novo mesto' *Arheološki Vestnik* 24 (1973) 309–26; T. Knez *Novo Mesto I: Halštatski grobovi = Carniola Archaeologica* I (Dolenski musej, Novo mesto 1986). HALLSTATT: H. Polenz 'Einige Bemerkungen zum figuralverzierten Bronzedeckel aus Grab 697' *Metteilungen der Anthropologischen Gesellschaft in Wien* 108 (1978) 127–39 argues that the animals on the Grave 697 situla lid are horses, not dogs.

Hallstatt D 'Princely' Culture

K. Spindler *Die frühen Kelten* (Reclam, Stuttgart 1983) is the only, if controversial, overview. H.G.H. Härke *Settlement Types and Patterns in the West Hallstatt Province = BAR Internat. Series* 57 (1979) covers settlement. F. Fischer with J. Biel 'Frühkeltische Fürstengräber in Mitteleuropa' *Antike Welt* 13 (1982), a special issue, is devoted to the grave finds – including articles on the Magdalenenberg, the Heuneburg, Eberdingen-Hochdorf, Hohenasperg, Burgundy and Switzerland.

IMPORTANT REGIONAL STUDIES: these include K. Bittel et al. (ed.) *Die Kelten in Baden-Württemberg* (Theiss, Stuttgart 1981); G. Kossack *Gräberfelder der Hallstattzeit an Main und frankische Saale* (Michael Lassleben, Kallmünz 1970); G. Wamser 'Zur Hallstatt-Kultur in Ostfrankreich: die Fundgruppen im Jura und Burgund' *56 Ber. d. RGK* (1975) 1–177; W. Torbrügge *Die Hallstattzeit in der Oberpfalz* I *= Materialhefte zur Bayerischen Vorgeschichte* 39 (Kallmünz 1979); L. Pauli 'Untersuchungen zur Späthallstattkultur in Nordwürttemberg' *= HBA* 2:1 (1972); N. Friedin *The Early Iron Age in the Paris Basin: Hallstatt C and D = BAR Internat. Series* 131 (1982).

Hallstatt D: Specific Sites

HEUNEBURG: W. Kimmig *Die Heuneburg an der oberen Donau = Führer zu vor- und frühgeschichtlichen Denkmälern in Baden-Württemberg* I 2nd ed. (Theiss, Stuttgart 1983); on the pottery mould see W. Kimmig and O.-W. von Vacano 'Zu einem Gussformfragment einer etruskischen Bronzekanne von der Heuneburg' *Germania* 51 (1973) 72–85; on pottery H.W. Dämmer *Die bemalte Keramik der Heuneburg: die Funde aus der Grabungen von 1950–73* 2 vols. *= Römisch-Germanische Forschungen* 37 *= Heuneburgstudien* IV (Philipp von Zabern, Mainz 1978).

MAGDALENENBERG: K. Spindler *Magdalenenberg; der hallstattzeitliche Fürstengrabhügel bei Villingen* vols 1–6 (Neckar Verlag, Villingen 1971–80); for a shorter version K. Spindler *Der Magdalenenberg bei Villingen = Führer zu vor- und frühgeschichtlichen Denkmälern in Baden-Württemberg* 5 (Theiss, Stuttgart 1976).

BRITZGYBERG: R. Schweitzer 'Le Britzgyberg; der Fürstensitzstation du Hallstatt' *Bulletin du Musée Historique de Mulhouse* 81 (1973) 43–64.

EBERDINGEN-HOCHDORF: J. Biel 'The late Hallstatt chieftain's grave at Eberdingen-Hochdorf' *Antiquity* 55 (1981) 16–18; J. Biel 'Ein Fürstengrabhügel der späten Hallstattzeit bei Eberdingen-Hochdorf, Kr. Ludwigsburg' *Germania* 60 (1982) 61–104; J. Biel *Der Keltenfürst von Hochdorf* (Theiss, Stuttgart 1985); *Der Keltenfürst von Hochdorf: Methode und Ergebnisse der Landesarchäologie* (exhibition catalogue) (Landesdenkmalamt Baden-Württemberg 1985).

HIRSCHLANDEN STATUE: H. Zürn 'An anthropological Hallstatt stele (Hirschlanden)' *Antiquity* 38 (1964) 224–6; W. Kimmig 'Der Krieger von Hirschlanden' *Le rayonnement des civilisations grecques et romaines sur les cultures périphériques. 8me Congrès International d'Archéologie Classique Paris 1963* (Paris 1965) 94–101; H. Zürn *Hallstattforschungen in Nordwürttemberg (Asperg, Hirschlanden, Mühlacker) = Staatl. Amt. für Denkmalpflege Reihe A*, 16 (Stuttgart 1970); H. Zürn 'Die hallstattzeitliche Kriegerstele von Hirschlanden' *Ausgrabungen in Deutschland ... 1950–75 = Monographien des RGZM Mainz* 1 (1975) 212–5; J. Beeser 'Der Kouro-Keltos von Hirschlanden' *Fundberichte zur Baden-Württemberg* 8 (1983) 21–46; C. Eibner 'Die hallstattzeitliche Kriegerstele von Hirschlanden – Ehemals ein griechischer Kouros?' *Pro Arte Antiqua: Festschr. für Hedwig Kenner* (Vienna 1982) 117–22.

VIX: R. Joffroy *Le Trésor de Vix (Côte d'Or)* (Presses Universitaires de France, Paris 1954); R. Joffroy *L'Oppidum de Vix et la civilisation hallstattienne finale dans l'est de la France* (Bernigaud, Dijon 1960); R. Joffroy *Vix et ses Trésors* (Tallandier, Paris 1979) (text as 1960); J.V.S. Megaw 'The Vix burial' *Antiquity* 40 (1966) 38–44; J. Driehaus 'Zum Krater von Vix: Fragen en die Klassische Archäologie' *HBA* 8 (1981) 103–13 opposes the view of recent Greek participation in transportation and assemblage of the *krater* as expressed e.g. by C. Rolley *Les vases de bronze de l'Archaïsme recent en Grand Grèce* (Les Belles Lettres, Paris 1982).

GOLD: for a summary see W. Drack 'Gold' in Lessing 64–71; W. Kimmig and W. Rest 'Ein Fürstengrab der spätem Hallstattzeit von Kappel an Rhein' *Jahrb. d. RGZM Mainz 1953*, 1 (1954) 202ff. make stylistic divisions among Hallstatt gold material; W. Kimmig 'Die Goldschale von Zürich-Altstetten: Bemerkungen zu ihrer Datierung und kulturhistorischer Einordnung' in *Homenaje al Prof. Martin Almagro Basch* II (Ministerio de Cultura, Madrid 1983) 101–18 deals with more than the Altstetten bowl, rejecting a Spanish origin for such goldwork (cf. K. Spindler *Die Frühen Kelten* (Reclam, Stuttgart 1983) on gold and silver); for 'transvestism' in Hallstatt grave evidence see L. Pauli as cited under 'Amulets' below.

ANTENNAE-DAGGERS of HALLSTATT D: S. Sievers *Die mitteleuropäischen Hallstattdolche = Kleine Schriften aus dem Vorgeschichtlichen Seminar Marburg* 7 (1980); *Hallstattkultur Symposium* 398–410; S. Sievers *Die mitteleuropäischen Hallstattdolche; ein Beitrag zur Waffenbeigabe im Westhallstattkreis = Prähistorische Bronzefunde Abt.* 6 Bd 6 (Beck, Munich 1982).

BELT-PLAQUES: F. Maier 'Zur Herstellungstechnik und Zierweise der späthallstattzeitlichen Gürtelbleche Südwestdeutschlands' *Ber. d. RGK* 39 (1958) 131–249; I. Kilian-Dirlmeier *Die hallstattzeitlichen Gürtelbleche und Blechgürtel Mitteleuropas = Prähistorische Bronzefunde* XII, 1 (Munich 1972).

TEXTILES: this field is a speciality of H.J. Hundt. See e.g. 'Die Webkunst' in Lessing 88–94; 'Die Textilien im Grab von Hochdorf' 106–115 in Eberdingen-Hochdorf catalogue cited above.

HALLSTATT D POTTERY: there are few recent studies of Hallstatt D pottery apart from that by Dämmer cited above under 'Heuneburg'; see also J. Keller *Die Alb-Hegau Keramik der älteren Eisenzeit = Tübinger Forschungen zur Archäologie und Kunstgeschichte* 18 (Reutlingen 1939). The Burrenhof pottery is probably from the Heuneburg.

AMULETS: L. Pauli *Keltischer Volksglaube: Amulette und Sonderbestattungen am Dürrnberg bei Hallein und im eisenzeitlichen Mitteleuropa = Münchner Beiträge zu Vor- und Frühgeschichte* 28 (Munich 1975).

Trade and Social Structure

The question of the nature and role of trade in Hallstatt D society, and its connection both with social structure and with the rise and collapse of that area has been a hard-fought battle in recent years. Franz Fischer 'KEIMHΛIA: Bemerkungen zur Kulturgeschichtlichen

Interpretation des sogenannten Südimports in der späten Hallstatt- und frühen Latène-Kultur des westlichen Mitteleuropa' *Germania* 51 (1973), 436–59 suggested, on Homeric analogies, that southern imports were not the result of modern-style commerce, but the result of gift-exchange between high-ranking individuals. S. Frankenstein and M. Rowlands 'The internal structure and regional context of Early Iron Age Society in south-western Germany' *Bull. Institute of Archaeology* 15 (1978) 73–112 used ethnographic parallels to create a model by which luxury goods circulated in patterns to reinforce the prestige of certain individuals and intensify controlled production for exchange leading to 'proto-urbanization'; shifts in patterns of southern export trade led to the collapse of Hallstatt D culture when such goods could no longer be obtained. Peter Wells, especially in *Culture contact and culture change; early Iron Age Central Europe and the Mediterranean* (Cambridge U.P. 1980) and *Farms, Villages and Cities: commerce and urban origins in Late Prehistoric Europe* (Cornell U.P. 1984) has emphasized the importance of basic economic production rather than luxury trade, the profit motive and entrepreneurial skills in barbarian Europe as engines of changes, and briefly offers 'readjustment' to changed patterns as the reason for the end of Hallstatt D. Chris Gosden 'Gifts and Kin in early Iron Age Europe' *Man* 20 (1985) 475–93 replaces ethnographic models by models based on Early Christian Irish written sources, arguing that Hallstatt D social structure would not have produced such patterns of exchange as those postulated by Rowlands. Ludwig Pauli in *Der Dürrnberg bei Hallein* III (Beck, Munich 1978), in 'Das keltische Mitteleuropa vom 6. bis zum 2. Jahrhundert v. Chr.' *KM* 25–36 and in a recent seminar paper has proposed yet another model by which the structure of Celtic society was based on specific types of relations with the Mediterranean world – whether by trade with the south, exaction of tribute in return for trade, or invasion.

Other recent works of importance include Heinrich Härke *Settlement Types and Settlement Patterns in the Western Hallstatt Province = BAR Internat. Ser.* 57 (1979) and 'Höhensiedlungen im Westhallstattkreis – ein Diskussions-beitrag' *AK* 13 1983, 461–77; Wolfgang Kimmig 'Die griechische Kolonisation im westlichen Mittelmeergebiet und ihre Wirkung auf die Landschaften des westlichen Mitteleuropa' *J. RGZM* 30 (1983) 5–78; Konrad Spindler, most recently in *Die frühen Kelten* (Reklam., Stuttgart 1983); Daphne Nash 'Celtic territorial expansion and the Mediterranean World' in T.C. Champion and J.V.S. Megaw (eds.) *Settlement and Society* (Leicester U.P. 1985) 45–67.

This question can be further complicated by the debate over how far, if at all, Hallstatt D culture overlapped with that of La Tène A, a question not explored here. W. Dehn and O.-H. Frey 'Southern Imports and Early La Tène Chronology of Central Europe' in D. and F.R. Ridgway (eds.) *Italy before the Romans* (Academic Press, London 1979) 489–511 accept some overlap; the most extreme overlap – to about 350 BC – is claimed by Spindler *Die frühen Kelten* (Reklam., Stuttgart 1983). Further studies in *HBA* 2:2 (1972) cover the problem generally as well as in specific areas.

SOUTH GERMAN DENDROCHRONOLOGY: on the somewhat confused state, Ernst Hollstein *Mitteleuropäische Eichenchronologie = Trierer dendrochronologische Forschungen zur Archäologie und Kunstgeschichte; Trierer Grabungen und Forschungen* 11 (Mainz 1980). GREEK COLONIES: for their speed, J. Boardman *The Greeks Overseas* new enlarged ed. (Thames and Hudson, London 1980). ETRUSCANS: D. and F.R. Ridgway (eds.) *Italy Before the Romans* (Academic Press, London 1979); Mauro Cristofani *The Etruscans: a new investigation* (Orbis, London 1979); M. Grant *The Etruscans* (Weidenfeld and Nicolson, London 1980); O.J. Brendel *Etruscan Art* (Penguin, Harmondsworth 1978). Among the flood of publications for the 1985 Year of the Etruscans the one of most value is Mauro Cristofani *Civiltà degli etruschi* (Electa, Milan 1985); see too L. Bonfante (ed.) *Etruscan Life and Afterlife: a handbook of Etruscan Studies* (Aris and Phillips, London 1986) and for contact between Etruscans and non-Etruscans in the north of Italy a further important catalogue, R. De Marinis *Gli Etruschi a Nord del Po* (Comune di Mantova, Mantua 1986).

SAAR/HUNSRÜCK-EIFEL: on whether iron was the reason for Celtic settlement there J. Driehaus 'Fürstengräber und Eisenerze zwischen Mittelrhein, Mosel und Saar' *Germania* 43 (1965) 32–49. GRAVE-ROBBING: J. Driehaus 'Der Grabraub in Mitteleuropa während der älteren Eisenzeit' in H. Jankuhn et al. (eds.) *Zum Grabfrevel in vor- und frühgeschichtlicher Zeit* (Vandenhoeck and Ruprecht, Göttingen 1978) 18–47.

CHAPTER 2

Southern Connections of Early La Tène Culture

There is once more a large and diffuse amount of literature. Recent treatments with bibliographies of earlier works include O.-H. Frey 'Zum Handel und Verkehr während der Frühlatènezeit in Mitteleuropa' and D. Timpe 'Der keltische Handel nach historischen Quellen' both in K. Düwel et al. (eds.) *Untersuchungen zu Handel und Verkehr der vor- und frühgeschichtlichen Zeit in Mittel- und Nordeuropa* 1 (Vandenhoeck and Ruprecht, Göttingen 1985). 231–57, 258–84. Important for transalpine trade is L. Pauli 'Die Golasecca-Kultur und Mitteleuropa: ein Beitrag zur Geschichte des Handels über die Alpen' = *HBA* 1:1 (1971). The Dehn and Frey paper cited under ch. 1 is crucial for the dating of Early La Tène by these imports: W. Dehn and O.-H. Frey 'Southern imports and the Hallstatt and Early La Tène Chronology of Central Europe' in D. and F.R. Ridgway (eds.) *Italy Before the Romans* (Academic Press, London 1979) 489–503.

Eastern and Western Burial Zones

These are surveyed in H. Lorenz 'Regional organisation in the western Early La Tène province; the Marne-Mosel and Rhine-Danube groups' in Champion and Megaw 109–22, an English summary of his 'Totenbrauchtum und Tracht: Untersuchungen zur regionaler Gliederung in der frühen Latènezeit' *Ber. d. RGK* 59 (1978) 1–380. RHINELAND: this area has been covered with exemplary scholarship in A. Haffner *Die westliche Hunsrück-Eifel-Kultur = Römisch-Germanische Forschungen* 36 (1976).

MARNE/CHAMPAGNE: D. Bretz-Mahler *La Civilisation de La Tène I en Champagne = 23me supplément à Gallia* (1971) though interesting on social structure has poor illustrations and less detailed information than Haffner. A. Thenot *La Civilisation dans l'Est de la France d'après la Collection de Baye au Musée des Antiquités Nationales à St Germain-en-Laye* 2 vols. (Fondation Singer-Polignac, Paris 1982) is much fuller than its title suggests; P. Sankot 'Le rite funéraire des nécropoles laténiennes en Champagne' *EC* 15 (1976–7) 49–94. CHRONOLOGY: for this French region see J.-J. Hatt and P. Roualet 'La chronologie de La Tène en Champagne' *Revue archéologique de l'Est* 28 (1977) 7–136; A. Duval 'Regional Groups in Western France' in S. Macready and F.H. Thomson (eds.) *Cross-Channel Trade Between Gaul and Britain in the Pre-Roman Iron Age* (Society of Antiquaries, London 1984) 78–91; J.-J. Hatt 'Réflexions sur l'Origine et la formation de la Civilisation de la Tène' in A. Bocquet et al. (eds.) *Eléments de Pré- et Protohistoire Européenne: Hommages à J.-P. Millotte = Annales Littéraires de l'Université de Besançon* 299 (1985) 351–6. BOHEMIA: J. Meduna *Die latènezeitlichen Siedlungen und Gräberfelder in Mähren = Fontes Archaeologiae Moravicae* XI (Aú ČSAV, Brno 1980) and C. Gosden 'Bohemian Iron Age Chronologies and the seriation of Radovesice' *Germania* 62 (1984) 289–309 reassess Iron Age chronology in this region to show Early La Tène settlement in Bohemia.

THE DÜRRNBERG AND ITS IMPORTANCE: finds to 1972 are discussed in E. Penninger *Der Dürrnberg bei Hallein* I (Beck, Munich 1972); F. Moosleitner, L. Pauli, E. Penninger *Der Dürrnberg bei Hallein* II (Beck, Munich 1974); L. Pauli *Der Dürrnberg bei Hallein* III (Beck, Munich 1978). See also F. Moosleitner *Die Schnabelkanne von Dürrnberg* (Salzburger Museum C.A. 1985) for further bibliography, which does not, however, include F. Fischer 'Württemberg und der Dürrnberg bei Hallein' *Fundberichte aus Baden-Württemberg* 9 (1984) 223–48. *APAS* is a useful recent catalogue of Dürrnberg material.

Early La Tène Art

For general works the starting point is, as always, Jacobsthal *ECA*.

Important recent articles are J.V.S. Megaw 'Style and style groupings in continental early La Tène Art' *World Archaeology* (3 (1972) 276–92; O.-H. Frey and F. Schwappach 'Studies in early Celtic design' *World Archaeology* 4 (1973) 339–56; F.Schwappach 'Floral Decoration and Arc-Designs of the "Early Style" of Celtic Art: ornaments of the Western and Eastern Circles of La Tène' *EC* 13 (1973) 710–32; P.-M. Duval 'Deux éléments fondamentaux du Premier Style celtique' *EC* 14 (1974) 1–19; F. Schwappach 'Ostkeltisches und Westkeltisches Ornament auf einem älterlatènezeitlichen Gurtelhaken von Mühlacker, Kr. Vaihingen' *Fundberichte aus Baden-Württemberg* 1 (1974) 337–72; F. Schwappach 'L'art ornemental du Premier Style celtique' in Duval and Hawkes 61–110.

BOHEMIA: V. Kruta 'Le Premier Style laténien en Bohême' in Duval and Hawkes 111–30; V. Kruta *L'Art Celtique en Bohême: les parures métalliques du Ve au IIe siècle avant notre ère* (Honoré Champion, Paris 1975) lists all Early Style metalwork in Bohemia. COMPASS DESIGN: M. Lenerz-de Wilde *Zirkelornamentik in der Kunst der Latènezeit = Münchner Beiträge zur vor- und Frühgeschichte* 25 (1977). KLEINASPERGLE: the definitive publication of this crucial nineteenth-century find is W. Kimmig (ed.) *Das Kleinaspergle: Ein Furstengrabhügel beim Hohenasperg, Kr. Ludwigsburg = Forschungen und Berichte zur Vor- und Frühg. in Baden-Württemberg* 30 (1988).

Rhineland Sheet Goldwork

SCHWARZENBACH: O.-H. Frey 'Die Goldschale von Schwarzenbach' *HBA* 1 (1971) 85–100 deals also with much of the other goldwork. EIGENBILZEN: W. Kimmig 'Das Fürstengrab von Eigenbilzen: neue Überlegung zu einem alten Fund' *Bull. des Musées Royaux d'Art et d'Histoire, Bruxelles* 54 (1983) 37–53. GOLD PLAQUES: A. Haffner 'Die frühlatènezeitlichen Goldscheiben vom Typ Weiskirchen' in *Festschrift 100 Jahre Rheinisches Landesmuseums Trier* (Philipp von Zabern, Mainz 1979) 281–96 covers most of these objects but see also on Chlum, J. Břeň 'Výzdoba šperku z Chlumu u Zvíkovce, okr. Rokycany' *Praehistorica VIII = Varia Archaeologica 2 = Sborník k poctě 80. narozenin Akademika Jana Filipa* (Prague 1981) 179–82 and, on the Uetliberg, W. Drack 'Der frühlatènezeitliche Fürstengrabhügel auf dem Uetliberg' *Zeitschrift für Schweizerische Archäologie und Kunstgeschichte* 38 (1981) 1–28; W. Kimmig *Frühe Kelten in der Schweiz im Spiegel der Ausgrabungen auf dem Uetliberg* (Selbstverlag der Stiftung für die Erforschung des Uetlibergs, Zürich 1983). WEISKIRCHEN: on drinking horns see L. Frey-Asche 'Zu einem goldenen Trinkhornbeschlag aus Weiskirchen' in H.A. Cahn and E. Simons (eds.) *Tainia = Festschrift Roland Hampe* (Philipp von Zabern, Mainz 1980) 121–32. On the flagon A. Haffner 'L'Oenochoé de Weiskirchen I: Etude technique' in *Les Ages du Fer dans la Vallée de la Saône = 6e supplément à Revue archéologique de l'Est* (1985) 279–82. A full publication by Professor Haffner of these Weiskirchen graves is in progress. AMEIS-SIESBACH SWORD: Haffner ... *Hunsrück-Eifel Kultur* (above) (1976) 204–5 and Taf. 8; a better illustration in A. Haffner 'Aus Vor- und Frühgeschichte' in *Kunst und Kultur im Birkenfelder Land* (1982) 22. REINHEIM: J. Keller *Das keltische Fürstengrab von Reinheim* I (RGZM, Mainz 1965); *KM* no. 33.

Marne/Champagne and Horse-Harness

LA BOUVANDEAU: *KM* no. 31; Megaw *AEIA* no. 112. SOMME-BIONNE: Megaw *AEIA* no. 111. CUPERLY: *KM* no. 154, L'EGLISE: A. Cahen-Delhaye *Tombelles de la Tène à l'Eglise: Inventaire = Archaeologia Belgica* 245 (1981). DANUBE HORSE-BIT: L. Pauli 'Eine frühkeltische Prunktrense aus der Donau' *Germania* 61 (1983) 459–86. MAINZ: *KM* no. 155, VILLENEUVE-RENNEVILLE: A. Brisson et al. 'Le cimetière gaulois La Tène Ia du Mont-Gravet, à Villeneuve-Renneville (Marne): suite et fin' *Mémoires de la Société d'Agriculture, Commerce, Sciences et Arts du département de la Marne* 87 (1972) 9–48. VERT-LA-GRAVELLE SWORD: Jacobsthal *ECA* no. 90. BERRU HELMETS: U. Schaaff 'Frühlatènezeitliche Grabfunde mit Helmen vom Typ Berru' *Jahrb. d. RGZM* 20 (1973) 81–106.

The Orientalizing Style

GENERAL: Works arguing for direct connections with the east are, most recently, N. Sandars 'Orient and Orientalising: recent thoughts reviewed' in Duval and Hawkes 41–60; F. Fischer 'Thrakien als Vermittler iranischer Metallkunst an die frühen Kelten' and H. Luschey 'Thrakien als Ort der Begegnung der Kelten mit der iranischen Metallkunst' both in R.M. Boehmer and H. Hauptmann (eds.) *Beiträge zur Altertumskunst Kleinasiens: Festschrift für Kurt Bittel* (Philipp von Zabern, Mainz 1983) 191–202 and 313–29; James E. Dean 'The Animal style in Celtic and Thracian art' in J.T. Koch and J. Ritmueller (eds.) *Proceedings of the Harvard Celtic Colloquium May 6–7 1983* (Dept. of Celtic Languages and Literatures, Harvard University, Cambridge, Mass.) 149–68. Works arguing against include Castriota – the reference on p. 65 is from his study, p. 259; J.V.S. Megaw 'The orientalising theme in Celtic art: East or West' in Fitz 15–33; F. Schwappach 'Zu einigen Tierdarstellungen der Frühlatènekunst' *HBA* 4 (1974) 103–40; H.G. Hüttel 'Keltische Zierscheiben und thrakischer Pferdegeschirrschmuck' *Germania* 56 (1978) 150–71 – which generally emphasize transmission by way of the orientalizing phase of Etruscan art.

ON THE VETTERSFELDE FIND: A. Greifenhagen 'Centenarium eines Goldfisches: hundert Jahre Fund von Vettersfelde' *Antike Welt* 13 (1982) 3–9. WEISKIRCHEN BELT PLAQUE: *KM* no. 24. PARSBERG BROOCH: *KM* no. 119; Megaw *AEIA* no. 63. BELT HOOKS: M. Lenerz-de Wilde 'Die frühlatènezeitlichen Gürtelhaken mit figuraler Verzierung' *Germania* 58 (1980) 61–103; Megaw *AEIA* nos. 95–99; *KM* nos. 128–31. STUPAVA: Megaw *AEIA* no. 64; *KM* no. 132. HOCHSCHEID SWORD: A. Haffner 'Die frühkeltische Fürstengräber von Hochscheid – "Fuckerichsheide"' in *Westlicher Hunsrück = Führer zu vor- und frühgeschichtlichen Denkmälern* 34 (Philipp von Zabern, Mainz 1977) 163–71.

GLAUBERG TORC: O.-H. Frey 'Zu einem bedeutender Zeugnis der frühen keltischen Kunst vom Glauberg' *Wetterauer Geschichtsblätter* 30 (1981) 13–21.

THRACIAN, DACIAN AND SCYTHIAN ART: good illustrations can be found in I. Venedikov *Thracian Treasures from Bulgaria* (British Museum, London 1976); *From the Lands of the Scythians (exhibition catalogue) = Metropolitan Museum of Art Bulletin* 23 (1973–4); B. Piotrovsky, L. Galanina and N. Grach *Scythian art* (Phaidon, Oxford/Aurora, Leningrad 1987). An older, but still stimulating book, is D. Carter *The symbol of the Beast: the animal style art of Eurasia* (Ronald Press Co., New York 1957). On the Scythians R. Rolle *Die Welt der Skythen* (Bucher, Luzern and Frankfurt 1980); on Thracians in eastern Europe M. Dušek *Die Thraker im Karpatenbecken* (Grüner, Amsterdam 1978).

DÜRRNBERG AND BASSE-YUTZ FLAGONS: F. Moosleitner *Die Schnabelkanne vom Dürrnberg: ein Meisterwerk keltischer Handwerkskunst* (Salzburger Museum C.A. 1985); *APAS* 35–65 and no. 71; J.V.S. and M.R. Megaw 'Italians and Greeks bearing gifts: the Basse-Yutz finds reconsidered' in J.-P. Descoeudres (ed.) *Greek Colonists and Native Populations* (Oxford U.P. 1988); J.V.S. Megaw and M.R. Megaw (ed.) *The Basse-Yutz (Moselle) 1927 find in the British Museum = Soc. Antiq. Occ. Paper* (1989).

Faces

J.V.S. Megaw 'Two La Tène finger rings in the Victoria and Albert Museum, London: an essay on the human face and Early Celtic Art' *Praehistorische Zeitschrift* 13/14 (1965–66) 96–166 deals extensively with these pieces; J.V.S. Megaw 'The Human Face in early Celtic art: some problems of analysis' *Actes du VIIe Congrès International UISPP Prague 1966* (Prague 1970) 817–20; J.V.S. Megaw 'Cheshire Cat and Mickey Mouse: analysis, interpretation and the art of the La Tène Iron Age' *PPS* 36 (1970) 261–79; M. Lenerz-de Wilde 'Le "style de Cheshire Cat"; un phénomène caractéristique de l'art celtique' in Duval and Kruta 101–14; F.-W. von Hase 'Unbekannte frühetruskische Edelmetallfunde mit Maskenköpfen: mögliche Vorbilder keltischer Darstellungen *HBA* 3 (1973) 51–64 points to Etruscan parallels.

BAD DÜRKHEIM: J.V.S. Megaw 'Doppelsinnigheit in der keltischen Kunst, dargestellt an einem Beispiel aus dem Fürstengrab von Bad

Dürkheim' *Pfälzer Heimat* 3 (1969) 85–6.

HERZOGENBURG: J.V.S. Megaw 'Zum Stil des bronzenenknaufbeschlags eines Frühlateneschwertes von Herzogenburg, NÖ' in J.W. Neugebauer with A. Gattringer *Herzogenburg-Kalkofen: ein ur- und frühgeschichtlicher Fundplatz im untern Traisental = Fundberichte aus Österreich: Materialhefte* A1 (1981) 39–41.

Statues

PFALZFELD: *KM* no. 16; H.E. Joachim 'Zur Deutung der keltischen Säulen von Pfalzfeld und Irlich' *AK* 4 (1974) 229–32. HOLZGERLINGEN: Megaw *AEIA* no. 14; *KM* no. 17. HEIDELBERG: Megaw *AEIA* no. 49. LEICHLINGEN: Megaw *AEIA* no. 85. An important overview is W. Kimmig 'Eisenzeitliche Grabstelen in Mitteleuropa' in *Studi di Paletnologia in Onore di Salvatore M. Puglisi* (Università di Roma 1985) 591–615.

Riders and Warriors

KÄRLICH: J. Driehaus 'Eine frühlatènezeitliche Reiterdarstellung aus Kärlich' *Bonner Jahrb.* 165 (1965) 57–71; H.E. Joachim 'Zur frühlatènezeitlichen Reiterfigur von Kärlich, Ldkr. Koblenz' *Jahrb. des RGZM* 17 (1970) 94–103. SPAIN: C. Angoso and E. Cuadrado 'Fibulas ibericas con escenas venatorias' *Boletin de la Asociacion Española de Amigos de la Arqueologia* 13 (May 1981) 18–30. HALLSTATT GRAVE 994: not specifically on the sword, W. Dehn 'Ein keltisches Häuptlingsgrab aus Hallstatt' *Krieger und Salzherren* (RGZM, Mainz 1970) 72–81 and *KM* no. 115. MANĚTÍN-HRÁDEK BROOCH: E. Soudská 'Hrob s maskovitou sponou z Manětína-Hrádku' *Archeologicke rozhledy* 20 (1968) 451–69; *KM* no. 75.

Brooches

S. Kurz 'Figürliche Fibeln der Frühlatènezeit in Mitteleuropa' *Fundberichte aus Baden-Württemberg* 9 (1984) 249–278 lists 167 brooches but does not illustrate them. On style see J.V.S. Megaw 'An Early La Tène *Maskenfibel* from Slovenské Pravno, okr. Martin, Slovakia' *EC* 19 (1982) 7–34. HORSE BROOCHES: B.W. Bahn and H. Ullman 'Eine Pferdchenfibel von der Steinsburg', *Alt-Thüringen* 21 (1986) 209–27. For some further illustrations see Megaw *AEIA* nos. 89–94 and 101, *KM* nos. 23, 33, 117–24; *APAS* figs. 54, 59–63 and nos. 13–17, 23–30, 43, 51–62. VAL-DE-TRAVERS: W. Dehn 'Die Doppelvogelkopffibel aus dem Val-de-Travers', *Helvetia Antiqua* (1966) 137–46.

Neckrings

Some brief discussion in J.V.S. Megaw 'Style and Style Groupings in Early Celtic Art' *World Archaeology* 3 (1972) 276–92. On Erstfeld and its origins see R. Wyss *Die Goldfund von Erstfeld: frühkeltische Goldschmuck zu den Zentralalpen* = *Arch. Forschungen* 1 (Zürich 1975) and *KM* no. 187. BESSERINGEN: Megaw *AEIA* no. 56. BAD DÜRKHEIM: Megaw *AEIA* no. 54; *KM* no. 29 (no illustrations). RODENBACH: Megaw *AEIA* no. 55. REINHEIM: Megaw *AEIA* nos. 79–83; *KM* no. 33; J. Keller *Das keltische Grab von Reinheim* I (RGZM, Mainz 1965).

Pottery

The key publications are F. Schwappach *On the Chronology of the eastern Early La Tène Pottery* (Moreland, Bad Bramstedt 1979); F. Schwappach 'Die stempelverzierte Latène-Keramik aus den Gräbern von Braubach' *Bonner Jahrb.* 177 (1977) 119–83; F. Schwappach 'Frühkeltischen Ornament zwischen Marne, Rhein und Moldau' *Bonner Jahrb.* 173 (1973) 53–111; F. Schwappach 'L'art ornemental du "Premier Style" Celtique' in Duval and Hawkes 61–110; Schwappach in these and other publications has examined the connections between pottery and metalwork designs. See too D. Linksfeller 'Die stempelverzierte Keramik in Böhmen und Mähren' *Arch. Informationen* 4 (1976) 82–108; R. and D.W. Müller 'Stempelverzierte Keramik aus einem Randgebiet der Keltiké' *Alt-Thüringen* 14 (1977) 194–243.

LINSENFLASCHEN: T. Vogt 'Zur Problematik der frühlatènezeitlichen Linsenflaschen' *Jahrb. Mitteldt. Vorgeschichte* 53 (1969) 415–36; for continuity of local tradition in the Matzhausen flask rather than southern influence H.P. Uenze 'Zu einigen bildlichen Darstellungen der Hallstattzeit aus Nordbayern' *Hallstattkultur Symposium* 375–88; see also L. Pauli 'Die frühkeltische Tonflasche aus Matzhausen' in S. Rieckhoff-Pauli and W. Torbrügge (eds.) *Regensburg-Kelheim-Straubing* I = *Führer zu archäologischen Denkmälern in Deutschland* 5 (Theiss, Stuttgart 1984) 198–204. DÜRRNBERG: for the 'pilgrim-flask' from grave 44/2 see *KM* no. 35; for discussion M.E. Mariën 'Eigenbilzen et Hallein' in *Collection Latomus, Hommages à Albert Grenier* 58 (1962) vol. III 1113–16.

Some discussion of engraving in Early La Tène art in J.V.S. Megaw 'Une épée de La Tène I avec fourreau décoré' *Revue archéologique de l'Est et du Centre-Est* 19 (1968) 129–44. RADOVESIC: J. Waldhauser 'Keltské sídliště u Radovesic v severozápadních Čechách' *Arch. rozhledy* 29 (1977) 144–77; J.V.S. Megaw 'Une "Volière" celtique: quelques notes sur l'identification des oiseaux dans l'art celtique ancien' *Revue archéologique de l'Est* 32 (1981) 137–43.

Brittany

P.-R. Giot, J. Briard and L. Pape *Protohistoire de la Bretagne* (Ouest-France, Rennes 1979) provides an authoritative overview and bibliography. On the pottery F. Schwappach 'Stempelverzierte Keramik von Armorica' *Fundberichte aus Hessen* Beiheft 1 (1969) 213–87; P.-R. Giot 'Ombres et lumières sur la chronologie de la céramique armoricaine de l'âge du fer' *Annales de Bretagne* 78 (1971) 73–98; P.-R. Giot, Y. Lecerf, Y. Onnée *Céramique Armoricaine de l'Age du Fer* (Université de Rennes 1971); *Au Temps des Celtes du Ve au Ier siècle avant J.C.* exhibition catalogue (Abbaye de Daoulas, Finistère, 1986) ranges much more widely but takes Brittany as its centre.

Cerrig-y-Drudion

I.M. Stead 'The Cerrig-y-Drudion "Hanging Bowl"' *Antiquaries Journal* 62 (1982) 221–34.

Reinheim and Waldalgesheim Flagons

J. Keller *Das keltische Fürstengrab von Reinheim* I (RGZM, Mainz 1965); H.E. Joachim 'Die Verzierungen auf der keltischen Röhrenkanne von Waldalgesheim' *AK* 8 (1978) 119–25; M. Lenerz-de Wilde 'Zur Verzierung der Röhrenkanne aus dem Fürstengrab von Waldalgesheim' *AK* 9 (1979) 313–16; *KM* nos. 33–4.

PRUNAY AND RELATED POTS: Megaw *AEIA* no. 154 wrongly gives département as Cher not Marne: *Gauls Provincial* no. 87; J.-J. Charpy and P. Roualet *Céramique peinte gauloise en Champagne du VIe au Ier Siècle avant Jésus-Christ* (Musée d'Epernay, 1987) esp. nos. 88, 90. KŠICE BROOCH: Megaw *AEIA* no. 104. MÂCON TORC: J.V.S. Megaw 'Ein verzierter Frühlatène-Halsring im Metropolitan Museum of Art, New York' *Germania* 45 (1967) 50–3.

On the transition towards Waldalgesheim style see next chapter.

AUVERS DISC: Megaw *AEIA* no. 42. P.-M. Duval 'Deux éléments foundamentaux du Premier style celtique' *EC* XIV (1974) 8–19. ST-JEAN-SUR-TOURBE DISC: *KM* no. 30. BESANÇON FLAGON: O.-H. Frey 'Eine etruskische Bronzeschnabelkanne' *Annales Littéraires de l'Université de Besançon* 2nd Ser. 2 (1955) 4–30; 'Zur Bronzeschnabelkanne in Besançon' *Ann. Litt. d'l'Univ. de Besançon* 294 = H. Walter (ed.) *Homages à Lucien Lerat* I 293–308 (Besançon 1984).

CHAPTER 3

Celtic Expansion

Duval and Kruta 1979 deals largely with this period and with that covered by Chapter 4, with valuable essays on southwest Europe, Italy, Hungary, Bohemia and Jugoslavia, while W. Dehn deals with the general character of Celtic wanderings. See also T.C. Champion 'Mass migration in later prehistoric Europe' in P. Sörbom (ed.) *Transport Technology and Social Change* (Stockholm 1980) 31–42. F.W. Walbank et al. (eds.) *The Cambridge Ancient History* VII part 1: *The Hellenistic World* 2nd ed. (Cambridge U.P. 1984) describes Celtic expansion into Anatolia and Greece, pp. 114–17, 415–25. For the nature of Celtic expansion, deemed land-seeking in the 5th to 4th century, booty-seeking thereafter, and the armed groups involved, K.

Peschel 'Kriegergrab, Gefolge und Landnahme bei den Latènekelten' *Ethnographische-Archäologische Zeitschrift* 25 (1984) 445–69. On Celts as mercenaries, see E.T. Griffiths *The Mercenaries of the Hellenistic World* (Oxford U.P. 1935) especially pp. 118 and 352–3.

Social and burial change is more fully documented under Chapter 4 but see G. Bergonzi 'Münsingen-Rain (Svizzeria) e Dürrnberg presso Hallein (Austria): alcune osservazione sulla struttura sociale nel La Tène antico' in *Popoli e facies* 49–58 and W. Krämer *Die Grabfunde von Manching und die Flachgräber in Sudbayern = Ausgrabungen in Manching* 9 (Franz Steiner Verlag, Stuttgart 1985), who also has a useful discussion on chronology, relative and absolute.

Origins of the Vegetal Style

Castriota 274–372 emphasizes the continuity with earlier Celtic art. O.-H. Frey 'Du premier style au style de Waldalgesheim' in Duval and Hawkes 141–65. The collection of articles in Duval and Kruta 1982 is invaluable for this and the following chapter. On the classical origins of tendril design O.-H. Frey 'Akanthusornamentik in der keltischen Kunst' *HBA* 4 (1974) 141–57; see also V. Kruta 'Remarques sur l'apparition du rinceau dans l'art celtique' *EC* 14 (1974) 21–30.
MÜNSINGEN AND DUCHCOV fibulae: for their implications, see F.R. Hodson *The La Tène cemetery at Münsingen-Rain = Acta Bernensia* V (Bern 1968); V. Kruta 'Remarques sur les fibules de la trouvaille de Duchcov (Dux), Bohême' in P.-M. Duval et al. *Recherches d'Archéologie celtique et gallo-romaine* (Librairie Droz, Paris 1973) 1–33; V. Kruta 'Duchcov-Münsingen: nature et diffusion d'une phase laténienne' in Duval and Kruta 1979, 81–115, emphasizes the Italian origins.
CELTS IN ITALY: *I Galli*; *Les Celtes en Italie = Dossiers Histoire et Archéologie* 112 (Jan. 1987); R. de Marinis 'The La Tène Cultures of the Cisalpine Gauls' *Keltske Studije* (Posavski muzej, Brežice 1977) 23–50; P.F. Stary 'Keltische Waffen auf der Apennin-Halbinsel' *Germania* 57 (1979) 99–110; D. Vitali (ed.) *Celti ed Etruschi nell'Italia centro-settentrionale = Realtà regionale: Fonti e Studi* 10 (University Press, Bologna 1987). Of the many writings of V. Kruta on Celtic settlement in Italy and on Italy as the birthplace of the Vegetal Style see esp. 'Les Boïens de Cispadane' *EC* 17 (1980) 7–32; 'Les Sénons de l'Adriatique' *EC* 18 (1981) 7–38; 'Aspects unitaires et Faciès dans l'art celtique du IVe et IIIe siècles avant notre ère' in Duval and Kruta 1982, 35–75; 'Faciès celtique de la Cisalpine au IVe siècle avant notre ère' in *Popoli e Facies* 1–15. Some doubts about this exclusively Italian origin have been expressed by Castriota; C. Peyre 'Y a-t-il un contexte italique au Style de Waldalgesheim?' in Duval and Kruta 1982, 51–84; J.-J. Hatt, review of V. Kruta *Les Celtes*, *Rev. Arch. de l'Est* 31 (1980) 261–9.

Italo-Celtic Helmets

GENERAL: U. Schaaff 'Keltische Eisenhelme aus vorrömischer Zeit' *Jahrb. des RGZM* 21 (1974) = *Festschrift Hundt* 1, 149–204.
MONTE BIBELE: D. Vitali 'L'Elmo della Tomba 14 di Monte Bibele a Monterenzio (Prov. di Bologna)' *EC* 19 (1982) 35–47; D. Vitali *Monte Bibele = Marburger kleine Schriften* 16 (1985). UMBRIA: Schaaff no. 33. GOTTOLENGO: Schaaff no. 23. CANOSA: Schaaff no. 36. AGRIS: J. Gomez de Soto 'A helmet from La Rochefoucauld' *Current Archaeology* 7, 301; J. Gomez de Soto 'Un casque princier gaulois' *Archéologia* 164 (1982) 6–7; C. Eluère 'Two unique golden helmets' *Gold Bulletin* (Marshalltown, S. Africa) 17 (1985) 110–11; Daoulas no. 59.01; J. Gomez de Soto 'Le Casque du IVe siècle a.n.è. de la Grotte des Perrats à Agris, France' *AK* 16 (1986) 179–83 has the first photographs of the helmet since its restoration by the RGZM, Mainz.
AMFREVILLE: V. Kruta 'Le casque d'Amfreville-sous-les-monts et quelques problèmes de l'art du IVe siècle a.n.è.' *EC* 15 (1978) 405–24; A. Duval et al. 'Zum keltischen Helm von Amfreville' *AK* 16 (1986) 83–4 has colour photographs of it as recently restored. See also C. Eluère et al. 'Un chef d'oeuvre de l'orfevrerie celtique' *Bull. Soc. Prehist. Française* 84 (1987) 8–22. A. Duval and J. Gomez de Soto 'Quelques considérations sur les casques celtiques d'Amfreville (Eure) et d'Agris (Charente)' *Revue Aquitania* Supplément 1 (1986) 239–44, have argued not only for local manufacturers of these helmets

in France, but, less convincingly for a date as late as the last quarter of the third century BC for the creation of the Amfreville helmet.

Waldalgesheim

E.M. Jope 'The Waldalgesheim Master' in J. Boardman et al. (eds.) *The European Community in Later Prehistory: Studies in Honour of C.F.C. Hawkes* (Routledge and Kegan Paul, London 1971) 167–180, suggested that the whole find came from one craftsman. J. Driehaus 'Zum Grabfund von Waldalgesheim' *HBA* 1 (1971) 101–11 clearly demonstrates several different hands. J. Driehaus 'Gerätespuren und Handswerksgerät: Ein Beitrag zur Metallbearbeitung während der späten Hallstatt und frühen Latènezeit' in H. Jankuhn et al. (eds.) *Das Handwerk in Vor- und frühgeschichtlicher Zeit* (Vandenhoek und Ruprecht, Göttingen 1983) 50–66, is mainly about Waldalgesheim and identifies eight styles of metalworking in the grave finds, though the grounds for differentiation in some cases (e.g. between armring and neckring) are occasionally dubious. On the date of the imported situla G. Zahlhaas 'Der Bronzeeimer von Waldalgesheim' *HBA* 1 (1971) 115–29 suggests a date of 380–70 BC while W. Schiering 'Zeitstellung und Herkunft der Bronzesitula von Waldalgesheim'. *HBA* 5 (1975) 77–97, suggests, as Jacobsthal did, a date later in the fourth century and a Tarentine origin.

Vegetal Style Developments in Italy

MOSCANO DI FABRIANO: O.H. Frey 'Das keltische Schwert von Moscano di Fabriano' *HBA* 1 (1971) 173–9; also from the grave but not published is a Münsingen brooch with vegetal decoration on the bow. A better drawing than Frey's is in J.V.S. Megaw 'Finding Purposeful Patterns: further notes towards a methodology of Pre-Roman Celtic Art' in Duval and Kruta 1982, 213–29, at 227 fig. 2. FILOTTRANO: Megaw *AEIA* nos. 128, 137. COMACCHIO: Megaw *AEIA* no. 117.

Fibulae

V. Kruta 'Les fibules laténiennes à décor d'inspiration végétale au IVe siècle a.n.è.'

Rings

DÜRRNBERG: *KM* no. 161. STETTLEN-DEISSWIL: *KM* no. 160. ETOY: J.V.S. Megaw 'Two La Tène fingerrings . . . in the Victoria and Albert Museum' *Praehistorische Zeitschrift* 54/4 (1965/6) cat. no. 24 and 145 ff.

Swords

ST GERMAINMONT: V. Kruta et al. 'Les fourreaux d'Epiais-Rhus (Val d'Oise) et de Saint-Germainmont (Ardennes) et l'art celtique du IVe siècle avant J.-C.' *Gallia* 42 (1984) 1–20. Other French stamped examples A. Duval and V. Kruta 'Objets d'une nécropole de La Tène à Larchant (Seine et Marne)' *Antiquités Nationales* 8 (1976) 60–68. To the small number of stamped swords with vegetal decoration they record can be added the stray find from Manching previously illustrated only in J. Filip *Keltové v střední Evropě* (1956) obr. 4:3 and that from MANCHING-STEINBICHL: Grave 27: G. Jacobi 'Verzierte Schwertscheide vom Frühlatèneschema aus den Flachgräbern von Manching' *Germania* 60 (1982) 565–6 which has better illustrations than W. Krämer *Die Grabfunde von Manching und die Flachgräber in Sudbayern = Die Ausgrabungen in Manching* 9 (Franz Steiner Verlag, Stuttgart 1985) 82–3 and Taf. 108.

Central and Eastern Europe

F. Schwappach 'Stempel des Waldalgesheimstils an einer Vase aus Sopron-Bécsidomb (West Ungarn)' *HBA* 1 (1971) 131–79 is a great deal more wide-ranging than its title. E. Jerem 'Stempelverziertes Gefäss aus Écs' *Mitteil. d. Arch. Inst. der Ungarischen Akademie der Wissenschaften* 5 (1974/5) 45–57 demonstrates the changes in Hungarian pottery decoration at this time. J.V.S. Megaw 'The decoration on the sword scabbard from Jenišův Újezd, gr. 115' in J. Waldhauser (ed.) *Das keltische Gräberfeld bei Jenišův Újezd* II (Krajské Museum, Teplice 1978) 106–13 makes the comparison with the Bussy-le-Château sword.
SOPRON-KRAUTACKER: on the kilns and the pot from Hidegség: E. Jerem 'An early Celtic pottery workshop in north western Hungary:

some archaeological and technical evidence' *Oxford J. Arch.* 3 (1984) 57–80.

Torcs

Paul Jacobsthal 'Kelten in Thrakien' in *Epitymbion Chrestou Tsounta = Archeion tou Thrakikou Laographikou Kai Gloss. Thes* (Athens 1940) 391–400 first drew attention to the similarity between the torc from Tsibur Varos and the Alsópól pot. DISC TORCS (SCHEIBENHALSRINGE): for the Upper Rhine, with reference to earlier writings, U. Schaaff 'Frülatènezeitliche Scheibenhalsringe vom südlichen Mittelrhein' *AK* 4 (1974) 151–6; W. Kimmig 'Ein Frühlatènefund mit Scheibenhalsring von Sulzfeld, Kr. Sinsheim (Baden Württemberg)' *AK* 5 (1975) 283–98; F. Müller 'Keltische Scheibenhalsringe: ein oberrheinisches Erzeugnis mit weiter Verbreitung' *AK* 15 (1985) 85–9. MARNIAN TORCS: V. Kruta and P. Roualet 'Une série de torques marniens à décor de style végétal continu' in Duval and Kruta 1982, 115–35. TORQUES TERNAIRES: see entry in Megaw *AEIA* no. 143 and recent additions in *Gauls Provincial* nos. 67–73, 122–4.

CHAPTER 4

Later Celtic Expansion

It is in this period that one can, for the first time, see clear evidence for Celtic expansion into central and eastern Europe and the mingling of Celts with local populations to produce new cultural elements and art styles. The process and dating is complex and still disputed but key writings with further references, especially to the flat grave fields and their social and ethnic significance can be found in J. Bujna 'Spiegelung der Sozialstruktur auf Latènezeitlichen Gräberfeldern im Karpathenbecken' *Památky Archeologické* 73 (1982) 312–41, an extremely important study though its bibliography goes up only to 1977, since it derives from an earlier dissertation. See also H. Lorenz 'Regional organization in the Western Early La Tène province' in Champion and Megaw, 109–22; F. Fischer 'Der Handel der Mittel- und Spät-Latènezeit in Mitteleuropa aufgrund archäologische Zeugnisse' in K. Düwel et al. ((eds.) *Untersuchungen zu Handel und Verkehr der vor- und frühgeschichtlichen Zeit in Mittel- und Nordeuropa* (Vandenhoek und Ruprecht, Göttingen 1985) 285–98. JUGOSLAVIA: M. Guštin 'Die Kelten in Jugoslavien: übersicht über das archäologische Fundgut' *Jahrb. des RGZM* 31 (1984) 305–63. On the Scordisci, J. Todorović *Skordisci* (Novi Sad, Belgrade 1974). See also P. Papazoglu *The Central Balkan Tribes in Pre-Roman times* (Hakkert, Amsterdam 1978); A. Stipčević *The Illyrians: History and Culture* tr. S.Č. Burton (Noyes Press, Park Ridge NJ 1977). ROMANIA: V. Zirra 'Beiträge zur Kenntnis des keltischen Latène in Rümänien' *Dacia* 15 (1971) 1–68; V. Zirra 'The Eastern Celts of Romania' *J. Indo-European Studies* 4 (1976) 1–41; V. Zirra 'Le problème des Celtes dans l'espace du Bas-Danube' *Thraco-Dacia* (1976) 175–82; J. Nandris 'The Dacian Iron Age: a comment in a European context' in H. Mitscha-Märheim et al. *Festschrift für Richard Pittioni = Arch. Austriaca* Beiheft 13 (1976) 723–36. HUNGARY: B. Maráz 'La Tène-Kori magányos sírok és kis temetök Dél-Alföldrol' *A. Békés. Megyei Múzeumok Közleményei* 2 (1973) 41–62. SLOVAKIA: B. Benadik 'Doba Laténska' *Slovenska Archeologia* 28 (1980) 191–5.

Further west, changes in grave practices and social structure are recorded in W. Krämer *Die Grabfunde von Manching und die Latènezeitlichen Flachgräber in Südbayern = Manching* 9 (Franz Steiner Verlag, Stuttgart 1985); P. Sankot 'Studien zur Sozialstruktur der nordalpinen Flachgräber der La-Tène-Zeit im Gebiet der Schweiz' *Zeitschrift für Schweizerische Archäologie und Kunstgeschichte* 37 (1980) 19–71. P. Hinton 'An analysis of the burial rites at Munsingen–Rain: an approach to the study of iron age society' *Revue Aquitania* Supplément I (1986) 351–8. For France there are a number of regional studies but as yet no overview; the closest is A. Duval 'Aspects de La Tène Moyen dans le Bassin Parisien *Bull. de la Société préhistorique française* 73 (1976) 457–84.

On the pitfalls involved in inferring social structure from burials see F.R. Hodson 'Inferring status from Burials in Iron Age Europe: some recent attempts' in B.C. Burnham and J. Kingsbury (eds.) *Space,*

Hierarchy and Society: Interdisciplinary Studies in Social Area Analysis = BAR Internat. Series 59 (1979) 23–30.

On the general eastern expansion of Celtic art see *Keltoi, KKM* and Szabó. A recent treatment of the Carpathian basin is M. Szabó 'Nouvelles vues sur l'art des Celtes orientaux' *EC* 22 (1985) 53–72 which deals briefly with the dating of Hungarian sword styles and of eastern pottery. GREECE AND ASIA MINOR: W. Krämer 'Keltische Hohlbückelringe vom Isthmus von Korinth' *Germania* 39 (1961) 32–42; J.V.S. Megaw 'Two finds of the Celtic Iron Age from Dodona' in K. Jazdzewski (ed.) *Liber Iosepho Kostrzewski Octogenario a veneratoribus Dicatus* (Warsaw 1968) 185–93; U. Schaaff 'Ein keltischer Hohlbückelring aus Kleinasien' *Germania* 50 (1972) 94–8; F. Maier 'Keltische Altertümer in Griechenland' *Germania* 51 (1973) 459–77; K. Bittel 'Die Galater in Kleinasien, archäologisch gesehen' in *Assimilation et résistance à la culture gréco-romaine dans le monde ancien = Travaux du VI.ᶜ Congrès international d'Etudes Classiques* (Madrid 1974) 241–49; H. Polenz 'Gedanken zu einer Fibel von Mittellatèneschema aus Kayserli in Anatolien' *Bonner Jahrb.* 178 (1978) 181–220. PERGAMON SCULPTURES: *I Galli* 231–57; E. Künzl *Die Kelten des Epigonos von Pergamon = Beiträge zur Archäol.* 4 (Triltsch, Würzburg 1971). MŠECKÉ ZEHROVICE HEAD: Megaw 1970. no. 171.

Swords

The most recent brief attempt at overall classification and methodology of the art is P.-M. Duval 'La decoration des fourreaux d'épée laténiens en Europe du Centre-Est et en Europe Occidentale' in Fitz, 9–14. On sword-smithing techniques see R. Wyss 'Belege zur keltischen Schwertschmiedekunst' in E. Schmid et al. (eds.) *Provincalia: Festschrift fur Rudolf Laur-Belart* (Schwabe, Basel 1968) 664–80.

Dragon Pairs

The starting point is J.M. de Navarro *The Finds from the Site of La Tène I: Scabbards and the Swords found in them.* (Oxford U.P., London 1972).

For more westerly distributions E. Petres 'Notes on scabbards decorated with dragons and bird-pairs' Duval and Kruta 1982, 161–74; A. Bulard 'Fourreaux ornés d'animaux fantastiques découverts en France' *EC* 16 (1979) 27–52; A. Bulard 'A propos des origines de la paire d'animaux fantastiques sur les fourreaux d'épée laténiens' in Duval and Kruta 1982, 149–60; I.M. Stead 'Celtic Dragons from the River Thames' *Antiquaries Journal* 64 (1984) 269–79; A. Rapin 'Le fourreau d'épée à "lyre zoomorphe" des Jogasses à Chouilly (Marne)' *EC* 22 (1985) 9–25.

Further east, V. Zirra 'Noi necropole celtice în nord-vestul României (cimitirele biriturale de la Sanislău și Dindești *Satu Mare: Studii și comunicări* (Muzeul Judetului, Satu Mare 1972) 151–205.

Hungarian Sword Styles

The basic introduction is Jacobsthal *ECA* 95–7; see also M. Szabó 'The origins of the Hungarian sword style' *Antiquity* 51 (1977) 211–19 and M. Szabó 'Remarques sur la classification des fourreaux d'épée dit Hongrois' in Duval and Kruta 1982, 175–90. JUGOSLAV SWORDS: J. Todorović 'Classification des épées celtiques dans les Balkans et la Pannonie du Sud' *Arch. Iugoslavica* 6 (1965) 71–4; M. Guštin 'Zeitliche Einordnung der verzierten keltischen Schwerter aus Jugoslawien' in Duval and Kruta 1982, 191–202. SLOVAKIA: J.V.S. Megaw 'The decorated Sword-Scabbards of iron from Cernon-sur-Coole (Marne) and Drňa, Rimavska Sobota (Slovakia)' *HBA* 3 (1973) (pub. 1977) 119–37; L. Zachar 'Datovanie pošiev keltských mečov z Drňa a Košíc' *Zbornik slovenského národneho Muzea* 68 (1978) 55–80. CIUMEȘTI: V. Zirra *Un cimitir celtic în nord-vestu României* (Muzeul Regional Maramureş, Baia Mare, n.d. [1967]; M. Rusu 'Das keltische Fürstengrab von Ciumeşti in Rumänien' *Ber. d. RGK* 1969 50 (1971) 267–300 and M. Rusu and O. Bandula *Morminтul Unei Căpitenei Celtice de la Ciumeşti* (Muzeul Judeţean Maramureş, Baia Mare 1970). DOBOVA: M. Guštin 'Keltische Gräber aus Dobova, Slovenia' *AK* 11 (1981) 223–9 on Dobova grave 10; M. Guštin 'La tomba n.6 di Dobova e l'ornamento delle lance La Tène' in

Popoli et Facies 100–3. JORESSANT AND CSABRENDEK OR 'HUNGARY': the spears are briefly considered in A. Duval 'Note sur une pointe de lance provenant de Rebourseaux (Yonne)' in Duval and Kruta 1982, 137–47. WALDENBUCH: Megaw *AEIA* no. 142. CONFLANS BROOCHES: V. Kruta 'Les deux fibules laténiennes de Conflans (Marne)' *EC* 14 (1975) 377–89. SCORDISCI: J. Todorović *Skordisci: Istorija i kultura* (Novi Sad, Belgrade 1974); B. Jovanović 'The Scordisci and their art' *Alba Regia* 14 (1975) 167–76.

The Saône Valley

L. Bonnamour and A. Bulard 'Une épée celtique à fourreau décoré, découverte à Montbellet (Saône-et-Loire)' *Gallia* 34 (1976) 279–84; A. Bulard 'Une pointe de lance laténienne ornée de Saunières (Saône-et-Loire)' *EC* 15 (1978) 483–9. See too L. Bonnamour and J.-P. Guillamet *La Vallée de la Saône aux âges du fer (VIIᵉ – Iᵉʳ siècle a.n.è.)* (exhibition catalogue) (Musée Denon, Chalon-sur-Saône 1983) which contains an essay on 'Les découvertes des âges du fer dans le lit de la Saône' by L. Bonnamour (pp. 62–78) and a full bibliography.

Swiss Sites and Swords

On the swords J.M. de Navarro *The Finds from the Site of La Tène I: Scabbards and the swords found in them* (Oxford U.P., London 1972). On Cornaux and the 'catastrophe theory' H. Schwab 'Entdeckung einer keltischen Brücke an der Zihl und ihre Bedeutung für la Tène' *AK* 2 (1972) 289–94; H. Schwab 'Neue Ergebnisse zur Topographie von la Tène' *Germania* 52 (1974) 348–67. For rebuttal of this theory L. Berger and M. Joos 'Zur Wasserführung der Zihl bei der Station La Tène' in K. Stüber and A. Zürcher (eds.) *Festschrift Walter Drack zu seinem 60 Geburtstag: Beiträge zur Archäologie und Denkmalpflege* (Stäfa, Zürich 1977) 68–76. OBERMENZING: the surgeon's grave J.M. de Navarro 'A Doctor's Grave of the Middle La Tène Period from Bavaria' *PPS* 21 (1955) 231–48. GROITZSCH: W. Coblenz 'Zum Waffengrab aus der Latènezeit von Groitzsch, Kr. Borna' *Arbeit und Forschungsberichte zur sächsischen Denkmalpflege* 19 (1970) 69–103. GOURNAY: A. Rapin 'Un sanctuaire gaulois à Gournay-sur-Aronde (Oise)' *Gallia* 38 (1980) 1–25; A. Rapin et al. 'Das keltische Heiligtum von Gournay-sur-Aronde' *Antike Welt* 13 (1982) 39–60; J.-L. Brunaux et al. *Gournay I: les fouilles sur le sanctuaire et l'oppidum (1975–84) = Rev. archéol. de Picardie* numéro special 1985.

Plastic Style Art

LA CHARME: for the bracelet *Gauls Provincial* no. 75; Megaw *AEIA* no. 140. DAMMELBERG; Megaw *AEIA* no. 148. CLONMACNOIS: Raftery 1 no. 451; Raftery 2, 175–81.

'Plastic' Armrings and Anklets

In general see U. Schaaff 'Zur Tragweise keltischer Hohlbückelringe' *AK* 2 (1972) 155–8. V. Kruta has suggested that the appearance of such ring ornaments in France suggests the influx of Danubian Celts – e.g. in 'Le port d'anneaux de cheville en Champagne et le problème d'une immigration danubienne au IIIᵉ siècle avant J.-C.' *EC* 22 (1985) 27–51. TARN: on the anklet see Megaw *AEIA* no. 175. KLETTHAM: Megaw *AEIA* no. 176. PALÁRIKOVO: *KM* no. 107 – this is a 'filigree' example, a technique documented below. BOUQUEVAL: on the bowl, see R. Guadagnin 'La nécropole celtique de Bouqueval' *Jeunesse Préhistorique et Géologique de la France* 8 (1978, published 1984) 12–65.

'Disney' or Animal 'Plastic' Style

J.V.S. Megaw 'Cheshire Cat and Mickey Mouse . . .' *PPS* 36 (1970) 261–79; V. Kruta 'Débuts et développements du "style plastique" en Bohême' *EC* 13 (1973) 644–59. BRÁ: O. Klindt-Jensen *Bronzekedelen fra Brå* (University Press, Aarhus 1958). BRNO-MALOMĚŘICE: Megaw *AEIA* nos. 158–60. DÜRRNBERG 'crocodile': *KM* no. 138, *APAS* no. 65. MANCHING: W. Krämer and F. Schubert 'Zwei Achsnägel aus Manching: Zeugnisse keltischer Kunst der Mittellatènezeit' *Jahrb. d. Deutschen Arch. Inst.* 94 (1979) 366–89. PARIS: Megaw *AEIA* nos. 166–8. PORT: H. Dannheimer 'Zu zwei keltischen Fundstücken aus der Münchner

Schotterebene' *AK* 5 (1975) 59–67. RAKÓS DEER: Szabó nos. 25–6, cf. E. Petres 'Angaben zum römerzeitlichen Fortleben der keltischen Plastik in Pannonien' *Alba Regia* 14 (1975) 225–34 on date. Another such French piece in A. Duval and J.C. Blanchet 'La tombe à char d'Attichy (Oise)' *Bull. de la Société Préhistorique française* (1974) 401–8.

Filigree in Eastern and Western Celtic Art

M. Szabó 'Sur la question du Filigrane dans l'art des Celtes orientaux' *Alba Regia* 14 (1975) 147–65, which also deals with the Szárazd-Regöly gold mentioned in Chapter 5 as well as with the Palárikovo anklet above. For western examples see *Gauls Provincial* nos. 138–43; A. Duval 'Deux objets pseudo-filigranés de la Tène' *Antiquités Nationales* 9 (1977) 40–45 and A. Duval 'Nouvel objet "pseudo-filigrane" . . .' *Antiquités Nationales* 11 (1979) 43–5. LABATLAN POT: M Szabó 'Tierkampszene auf einer keltischen Urne' *Folia Archeologica* 24 (1973) 43–56. JÁSZBERÉNY DRINKING HORN: G. Kaposvári 'A Jászberény-Cserőhalmi Kelta Temető' *Arch. Értesítő* 96 (1969) 178–98; M. Szabó 'Éléments régionaux dans l'art des Celtes orientaux' *EC* 13 (1973) 750–74 at pp. 768–70; W. Krämer 'Zwei Achsnägel aus Manching' *Jahrb. d. Deutschen Arch. Inst.* 94 (1979) 366–89 at pp. 386–8. BELT CHAINS: J. Reitlinger 'Die latènezeitl. Funde des Braunauer Heimathauses' *Jahrb. des Oberösterreich. Musealvereines* 111 (1966), 165–236; I Stanczik and A. Vaday 'Keltische Bronzegürtel "Ungarischen" Typs im Karpatenbecken' *Folia Archaeologica* 22 (1971) 7–27; B. Jovanović 'Les Chaines de Ceintures chez les Scordisques' *EC* 20 (1983) 43–57.

East Celtic Pottery and Hellenistic Influence

V. Kruta and M. Szabó 'Canthares danubiens du IIIᵉ siècle a.n.è.: un exemple d'influence hellénistique sur les Celtes orientaux' *EC* 19 (1982) 51–67; *KKM* nos. 47–59; M. Szabó 'Celtic Art and History in the Carpathian Basin' *Acta Archaeologica* 24 (1972) 385–93. NOVO MESTO POT: T. Knez and M. Szabó 'Ein keltischer Kantharos aus Novo mesto' *Arch. Iugoslavica* 20/21 (1980–81) 80–88.

CHAPTER 5

General; and Oppida Culture

B. Chropovsky (ed.) *Symposium: Ausklang der Latène-Zivilisation und Anfänge der germanischen Besiedlung im mittleren Donaugebiet* (Veda, Bratislava 1977); S. Rieckhoff-Pauli 'Das Ende der keltischen Welt' *KM* 37–47; J. Werner *Spätes Keltentum zwischen Rom und Germanien: Gesammelte Aufsätze zur Spätlatènezeit = Münchner Beiträge zur Vor- und Frühgeschichte*, Ergänzungsband 2 (1979). Of the voluminous writings on oppida, with full bibliographies, P. Wells *Farms, Villages and Cities: Commerce and Urban Origins in Late Prehistoric Europe* (Cornell U.P., Ithaca/London 1984) and J. Collis *Oppida: Earliest Towns North of the Alps* (Dept. of Prehistory and Archaeology, University of Sheffield 1984). O.-H. Frey 'Die Bedeutung der Gallia Cisalpina für die Entstehung der Oppida-Kultur' in *Studien zu Siedlungsfragen der Latènezeit = Veröffentlichung des Vorgeschichtlichen Seminars Marburg*, Sonderband 3 (Marburg 1984) 1–38 presses Italian models for oppida formation, J. Nandris 'The Dacian Iron Age: a Comment in a European Context' in H. Mitscha-Märheim et al. (eds.) *Festschrift für Richard Pittioni = Arch. Austriaca* Beiheft 13 (1976) 723–36 points to the importance of Dacian influence, particularly in the east of the Celtic world, and R. Pleiner *Otázka Státu ve Staré Galii* (Academia, Praha 1979) gives a specifically Marxist economic explanation. K. Pieta *Die Púchov-Kultur* (Academia Scientarum Slovaca, Nitra 1982) on Slovakia; M. Guštin 'Die Kelten in Jugoslavien' *Jahrb. d. RGZM* 31 (1984) 305–64; E. Petres 'The Late Pre-Roman Iron Age in Hungary with special reference to Oppida' and J. Břeň 'Earliest Settlements with Urban Character in Central Europe' both in B. Cunliffe and T. Rowley (eds.) *Oppida in Barbarian Europe = BAR Suppl. Series* 11 (1976) 51–80, 81–94 comment on the less intensively studied areas in eastern Europe. F. Fischer 'Das Handwerk bei den Kelten zur Zeit der Oppida' in H. Jankuhn et al. (eds.) *Das Handwerk in vor- und frühgeschichtlicher Zeit* (Vandenhoek und Ruprecht, Göttingen 1983)

34–49 deals with the crafts of the oppida. Most recently for Gaul with a useful discussion of the origin of towns see C. Goudineau and V. Kruta 'Les antécédents: y a-t-il une ville protohistorique ?' in G. Duby (ed.) *Histoire de la France urbaine* I (Seuil, Paris 1981) 139–231. DACIAN EXPANSION: H. Daicoviciu *Dacia de la Burebista la cuceriea Romana* (Editura Dacia, Cluj 1972); B. Jovanović 'The Scordisci and the Dacians during the first century BC' *Journal of Indo-European Studies* 4 (1976) 81–96. GERMANIC PEOPLES: R. Hachmann *The Germanic Peoples* tr. J. Hogarth (Barrie and Jenkins, London 1974) is a readable account and more reliable than H. Schutz *The Prehistory of Germanic Europe* (Yale U.P., New Haven/London 1983). See also M. Todd *The Northern Barbarians 100 BC–AD 300* (Hutchinson, London 1975), and on the invasion of the Cimbri and Teutones E. Demongeot 'L'invasion des Cimbres-Teutons-Ambions et les Romains' *Latomus* 37 (1978) 910–38.
ROME: the basic source is Caesar's *De Bello Gallico* of which the best modern edition is Julius Caesar *The Battle for Gaul* tr. A. and P. Wiseman, intro. by B. Cunliffe (Chatto and Windus, London 1980). A recent assessment of Germanic and Roman invasions of Gaul and Switzerland in A. Furger-Gunti *Die Helvetier: Kulturgeschichte eines Keltenvolkes* (Neue Zürcher Zeitung, Zürich 1984) on the Helvetii; also A. Duval 'Autour de Vercingetorix: de l'archéologie à l'histoire économique et sociale' in J. Collis et al. (eds.) *Le deuxième âge du fer en Auvergne et en Forez* (John Collis Publications, University of Sheffield 1982) 298–335; A. Mócsy *Pannonia and Upper Moesia: a history of the Middle Danube Provinces of the Roman Empire* tr. S. Frere (Routledge and Kegan Paul, London/Boston 1974).
RELIGION IN GAUL; P-M. Duval *Les Dieux de la Gaule* (Presses Universitaires de France, Paris 1957); F. Benoit *Art et Dieux de la Gaule* (Arthaud, Paris 1969); E. Thevenot *Divinités et sanctuaires de la Gaule* (Fayard, Paris 1968); S. Piggott *The Druids* (Thames and Hudson, London 1975).
MAGDALENSBURG: A. Obermayr *Kelten und Römer am Magdalensburg* (Österreichischer Bundesverlag, Vienna 1971); G. Alfoldy *Noricum* tr. A. Birley (Routledge and Kegan Paul, London 1974).

On the use of writing in the oppida, see G. Jacobi 'Zum Schriftgebrauch in keltischen Oppida nördlich der Alpen' *HBA* 4 (1974) 171–81; W. Krämer 'Graffiti auf Spätlatènekeramik aus Manching' *Germania* 60 (1982) 489–99.

Late La Tène Pottery

MANCHING: I. Kappel *Die Graphittonkeramik von Manching* (Steiner, Wiesbaden 1969) has looked at the clay sources for Manching ceramics; F. Maier *Die bemalte Spätlatènekeramik von Manching* (Steiner, Wiesbaden 1970) at the painted pottery. BASEL GASFABRIK: E. Major *Gallische Ansiedlung mit Gräberfeld bei Basel* (Frobenius, Basel 1940); A. Furger-Gunti and L. Berger *Katalog und Tafeln der Funde aus dem spätkeltischen Siedlung Basel-Gasfabrik = Basler Beiträge zur Ur- und Frühgeschichte* 7 (1980). LOIRE: R. Périchon *La céramique peinte celtique et gallo-romaine en Forez et dans le Massif Central = Centre d'Etudes Foréziennes: Thèses et Mémoires* 6 (1978). HUNGARY: E.B. Bonis *Die spätkeltische Siedlung Gellérthegy-Tabán in Budapest* (Akadémiai Kiadó, Budapest 1969). Slightly later, but similar to figural pottery at Roanne, is that described in E. Maroti and A. Vaday 'Kora Császárkori Figurális Díszítésű, Festett Kerámia Pannoniában és a Szarmata Barbaricumban' *Studia Comitatensia* 9 (1980) 79–92.

Sword Stamps

R. Wyss 'Technik, Wirtschaft, Handel und Kriegswesen der Eisenzeit' in W. Drack *Archäologie der Schweiz IV: Die Eisenzeit* (Basel 1974) 105–138. J.M. De Navarro *The Finds from the Site of La Tène I: Scabbards and the Swords found in them* (Oxford U.P. 1972) 151–200; R. Wyss 'Das Schwert von Korisios: zur Entdeckung einer griechischen Inschrift' *Jahrbuch d. Bernischen Historischen Museums* 34 (1954) 201–221; R.G. Livens 'Who was Korisios?' *Antiquity* 46 (1972) 56–7; M. Tizzoni 'I Marchi delle Spade La Tène conservate al civico Museo Archeologico di Milano' *EC* 21 (1984) 95–110. On the Manching lead weight, T. Müller and W. Rasmüller (eds.) *Ingolstadt* (Donau Courier, Ingolstadt 1976) 37.

Animal Representations

G. Jacob-Friesen 'Zu einigen Tier-und Menschenkopfattaschen der Spätlatènezeit' *Kölner Jahrbuch für Vor- und Frühgeschichte* 13 (1972/3) 50–8. WELTENBURG: W. Krämer 'Der keltische Bronzestier von Weltenburg in Niederbayern' *Germania* 28 (1944/50) 210–3. FIREDOGS: S. Piggott 'Firedogs in Iron Age Britain and beyond' in J. Boardman et al. (eds.) *The European Community in Later Prehistory: Studies in Honour of C.F.C. Hawkes* (Routledge and Kegan Paul, London 1971) 245–70. BOARS K. Gschwantler 'Eine bronzene Eberstatuette aus Enns-Lauricum' *Alba Regia* XXI (1984) 71–77. BÁTA: *KM* no. 177. The boar and the Rákos deer are dealt with by E.F. Petres 'Ausgaben zum Römerzeitlichen Fortleben der keltischen Plastik in Pannonien' *Alba Regia* 14 (1975) 225–234. EUFFIGNEIX: *KM* no. 15; Megaw *AEIA* no. 226. NEUVY boar: Megaw *AEIA* no. 238. HEIDETRÄNK: A. and M. Müller-Karpe 'Neue latènezeitliche Funde aus dem Heidetränk-Oppidum in Taunus' *Germania* 55 (1977) 33–55; F. Maier *Das Heidletränk-Oppidum = Führer zur hessischen Vor- und Frühgeschichte* 4 (Theiss, Stuttgart 1985) esp. 96f. WALLERTHEIM DOG: H. Polenz 'Latènezeitlichen Hundeplastiken aus Süd- und Rheinhessen' *Fundberichte aus Hessen* 14 (1974) 255–307. NOVO MESTO, MIHOVO AND SMARJETA HELMETS: U. Schaaff with T. Knez 'Ein spätkeltisches Kriegergrab mit Eisenhelm aus Novo Mesto' *Situla* 20/21 (1980) 398–413. FELLBACH-SCHMIDEN: the fullest publication is D. Planck et al. 'Ein neuentdecktes Viereckschanz in Fellbach-Schmiden, Rems-Murr-Kreis; Vorbericht der Grabungen 1977–80' *Germania* 60 (1982) 105–91. MIHOVO SCABBARD: H.J. Windl 'Ein verzierter Schwertscheidebeschlag aus dem Gräberfeld von Mihovo, Unterkrain (Dolejnsko)' *Mitteilungen der Anthropologischen Gesellschaft in Wien* 106 (1976) 42–7.

Humans

DONNERSBERG: H. Polenz 'Ein maskenvierzierter Achsnagel der spätlatènezeit vom Donnersberg im Pfalz' *Germania* 52 (1974) 386–400. URACH: F. Fischer *Der Heidengraben bei Grabenstetten = Führer zu vor- und frühgeschichtlichen Denkmälern in Württemberg und Hohenzollern* 2 (1979) 108–110. ZEMPLÍN: Megaw *AEIA* no. 199. ANTHROPOID-HILTED SWORDS: R.R. Clarke and C.F.C. Hawkes 'An Iron Anthropoid Sword from Shouldham, Norfolk, with related Continental and British Weapons' *PPS* 21 (1955) 198–227; E.F. Petres 'Some remarks on anthropoid and pseudoanthropoid hilted daggers in Hungary' in Duval and Kruta 1979, 171–6.
STARÉ HRADISKO: on the oppidum J. Meduna 'Das keltische Oppidum Staré Hradisko In Mähren' *Památky* 48 (1970) 34–59; J. Meduna, *Staré Hradisko II = Fontes Archaeologiae Moraviace V* (Archaeological Institute, Brno 1970). MANERBIO: V. Kruta 'Le Falere di Manerbio' *Atti Conv. XIX Centenario ... Capitolium di Brescia 27–30 Sept. 1973* (1975) II 43–52. DEJBJERG: Megaw *AEIA* no. 203; S. Piggott, *The Earliest Wheeled Transport* (Thames and Hudson, London 1983), 225 ff.

Sculpture in France

M. Pobe and J. Roubier *The Art of Roman Gaul* (Readers Union/Galley Press, London 1962); H.-P. Eydoux *La France Antique* (Plon, Paris 1962).
SOUTH OF FRANCE: F. Salviat 'La sculpture préromaine en Provence' in *Au temps des gaulois en Gaule meridionale = Dossiers de l'Archéologie* 35 (June 1979) 31–51 and 111; *Gauls Provincial* 129–40; F. Benoit *L'art primitif méditerranéen de la Vallée du Rhône = Annales de la Faculté des Lettres Aix-en-Provence* 9 (1955); F. Salviat *Entremont antique* (Les Amis d'Entremont, Aix-en-Provence 1973); F. Salviat and J. Marcadé 'Le relief d'Aubergue et les têtes coupées d'Entremont' *Revue Archéologique de Narbonnaise* 9 (1976) 81–7. LINSDORF: I.M. Stead 'The Linsdorf Monster' *Antiquity* 59 (1985) 40–42. EUFFIGNEIX: Megaw *AEIA* no. 226; *KM* no. 15. BOURAY: Megaw *AEIA* no. 232; *KM* no. 14. NEUVY: Megaw *AEIA* no. 237; *Gauls Provincial* 199–201. CHAMALIÈRES: *Musée Bargoin, ex-voto gallo-romains* (Catalogue) (Clermont-Ferrand 1980); see also *Gauls Provincial* 204–7 and A.-M. Romeuf 'Ex-voto en bois de Chamalières (Puy-de-Dôme) et des Sources de la Seine: essai de

comparaison' *Gallia* 44 (1986) 65–89. SOURCES-DE-LA SEINE: S. Deyts *Les Bois Sculptés des Sources de la Seine* = *Gallia*, 42ᵉ supplément (CRNS, Paris 1983).

Cauldrons

RYNKEBY: Megaw *AEI* A no. 222. GUNDESTRUP: this is one of the most debated pieces illustrated. Megaw *AEI* A, nos. 131–3 summarizes the bibliography to 1969. Of the fuller publications since, T.G.E. Powell 'From Urartu to Gundestrup' in J. Boardman et al. (eds.) *The European Community in Later Prehistory: Studies in Honour of C.F.C. Hawkes* (Routledge and Kegan Paul, London 1971) 181–210 and C. Bémont 'Le Bassin de Gundestrup: remarques sur les décors végétaux' *EC* 16 (1979) 69–99 point to an eastern European origin, A.K. Berquist and T.F. Taylor 'The origin of the Gundestrup Cauldron' *Antiquity* 61 (1987) 10–24 do likewise. J.J. Hatt 'Eine Interpretation der Bilder und Szenen auf dem Silberkessel von Gundestrup' *KM* 68–75 and G.S. Olmstedt *The Gundestrup Cauldron . . . Narration of a Gaulish Version of the 'Táin Bó Cúailnge'* = *Collection Latomus* 162 (Brussels 1979) suggest an origin in France. R. Pittioni *Wer hat wann und wo den Silberkessel von Gundestrup angefertigt?* (Verlag der Österreichischen Akademie der Wissenschaften, Vienna 1984) claims Roquepertuse in southern France as the origin. On the technique, see A. Villemess 'Hvad nyt om Gundestrupkarret?' *Nationalmuseets Arbejdsmark 1978* (1979), 78–84. On comparison with Thracian coins D.F. Allen 'The Sark Hoard' *Archaeologia* 103 (1971) 1–31. On Thraco-Getic art D. Berciu *Arta Traco-Getica* (Bucarest 1969); P. Alexandrescu 'Un art thraco-gète?' *Dacia* 18 (1974) 278–81. D. Berciu *Contribution à l'étude de l'Art thraco-gète* (Editura Academiei Republicii Socialiste România, Bucarest 1974) puts the Gundestrup cauldron in the first century A D. See also A. Fol, B. Nikolov and R.F. Hoddinott *The new Thracian treasure from Rogozen, Bulgaria* (British Museum Publications, London 1986) for a fifth-fourth century B C find, 'possibly exhibiting Celtic elements'.

Trichtingen Ring

L.P. Goessler *Der Silberring von Trichtingen* (Walter de Gruyter, Berlin and Leipzig 1929); F. Fischer *Der Trichtinger Ring und seine Probleme* = *Kolloquium 70. Geburtstag Prof. Dr. K. Bittel* (Heimat- und Altertumsverein, Heidenheim an der Brenz 1978). The discussion in Fischer makes clear the division between Celtic specialists who place the ring in the first century B C and classical and oriental scholars who would prefer to place it at a much earlier date and give it an oriental pedigree.

Coins

The literature is so vast that only a small selection is presented here. Brief introductions can be found in D.F. Allen *An Introduction to Celtic Coins* (British Museum, London 1978); D.F. Allen *The Coins of the Ancient Celts* ed. D. Nash (Edinburgh U.P. 1980) with a very valuable bibliography; D. Nash 'The Celts' in M.J. Price (ed.) *Coins: an illustrated survey 650 BC to the present day* (Methuen, London 1980) 74–85; P. La Baume *Keltische Münzen: ein Brevier* (Klinkhardt and Biermann, Braunschweig 1960); H. Polenz (ed.) *Münzen der Kelten: exhibition catalogue Westfälisches Museum für Archäologie* 5 July-4 October 1981 (Landschaftsverband Westfalen Lippe, Munster 1981); *KM* 101–110, 316–335; *KKM* nos. 174–213; Szabo nos. 1, 53–68.

A very full treatment of numismatic methodology appears in J. Colbert de Beaulieu *Traité de Numismatique Celtique* I *Méthodologie des Ensembles* = *Annales Littéraires de l'Université de Besançon* 135 (Les Belles Lettres, Paris 1973). A brief overview of the function and origins of Celtic coinage is D.F. Allen 'Wealth, Money and Coinage in a Celtic Society' in J.V.S. Megaw (ed.) *To Illustrate the Monuments; essays on archaeology presented to Stuart Piggott . . . on the occasion of his 65th birthday* (Thames and Hudson, London 1976) 199–208.

An important new series based on the work of the late Derek Allen has just commenced publication: *Catalogue of the Celtic Coins in the British Museum* I– (British Museum Publications, London 1987–). Important regional studies include, on western Europe, H. de la Tour *Atlas de Monnaies Gauloises* (Paris 1892, reprinted Spink, London 1965). B. Cunliffe (ed.) *Coinage and Society in Britain and Gaul: some current problems* = *CBA Research Report* 38 (1981) contains some valuable articles; two by D. Nash and S. Scheers usefully summarize much longer works: D. Nash *Settlement and Coinage in Central Gaul c. 200–50 B.C.* 2 vols. = *BAR Suppl. Series* 39 (1978) and S. Scheers *Traité de Numismatique Celtique* II: *La Gaule belgique* = *Annales Littéraires de l'Université de Besançon* 195 (Les Belles Lettres, Paris 1977). B. Ployart *Choix de Monnaies Gauloises* (Bibliothèque Nationale, Paris 1980); G. Grasmann et al. (eds.) *Keltische Numismatik und Archäologie: Veröffentlichung der Referate des Kolloquiums keltische Numismatik 4–8 Februar 1981* = *BAR Internat. Series* 200 (1984) has many valuable essays, mostly on western Europe; C. Haselgrove 'Warfare and its Aftermath as reflected in the Precious Metal Coinage of Belgic Gaul' *Oxford J. Arch.* 3 (1984) 81–106.

EASTERN AND CENTRAL EUROPE: C. Preda *Monedele Geto-Dacilor* (Editura Academiei Republicii Socialiste Romania, Bucharest 1973). R. Forrer *Keltische Numismatik der Rhein und Donaulandes* 2 vols. (Akademische Druck- und Verlagsanstalt, Graz 1968) has been valuably updated by K. Castelin since its original publication in 1908. The earliest eastern coins are discussed in M. Szabó 'Audoleon und die Anfänge der ostkeltischen Münzprägung' *Alba Regia* 20 (1983) 43–56 and V. Kruta 'Archéologie et Numismatique: la phase initiale du monnayage celtique' *EC* 19 (1982) 69–82.

For stylistic rather than numismatic approaches to Celtic coins, P.-M. Duval 'Matériaux pour l'étude stylistique des monnaies celtiques' Duval and Hawkes 247–63; E. Kolníková 'Münzkunst der Kelten in der Slowakei' in T. Hackens and R. Weiller (eds.) *Proceedings of the 9th International Congress of Numismatics, Berne, September 1979* (Louvain-la-Neuve 1982) 679–87; L. Lengyel *L'art gaulois dans les médailles* (Corvina, Montrouge-Seine 1954).

Attempts to interpret the symbolism of coins with reference to Celtic religion include M.E.P. König 'Keltische Münzbilden' *IPEK* 21 (1964–5) 65–77; M.E.P. König 'Celtic Coins: a new interpretation' *Archaeology* 19 (1966) 24–30; L. Lengyel *Le Secret des Celtes* (R. Morel, Forcalquier 1969); P.-M. Duval 'Observations sur la mythologie celtique: les sources numismatiques' *EC* 19 (1982) 93–105.

Coins from graves (e.g. Giengen and Châtenay-Mâcheron) rather than from the more common hoards are dealt with by H. Polenz 'Münzen in latènezeitlichen Gräbern Mitteleuropas aus der Zeit zwischen 300 and 50 vor Christi Geburt' *Bayerische Vorgeschichtsblätter* 47 (1982) 27–222. See also J. Biel 'Ein Mittellatènezeitliches Brandgräberfeld in Giengen-an-der-Brenz, Kr. Heidenheim' *AK* 4 (1974) 225–7.

A. Furger-Gunti 'Frühe Auxilien am Rhein, keltische Münzen in römischen Militarstationen' *AK* 11 (1981) 231–46 suggests that Roman auxiliaries on the Rhine were paid in Celtic coins. On Eggendorf, F. Felgenhauer 'Gemmenabdrücke als Verzierung auf Latène-keramik' *Jahresheften d. Österr. Arch. Inst.* LV (1987) 160–71.

Torcs with Coins

TAYAC: H.-J. Kellner 'Der Fund von Tayac: ein Zeugnis der Cimbernzuges?' *Jahrbuch für Numismatik und Geschichte* 20 (1970) 13–47; *Gauls Provincial* 123–5. NIEDERZIER: H.-E. Joachim and V. Zedelius 'Ein bedeutender keltischer Verwahrfund aus Niederzier, Kr. Düren' *Gymnasium* 87 (1980) 205–10. ST. LOUIS: A. Furger-Gunti 'Der "Goldfund von Saint-Louis" bei Basel und ähnliche keltische Schatzfunde' *Zeitschrift für Schweizerische Archäologie und Kunstgeschichte* 39 (1982) 1–47 attempts a general explanation for the deposition of rings and coins. MAILLY-LE-CAMP: R. Joffroy 'Le torque de Mailly-le-Camp (Aube)' and M. Lejeune 'Les graffites gallo-grecs du torque de Mailly-le-Camp' both in *Monuments et Mémoires (Piot)* 56 (1969) 45–76.

Buckets

In general M. Vidal 'Le seau de bois orné de Vieille-Toulouse (Haute-Garonne): étude comparative de La Tène III' *Gallia* 34 (1976) 167–200.

GOEBLINGEN-NOSPELT: G. Thill 'Die Metallgegenstände aus vier spätlatènezeitlichen Brandgräbern bei Goeblingen-Nospelt' *Hémecht* 19 (1967) 87–95; J. Metzler 'Treverische Reitergräber von Goeblingen-Nospelt' in *Trier: Augustusstadt der Treverer: Stadt und Land in vor- und frührömischer Zeit* (exhibition catalogue Rheinisches Landesmuseum Trier) (von Zabern, Mainz 1984) 87–99. BALDOCK AND AYLESFORD: I.M. Stead 'The Reconstruction of Iron Age Buckets from Aylesford and Baldock' *British Museum Quarterly* 35 (1971) 250–282 deals with all the Late La Tène pre-Roman British buckets. BUCKET DECORATION: W. Meier-Arendt 'Eine spätlatènezeitliche Henkelattasche aus der Kölner Innenstadt' *Kölner Jahrb. für Vor- und Frühgeschichte* 12 (1971) 50–51; also H.-E. Joachim 'Ein merkwürdiger Gegenstand: spätlatènezeitliche Bronze von Rheinbach-Flerzheim, Rhein-Sieg-Kreis' *Das Rheinische Landesmuseum Bonn* 3 (1983) 36–8 on the 'leaf-crown' as prototype for Aylesford and Baldock etc. H. Polenz 'Ein maskvierzierter Achsnagel der Spätlatènezeit vom Donnersberg in der Pfalz' *Germania* 52 (1974) 386–400 sees the 'headdresses' as helmets rather than leaf crowns. GOEBLINGEN-NOSPELT SWORD: see above under buckets. This sword and that from Hammersmith are clearly in the same tradition as the Norican swords described by J. Werner 'Spätlatène-Schwerter norischer Herkunft' in his *Spätes Keltentum zwischen Rom und Germanien* (Beck, Munich 1979) 165–197, though E.M. Jope in 'The Beginnings of La Tène Ornamental Style in the British Isles' *Problems of the Iron Age in Southern Britain = Inst. Arch. Univ. London Occasional Paper* no. 11 (n.d.) and 'Daggers of the Early Iron Age in Britain' *PPS* 27 (1961) has, wrongly in our opinion, put the Hammersmith openwork scabbard very much earlier. ALTENBURG-NIEDENSTEIN: *KM* no. 171.

On connections between Britain and Gaul see the useful collection of essays in S. Macready and F.H. Thompson (eds.) *Cross-Channel Trade between Gaul and Britain in the Pre-Roman Iron Age* (Society of Antiquaries, London 1984).

CHAPTER 6

To keep the bibliography of this chapter within reasonable proportions few references will be given on general archaeology.

General Iron Age in Britain and Ireland

The quotation on p. 189 comes from S. Piggott *Ancient Europe: a survey* (Edinburgh U.P. 1965) 229.

On language, the basic text remains K. Jackson *Language and History in Early Britain: a chronological survey of the Brittonic languages 1st to 12th centuries AD* (Edinburgh U.P. 1953); see also G. Price *The Languages of Britain* (Edward Arnold, London 1984).

Basic surveys of the British Iron Age are D.W. Harding *The Iron Age in Lowland Britain* (Routledge and Kegan Paul, London 1974); B.W. Cunliffe *Iron Age Communities in Britain* 2nd ed. (Routledge and Kegan Paul, London 1978); J.V.S. Megaw and D.D.S. Simpson (eds.) *Introduction to British Prehistory* (Leicester U.P. 1979), ch. 7 with a full bibliography to the date of publication. Some interesting ideas appear in John Collis (ed.) *The Iron Age in Britain: a review* (Department of Prehistory and Archaeology, University of Sheffield 1977) and R. Bradley *The social foundations of prehistoric Britain: themes and variations in the archaeology of power* (Longman, London 1984) esp. ch. 6. IRELAND: all previous work has been superseded by two monographs by Barry Raftery, cited below under 'Art'. See also J.P. Mallory 'The origins of the Irish' *J. Irish Arch.* 2 (1984) 65–9. SCOTLAND: this area is not so well served. The most recent short publication is S. Piggott with J.N.G. Ritchie *Scotland Before History* 2nd rev. ed. (Edinburgh U.P. 1983) originally published in 1952 but now with new bibliography and gazetteer; A.L.F. Rivet (ed.) *The Iron Age in Northern Britain* (Edinburgh U.P. 1966) is also still useful. On Wales, H.N. Savory 'La Tène Wales' *EC* 13 (1973) 685–709; more recently the same writer's *Guide Catalogue of the Early Iron Age collections* (National Museum of Wales, Cardiff 1976) and 'The early Iron Age in Wales' in J.A. Taylor (ed.) *Culture and environment in prehistoric Wales = BAR* 76 (1980) 287–310 – though we do not follow Savory on the 'Welshness' of Welsh Iron Age art.

The idea of cumulative Celticity: C.F.C. Hawkes 'Cumulative Celticity in Pre-Roman Britain' *EC* 13 (1973) 590–611. ARRAS CULTURE: I.M. Stead *The Arras Culture* (Yorkshire Philosophical Society, York 1979). IMPORTS: I.M. Stead 'Some Notes on Imported Metalwork in Iron Age Britain' in S. Macready and F.H. Thompson (eds.) *Cross-Channel Trade between Gaul and Britain in the Pre-Roman Iron Age* (Society of Antiquaries, London 1984) 43–66. METALWORKING: R.F. Tylecote *The Prehistory of Metallurgy in the British Isles* (Institute of Metals, London 1986) ch. 6 'The coming of iron'.

Celtic Religion

The fundamental text is A. Ross *Pagan Celtic Britain* (Routledge and Kegan Paul, London 1967); see also S. Piggott *The Druids* rev. ed. (Thames and Hudson, London 1975); G.A. Wait *Ritual and Religion in Iron Age Britain = BAR* 149 (1985) 2 vols.; M.J. Green *The Gods of the Celts* (Alan Sutton, Gloucester 1986) and *The Gods of Roman Britain* (Shire Publications, Princes Risborough 1983), which summarizes her *The Religions of Civilian Roman Britain = BAR* 24 (1976); G. Webster *The British Celts and their gods under Rome* (Batsford, London 1986).

Celtic Art in Britain and Ireland

Leeds and Fox are pioneering studies, the latter now somewhat superseded in its attempt to discover 'schools' of art. Kilbride-Jones deals mostly with the period after the Roman arrival; it is idiosyncratic though interesting and with splendid drawings. Stead is a good short paperback, while Megaw 1986 provides another short paperback survey. Macgregor is essential on Scotland and northern England and Raftery 1 and Raftery 2 on Ireland.

The definitive work on Celtic art in the British Isles will be the long-awaited completion by Professor E.M. Jope of the work left unfinished by Paul Jacobsthal by his death in 1957. There are further valuable catalogues for this chapter and the following one, for example, *Ancient Treasures of Scotland* (ATS), *Frühe Irische Kunst* (FIK) and *Irische Kunst* (IK). Savory is valuable on Wales, though difficult to use. An unpublished Ph.D. thesis is also of major importance, M.G. Spratling *Southern British Decorated Bronzes of the Late Pre-Roman Iron Age* (Institute of Archaeology, University of London, 1972).

ORIGINS OF CELTIC ART IN BRITAIN AND IRELAND: O.-H. Frey with J.V.S. Megaw 'Palmette and Circle: Early Celtic Art in Britain and its Continental Background' *PPS* 42 (1976) 47–65, and J.V.S. Megaw 'From Transdanubia to Torrs . . .' in A. O'Connor and D.V. Clarke (eds.) *From the Stone Age to the Forty-Five: Studies Presented to R.B.K. Stevenson* (John Donald, Edinburgh 1983) 127–48; Megaw 1986 puts the traceable start of insular Celtic art fairly late, and derives it primarily from continental Sword Styles, as generally does Stead 1985. E.M. Jope 'The Southward Face of Celtic Britain 300 BC–AD 50: Four British Parade Shields' in *I Celti e la Loro Cultura nell' epoca pre-romana et romana Nella Britannia = Academia Nazionale dei Lincei* 237 (1978) 27–36 stresses direct Italian origins and an earlier start. Stead 1985 avoids the issue of stating date. CERRIG-Y-DRUDION: I.M. Stead 'The Cerrig-y-Drudion "Hanging Bowl"' *Antiquaries Journal* 62 (1982) 221–34. NEWNHAM CROFT: Megaw *AEIA* no. 131; Stead 1985, 17–18; Megaw 1986, 24; BRENTFORD HORN-CAP: Megaw *AEIA* no. 130; P.-M. Duval 'L' Ornement de Char de Brentford (Middlesex)' in P.-M. Duval et al. *Recherches d'archéologie celtique et gallo-romaine* (Librairie Droz, Paris and Geneva 1973) 1–10; I.M. Stead 'Some Notes on Imported Metalwork . . .' see above under 'imports'. WISBECH: Stead 1985 pl. 18; Megaw 1986, 15 and pl. 5. STANDLAKE: Megaw *AEIA* no. 250; Stead 1985, 17; Megaw 1986, 13–14 and pl. 4. FOVANT: Stead 1985 19–20, pl. 23. LADDERING: Stead 'Some Notes on Imported Metalwork . . .', 47–8; on the most recently discovered 'laddered' sword, from Little Wittenham, A. Sherratt 'A Newly Discovered La Tène Sword and Scabbard' *Oxford J. Archaeology* 2 (1983) 115–8; Stead 1985, 48–9; Megaw 1986, 31.

Northern Ireland, Torrs, Witham, Wandsworth Group

See the general papers by Frey with Megaw, and Megaw (1983) above under 'Origins'. NORTHERN IRISH SCABBARDS: Raftery 1 nos. 238–242, 260–272 and figs. 107–11; Raftery 2, 75–87 and pls. 26–31. WETWANG: J. Dent 'Three cart burials from Wetwang, Yorkshire' *Antiquity* 59 (1985) 85–92. TORRS: R.J.C. Atkinson and S. Piggott 'The Torrs Chamfrein' *Archaeologia* 96 (1955) 197–235; J.V.S. Megaw 'From Transdanubia to Torrs' (see above under 'Origins . . .') reviews the writings on this subject as well as discussing it directly; see also E.M. Jope 'Torrs, Aylesford, and the Padstow Hobby-Horse' in the same volume. LOUGHNASHADE HORN: Raftery 1 no. 781 and figs. 201–2; Raftery 2, 135–43; also *TEIA* no. 22, *IK* no. 31. B. Raftery 'The Loughnashade horns' *Emania* 2 (1987) 21–24 prefers a date in the first century BC or AD. WITHAM SCABBARD: Megaw *AEIA* no. 250; Stead 1985, 20–1; Megaw 1986 15 and pl. 6.

SHIELDS: the four shields from Wandsworth, Witham and Battersea have been discussed by E.M. Jope 'Southward Face of Roman Britain' quoted above under 'Origins'; see also Brailsford 10–24. WITHAM: E.M. Jope 'The Witham Shield' in G. de G. Sieveking (ed.) *Prehistoric and Roman Studies = British Museum Quarterly* 35 (1971) 61–9; Megaw *AEIA* no. 252 and col. pl. VII; Megaw 1986, 16–18 and pl. 8. WANDSWORTH LONG BOSS: E.M. Jope 'The Wandsworth Mask Shield and its European Sources of Inspiration' in Duval and Hawkes 167–84; Megaw *AEIA* no. 255 first commented on the teeth. BATTERSEA: Brailsford 25–31; I.M. Stead *The Battersea Shield* (British Museum Publications, London 1985). WANDSWORTH ROUND BOSS: Megaw *AEIA* no. 247; Stead 1985, 54, 56 and pl. 76; Megaw 1986, 15 and pl 7.

CASTIGLIONE DELLE STIVIERE: Jacobsthal *ECA* no. 398; Dr. R. de Marinis and Dr. M. Tizzoni have been good enough to furnish the opinion that the piece is a carnyx or warhorn, not an askos. LLYN CERRIG BACH: Sir Cyril Fox *A Find of the Early Iron Age from Llyn Cerrig Bach, Anglesey* (National Museum of Wales, Cardiff 1946); Megaw *AEIA* no. 254.

Britain in the First Century BC

HILLFORTS AND OPPIDA: of the voluminous literature on this subject, basic information can be found in J. Collis *Defended Sites of Late La Tène = BAR Suppl. Series* 2 (1975) 210–31 and B. Cunliffe 'The Origins of Urbanisation in Britain' in B. Cunliffe and T. Rowley (eds.) *Oppida in Barbarian Europe = BAR Suppl. Series* 11 (1976) 135–61. TRADE: see papers by J. Collis and C. Haselgrove in the above volume; S. Macready and F.H. Thompson (eds.) *Cross-Channel Trade between Gaul and Britain in the pre-Roman Iron Age* (Society of Antiquaries, London 1984), in which D. Nash repeats her idea of agrarian/warrior-agrarian societies, and B. Cunliffe suggests the Belgae were in Wessex, not in the southeast, as well as detailing the connections between Wessex and Armorica; B. Cunliffe 'Britain, the Veneti and beyond' *Oxford J. Arch.* 1 (1982) 39–68; B. Cunliffe 'Ictis, was it here?' *Oxford J. Arch.* 2 (1983) 123–6; and C.F.C. Hawkes 'Ictis disentangled, and the British tin trade' *Oxford J. Arch.* 3 (1984) 211–33; R.D. Penhallurick *Tin in Antiquity* (Institute of Metals, London 1986). BELGIC INVASIONS AND SETTLEMENT: on the current state of discussion, C.F.C. Hawkes 'New thoughts on the Belgae' *Antiquity* 42 (1968) 6–19; R. Hachmann 'The problem of the Belgae seen from the Continent' *Bull. Institute of Archaeology* 13 (1976) 117–37; I.M. Stead 'The earliest burials of the Aylesford culture' in G. de G. Sieveking et al. (eds.) *Problems in Economic and Social Archaeology* (Duckworth, London 1976) 401–16. Bearing on this period, though basically on AD 43 and the Roman period, is the series published by Alan Sutton Ltd, Gloucester, especially K. Branigan *The Catuvellauni* (1985); also R. Dunnett *The Trinovantes* (1975), Alec Detsicas *The Cantiaci* (1977), B. Cunliffe *The Regni* (1973), M. Todd *The Coritani* (1973).

Coins

As well as the general works cited under Chapter 5, R.P. Mack *The Coinage of Ancient Britain* 3rd ed. (Spink, London 1975) is a standard reference. See too D.F. Allen 'The Origins of coinage in Britain: a re-appraisal' in S.S. Frere (ed.) *Problems of the Iron Age in southern Britain = Univ. London Inst. of Archaeology Occasional Paper* 11

(n.d.). 97–302. Other important recent works include J.P.C. Kent 'The Origin and Development of Celtic Gold Coinage in Britain' in *Centenaire de l'Abbé Cochet = Actes du Colloque International d'Archéologie* (Rouen 1978) 313–24; W.J. Rodwell 'Coinage, oppida and the rise of Belgic power in S.E. Britain' in B.W. Cunliffe and R.T. Rowley (eds.) *Oppida in Barbarian Europe = BAR Suppl. Series* 11 (1976) 181–367; C.C. Haselgrove 'The significance of coinage in pre-Conquest Britain' in B.C. Burnham and H. Johnson (eds.) *Invasion and response; the case of Roman Britain = BAR* 73 (1979) 197–210; B. Cunliffe (ed.) *Coinage and Society in Britain and Gaul: some current problems = CBA Research Report* 38 (1981) contains a number of extremely important articles, including clear statements of the debate between the makers of Procrustean models and the collectors of 'facts'. Most recently C. Haselgrove *Iron Age Coinage in South-East England = BAR* 174 (1987).

On the 'potin' or cast bronze coins see D.F. Allen 'British Potin Coins: A Review' in D. Hill and M. Jesson (eds.) *The Iron Age and its Hillforts* (Southampton University Archaeological Soc., 1971) 127–54; R.D. Van Arsdell 'An industrial engineer (but no papyrus) in Celtic Britain' *Oxford J. Arch.* 5 (1986) 205–21.

Gussage All Saints

G. Wainwright and M.G. Spratling 'The Iron Age Settlement of Gussage All Saints' *Antiquity* 47 (1973) 109–30; G.D. Wainwright et al. *Gussage All Saints: An Iron Age Settlement in Dorset = Dept. of Environment Archaeological Reports* 10 (H.M.S.O., London 1979); J. Foster *The Iron Age Moulds from Gussage All Saints = British Museum Occasional Paper* 12 (1980).

Mature Celtic Insular Art:
(A) Ireland

LOUGH CREW BONE PIECES: Raftery 1 nos. 621–780 and figs. 187–200; Raftery 2, 251–63 and pls. 80–1. SPOONS AND SCOOPS: Raftery 1 nos. 822–7 and figs. 226–7; Raftery 2, 264–6 and pls. 82–3; MacGregor 145–6. MEARE AND GLASTONBURY POTS: D.P.S. Peacock 'A Contribution to the Study of Glastonbury ware from South-Western Britain' *Antiquaries Journal* 49 (1969) 41–61; Megaw *AEIA* no. 295. IRISH CARVED STONES: Raftery 1 nos. 835–9 and figs. 232–6; Raftery 2, 291–303 and pls. 102–6. TUROE: M.V. Duignan 'The Turoe Stone: its place in insular Celtic art' in Duval and Hawkes 201–18; J. Waddell 'From Kermaria to Turoe' in B.G. Scott (ed.) *Studies on Early Ireland: Essays in Honour of M.V. Duignan* (Association of Young Irish Archaeologists, Belfast 1982) 21–8.

BROIGHTER TORC AND BOAT: Raftery 1 nos. 450, 456–9, 575, 834 and figs. 141–2, 146, 179, 231; Raftery 2, 181–92 and pls. 61–2; *TEIA* no. 21; *IK* no. 30; R.B. Warner 'The Broighter Hoard: a Reappraisal and the Iconography of the Collar' in B.G. Scott (ed.) *Studies on Early Ireland* 29–38; A.W. Farrell and S. Penny 'The Broighter Boat: a Reassessment' *Irish Archaeol. Res. Forum* 2 (1975) 15–28.

(B) England and Wales

MIRRORS: general technical, P. Lowery, R.D.A. Savage and R.L. Wilkins 'A Technical Study of the Designs on the British Mirror Series' *Archaeologia* 105 (1976) 99–126; general, Sir C. Fox 'Celtic Mirror Handles in Britain, with special reference to the Colchester handle' *Arch. Cambrensis* 103 (1948) 24–44 and *Pattern and Purpose* (National Museum of Wales, Cardiff 1958) 84–104. ASTON: T. Rook et al. 'An Iron Age Bronze Mirror from Aston, Hertfordshire' *Antiquaries Journal* 62 (1982) 18–33. DORTON: M. Farley 'A Mirror Burial at Dorton, Buckinghamshire' *PPS* 49 (1983) 269–402. HOLCOMBE: A Fox 'The Holcombe Mirror' *Antiquity* 46 (1972) 293–6; Brailsford 62–6; P. Lowery and R. Savage 'Celtic Designs with Compasses as seen on the Holcombe Mirror' in Duval and Hawkes 219–29. GREAT CHESTERFORD: Sir C. Fox 'A Celtic Mirror from Great Chesterford' *Antiquity* 34 (1960) 207–10. OLD WARDEN: M. Spratling 'The Late Pre-Roman Iron Age Bronze Mirror from Old Warden' *Bedfordshire Arch. J.* 5 (1970) 9–16. NIJMEGEN: G.L. Morgan *Descriptions of the Collections in the Rijksmuseum G.M. Kam at Nijmegen IX: The Mirrors* (Ministry of Culture, Recreation and Social Welfare 1981) 111–6. DESBOROUGH: illustrated in Brailsford 67–8.

BIBLIOGRAPHY

Swords, Spears and Shields

THAMES: Megaw *AEIA* no. 257. LITTLE WITTENHAM: A. Sherratt 'A newly discovered La Tène sword and scabbard' *Oxford J. Arch.* 2 (1983) 115–8. HENLEY: R.A. Rutland 'An Iron Age Sword and Scabbard from the Thames at Henley, Oxon' *Antiquaries Journal* 52 (1972) 345–6. BUGTHORPE: Megaw *AEIA* no. 259. TAL-Y-LLYN: H. Savory 'The La Tène Shield in Wales' in Duval and Hawkes 185–99; Megaw *AEIA* no. 262.

Snettisham Ipswich 'Style'

SNETTISHAM: R.R. Clarke 'The Early Iron Age Treasure from Snettisham, Norfolk' *PPS* 20 (1954) 27–86; Brailsford 55–61; more recently P.R. Sealey 'The Later History of Icenian Electrum Torcs' *PPS* 45 (1979) 165–78 has argued strongly for an Icenian origin for this and the other torcs of this group. IPSWICH: J. Brailsford and J.E. Stapley 'The Ipswich Torcs' *PPS* 38 (1972) 219–34; Brailsford 44–54; E. Owles 'The Ipswich Gold Torcs' *Antiquity* 43 (1969) 208–12 points to the contrast between the splendour of the torcs and the poverty and paucity of evidence for everyday life in E. Anglia. NETHERURD: MacGregor 94–6 and pl. Ib, nos. 191–4. SEDGFORD: J.W. Brailsford 'The Sedgford Torc' in G. de G. Sieveking (ed.) *Prehistoric and Roman Studies = British Museum Quarterly* 35 (1971) 16–19. WATERLOO HELMET: Megaw *AEIA* no. 294; Brailsford 32–9.

Horse Harness

M. Spratling *Southern British Decorated Bronzes* (unpublished Ph.D. thesis, Institute of Archaeology, University of London, 1972), is valuable. On enamelling in the late Iron Age see J.D. Bateson *Enamelworking in Iron Age, Roman and Sub-Roman Britain: the products and techniques = BAR* 93 (1981) 17–18. Quadrilobe mounts are discussed in G. Leman-Delerive et al. 'Une plaque émaillée celtique découverte à Paillart (Oise) *Gallia* 44 (1986) 29–53. SANTON: Megaw *AEIA* 263 and pl. VIIIa. POLDEN HILLS: J.W. Brailsford 'The Polden Hill Hoard, Somerset' *PPS* 41 (1975) 222–34. ISLEHAM SWORD: I.M. Stead et al. 'An Iron Age Sword and Scabbard from Isleham' *Procs. Cambridge Antiquarian Soc.* 70 (1980) 61–74.

Men and Beasts

Fox 72–83 discusses such representations generally, see also G. Jacob-Friesen 'Zu einigen Tier- und Menschenkopfattaschen der Spät-latènezeit' *Kölner Jahrbuch für Vor- und Frühgeschichte* 13 (1972/3) 50–58. KESHCARRIGAN: Raftery 1 no. 567 and fig. 175; Raftery 2, 214–23 and pl. 69; *TEIA* no. 20; *IK* no. 33. FELMERSHAM: Megaw *AEIA* no. 276; J.V.S. Megaw 'The Felmersham fish-head spout: a suggested reconstruction' *Antiquaries Journal* 50 (1970) 86–8; D. Kennett 'Felmersham and Ostia, a Metalwork comparison' *Bedfordshire Arch. J.* 11 (1976) 19–22. ŁĘG PIEKARSKI: J.V.S. Megaw 'A British Bronze Bowl of the Iron Age in Poland' *Antiquaries Journal* 43 (1963) 27–37; Megaw *AEIA* no. 277; on other boars, J. Foster *Bronze Boar Figurines in Iron Age and Roman Britain = BAR* 39 (1977). BALLYBOGEY MIRROR: Raftery 1 no. 537 and fig. 163; Raftery 2, 208–10 and pl. 66. IRISH HORSE-BIT: Raftery 1 no. 42 and fig. 11; Raftery 2, 20–21 and pl. 1; B. Raftery 'A Decorated Iron Age Horse-bit from Ireland' *Procs. Royal Irish Acad.* 74 C. (1974) 1–10. MELSONBY HORSE MASK: M. MacGregor 'The Iron Age Metalwork Hoard from Stanwick, North Riding, Yorkshire' *PPS* 28 (1962) 17–57. ALDBOROUGH: Megaw *AEIA* no. 264; MacGregor no. 61. MELSONBY HUMAN: Megaw *AEIA* no. 264. TAL-Y-LLYN HUMAN: Megaw *AEIA* no. 266; H. Savory 'The La Tène Shield in Wales' in Duval and Hawkes 185–99. TRE'R CEIRI FACE: Megaw *AEIA* no. 304. RALAGHAN: Raftery 1 no. 828 and fig. 228; Raftery 2, 308 and pl. 112. TANDERAGEE: Megaw *AEIA* no. 285. SUTHERLAND STONE HEAD: Megaw *AEIA* no. 286.

Roman Conquest and Occupation

Good introductory accounts in John Wacher *The Coming of Rome* (Routledge and Kegan Paul, London 1979) now available as a Paladin paperback; Graham Webster *The Roman Invasion of Britain* (Batsford, London 1980).

On Britain under the Romans: S.S. Frere *Britannia: a history of Roman Britain* rev. ed. (Routledge and Kegan Paul, London 1978); J. Wacher *Roman Britain* (Dent, London 1978); B. Burnham and C. Johnson (eds.) *Invasion and response: the case of Roman Britain = BAR* 73 (1979).

Art of the Celts in Roman Britain

J.M.C. Toynbee *Art in Britain under the Romans* (Clarendon Press, Oxford 1964) is valuable, as is J.M.C. Toynbee *Art in Roman Britain* (Phaidon, London 1962) which is basically a catalogue; less useful is C. Lindgren *Classical Art Forms and Celtic Mutations* (Noyes Press, Park Ridge N.J. 1980); on the new 'schools of art' see MacGregor 184–5. DOWGATE PLAQUE: J.V.S. Megaw and R. Merrifield 'The Dowgate Plaque. A bronze Mount of the British Iron Age from the City of London' *Arch. J.* 126 (1969) 154–9 also deals with the Silchester disc. AESICA BROOCH: Toynbee 1962 no. 130 and pl. 154; Megaw *AEIA* no. 305; MacGregor 119–23, no. 251 and pl. XII; D. Charlesworth 'The Aesica Hoard' *Archaeologia Aeliana* 5th ser, 1 (1973) 225–34; Kilbride-Jones 21–2, 26–7, 84–5. DRAGONESQUE BROOCHES: R.W. Feachem 'Dragonesque Fibulae' *Antiquaries Journal* 48 (1968) 100–3; MacGregor 127–9; Kilbride-Jones 170–83. CARMARTHEN BROOCH: G.C. Boon and H.N. Savory 'A Silver Trumpet-Brooch with Relief Decoration, Parcel-Gilt, from Carmarthen and a Note on the Development of the Type' *Antiquaries Journal* 55 (1975) 41–61. ELMSWELL PLAQUE: Toynbee 1962 no. 123 and pl. 142; Megaw *AEIA* no. 303; MacGregor 158–9, no. 336; Kilbride-Jones 78–83. CASKET STRIPS: Megaw *AEIA* no. 300 and Megaw and Merrifield (above under 'Dowgate'). STICHILL COLLAR: Megaw *AEIA* no. 298; MacGregor 99–101 no. 210 and pl. IIa; Kilbride-Jones 73–4. LINCOLN SEAL-BOX: MacGregor 101. DESKFORD CARNYX: Megaw *AEIA* no. 242; MacGregor 87–8, no. 188 and pl VId. MORTONHALL SWORD: MacGregor 81–3, no. 149 and pl. IIIb; *ATS* no. 29; Kilbride-Jones 120–1, 129 and fig. 32:5. CULBIN SANDS ARMLET: Megaw *AEIA* no. 302; Macgregor 103–5 no. 214 and pl. VIc. MASSIVE ARMLETS: Megaw *AEIA* 173–4 and pl. VIIIb; MacGregor 106–10, nos. 240–1; Brailsford 73–82. NORRIES LAW: MacGregor no. 349.

West Britain

MOEL HIRADDUG: Megaw *AEIA* no. 268; H. Savory 'The La Tène Shield in Wales' in Duval and Hawkes 185–99. TRAWSFYNYDD: Megaw *AEIA* no. 296; P. Webster 'Roman and Iron Age Tankards in Western Britain' *Bulletin of the Board of Celtic Studies* 26 (1975) 231–6. CAPEL GARMON: S. Piggott 'Firedogs in Iron Age Britain and Beyond' in J. Boardman et al. (eds.) *The European Community in Later Prehistory: Studies in Honour of C.F.C. Hawkes* (Routledge and Kegan Paul, London 1971) 245–70; Savory no. 31 and pl. VIa. WRAXALL COLLAR: J.V.S. Megaw 'A Group of Later Iron Age Collars in Western Britain' in G. de G. Sieveking (ed.) *Prehistoric and Roman Studies = British Museum Quarterly* 35 (1971) 145–55.

Ireland

ATTYMON HORSE-BITS: Raftery 1 nos. 102–3 and figs. 37, 97A; Raftery 2 figs. 19, 24; *TEIA* no. 26; *IK* nos. 38a, 38b. ATTYMON PENDANTS: Raftery 1 nos. 200–1 and figs. 79, 80, 97A; Raftery 2, 45–57 and pl. 16; *IK* nos. 38c and 38d. LAMBAY ISLAND: Raftery 1 no. 794 and fig. 159; Raftery 2, 282–4 and pl. 96; see also E. Rynne 'The La Tène and Roman Finds from Lambay, Co. Dublin: a reassessment' *Procs. Royal Irish Acad.* 76C (1976) 231–45. LOUGHAN ISLAND (BANN) DISC: Raftery 1 no. 793 and fig. 213; Raftery 2, 268–75 and pl. 88; P.-M. Duval 'Un motif celtique: le triscèle du disque de la Bann' *EC* 20 (1983) 81–90. PETRIE CROWN: Raftery 1 no. 821 and figs. 223–5; Raftery 2, 268–75 and pls. 85–7; *TEIA* no. 24; *IK* no. 36. CORK HORNS: Raftery 1 no. 820 and figs. 219–22; Raftery 2, 268–75 and pl. 84. On the technique of these last three pieces see M.J. O'Kelly 'The Cork Horns, the Petrie Crown and the Bann Disc: the Technique of their Ornamentation' *J. Cork Hist. and Arch. Soc.* 66 (1961) 1–12. MONASTEREVIN DISCS: Raftery 1 no. 792 and fig. 212; Raftery 2, 276–82.

Scotland and England

WEST LOTHIAN: on the patera, Toynbee 1962, no. 113 and pl. 125; on other such cups see J.D. Cowen and I.A. Richmond 'The Rudge Cup' *Archaeologia Aeliana* 12 (1935) 310–42; J. Heurgon 'The Amiens Patera' *Journal of Roman Studies* 41 (1951) 22–4. *Trompetenmuster* and the 'factory'; in general J. Oldenstein 'Zur Aüsrustung der römischer Auxiliareinheiten' *Ber. d. RGK* 7 (1976) 49–284; L. Berger 'Die Thekenbeschlage des Gemellianus von Baden-Aquae Helvetiae' *Studien zu Unserer Frühgeschichte* (Aktiengesellschaft Oederlin et Cie. Baden, n.d.) 9–32 is an enlarged version of an article of the same title in *Jahrb. der Schweizerischen Gesellschaft für Urgeschichte* 46 (1957) 24–39. SOUTH SHIELDS: MacGregor 186–8, fig. 9:12 and pl. XVIb. NIDA-HEDDERNHEIM: I. Huld-Zetsche '150 Jahre Forschungen in Nida-Heddernheim' *Nassaue Annalen* 90 (1979) 5–38. KELVEDON SHERD: K. and W. Rodwell 'Kelvedon' *Current Archaeology* 48 (1975) 25–9. CADBURY MASK: L. Alcock '*By South Cadbury is that Camelot*': *excavations at Cadbury Castle 1966–70* (Thames and Hudson, London 1972) 167–72 and pl XII.

EPILOGUE

The quotations at the opening come from R.G. Collingwood and J.N.L. Myres *Roman Britain and the English Settlements* (Oxford U.P. 1936) 259. S.S. Frere *Britannia* rev. ed. (Routledge and Kegan Paul, London 1978) 355; T.D. Leeds *Celtic Ornament* (Clarendon Press, Oxford 1933) 62; J.M.C. Toynbee *Art in Britain under the Romans* (Clarendon Press, Oxford 1964) 21; J.M. de Navarro 'Celts in Britain and Their Art' in M.P. Charlesworth et al. *The Heritage of Early Britain* (Bell, London 1952) 56–81 at p. 81.

The Decline of Rome and the Coming to Britain of the Germanic People

M. Dillon and N. Chadwick *The Celtic Realms* (Weidenfeld and Nicolson, London 1967) is almost entirely on this post-Roman period, though its attempts to link archaeology and history is no longer widely accepted. C. Thomas *Britain and Ireland in Early Christian Times, AD400–800* (Thames and Hudson, London 1971); L. Alcock *Arthur's Britain* (Penguin, Harmondsworth 1973); M. Todd *The Northern Barbarians* (Hutchinson, London 1975); D. Wilson (ed.) *The Archaeology of Anglo-Saxon England* (Methuen, London 1976); P.J. Casey (ed.) *The End of Roman Britain = BAR* 71 (1979); S. Johnson *Later Roman Britain* (Routledge and Kegan Paul, London 1980); C. Arnold *Roman Britain to Saxon England* (Croom Helm, London 1984) is an interesting if exasperating study in migration theory; J.N.L. Myres *The English Settlements = Oxford History of England* Ib (1986) and C. Thomas *Celtic Britain* (Thames and Hudson, London 1986) (on 5th–7th centuries AD) are the two most recent treatments.

On Ireland M. and L. De Paor *Early Christian Ireland* rev. ed. (Thames and Hudson, London 1978); K. Hughes *Early Christian Ireland: Introduction to the Sources* (Cambridge U.P. 1972).

Christianity

M.W. Barley and R.P.C. Hanson (eds.) *Christianity in Britain, 300–700* (Leicester U.P. 1968); C. Thomas *Christianity in Roman Britain to AD 500* (Batsford, London 1981) is extremely wide-ranging, and deals with matters such as St Ninian and St Patrick; of Ludwig Bieler's extensive and distinguished writings on the early Irish Church see *St. Patrick and the Coming of Christianity = History of Irish Catholicism* Ii (Dublin 1967); *The Patrician Texts in the book of Armagh = Scriptores Latini Hiberniae* X (Dublin 1979); for St Patrick E.A. Thompson *Who was St. Patrick?* (Boydell and Brewer 1986); L. Bieler *Ireland: Harbinger of the Middle Ages* (Oxford U.P.) 1963) remains a lucid and readable exposition of the spread of Irish Christianity to Britain and Europe; N. Chadwick *The Age of the Saints in the Celtic Church* (Oxford U.P., London 1961); see also C. Thomas *Celtic Britain* (1986).

Art of the Post-Roman Period in Britain

T.D. Kendrick *Anglo-Saxon Art to A.D. 900* (Methuen, London 1938); D.M. Wilson *Anglo-Saxon Art from the Seventh Century to the Norman Conquest* (Thames and Hudson, London 1984); G. Speake *Anglo-Saxon Animal art and its Germanic Background* (Clarendon Press, Oxford 1980). For Celtic art see Leeds 137–64; C. Nordenfalk

Celtic and Anglo-Saxon Painting (Chatto and Windus, London 1977). Continental context and workshops are discussed in H. Roth *Kunst und Handwerk im Frühmittelalter* (Theiss, Stuttgart, 1986). IRELAND: F. Henry *Irish Art in the Early Christian Period to A.D. 800* (Methuen, London 1965) is, though a translation of a much earlier work, still absolutely essential. See also G.F. Mitchell 'Foreign Influences and the Beginnings of Christian Art' *TEIA* 54–60 and L. de Paor 'The Christian Triumph: The Golden Age' *TEIA* 93–104; M. Ryan 'Das frühchristliche Irland (*ca.* 400–1000 n.Chr.)' *IK* 31–3; M. Ryan 'Metallhandwerk und künstlerischer Stil im frühen Mittelalter (7.–10. Jahrhundert n.Chr.)' *IK* 34–45. An important collection of papers demonstrating the many points of continuing debate is M. Day (ed.) *Ireland and insular art, AD 500–1200* (Royal Irish Academy, Dublin 1987).

HANGING-BOWLS: T.D. Kendrick 'British Hanging Bowls' *Antiquity* 6 (1932) 161–84; Henry 68–75; F. Henry 'Hanging-bowls' *J. Royal Soc. Antiquaries Ireland* 66 (1936) 209–46; E. Fowler 'Celtic Metalwork of the Fifth and Sixth Centuries AD' *Archaeological Journal* 120 (1963) 98–160; Kilbride-Jones 236–57; D. Longley *Hanging-bowls, penannular brooches and the Anglo-Saxon connection = BAR* 22 (1975); R.L.S. Bruce-Mitford 'Ireland and the hanging-bowls – a review' in Day (ed.) *Ireland and insular art AD 500–1200*, 30–39. HITCHIN: Leeds pl. III: 6.

SUTTON HOO: this site, though excavated before World War II, is only recently fully published. R. Bruce-Mitford et al. *The Sutton Hoo Ship Burial* (British Museum Publications, London 1975, 1978 and 1983) now runs to three volumes. For blistering attacks on the delays, the cost of the volumes and the suppression of information see most recently J. Werner *The Sutton Hoo Ship-Burial: Research and Publication between 1939 and 1980* (privately printed in Oxford, 1985), a translation by C.F.C. and S. Hawkes from its original publication in *Germania* 60 (1982) 193–209 and Werner's further detailed review 'Nachlese zum Schiffsgrab von Sutton Hoo' *Germania* 64 (1986) 465–497; see also the review by C.M. Hills *Antiquity* 59 (1985) 60–61. More accessible, and cheaper for the general reader, are R. Bruce-Mitford *The Sutton Hoo Ship Burial: a handbook* 3rd ed. (British Museum Publications, London 1979); A. Care-Evans *The Sutton Hoo Ship Burial* (British Museum Publications, London 1986) offers a revised version, which has also been the subject of some adverse criticism. SWALLOWCLIFFE DOWN: G. Speake *Anglo-Saxon Animal Art and its Germanic Background* (Clarendon Press, Oxford 1980) 65, 93, pl. 16i. IRISH LATCHET: Henry 68–9 and pl. 13; *TEIA* no. 25; *IK* no.39; Kilbride-Jones 211–13.

PENANNULAR BROOCHES: in general, E. Fowler 'Celtic Metalwork of the Fifth and Sixth Centuries AD' *Archaeological Journal* 120 (1963) 98–160; H.E. Kilbride-Jones *Zoomorphic Penannular Brooches* (Society of Antiquaries, London 1980). RIVER SHANNON: Henry 86; Kilbride-Jones in Brooches above, no. 66–7 (one of a pair); *IK* no. 44. LAGORE DISC: Henry pl. 28; Kilbride-Jones 232–3. BALLINDERRY: Henry pl. 24; Kilbride-Jones, *Brooches* above 56 and no. 89; *IK* no. 45.

Manuscripts

C. Nordenfalk *Celtic and Anglo-Saxon Painting* (Chatto and Windus, London 1977); J.J.G. Alexander *A Survey of Manuscripts Illuminated in the British Isles* 6; *6th to 9th Century* (Harvey Miller, London 1978) has excellent bibliographies; U. Roth 'Studien zur Ornamentik frühchristlicher Handschriften des insularen Bereichs' *Ber.d.RGK* 60 (1979) 5–225 who here and in her contribution to *Ireland and insular art, AD500–1200* favours an early (AD 600) date for Durrow; B. Meehan 'Irische Handschrifte im frühen Mittelalter' *IK* 48–55; G. Henderson *From Durrow to Kells: the insular Gospel-Books 650–800* (Thames and Hudson, London 1987). CATHACH OF ST COLUMBA: H.J. Lawley 'The Cathach of St. Columba' *Procs. Royal Irish Acad.* C33 (1916/17) 241–443; Henry 58–63 and pls. 9, 12; Roth (above) 61–88 and pls. 23–31. BOOK OF DURROW: A.A. Luce et al. *Evangeliorum Quattuor Codex Durmachensis* (Urs Graf Verlag, Olten and Lausanne 1960) 2 vols. is the facsimile edition; Roth (above) 122–221; Henderson (above) 18–55; shorter discussion and illustrations Henry 165–75; *TEIA* no. 27; *IK* no. 43. RINNAGAN PLAQUE: Henry 114 and pl. 46, 48; *TEIA* no. 29; *IK* no. 47.

LAGORE BUCKLE: Henry pl. 28; *IK* no. 49; for the background, H. O'N. Hencken 'Lagore Crannóg: an Irish Royal Residence of the 7th to 10th centuries AD' *Procs. Royal Irish Acad.* 53C (1950/51) 1–247. TARA BROOCH: Henry 108–10 and pl. 38; *TEIA* no. 32; *IK* no. 48. See also N. Whitfield 'The Finding of the Tara brooch' *J. Royal Soc. Antiquaries Ireland* 104 (1974) 120–42; N. Whitfield 'The Original Appearance of the Tara Brooch' *J. Royal Soc. Antiquaries Ireland* 106 (1976) 5–30. LINDISFARNE AND LICHFIELD GOSPELS: T.D. Kendrick et al. (eds.) *Evangeliorum Quattuor Codex Lindisfarnensis* (Urs Graf Verlag, Olten and Lausanne 1956, 1960) 2 vols. is another superb facsimile with the second volume containing a commentary, but, since only seven hundred copies were printed, it is rarely available outside major libraries; J. Backhouse *The Lindisfarne Gospels* (Phaidon, Oxford 1981) is shorter but more easily available. Lichfield is not published in facsimile but see Alexander *Insular Manuscripts* no. 21 and Henderson *Durrow to Kells* 122–129.

BOOK OF KELLS: E.H. Alton et al. (eds.) *Evangeliorum Quattuor Codex Cenannensis* (Urs Graf Verlag, Berne 1950) is once again the earliest facsimile edition with commentary; F. Henry *The Book of Kells* (Thames and Hudson, London 1974) is slightly shorter and P. Brown *The Book of Kells: Forty-Eight pages and details* (Thames and Hudson, London 1980) is a brief introduction; see also Henderson *Durrow to Kells* 130–198; specifically on the Chi-Ro page S. Lewis 'Sacred Calligraphy: the Chi-Ro page in the Book of Kells' *Traditio* 36 (1980) 139–59.

The statement on Llyn Cerrig Bach comes from I. Finlay *Celtic Art* (Faber, London 1973) 86.

For the 'Eire Page' and the Celtic revival generally see J. Sheehy *The Rediscovery of Ireland's Past: the Celtic Revival 1830–1930* (Thames and Hudson, London 1980); ch. 7 'The Celtic Revival' in B. de Breffny (ed.) *The Irish World* (Thames and Hudson, London 1977).

Sources of Illustrations

Unless otherwise indicated, the source of the photograph is the same as the location given for the object concerned.

Colour Plates

I From Kemble, Franks and Latham, *Horae Ferales*, London 1863. II Slovenské Národné Múzeum, Bratislava. Photo Marta Novotná. III British Museum, London. Photo J.V.S. Megaw. IV Courtesy Trustees of the British Museum. V,VI Salzburger Museum Carolino-Augusteum, Salzburg. Photo Eric Schaal. VII Naturhistorisches Museum, Vienna. Photo J.V.S. Megaw. VIII Archeologický ústav SAV, Nitra-Hrad. Photo Archeologický ústav SAV (Jozef Krátky), IX Schweizerisches Landesmuseum, Zürich. X,XI Musée Municipal, Angoulême. Photo courtesy Römisch-Germanisches Zentralmuseum, Mainz. XII,XIII Rheinisches Landesmuseum, Bonn. Photo Archäologie Bild, Berlin. XIV Rheinisches Landesmuseum, Bonn. XV Archeologický ústav SAV, Nitra-Hrad. Photo Archeologický ústav SAV (Jozef Krátky). XVI Mittelrheinisches Landesmuseum, Mainz. XVII Národní Muzeum, Prague. Photo L'Univers des Formes-La Photothèque. XVIII Musée des Antiquités Nationales, St-Germain-en-Laye. XIX,XX Courtesy Trustees of the British Museum. XXI University Museum of Archaeology and Anthropology, Cambridge. Photo L.P. Morley. XXII,XXIII Courtesy Trustees of the British Museum. XXIV Trinity College, Dublin. Photo courtesy the Board of Trinity College.

Monochrome Illustrations

Title page Bundesdenkmalbamt, Vienna. Photo Dr. J.-W. Neugebauer. 1 From Kemble, Franks and Latham, *Horae Ferales*, London 1863. 2 Map Simon S.S. Driver after P.-M. Duval. 3 Württembergisches Landesmuseum, Stuttgart. Photo Württembergisches Landesmuseum (courtesy Prof. W. Kimmig). 4 Landesmuseum Joanneum, Graz. Photo E. Lessing. 5–7 Naturhistorisches Museum, Vienna. 8 Germanisches Historisches Museum, Nürnberg. 9 Courtesy Trustees of the British Museum. 10 Naturhistorisches Museum, Vienna. 11 Slovenské Národné Múzeum, Bratislava. 12 Naturhistorisches Museum, Vienna. 13 Württembergisches Landesmuseum, Stuttgart. Photo Landesbildstelle Baden-Württemberg (Dr H. Hell). 14 Map Joanna Foale. 15,16 Ferenc Liszt Múzeum, Sopron. Photo Belzeaux-Zodiaque. Drawing after C. Dobiat. 17 Naturhistorisches Museum, Vienna. Drawing after A. Gallus. 18 Prähistorische Staatssammlung, Munich. 19 Landesmuseum Joanneum, Graz. 20 Landesmuseum Joanneum, Graz. Photo E. Lessing. 21,22 Naturhistorisches Museum, Vienna. 23

Narodni Muzej, Ljubljana. 24 Dolenjski muzej, Novo mesto. 25 Museo Civico, Bologna. Photo Mladen Grčevic. 26 Dolenjski muzej, Novo mesto. 27–29 Naturhistorisches Museum, Vienna. 30 Badisches Landesmuseum, Karlsruhe. Photo Landesbildstelle Baden-Württemberg (Dr Helmut Hell). 31 Württembergisches Landesmuseum, Stuttgart. Photo Landesdenkmalamt Baden-Württemberg. 32 Franziskaner Museum, Villingen-Schwenningen. Photo Fred Hügel, Villingen. 33–37 Württembergisches Landesmuseum, Stuttgart. Photos Landesdenkmalamt Baden-Württemberg. 38 Württembergisches Landesmuseum, Stuttgart. 39 Hegau Museum, Singen. Photo courtesy Förderkreis für die ur- und frühg. Forschung in Baden e.V. 40 Württembergisches Landesmuseum, Stuttgart. Photo Landesdenkmalamt Baden-Württemberg. 41 Württembergisches Landesmuseum, Stuttgart. Photo Landesbildstelle Baden-Württemberg. 42 Schweizerisches Landesmuseum, Zurich. Photo Landesbildstelle Baden-Württemberg (Dr H. Hell). 43 Musée de Châtillon-sur-Seine. Photo Giraudon, Paris. 44 Musée de Châtillon-sur-Seine. Photo E. Lessing. 45 Rheinisches Landesmuseum, Bonn. Photo J.V.S. Megaw. 46 Württembergisches Landesmuseum, Stuttgart. Photo Landesbildstelle Baden-Württemberg (Dr H. Hell). 47 Württemberg Landesmuseum, Stuttgart. 48 Rheinisches Landesmuseum, Bonn. Photo J.V.S. Megaw. 49 Musées Royaux d'Art et d'Histoire, Brussels. Drawing Simon S.S. Driver. 50 Drawing Simon S.S. Driver after J. Břeň. 51 Antikenabteilung, Stiftung Preussischer Kulturbesitz, Staatliches Museum, Berlin. Photo Ute Jung. 52 Map Joanna Foale. 53, 54 Rheinisches Landesmuseum, Trier. 55 Národní Muzeum, Prague. Drawing after J. Břeň. 56 Heimatmuseum Birkenfeld. Drawing Simon S.S. Driver after A. Haffner. 57 Rheinisches Landesmuseum, Trier. Drawing Simon S.S. Driver after A. Haffner. 58 Musée des Antiquités Nationales, St-Germain-en-Laye. Photo Inge Kitlitschka-Strempel. 59 Musée des Antiquités Nationales, St-Germain-en-Laye. Photo Belzeaux-Zodiaque. 60 Musée des Antiquités Nationales, St-Germain-en-Laye. 61 British Museum, London. Drawing after O.-H. Frey. 62 Mittelrheinisches Landesmuseum, Mainz. Photo Alfons Coreth, Salzburg. 63 Musée des Antiquités Nationales, St-Germain-en-Laye. 64 Musée des Beaux-Arts et d'Archéologie, Besançon. 65 Rheinisches Landesmuseum, Trier. Photo Alfons Coreth, Salzburg. 66 Courtesy Trustees of the British Museum. 67 Germanisches Nationalmuseum, Nürnberg. Photo Dr Carl Albiker, Karlsruhe. 68 Museo Civico 'G. Chierici', Reggio Emilia. 69 Prähistorisches Staatssammlung, Munich. Photo courtesy Römisch-Germanische Kommission (E. Neuffer). **70** Naturhistorisches Museum, Vienna. Photo Foto Meyer, Vienna. **71** Wetterau Museum, Friedberg, Hessen. Photo Department of Illustration, University of Sydney. **72** Slovenské Národné Múzeum, Bratislava. Photo W. and B. Forman (courtesy Artia Prague). **73** Drawing M.E. Weaver. **74** Historisches Museum der Pfalz, Speyer. **75** Národní Muzeum, Prague. Photo Aú ČSAV, Prague. **76** Antikenabteilung, Stiftung Preussischer Kulturbesitz, Staatliches Museum, Berlin. Photo Ute Jung. **77** Photo Foto Penz, St Pölten. **78,79** Historisches Museum der Pfalz, Speyer. Photos Dr Karl Albiker, Karlsruhe. **80** Victoria and Albert Museum, London. Crown Copyright Reserved. **81** Keltenmuseum, Hallein. Photo courtesy Dr E. Penninger. **82** Badisches Landesmuseum, Karlsruhe. Photo Landesbildstelle Baden-Württemberg (Dr H. Hell). **83** Rheinisches Landesmuseum, Bonn. **84** Württembergisches Landesmuseum, Stuttgart. Photo Landesbildstelle Baden-Württemberg (Dr H. Hell). **85,86** Salzburger Museum Carolino-Augusteum. Photos (above) Oscar Anrather, Salzburg; (below) courtesy Dr E. Penninger. **87,88** British Museum, London. Photos (above) J.V.S. Megaw; (below) courtesy Trustees of the British Museum. **89** Salzburger Museum Carolino-Augusteum. Photo courtesy Dr E. Penninger. **90** Formerly Museum für Vor-und-Frühgeschichte, Berlin: now destroyed. Photo courtesy Römisch-Germanische Kommission (E. Neuffer). **91** Musée des Antiquités Nationales, St-Germain-en-Laye. Photo courtesy Römisch-Germanische Kommission (E. Neuffer). **92** Naturhistorisches Museum, Vienna. Drawing courtesy Römisch-Germanisches Zentralmuseum, Mainz. **93** Museo Arqueológico Nacional Madrid. Photo courtesy Dr M. Lenerz de Wilde. **94** Mittelrheinisches Museum, Koblenz. Drawing after Dr J. Driehaus. **95** Römisch-Germanische Kommission. Photo courtesy Römisch-Germanische Kommission (E. Neuffer). **96** Museo Arqueológico Nacional, Madrid. Photo courtesy Dr M. Lenerz de Wilde. **97** Regensburg Museum. **98** Rheinisches Landesmuseum, Trier. **99** Aú ČSAV, Prague. **100** Rheinisches Landesmuseum, Trier. **101** Keltenmuseum, Hallein. Photo courtesy Dr E. Penninger. **102** Magyar Nemzeti Múzeum, Budapest. **103** Badisches Landesmuseum, Karlsruhe. Photo Landesbildstelle Baden-Württemberg (Dr H. Hell). **104** Národní Muzeum, Prague. Photo J.V.S. Megaw. **105** Musée cantonal d'archéologie, Neuchâtel. Photo Schweizerisches Landesmuseum, Zürich. **106** Západočeské Muzeum, Plzeň. Photo Aú ČSAV, Prague. **107** Keltenmuseum, Hallein. Photo courtesy Dr E. Penninger. **108** Musée Municipal, Châtillon-sur-Seine. Photo Musée des Antiquités Nationales, St-Germain-en-Laye. **109** Museum für Vor- und Frühgeschichte, Saarbrücken. **110** Badisches Landesmuseum, Karlsruhe. Photo Landesbildstelle Baden-Württemberg (Dr H. Hell). **111** Národní Muzeum Prague. Photo Národní Muzeum, Prague. **112** Germanisches Nationalmuseum, Nürnberg. Photo Dr Carl Albiker, Karlsruhe. **113** Vorgeschichtliches Museum, Friedrich-Schiller-Universität, Jena. **114** Historisches Museum der Pfalz, Speyer. **115** Formerly Museum für Vor- und Frühgeschichte, Berlin: now lost. Photo Dr O. Doppelfeld. **116–118** Museum für Vor- und Frühgeschichte, Saarbrücken. **119,120** Schweizerisches Landesmuseum, Zürich. **121,122** Museum für Vor- und Frühgeschichte, Staatlichen Museen, Berlin. Photo Alfons Coreth, Salzburg; Drawing courtesy Römisch-Germanisches Zentralmuseum, Mainz. **123** Krajské Museum, Teplice. Drawing Dr J. Waldhauser. **124** Formerly Krajské Muzeum, Teplice: now lost. Photo Aú ČSAV, Prague. **125** Aú ČSAV, Brno. **126** Ferenc Liszt Múzeum, Sopron. Photo MTA Régészeti Intézete. **127** Aú ČSAV, Brno. **128,129** Keltenmuseum, Hallein. Photos Alfons Coreth, Salzburg. **130** Museum Mannersdorf a. L. Photo Alfons Coreth, Salzburg. **131** Musée des Jacobins, Morlaix. Photo M.B. Cookson (courtesy of Sir Mortimer Wheeler). **132** Musée Préhistorique Finistérien, Quimper. Photo P.-R. Giot. **133** Musée des Antiquités Nationales, St-Germain-en-Laye. Photo Belzeaux-Zodiaque. **134** National Museum of Wales, Cardiff. **135** Metropolitan Museum of Art, New York (Fletcher Fund, 1947). **136** Rheinisches Landesmuseum, Bonn. **137,138** Museum für Vor- und Frühgeschichte, Saarbrücken. Photo Staatliches Konservatoramt, Saarbrücken. **139** Cabinet des Médailles, Bibliothèque Nationale, Paris. Photo L'Univers des Formes – La Photothèque. **140,141** (Left)

Museum für Vor- und Frühgeschichte, Saarbrücken. Drawing after M. Lenerz-de Wilde. (Right) Rheinisches Landesmuseum, Bonn. Drawing after H.-J. Joachim. **142** Musée des Antiquités Nationales, St-Germain-en-Laye. Drawing after P. Jacobsthal. **143** Musée des Beaux-Arts, Besançon. Drawing after O.-H. Frey. **144** Musée St Remi, Reims. Photo Musée des Antiquités Nationales, St-Germain-en-Laye. **145,146** Musée des Antiquités Nationales, St-Germain-en-Laye. Photo Inge Kitlitschka-Strempel (whole disc); Musée des Antiquités Nationales (detail). **147** Rheinisches Landesmuseum, Bonn. Photo J.V.S. Megaw. **148** Map Joanna Foale. **149** Antikenabteilung, Stiftung Preussischer Kulturbesitz, Staatlichen Museen, Berlin. Photo Jutta Tietz-Glagow. **150** Musée des Antiquités Nationales, St-Germain-en-Laye. Drawing after V. Kruta. **151** Musée St Rémi, Reims. Photo courtesy Trustees of the British Museum. **152** Museo di Monterenzio. Photo Soprintendenza Archaeologica dell'Emilia-Romagna. **153** Antikenabteilung, Stiftung Preussischer Kulturbesitz, Staatlichen Museen Berlin. Photo Ingrid Geske. **154** Musée des Antiquités Nationales, St-Germain-en-Laye. Photo Römisch-Germanische Zentralmuseum, Mainz. **155** Magyar Nemzeti Múzeum, Budapest. Photo Kálmán Kónya, Budapest. **156** Rheinisches Landesmuseum, Bonn. **157** Museo Nazionale delle Marche, Ancona. Photo Soprintendenza della Antichità delle Marche. **158** Museo nazionale delle Marche, Ancona. Photo L'Univers des Formes – La Photothèque. **159,160** Bernisches Historisches Museum, Bern. Photo Alfons Coreth, Salzburg. Drawings after O.-H. Frey. **161** Formerly Museum für Vor-und Frühgeschichte, Berlin: now lost. Photo courtesy Römisch-Germanische Kommission (E. Neuffer). **162** Keltenmuseum, Hallein. Photo Alfons Coreth, Salzburg. **163** Bernisches Historisches Museum, Bern. **164** Keltenmuseum, Ingolstadt. **165** Krajské Muzeum, Teplice. Photo courtesy Dr J. Waldhauser. **166** Magyar Nemzeti Múzeum, Budapest. Drawing after M. Szabó. **167** Burgenländisches Landesmuseum, Eisenstadt. Photo courtesy Dr E. Jerem. **168** Narodnija Archeologiceski Muzej, Sofia. Photo L'Univers des Formes – La Photothèque. **169** Magyar Nemzeti Múzeum, Budapest. Photo courtesy Römisch-Germanische Kommission (E. Neuffer). **170** Ferenc Liszt Múzeum, Sopron. Photo Ferenc Gelencsér. **171** Musée Denon. Chalon-sur-Saône. **172** British Museum, London. Photo J.V.S. Megaw. **173** Musée Historique Lorrain, Nancy. **174** Musée des Beaux-Arts, Troyes. Photo J. Bienaimé, Troyes. **175** British Museum, London. Photo J.V.S. Megaw. **176** Courtesy Trustees of the British Museum. **177** Private collection. Photo courtesy Trustees of the British Museum. **178** Národní Muzeum, Prague. Photo Aú ČSAV, Prague (J. Škoda). **179** Musei Capitolini, Rome. Photo Barbara Malter, Rome. **180** Map Joanna Foale. **181** Musée des Antiquités Nationales, St-Germain-en-Laye. Drawing after F. Schwappach. **182** (Above) Magyar Nemzeti Múzeum, Budapest. (Below) Naturhistorisches Museum, Vienna. Drawings Simon S.S. Driver after M. Szabó. **183** Musée des Antiquités Nationales, St-Germain-en-Laye. Photo Belzeaux-Zodiaque. **184** Musée Denon, Chalon-sur-Saône. **185** Musée des Beaux-Arts, Troyes. Photo L'Univers des Formes – La Photothèque. **186** Arheološki Muzej, Zagreb. **187** Gemerské múzeum, Rimavská Sobota. Photo J.V.S. Megaw. **188** Musée de Chálons-sur-Marne. Photo Centre de recherche d'histoire de la sidérurgie, Nancy (courtesy Professor P.-M. Duval). **189** Savaria Múzeum, Szombathely. Photo Ferenc Gelencsér. **190** (Left to right) Naturhistorisches Museum, Vienna; Römisch-Germanisches Zentralmuseum, Mainz; Magyar Nemzeti Múzeum, Budapest. Drawings Simon S.S. Driver after M. Szabó. **191** Bernisches Historisches Museum, Bern. Drawing Simon S.S. Driver after J.M. De Navarro. **192** Landesmuseum für Vorgeschichte, Dresden. **193** Württembergisches Landesmuseum, Stuttgart. Photo Landesbildstelle Baden-Württemberg (Dr H. Hell). **194** Narodni Muzej, Ljubljana. **195** Muzeul de Istorie a R.S., Romania. Photo L'Univers des Formes – La Photothèque. **196** Magyar Nemzeti Múzeum, Budapest. Drawing Simon S.S. Driver after M. Szabó. **197** Posavski Muzej, Brežice. Photo courtesy Dr M. Guštin. **198** Musée Cantonal Archéologique, Neuchâtel. **199** Prähistorische Staatssammlung, Munich. **200** Musée Cantonal Archéologique, Neuchâtel. **201** Schweizerisches Landesmuseum,

National Museum of Wales, Cardiff. **381** National Museum of Wales, Cardiff. **382** Royal Museum of Scotland, Edinburgh. Photo M.J.M. Murray. **383** National Museum of Ireland, Dublin. **384** Chapter House, Armagh Protestant Cathedral. Photo Dr Françoise Henry. **385** Museum of London. **386** Courtesy Trustees of the British Museum. **387** Reading Museum and Art Gallery. **388** Museum of Antiquities, University of Newcastle upon Tyne & Society of Antiquaries of Newcastle upon Tyne. Photo Museum of Antiquities, University of Newcastle upon Tyne. **389** Carmarthen Museum. Photo National Museum of Wales, Cardiff. **390** Kingston-upon-Hull Transport & Archaeology Museum. Photo courtesy Trustees of the British Museum. **391** University Museum of Archaeology and Anthropology, Cambridge. **392** Courtesy Trustees of the British Museum. **393** Royal Museum of Scotland, Edinburgh. Photo M.J.M. Murray. **394–396** Royal Museum of Scotland, Edinburgh. **397** Formerly Powysland Museum, Welshpool: now lost. Photo National Museum of Wales, Cardiff. **398** Merseyside County Museums, Liverpool. **399** City Museum, Bristol. **400–403** National Museum of Ireland, Dublin. **404** Ulster Museum, Belfast. **405** Royal Museum of Scotland, Edinburgh. **406** National Museum of Ireland, Dublin. Photo Belzeaux-Zodiaque.

407 British Museum, London. Photo courtesy Römisch-Germanische Kommission (E. Neuffer). **408** Mittelrheinisches Landesmuseum, Mainz. **409** Museum of Antiquities, University of Newcastle upon Tyne and Society of Antiquaries, Newcastle upon Tyne. **410** Royal Museum of Scotland, Edinburgh. **411** Colchester Museum. Photo G. Ager (courtesy Kirsty Rodwell). **412** Somerset County Museum, Taunton. Photo courtesy Prof. Leslie Alcock. **413** National Museum of Ireland, Dublin. Photo Belzeaux-Zodiaque. **414** Map Joanna Foale. **415** City Museum, Sheffield. **416** National Museum of Ireland, Dublin. Photo Belzeaux-Zodiaque. **417** Victoria and Albert Museum, London. Crown Copyright Reserved. **418** National Museum of Ireland, Dublin. **419** Avebury Museum. Photo Prof. Dr Helmut Roth. **420** National Museum of Ireland, Dublin. Photo Belzeaux-Zodiaque. **421,422** Royal Irish Academy, Dublin. Photo Belzeaux-Zodiaque. **423,424** National Museum of Ireland, Dublin. **425** Lichfield Cathedral Library, Lichfield, Staffordshire, England. Photo Colour Centre Slides Ltd (courtesy the Dean and Chapter, Lichfield Cathedral). **426** Trinity College, Dublin. Photo Green Studios, Dublin (courtesy the Board of Trinity College). **427** National Museum of Ireland, Dublin.

Acknowledgments

Over the past decade we have received practical support – and, even more important, valuable time – for the research required in preparing this book from, successively, the University of Leicester and the Flinders University of South Australia. Financial backing and assistance with travel has also come from the British Academy, the British Council, the Australian Research Grants Scheme and the Deutscher Akademischer Austauschdienst. The illustration credits due have, we trust, been fully indicated in the Sources of Illustrations. Of the many other individuals and institutions we can only mention here those to whom thanks is greatest since they have given most freely of their hospitality, resources, time and knowledge particularly in areas where, scientifically speaking only, we have felt least at home:

Dr Jörg Biel, Landesdenkmalamt Baden-Württemberg, Stuttgart; Anne Cahen-Delhaye, Musées Royaux d'Art et d'Histoire, Brussels; Professor B. Chropovský, Aú SAV, Nitra-Hrad; Ann Dornier, University of Leicester; Alain Duval, Musée des Antiquités Nationales, St-Germain-en-Laye; Professor P.-M. Duval, Paris; Professor Franz Fischer, Institut für Vor- und Frühgeschichte, Universität Tübingen; Professor Otto-Herman Frey, Vorgeschichtliches Seminar, Philipps-Universität, Marburg/Lahn and Dr Lore Frey-Asche; Dr Mitja Guštin, formerly Posavski Muzej, Brežice; Professor Alfred Haffner, Institut für Ur- und Frühgeschichte, Universität Kiel; Dr Erzsébet Jerem, MTA Régészeti Intézete, Budapest; Emeritus Professor E.M. Jope, Oxford; Professor Emeritus Wolfgang Kimmig, Tübingen; Dr Tone Knez, Dolenjske Muzej, Novo mesto; Dr Eva Kolníková, Aú SAV, Nitra-Hrad; Dr Vaclav Kruta, Ecole Pratique des Hautes Etudes, Paris and Dr Luana Kruta-Poppi; Dr Majolie Lenerz-de Wilde, Seminar für Ur- und Frühgeschichte, Universität Münster; Professor Ferdinand Maier, Römisch-Germanische Kommission, Frankfurt/Main; Dr Ivan Marazov, Arkheolog. Institut, Sofia; Dr Raffaele De Marinis, Soprintendenza Archaeologica della Lombardia, Milan; Dr Fritz Moosleitner, Salzburger Museum C.A., Salzburg; Dr Éva f. Petres, István Király Múzeum, Székesfehérvár; Dr Ernst Penninger, Keltenmuseum, Hallein; Professor Jozef Poulík, Aú ČSAV, Brno; Dr

Barry Raftery, University College, Dublin; Dr Anne Ross, Southampton; Professor Helmut Roth, Vorgeschichtliches Seminar, Universität Marburg/Lahn and Dr Uta Roth; Dr Franz Schubert, Römisch-Germanische Kommission, Ingolstadt; Professor Konrad Spindler, Institut für Ur- und Frühgeschichte, Universität Erlangen/Nürnberg and Dorothea Spindler; Dr M.G. Spratling, Cambridge; Dr I.M. Stead, British Museum, London; Professor Miklós Szabó, Eötvös Loránd Egyetem, Budapest and Dr Agnes f. Molnár; Dr Marco Tizzoni, Istituto Universitario di Bergamo; Dr Natalie Venclová, Aú ČSAV Prague; Dr Daniele Vitali, Istituto di Archeologia, Università di Bologna; Professor P.S. Wells, University of Minnesota and Joan Wells; Dr Herbert Werner, Amt der Salzburger Landesregierung (Kulturabteilung), Salzburg; and Dr Vlad Zirra, Institutul de Arheologie, Bucharest.

To Emeritus Professor Stuart Piggott, the late Professor T.G.E. Powell and the late Derek Allen, numismatist and musician, our debt is also great since in a very real sense they have represented a personal three-headed Celtic deity. Professor Emeritus Wolfgang Dehn and Frau Gerda Dehn first welcomed us twenty years ago to Marburg, the original seat of Paul Jacobsthal's researches into early Celtic art, and, with our old friends the Freys, have continued to make us at home ever since.

Like so many, we must thank John Hopkins, the former Librarian, and the staff of the Library of the Society of Antiquaries of London and Dr Eckehart Schubert and Frau D. Beck of the Römisch-Germanische Kommission, Frankfurt for keeping us supplied with bibliographical information. Our former Research Assistant, Susan Semmens, knows who did the essential groundwork in amassing the illustrations which form the core of this work. Fellow student and indexer-extraordinary Elizabeth Fowler has once more added her analytical skills, while the text was processed by several patient hands: first among many cipher experts our affectionate thanks go to Jane Pearson, one of three people in the world who can read Vincent's handwriting.

39/16